POMPEY

POMPEY
THE ROMAN ALEXANDER

PETER GREENHALGH

WEIDENFELD AND NICOLSON
LONDON

First published in Great Britain by
Weidenfeld and Nicolson Ltd
91 Clapham High Street
London SW4 7TA

ISBN 0 297 77640 1

Printed in Great Britain by
Butler & Tanner Ltd, Frome and London

To the memory of F.E. Adcock

His grave extends wherever land on Ocean floats,
The Roman name and Empire are its only bounds....
But if you think a stone deserves his sacred name,
Then add his great achievements, list his mighty deeds:
Fierce Lepidus subdued, the Alps, Sertorius,
The triumph of a knight who won a consul's war.
Recall the seas made safe for every nation's trade,
All Barbary subdued, the nomad tribes, the realms
Of East and North made pliant to the will of Rome.
Record how after every war he laid aside
His arms and donned again the civil robes of peace.
No tomb could do such greatness justice, let alone
A wretched stone that scarce has room for Pompey's name –
The name that men were wont to read on temple walls
And great triumphal arches raised with foreign spoils...

LUCAN, *Pharsalia*, 8.797–819

CONTENTS

LIST OF MAPS AND ILLUSTRATIONS

MAPS

ILLUSTRATIONS (*between pages 124 and 125*)

PREFACE

To do justice to the greatness of this man would require a
work of many volumes ...
Velleius Paterculus, *History of Rome*, 2.29.2

The life of Pompey the Great divides conveniently into two parts, and
I have therefore tried to do justice to it in two volumes. The first covers
the forty-seven years from his birth in 106 BC to the coalition with
Crassus and Caesar in 59 through which he asserted his political will in
a city-state aristocracy unwilling to accommodate a Roman Alexander
who had triumphed over the three parts of the inhabited world. The
second volume traces the development of Pompey's political supremacy
against the background of increasing corruption, constitutional manipulation and urban violence of the fifties, the rivalry of Caesar, and the
catastrophic Civil War which destroyed both Pompey and a decayed Republic which could control its empire more easily than its imperialists.

In reconstructing Pompey's life I have tried not to write for the academic
at the expense of the general reader or for the general reader at the
expense of the academic. To compartmentalize readers of historical biography by this literary apartheid has always seemed to me rather artificial
and offensive. There are of course some highly technical writings so eso-
teric that only specialists are likely to read them, but even these should
not be illiterate or more boring than they can help, and certainly biographies have no such excuse. That scholarship should be regarded as
a medicine which can be good only if unpalatable is a curiously puritanical hangover in a permissive age, and there is a suggestion of literary
insecurity among those who profess to be serious scholars but scorn read-
ability as somehow irrelevant or even inimical to their profession. On
the other hand it is equally offensive to patronize the non-specialist reader
by spoon-feeding him slops which may be easily assimilated but are pro-
foundly unsatisfying to the mature intelligence. The lover of history is
by definition intelligent, because the very word means 'inquiry', and only
the intelligent are curious. The historian is the inquiring writer whose
creativity is disciplined by fact rather than fiction, and the inquiring
reader should be able to see for himself how the picture has been reconstructed from the jigsaw-puzzle of the ancient sources, both literary and
non-literary, contemporary and non-contemporary, with many of the

pieces missing, others duplicated in conflicting shapes, and almost all of them warped by time and prejudice. The historian's scholarly responsibility to his non-specialist reader is not less but greater than to his fellow-specialist, and in attempting to share the fascinating process of historical reconstruction I have also tried to communicate by direct and indirect quotation the character of the ancient writers on whom I have drawn.

In dedicating this book to Sir Frank Adcock I remember as yesterday the awe with which a grammar schoolboy arrived to take up a scholarship at King's College, Cambridge, in 1964 and first met that great historian four times his own age. I remember too how quickly the awed admiration matured into a friendship which made a splendid nonsense of the generation-gap and which remains one of my most cherished memories. It is a great strength of the Oxbridge system that so much of the best education is informal. Every Monday evening, for example, classical undergraduates and dons were invited to have coffee and read a Greek play in the original in Adcock's rooms, and through those readings the Greek dramatists spoke to us with a spontaneity that few formal lectures could achieve. In the same way I believe I gained some of my best lessons in the art of history from accompanying 'the Adder' on afternoon perambulations round the Backs. His own rare combination of wordliness and scholarship gave him an insight into the mentality of the makers of history which is less readily available to historians of narrower experience, and I learnt from his lively wit and sparkling prose that history which is worth writing at all is worth trying to write well. In Adcock's lifetime there were two World Wars to take him from the cloistered atmosphere of Cambridge to the Bedlam of power-politics and that peculiarly human activity to which our species has always devoted more energy and resources than to the arts of peace. And just as my old friend freely acknowledged that his extra-mural experiences had made him a better historian, I too in my humbler way acknowledge the benefits of several years' intimacy with big business. If I had not been the veteran of so many take-over battles in the corridors of financial power I should not have begun to understand the megalomania of Pompey and his ambitious peers; and however well or badly this book is received, it would have been less good than it is but for my five years as a merchant-banker in the City of London. To the example and inspiration of Sir Frank Adcock I owe a great debt of gratitude, and I dedicate this book to his memory with affection and pride in having been his friend.

It is customary in prefaces to record dutiful thanks to wives and publishers at the very end, but in this case I put them first in my acknowledgements together with an orthopaedic surgeon, Mr Douglas Freebody. I had no sooner signed the contract to write this book in 1975 than I wrote off a whole year undergoing serious repairs to a disintegrating spine. It was a year I prefer to forget, although it was not without consolations: I have the doubtful distinction of having read the whole of Shakespeare, Dickens and Greek tragedy through prismatic spectacles while immobilized in a plaster bed, and I am able to refute with the authority of personal experience the fashionable theory that creative writers have often been inspired by pain: they succeed despite it, and would do even better without it. But happily I had a skilful surgeon, a loving wife, and a patient publisher, to whom I am deeply grateful for repeatedly extending my contract to take account first of my incapacity and then of the development of this work from a relatively modest undertaking into the very large biography which Velleius rightly believed necessary to do justice to Pompey the Great. The mutual trust and understanding between an author and his publisher is a precious thing, and it is no mere convention when I record my appreciation to Mrs Gila Falkus and her colleagues at Weidenfeld & Nicolson. To Douglas Freebody I owe the still positive pleasure which I feel in being able to sit and write without pain. And to my wife's devoted encouragement and help I and *Pompey* owe more than I could ever begin to express.

Special thanks are also due to my veteran typist and dear friend Mrs Irene Bosset. Like the ageless scholar to whose memory this book is dedicated she proves in her own way that we are all as young as we feel, and that an active mind and great industry are not the monopoly of youth. So great are her skill and loyalty that we have allowed no distance or difficulty to break up our partnership, and we have cheerfully spent a small fortune sending manuscripts and typescripts backwards and forwards between London and the distant parts of the globe in which I have written much of this book. I am also very grateful to Mr R. A. Gardner of the British Museum for the skill with which he photographed coins for me; to Mr Patrick Leeson for turning my crude drafts into such fine maps; to Mrs Myzka Sulkin for painstaking and sensitive editorial work; to Mrs E. Zingg, Miss R. Stolze, Mrs C. Kingdon and Mrs M. Black for supplementary typing; and to Mr C. J. van Niekerk for photocopying vast quantities of manuscripts and typescripts and for helping with all manner of postal and communication difficulties. I have not burdened academic friends with requests for help or opinions on my work in progress, but I owe a more general debt of gratitude to four distinguished men whose friendship and example have meant much to me at a difficult time in my life: they are Robert Clark, Robert Cook, Arnaldo Momigliano and Anthony Snodgrass, a banker and three scholars, none of whom can ever know how highly I value their friendship and admire their excellence in their different fields. And last but not least I record my warm thanks to the Provost and Fellows of King's College, Cambridge, who welcomed me as a member of their High Table and afforded me every facility to complete my research in my old College among old and new friends.

P.A.L.G.

THE LITERARY SOURCES

I write what I believe to be the truth, for the Greeks have
many stories which seem to me absurd.
Hecataeus of Miletus.

The reader who is not familiar with the sources for the history of the
late Roman Republic may find it helpful to read this very brief introduction to some of the more prominent ancient writers whose names will
be encountered in the text of this volume or its sequel. It is not intended
to be a comprehensive survey of the sources, which would require yet
another book to do it justice.

Of Pompey's contemporaries the two main writers whose works
survive are Marcus Tullius CICERO (106–43 BC) and Gaius Julius
CAESAR (100–44 BC), and as both of them are prominent characters in
the story of Pompey, their careers need no preliminary introduction
here. From Cicero we have numerous political and legal speeches together
with comments on them by ancient scholars, notably Q. ASCONIUS
Pedianus (9 BC–76 AD), whose extant observations on the speech in
defence of Milo are particularly valuable for the extraordinary circumstances of Pompey's third consulship in 52 BC. But even more valuable
than Cicero's speeches are his *Letters*, a vast corpus of correspondence
belonging to the period 68–43 BC. Among over nine hundred surviving
letters from Cicero to his banker-friend Atticus, his brother Quintus and
other relatives and friends of varying degrees of intimacy there are a few
received by him, including one or two from Pompey himself and a much
larger number from a witty and singularly uninhibited young politician
named Marcus CAELIUS Rufus (82–48 BC), whom Cicero asked to keep
him informed of affairs in Rome while he was away governing Cilicia
in 51–50 BC. Because Cicero's letters are not spread evenly over the period
68–43 there is a danger of overemphasizing episodes covered by them
in detail at the expense of others on which we have less information,
but the unique contemporary insight which they afford into the period
of Pompey's greatness makes this a risk that has to be run.

As if it was not bad enough for Pompey to lose his greatness to a
protégé, his memory has continued to be eclipsed in the judgement of
history by the fact that Caesar not only lent his name to centuries of autocracy but wrote a great mass of personal memoirs which none of the

contemporary eulogies of Pompey's achievements has survived to counterbalance. Caesar has left us seven books of memoirs of his conquest of
Gaul covering the years 58–52 BC (to which his officer Aulus HIRTIUS
added an eighth covering 52–50) and three books on his Civil War with
Pompey in 49–48 (to which other officers have added monographs on
his subsequent Alexandrian, African and Spanish campaigns). All are
written in the third person, which gives a veneer of objectivity to an essay
in self-congratulation while ensuring that the hero's name appears as
often as possible. The reliability of Caesar's commentaries will be discussed in the text and notes of the second volume.

Among contemporary writers whose work is less relevant to Pompey's
life or whose relevant work has not survived in more than fragmentary
form the names of Gaius Sallustius Crispus (SALLUST), Gaius
ASINIUS POLLIO, Marcus TERENTIUS VARRO, THEO-
PHANES of Mytilene and POSIDONIUS of Apamea will be encountered. Sallust (c. 86–35 BC) has left us monographs on the war with
Jugurtha in Africa and the Civil War of Catiline, together with fragments
of an annalistic history of Rome which he wrote covering events from
78 BC down to at least 67, the year of the latest datable fragment: the
fragments include an angry letter supposedly written by Pompey to the
Senate in Rome during his war against Sertorius in Spain. Asinius Pollio
(76 BC–4 AD), also a Caesarian in the Civil War though a rather more
successful one, wrote a history of Rome from 60 BC down to Philippi in
42, which seems to have been highly analytical and critical in method.
Unfortunately the work itself has not survived, but it was used by such
later writers as Plutarch and Appian, who are discussed below. Terentius
Varro (116–27 BC), perhaps the most prolific of all Roman writers, was
also a man of the world and a protégé of Pompey, who appointed him to
high command in the Pirate War and in Spain. Varro's insatiable erudi-
tion covered almost every subject of inquiry from agriculture to moral
philosophy, and he wrote a lost monograph on Pompey which was nevertheless available to other writers whose work has survived. Theophanes
of Mytilene accompanied Pompey on his Eastern campaigns, acted as his
official historian, and continued as one of Pompey's closest advisers. Posidonius (c. 135–50 BC) was the famous philosopher under whom Cicero
studied, and he became so enthusiastic a supporter of Pompey that he wrote
a monograph on Pompey's Eastern campaigns as an appendix to his
fifty-two books of Histories, which picked up where Polybius left off in
146 BC and went down to the dictatorship of Sulla. Unfortunately the works
of both Theophanes and Posidonius are lost, but they were used by other
writers whose work has survived, and both are mentioned by our main
non-contemporary source for Pompey's life, the biographer Plutarch.

PLUTARCH has left us not only a *Life* of Pompey but *Lives* of many of Pompey's contemporaries, including Marius, Sulla, Sertorius, Lucullus, Crassus, Cicero, Caesar, Cato, Antony and Brutus. He was born before 50 AD and died after 120 AD, and though he knew Athens well and travelled to Egypt and Italy, he spent most of his life in or near his home-town of Chaeronea in Boeotia. His purpose in writing *Parallel Lives* of prominent Greeks and Romans was to illustrate character, virtue and vice, and the historian who uses Plutarch must realize that he is not dealing with a biographer in the modern sense but with a didactic moral philosopher. All the same Plutarch was a very learned man who employed a wide range of sources, and his contribution to our knowledge of the personalities of the late Republic is invaluable. We have no other ancient biography of Pompey, and though Gaius SUETONIUS Tranquillus has left us one of Julius Caesar, it adds relatively little to the evidence of other sources for the purpose of this work. Suetonius, born about 69 AD, held high office in the imperial secretariat under the emperors Trajan (98–117 AD) and Hadrian (117–138 AD), and had access to official archives for his biographies of the *Twelve Caesars* from Julius Caesar to Domitian.

The principal ancient historians whose work has survived on the period of Pompey's lifetime are APPIAN and DIO Cassius, both of them writing in Greek. Appian was a native of Alexandria who practised as a lawyer in Rome in the second century AD and compiled a narrative history of Roman wars and conquests. His surviving books on the *Mithridatic Wars* and the *Civil Wars* are of great value to the biographer of Pompey. Dio, a native of Nicaea in Bithynia, was even later than Appian. As the son of the Roman governor of Cilicia and Dalmatia he was destined for a political career in Rome and eventually became consul with the emperor Alexander Severus in 229 AD, but he combined public life and authorship so energetically that he managed to write (among other things) an annalistic history of Rome in eighty books from earliest times to 229 AD. It took him ten years to research and twelve to write. Although he is writing over two centuries after our period and in very different political conditions, he is often shrewd in his judgements and uses good sources, mainly Livy or Livy's own sources. Much of his work survives only in wretched epitomes by Byzantine scholars, but from 67 BC to Pompey's death we are fortunate in having virtually the whole of Dio intact.

Next in importance to Appian and Dio among the surviving ancient historians of our period (though lagging well behind them) is VELLEIUS PATERCULUS, who served as an army-officer under Tiberius and reached the praetorship in 15 AD. He wrote a Roman history in two books, the first covering the period from Romulus to the destruction of Corinth and Carthage in 146 BC, the second from 146 BC to 30 AD and becoming more detailed as it approaches his own time. He was not the greatest historian who ever lived, but he was no fool, and his contribution is not unimportant. Very little is added by Annaeus FLORUS, an author of the second century AD who wrote a very brief, rhetorical and often inaccurate history of Roman wars and conquests from Romulus to Augustus in two books. The Jewish historian Flavius JOSEPHUS, born about 38 AD, is of a very much higher calibre, but since his interest was solely in Jewish history his *Jewish Wars* and *Jewish Antiquities* are of little use to us except for the one relevant part of Pompey's Eastern campaigns.

Our greatest loss among the ancient historians is LIVY. Titus Livius, whose life spanned the late Republic and early empire, wrote a gigantic history of Rome in a hundred and forty-two books from earliest times to 9 BC, and those who are acquainted with his surviving books on the Hannibalic wars will realize how much we miss by having little more than the forty-six tantalizing paragraphs summarizing the forty-six books which covered Pompey's lifetime. But Livy reaches us indirectly through his use by other writers whose work has survived, and not only prose-writers like the biographer Plutarch but also the poet Marcus Annaeus Lucanus, whose epic *On the Civil War*, commonly called the *Pharsalia*, makes the study of Pompey's final tragedy so rewarding a literary as well as historical experience.

LUCAN (39–65 AD) was only twenty-five when ordered to commit suicide as a conspirator against the emperor Nero, but his genius had flowered early and he had already written nearly ten books of the *Pharsalia*. His work was greatly admired by contemporaries (too greatly for easy co-existence with Nero's own literary pretensions), and though he tends to be neglected today, he was rightly appreciated in the Middle Ages and by the discriminating Elizabethans, among whom Marlowe translated the first book. To the biographer of Pompey his work is invaluable for its derivation from the lost Livy and for its refreshingly anti-Caesarian bias. As literature it is occasionally marred by purple passages and an excess of rhetoric, but at its best it is magnificent, and I have tried to convey some of its spirit through my own verse-translations in this book.

Last but not least I should mention a natural historian, a geographer and a collector of stratagems who made significant contributions to our study. The natural historian is the Elder PLINY (Gaius Plinius Secundus, c. 24–79 AD), Roman lawyer, soldier, statesman, favourite of the emperor Vespasian, scientist, scholar and historian. His industry and search for every kind of scientific knowledge were insatiable and ultimately fatal, for he perished investigating the eruption of Vesuvius which preserved Pompeii and Herculaneum for us in AD 79. From his enormous literary output the principal survivor is his *Natural History* in thirty-seven books, dedicated to the future emperor Titus in 77 AD and ranging over subjects as diverse as cosmology, geography, ethnology, physiology, zoology, botany, medicine, mineralogy, metallurgy and the history of art. The geographer STRABO (*c.* 64 BC–21 AD) has left us seventeen books of his *Geography*, which attempted a comprehensive survey of the political geography of the Roman world with details of economic and historical development, ethnology and culture. As a native of Amaseia in Pontus he is particularly valuable for our study of Pompey's Eastern campaigns and settlements. The collector of stratagems is Sextus Julius FRONTINUS, who became Roman governor of Britain during the principate of Vespasian (69–79 AD) and was put in charge of Rome's water-supply under Nerva (96–8 AD). His theoretical treatise *On Military Science* has perished, but we still have his works on *Aqueducts* and *Stratagems*, the latter providing many valuable references to Pompey's campaigns.

There are many more literary sources to which this biography is indebted than those listed above, but their contributions are relatively minor and their work generally inaccessible to any but the specialist scholar who will be familiar with them anyway. As for all the non-literary sources, notably inscriptions and coins, there is little of value that can be said about them by way of general introduction, and the reader will be guided to them in the notes.

1
A SCHOOLING IN WAR

Hitherto the political murders and seditions in Rome had
been intermittent domestic affairs on a relatively small scale,
but from now on the leaders of the factions began to assail
each other with great armies according to the laws of war,
and looked upon their country as the prize
in a contest of arms.
Appian, *Roman Civil Wars*, 1.55

When Gnaeus Pompeius was born in 106 BC, a colonial war in North
Africa was engaging the energies of the two men through whose future
rivalry he was destined to achieve greatness when he was barely twenty-
five. One was the Roman army's commanding officer, the proconsul
Gaius Marius, who had been elected to the consulship for the previous
year after promising the Roman people an early victory in this seemingly
endless war. The other was Lucius Cornelius Sulla, a young officer on
the proconsul's staff and as distant from his commanding officer in personality as in rank. Marius, already in his fifties, was the pure soldier,
down to earth, unsophisticated, an outsider in the Roman aristocracy
who had nevertheless reached the highest public office in recognition of
his military abilities. Sulla, nineteen years his junior, was a member of
a great family which had seen better days, a young roué as much at home
in the salon as the camp, polished, suave, almost effete in his manners.
They were alike only in their determination to succeed, Marius to redeem
his election promises, Sulla to make a name for himself that would end
the frustrating anonymity of a young nobleman whose fortune was not
commensurate with either his birth or talents.

The enemy was King Jugurtha of Numidia, a powerful native kingdom
covering most of what is now northern Algeria. Marius defeated his
armies, sacked his desert strongholds and seized the royal treasure, but
he was constantly denied the one success that would bring the war to
an immediate end and satisfy the Roman people – the capture of Jugurtha
himself. Then early in 105 he received secret overtures from Jugurtha's
father-in-law and ally, King Bocchus of neighbouring Mauretania, at a

time when Jugurtha was at the Mauretanian court. At the request of Bocchus he sent Sulla to act as intermediary and present his terms, which offered Bocchus the friendship of Rome and a slice of the Numidian kingdom in exchange for his son-in-law. It was a delicate and dangerous mission, but after some vacillation Bocchus agreed, and Sulla returned with the arch-enemy in chains.

Marius returned to Rome to celebrate a magnificent triumph, but his many political opponents made the best of his success by whispering that he was reaping rewards which truly belonged to Sulla. It was too much to expect a young man of Sulla's temperament to play down his own role in the victory, and the more he boasted, the less cordial became his relations with his old commanding officer. All the same, when Marius was called upon to repulse the advances of the Cimbri and Teutones, he swallowed hurt pride and looked to Sulla to command under him.

For several years the Romans had watched with increasing anxiety as hordes of these Northern tribes had migrated towards Italy and swept aside almost every Roman army that had dared to stand in their way. In the year of Marius' triumph over Jugurtha they inflicted on Rome her greatest military disaster since Cannae by annihilating an army of eighty thousand legionaries near the Rhône, and if the Cimbri had not then decided to invade Spain before Italy, they might have anticipated Alaric by five centuries. It was a formidable enemy which Marius now set out to defeat, and for two years Sulla deserved well of his general; but his successes irritated Marius, and when Sulla found that he was being denied further opportunities to demonstrate his ability he offered his services to the less successful army of the other consul of 102, Quintus Lutatius Catulus, who was only too glad to entrust his most critical enterprises to so competent an officer. As Sulla enhanced his reputation in the service of Catulus, Marius' resentment of him increased, even though Sulla presented no real challenge to his former general's monopoly of glory. It was Marius who annihilated the Teutonic hordes at Aquae Sextiae in 102 and, leading Catulus' army, the Cimbri at Vercellae in the following year; and it was to Marius alone that the Roman people gave the title 'Third Founder of Rome' when they elected him to a sixth consulship in 100. Yet it rankled with Marius that there had been one occasion in the war when his own troops had been dependent on surplus supplies furnished by Sulla for the army of Catulus, and it rankled with Sulla that Marius had seemed to be trying to retard his advancement. 'So slight and childish', says Plutarch, 'were the early occasions and causes of that hatred between them that would one day confound the whole state.'

In the years that followed this emergency there was a gradual reassertion of the senatorial establishment against popular champions like

Marius, who found his purely military abilities redundant in the politics of peacetime. He needed another war, and when he went on a tour of the East in 97 he did his best to provoke one by his arrogant behaviour to the formidable King of Pontus, but Mithridates was not yet ready to risk war with the Republic and refused to be drawn. Sulla, in the meantime, did all he could to advance his political career by cultivating the powerful and marrying for money. He was now in his forties and turning his once handsome face into a 'mulberry spotted with meal' as he made up for the years of penury which had cramped the style of his youth. By bribing the electorate he gained the praetorship for 93, and in the following year he recieved a governorship in Asia Minor which was worthy of his talents. His province was Cilicia, his brief to reinstate the pro-Roman king of neighbouring Cappadocia who had just been deposed in a *coup d'état* backed by the wily Mithridates, who was now emerging as the greatest threat to Rome's developing empire in the East.

Sulla quickly collected an army from allied states, restored the deposed monarch, and successfully defended him against a counter-invasion from Armenia. It was a splendid achievement in itself and had useful repercussions further afield, for it not only gave pause to Mithridates' expansionist policy in Asia Minor but brought the name of Rome to the attention of the vast central Asian empire of Parthia. The self-styled 'King of Kings' was so impressed that he sent an ambassador to confer with Sulla on the banks of the Euphrates, and Sulla, conscious that he was the first representative of Rome to come into formal diplomatic contact with Parthia, arranged a magnificent reception with three great thrones – one for his distinguished visitor, one for himself and one for the King of Cappadocia whom he had restored. He was well aware of the significance of seating arrangements on such occasions to the rulers of earth's proud empires, and when the Parthian ambassador allowed him to remain seated in the central position, it constituted a great diplomatic triumph for the Republic. It was enough to lose the ambassador his head in Babylon and make Sulla the toast of Rome.

Marius' jealousy was further aggravated when King Bocchus dedicated some statues on the Capitol to commemorate the African campaign. These gilded figures represented the king handing over Jugurtha to Sulla, and for Marius, who did not feature in the group, no studied insult could have re-opened old wounds half so effectively. In his fury he demanded the removal of the statues, but others supported Sulla's insistence that they should stay, and soon the whole city had taken sides over the issue. But before this elevated quarrel had reached what promised to be a violent climax, it was dramatically postponed by the outbreak of a war so serious that Rome found herself once more fighting for survival.

This time her enemies were even nearer home than the migrating Cimbri and Teutones had been. They were friends turned enemies, a powerful coalition of some of the most warlike tribes of Italy, whose just grievance was that they provided more than half the troops of the Roman armies but were constantly denied full citizenship. Enlightened members of the Roman aristocracy had been pressing for their enfranchisement for over thirty years, but the majority of the Senate were afraid of a large body of new voters outside their traditional patronage and the chauvinistic populace was reluctant to share its privileges and corn-dole, despite the fact that most of the new citizens would live so far from Rome that they would seldom, if ever, exercise their right to vote or claim a cheap meal. But the demand for citizenship had become a vital issue to the Italians, not only on principle but because it would protect them in their own communities from the high-handed behaviour of itinerant Roman magistrates and ensure them a fair share of the spoils of war. Late in 91 the distinguished promoter of yet another Franchise Bill fell dead with a shoemaker's knife in his hip, and their patience finally snapped. Several of the most powerful tribes promptly repudiated their alliance with Rome, established a rival capital in the Apennines, and faced the Republic with two years of the most bitter fighting it had known since Hannibal had invaded Italy nearly a hundred and thirty years before.

To meet this new emergency Rome deployed all her best generals including Pompey's father, Pompeius Strabo. Of Strabo's earlier career we can piece together very little except that he had served as quaestor in Sardinia in 104, had become praetor by 92, and had then, like Sulla, seen service abroad as governor of a province, most probably Macedonia which had once been governed by his father. Although Strabo was widely disliked, he was an excellent military commander, and he was sent to operate against the confederate forces in Picenum, to the north-east, where he had extensive family estates and where the rebels had opened hostilities with the massacre of all Roman citizens in the strategic town of Asculum. Pompey, now in his sixteenth year, accompanied him.

Strabo lost no time in raising an army from his clients and retainers, but on his way to Asculum he was checked and besieged in Firmum by an army of the Marsi. These were formidable enemies who justly claimed that there had never been a Roman triumph without them or over them, but eventually Strabo succeeded in breaking through and laid siege to Asculum, whose defenders hurled lead sling-bullets that still survive bearing the inscriptions 'for Pompeius' and 'for his guts'. In recognition of this and other services in the first year of the war he was elected to the consulship for 89, the first his family had ever achieved, and towards the end of that year he succeeded in taking Asculum after winning a great battle against a rebel relief-force. What part the young Pompey played in all this we do not know, but it would be out of character if he had not borne his share of the fighting besides serving as a member of his father's council-of-war – a capacity in which, so an inscription informs us, he witnessed the granting of Roman citizenship to some thirty Spanish cavalrymen in recognition of their outstanding bravery in the field.

But not all Rome's generals were as effective as Pompeius Strabo. One of the two consuls was killed and his army defeated in each year of the war, and Rome had been forced to contain the rebellion by conceding citizenship to all those tribes which had not revolted by the end of 90, and to all the rest who wanted it in the following year. It was therefore a particularly unnecessary war, a retrospective civil war that claimed 300,000 lives and taught Roman to fight against Roman on a scale that was soon to bring a new dimension to the increasingly violent politics of Pompey's lifetime. 'For hitherto,' says Appian, 'the political murders and seditions at Rome had been intermittent domestic affairs on a relatively small scale, but from now on the leaders of the factions began to assail each other with great armies according to the laws of war, and looked upon their country as the prize in a contest of arms.'

The first to do this was Sulla over a new quarrel with Marius. Both of them had performed great services in the Italian War and had actually joined forces on one occasion to win a battle against the Marsi, but whereas Marius had resigned his command at the end of the first year on the grounds of ill-health, Sulla, like Pompeius Strabo, had gone on to achieve even greater success in the second and the reward of the consulship for 88. Naturally it did not please Marius to see Sulla reaching the same level of dignity as himself (and divorcing his third wife in order to marry the more illustrious niece of his old enemy Metellus), but what really fuelled their quarrel was the Senate's appointment of Sulla to the command in the East which Marius had mentally reserved for himself ever since he had tried to provoke King Mithridates into war some ten years before.

Rome's preoccupation with a self-destructive war had finally convinced the expansionist King of Pontus that the time had come to take advantage of her unpopularity in the East. Beginning experimentally by repeating the take-over of Cappadocia, Mithridates had gone on to invade Bithynia and the whole of Roman Asia Minor. Everywhere he had been hailed as the great deliverer from the exactions of the Roman tax-gatherers and the even more rapacious money-lenders whose interests coincided. In a terrific outburst of anti-Roman feeling every Italian man, woman and child east of the Aegean had been put to the sword, and soon there were large Oriental armies sailing westwards to reverse the

conquests of Alexander. To the Greeks it seemed all too likely that
Mithridates would succeed where Xerxes had failed four centuries before.
Even as Sulla was preparing to sail to their defence, he received the grim
news that Athens had gone over to Mithridates and that all of southern
and central Greece was in enemy hands. Macedonia itself was about to
be invaded across the Hellespont, and though a Roman force was still
operating defiantly in Thessaly, it could not hope to hold out for long
without help. But such was the nature of politics in Rome's jealous aristocracy that Sulla was now faced with what he saw as an unenviable choice
between high treason and disgrace.

Despite his seventy years and recent ill-health Marius coveted the one
last triumph that would both seal his reputation as the greatest general
Rome had ever known and enrich his family with the wealth that only
an Eastern campaign could bring. He also wanted to teach Sulla and his
senatorial friends a lesson. It was only by convention that the Senate
enjoyed the patronage of military commands. Constitutionally Rome was
a democracy. The people were under no legal obligation to accept the
aristocracy's collective wisdom, or lack of it, and there was a vigorous
anti-senatorial faction only too pleased to be exploited by so distinguished and powerful an ally who also happened to be in sympathy with
one of its main aims, namely the equitable distribution of the newly
enfranchised Italians over all the thirty-five existing tribes instead of the
restricted allocation that had been favoured by more reactionary
members of the Senate.

The proposal to transfer the command to Marius was presented to
the popular assembly in a list of other proposals by the orator Sulpicius,
one of the ten tribunes of 88. Sulla, as consul, retaliated by retiring to
examine the heavens for omens, which meant a total suspension of public
business. Sulpicius replied with force, and as his well-drilled mob took
to the streets, all opposition was either trampled or put to flight. Sulla
himself was able to save his skin only by rushing into Marius' house to
beg his protection. The price for this, which was not negotiable, was the
immediate resumption of public business so that the Bill giving Marius
his coveted command could be passed. With the mob howling for his
blood outside, Sulla had only two choices, and chose to live.

A less self-confident or more scrupulous man would have accepted that
he had been outmanœuvred, but Sulla valued nothing more highly than
his dignity. That night he rode secretly out of Rome to ask his former
troops whom they wanted to lead them to plunder and glory in the East.
Fearing that Marius might choose other legions for this lucrative campaign, they made their decision by stoning to death the officers who came
to take command in his name, and before Marius and his friends in Rome

had time to organize an effective defence, there were six hostile legions outside the city-walls. Marius fled to Africa. Sulpicius was killed, and Sulla had the distinction of being the first Roman since Coriolanus to lead an army on Rome.

After first proclaiming the laws of Sulpicius void as having been passed under duress and then compounding the irony by forcing through some legislation of his own, Sulla marched his army to Brundisium (the modern Brindisi), and embarked for the war in Greece. But he was no sooner out of the way than one of the two consuls for 87, Lucius Cornelius Cinna, not only revived Sulpicius' legislation for the fair distribution of the new citizens but proposed the immediate recall of Marius and his friends. He in turn was opposed by his fellow-consul Octavius, who found support from a majority of the Senate and the old citizens, and succeeded in persuading a majority of the tribunes to veto his colleague's proposals. The outcome was that Cinna and his supporters were driven out of Rome, whereupon they began recruiting a large army from the newly enfranchised towns, won over some of the Roman forces that were still stamping out the embers of the Italian War, and sent for Marius to return from Africa. Octavius reacted by summoning reinforcements from loyal towns and recalling other armies which were still in the field in different parts of Italy; but with Sulla in Greece the only man who had a chance of resisting the Marians was Pompey's father, to whom both sides now made urgent appeals.

Pompeius Strabo had been in the field almost continuously since the December of 89, when he had brought his year as consul to a glorious close by celebrating his triumph over the Picentines of Asculum. During 88, in which he had received the surrender of two more of the rebel tribes, the Vestini and Paeligni, he had followed the course of Rome's domestic politics with a keen eye to his own advantage. He had no love for Sulla since that equally unscrupulous careerist had tried to transfer Strabo's army to the other consul of 88, a man whom Sulla felt he could trust while he was away in Greece. This would-be replacement was mysteriously murdered in a mutiny less than twenty-four hours after he had taken over, and though Strabo pretended to be furious, it is generally assumed that he was implicated. He promptly resumed command, and now that Sulla was overseas and Cinna was threatening Rome, he felt himself to be in a strong position to bargain for what he most wanted, which was a second consulship.

How far Strabo reached in his negotiations with each side is uncertain. By refusing for a long time to obey the summons of Octavius and the government in Rome he gave considerable strength to the Marian cause, but Cinna soon tired of his endless vacillations and came to the conclusion that it was only Strabo's authority that was preventing his troops from joining the Marians of their own accord. He suborned assassins in Strabo's camp and relied on sympathizers in the army to mutiny in his own favour as soon as the general was out of the way. But he had reckoned without the vigilance of Strabo's eighteen-year-old son, who was also a target of the conspiracy.

On the evening of the assassination attempt, which involved setting fire to Strabo's tent and stabbing his son in bed, the young Pompey was secretly informed of the plot while he was at dinner with his prospective murderer, his tent-mate Lucius Terentius. With remarkable sang-froid he showed no sign of discomposure. He drank even more freely than usual, showed great friendliness to Terentius, and retired to bed. But as soon as he was alone he quickly made up his couch to look as though he was in it, stole out unperceived to set a guard of trustworthy men round his father's tent, and returned to his own quarters. Eventually he saw a figure stealthily approach his couch and plunge a sword harmlessly into the heaped bedclothes. He was on Terentius in a moment and had soon disposed of him, but the commotion alerted the other conspirators, who took it as their signal to incite mutiny among the troops. Cinna had been correct in supposing that the majority were eager to join him. The uproar was so great that Strabo did not dare to leave his heavily guarded tent, but Pompey, who was loved by the troops as much as his father was feared, went up and down through the camp, appealed to the men with tears, and finally threw himself down at the camp-gates, where he cried out to those who were deserting their general that they must first trample on his son. Amazingly it worked. 'Everyone,' says Plutarch, 'drew back out of shame, and all but eight hundred of the men were reconciled to Strabo', who no longer hesitated to march to the defence of Rome.

Thanks to Strabo's vacillations the Marian forces had grown into an enormous army. Cinna alone is reported to have raised three hundred cohorts from the newly enfranchised Italians. Marius was back in Italy with a bodyguard of his former soldiers who had settled in Africa, and as he marched inland to join Cinna he attracted large numbers of Etruscan volunteers to his standard by the magnetism of his name and his promise to see that the new citizens were fairly distributed. Their combined forces were so great that they divided them into three. Marius took one to capture Ostia, the port of Rome; the second was entrusted to Quintus Sertorius, a brilliant young officer who was destined to play a major part in Pompey's early career; and with the third Cinna confronted Pompey's father, who had taken up a defensive position outside the Colline Gate. But Strabo was not in the least daunted by the odds against him. Just as he had seen the struggle between the supporters of Sulla and Marius solely in terms of his personal advancement, so his personal animosity towards the man who had tried to murder him now made him bold for any desperate enterprise that offered the chance of revenge.

An appalling battle ensued. According to Velleius Paterculus, 'words cannot express how disastrous to combatants and spectators alike was the result of this hideous struggle that began and ended under the walls and gaze of the city of Rome'. To Livy its horrors were typified by the story of a soldier who burst into tears when stripping the corpse of a slain opponent: as he removed the helmet, he saw the face of his own brother, and such was his revulsion and remorse that he committed suicide on the funeral pyre. And when at the end of the day the exhausted armies retired to cremate their dead, there was no clear advantage to either side, but only a new and more sinister enemy, a terrifying epidemic that proceeded to decimate the survivors.

The Marians' next attempt to shorten the siege came when Marius persuaded the officer commanding the defence forces on the Janiculum to open the gates to him as a personal favour. Marius in turn admitted Cinna, their troops began pouring into the city, and Octavius was on the point of defeat when Strabo appeared with reinforcements and managed to force the Marians out again. But it was Strabo's last battle, for soon afterwards he was dead. According to one tradition he was struck by lightning in a thunderstorm. Another suggests that he succumbed to the plague that was ravaging his camp, and it is not inconceivable that he was helped on his way by a Marian agent.

Although his death was a crippling blow to the defenders, our sources are unanimous in claiming that the only tears which were shed for Strabo outside the bosom of his own family were tears of joy. According to Plutarch 'the Romans have never shown so fierce a hatred of any general', while Velleius Paterculus maintains that 'the joy felt at his death nearly outweighed the feeling of loss for the citizens who had perished by the sword or the plague'. Velleius adds that 'the Roman people vented upon the dead body the hatred it had owed him while he lived', and Plutarch elaborates by describing how the corpse was dragged from the bier on its way to the pyre and 'heaped with insults'. The universal judgement on Pompey's father was that he was totally unprincipled, insatiably greedy for money and honours, yet a great soldier. How so eminently unlikable a general actually managed to command troops is a fascinating question which has been asked of many great military commanders in more modern times. Plutarch's answer was that 'while he lived, they feared him, for he was a very warlike man'. His was a natural authority, and because of his great ability as a soldier in a series of crises he rose to the highest office of state though almost friendless even among his peers.

The resistance in Rome soon collapsed after Strabo's death. Crowds of starving citizens and slaves flocked to join the Marian forces for the promise of food or freedom. Octavius refused all compromise, but the despairing Senate sent ambassadors to negotiate a settlement with Cinna and Marius, who demanded that their sentences of exile should be formally repealed. Significantly they refused to promise an end to bloodshed, and when they entered Rome they lost no time in avenging themselves on their enemies. Octavius stood his ground and lost his head, which went on display in the Forum. Nor was it the sole exhibit there, for there was a wholesale hunting down and killing of all those prominent supporters of Sulla who failed to anticipate their punishment by taking their own lives. Sulla was voted a public enemy, his house burnt to the ground, his property confiscated, and his legislation repealed. Cinna and Marius were elected consuls for 86, Cinna for the second time, Marius for the seventh, and the new regime provided a splendid opportunity for personal enemies to give a veneer of legality to the settling of old scores.

It was not long before young Pompey became the object of a lawsuit. He was arraigned as Strabo's heir on a charge of stealing public property, namely booty from the sack of Asculum three years earlier. But the charge failed. There had certainly been thefts, but most of them turned out to have been committed by a member of Strabo's household, and Pompey was able to prove it to the satisfaction of the court. He was then accused on his own account of being in possession of hunting-nets and books, trivial gifts which he had indeed received from his father out of the spoils of Asculum. But again he was acquitted, this time for lack of evidence since these particular items of public property had conveniently disappeared when Cinna's guards had ransacked his house on entering Rome.

All the same, it had been quite an ordeal for a nineteen-year-old. He had had powerful advocates in the orator Hortensius and the distinguished Lucius Marcius Philippus, formerly consul and now censor, but Plutarch also says that he had many direct exchanges with his accusers in which he impressed everyone by 'a sharpness of wit and degree of poise beyond his years'. Indeed, the judge himself, the aedile Antistius, was so taken with the young defendant that he decided to offer him his daughter in marriage before the trial was half over. Pompey accepted and a supposedly secret agreement was made between the two families, but the people soon got wind of the matter. Antistius aroused their suspicions by ill-concealed attempts to favour his future son-in-law during the trial, and when the day came on which he pronounced the acquittal, the crowded court broke out into the bawdy marriage hymn that well-wishers customarily sang to Roman newly-weds – only a little prematurely because Pompey and Antistia were married a few days later.

It was widely acknowledged that Antistia had made a good match. Pompey had inherited from his father the dignity of his rank and the wealth of his estates without any of those defects of personality that had made Strabo so universally hated. To charm, tact and utter reliability he added a degree of modesty which was quite remarkable in so handsome a young man, for Plutarch is insistent that his face was his fortune in those early days. 'His good looks,' says the biographer, 'played a great part in his popularity, and pleaded for him before he opened his mouth.' From his youth he is credited with a regal appearance. 'There was also the way his hair lifted from the forehead,' adds Plutarch, 'and the graceful contours of his face around the eyes that produced a resemblance to portraits of Alexander the Great.' And though Plutarch suggests that this resemblance was more talked about than apparent, the name Alexander stuck so firmly to Pompey that when Lucius Philippus was pleading on his behalf in court he was able to say that he was 'doing nothing strange if, being Philip, he loved Alexander'. But if there were many who applauded this clever remark, there was not one who realized how soon this young man's deeds would make the comparison with the conqueror of the East much more than a matter of mere physiognomy.

2
BEARDLESS *IMPERATOR*

What so novel as for a mere youth, a private citizen holding
no office, to raise an army at a time of crisis in the Republic,
command it in person, and wage war successfully under his
own direction?
Cicero, *For the Manilian Law*, 61

For three years Pompey was free to enjoy his married life in peace, but
in 84 the prospect of Sulla's return from the East revived the Civil War
and presented him with his father's problem of deciding which side to
join. While Sulla had been fighting King Mithridates in Greece and Asia
Minor, the Marians had had everything their own way in Rome. Marius
himself had succumbed to a heart-attack only days after entering his
seventh consulship, but Cinna had continued as consul in each of the
years 86–84, first with Valerius Flaccus as his colleague, then with
Papirius Carbo for the last two years. They had hoped that Sulla would
never return, for he had been faced not only with the formidable Mithridates but also with a Roman army which Flaccus had taken to Greece
in 86 to fight both of them. But Sulla had proved indestructible. 'In less
than three years,' says Appian, 'he had killed 160,000 men, recovered
Greece, Macedonia, Ionia, Asia and many other countries which Mithridates had occupied, and taken the king's fleet away from him.' As for
the Marian army which was to have fought him in Greece, it had preferred
to fight Mithridates instead, and when Sulla had made peace with the
defeated king in 84, it had promptly mutinied in his favour and joined
forces with him after killing its own commander.

When this news reached Rome along with a threatening letter from
Sulla to the Senate, the consuls Cinna and Carbo began a vast mobilization in Italy while the Senate sent envoys to Greece to attempt a reconciliation. But Sulla was implacable. When the envoys offered to guarantee
his security if he would return in peace and disband his army, he replied
that he would never be friends with criminals. 'And as for security,' he
added, 'I am in a far better position to offer it to you than you to
me.'

Seeing that war was inevitable, Cinna made the praiseworthy decision to spare Italy by fighting Sulla in Greece. He chose an Adriatic port as the assembly-point for his army and shipped his first detachment to Greece without problems, but the second was caught in a terrific storm which did nothing to hearten men who had little enough stomach for a war against the victors of Mithridates. When the survivors reached Italian *terra firma* again, they simply melted away to their homes, and this provoked a general mutiny among the rest of the army. Cinna called a parade with the intention of restoring discipline by a stern harangue, but feelings were running so high that when he ordered the arrest of a soldier who had struck one of his lictors, there was a great outburst of anger and Cinna was stabbed to death. It was not enough to stop the Civil War but more than enough to decide his fellow-consul Carbo to wait for Sulla in Italy.

In the meantime Pompey had changed sides. At first he had offered his services to Cinna. After all, if his father had fought against Cinna, he had been no friend of Sulla either, and on balance it seemed better to join an elected consul preparing to defend Rome than an outlaw, however artificial the legalities of the situation. But Pompey was mistaken if he thought that his acquittal in court had cleansed him from all taint of the Marian blood which Strabo had spilt so liberally three years before. He had no sooner joined Cinna's camp than he became the target of all kinds of new accusations, which so put him in fear of his life that he quietly retired to his family estates in Picenum. Plutarch even suggests that it was Pompey's mysterious disappearance and a suspicion that Cinna had made away with him that sparked off the mutiny in which Cinna was killed, but in the absence of confirmation from other sources it seems unlikely that Pompey was so very popular in Cinna's camp. On the contrary, it was clearly his unpopularity as Strabo's son that convinced him that he had no future in the Marian cause, for when we next hear of him, he is raising a private army in support of Sulla.

When news came in the spring of 83 that Sulla had left Athens for the port of Patras from where he intended to launch his invasion of Italy, Pompey disdained to join the exiles and other opponents of the Marian regime who were flocking to join him as fugitives requesting help. Having offered his services to one of his father's enemies and suffered a rebuff, he was not going to approach another without proving his worth, and he decided to join Sulla not as a suppliant but as an ally with an army of his own.

It was the sort of novelty which could happen only in civil war. Pompey was probably not yet twenty-three and had held not even the most junior public office, let alone been given legal authority to raise an army, yet he used his influence to stir up the Picentines whose traditional allegiance to his house had always been strong. At first his efforts were not taken seriously by Carbo's agents who were recruiting for the Marian armies in the same area, but they soon changed their attitude after a local wit had been lynched at a public meeting for making a snide remark about Pompey's youth – that he had 'evidently left his pedagogues to become a demagogue among them'.

At Auximum, where Pompey set up his tribunal in the market-place, eager young men were soon flocking to enlist under his colours. He supplied pay and provisions entirely from his own resources, and with a professionalism worthy of his father's training he organized the volunteers into centuries and cohorts, to which he appointed centurions and officers in regular fashion. Soon he was strong enough to order Carbo's recruiting officers out of the city, and when he had a sufficiently impressive force he marched it round the neighbouring towns and cities with such bravado that its numbers had grown to six thousand by the time he heard that Sulla had landed in Brindisi and was preparing to march on Rome.

In comparison with the two hundred and fifty cohorts of five hundred men which Appian gives as the size of the Marian forces, Pompey's one legion was little enough support for the forty thousand men whom Sulla had brought with him from Greece, but it was evidently considered sufficiently dangerous for the Marians to send no less than three armies to try to destroy it before it could leave Picenum. Unaware of the preparations being made to annihilate him, Pompey marched slowly southwards to join Sulla, 'not in haste nor even with a desire to escape observation, but taking his time, harrying the enemy, and doing his best to detach from Carbo's party all that part of Italy through which he passed'. Nor was he dismayed when his scouts reported that three hostile generals were closing in on him from different directions. Far from trying to escape by forced marches, he calmly collected his army together, picked the nearest of the enemy armies, and struck first. Leading the cavalry in person, he charged straight for the commander of the Marians' Celtic Horse and ran him through, with the result that the rest of the enemy cavalry were thrown into confusion, recoiled on to their own infantry, and turned the battle into a rout. It was a great success for Pompey and one that had wide repercussions, for it not only freed him from immediate danger but caused such disagreement on tactics among the three enemy generals that they quarrelled and retired, leaving a large number of cities eager to transfer their allegiance.

As a result of this success Pompey seems to have changed his mind about marching south to join Sulla in favour of consolidating his position

in Picenum, for he is next reliably reported fighting a battle on the River
Aesis that forms the boundary between Picenum and Umbria. This time
Carbo himself was directing operations and made a determined effort
to overwhelm him with a superior force of cavalry, but Pompey met their
attack with such vigour that he succeeded in driving them into difficult
ground, where he promptly attacked them with infantry as they struggled
to re-form. It was a fine piece of generalship. Hopelessly bogged down,
they had no choice but an unconditional surrender, which gave Pompey
his second victory in two battles, a valuable haul of armour and horses,
and one more to add to the growing catalogue of services which he would
be able to present to Sulla when they eventually met – assuming, of course,
that his commander-in-chief was still alive. For Pompey and Sulla knew
little about each other's progress, and Pompey must have been in constant
fear of hearing that a defeat of Sulla's army had left his one legion the
sole object of the Marian war-effort. But he need not have worried,
for Sulla had been doing very well since he had landed unopposed at
Brundisium and begun his long march to Rome.

Following the Appian Way Sulla had passed unchallenged through
Calabria and Apulia and crossed the Apennines into Campania before
being brought up short by two consular armies waiting for him in strategic positions, one holding the line of the River Volturnus, the other
near the town of Teanum. But neither of these numerically superior forces
was a match for Sulla's hardened veterans, whose general enjoyed that
perfect combination of the qualities of the lion and the fox which Machia-
velli considered indispensable to the successful prince. He routed the first
with a loss of only seventy of his own men to six thousand of the enemy,
if we may believe figures which came from his own memoirs. He then
crossed the Volturnus against the second, but instead of attacking at once,
he pitched camp and opened negotiations with the Marian consul Scipio
in order to gain time for his agents to organize a mutiny in the ranks
of an enemy already disheartened by the disaster which had overtaken
their comrades. This accomplished, he used a technical infraction of the
armistice as his excuse to resume hostilities, and as the two armies
approached each other, he had the satisfaction of seeing the enemy
general deserted by all his troops except his own son. It was an amazing
episode, at once a terrible condemnation of the ineffectual generalship
of the Marian army and a most valuable victory for Sulla, whose Machia-
vellian methods had not only got rid of a hostile army but doubled his
own.

But these successes in Campania were only the first encounters in what
promised to be a long and terrible struggle. If Sulla could now claim control of Calabria, Apulia and Campania in the south, by far the greater

part of Italy and Rome itself still adhered to the consuls. Latium, Umbria, Etruria and the Gauls of the Po valley were almost solidly of Marian sympathies, as was warlike Samnium which remained undefeated from the Italian War but had been left alone by the Marian regime. Indeed, the only territory in the whole of central or northern Italy to offer Sulla any encouragement was Picenum, where the son of his old enemy Pompeius Strabo had unaccountably begun recruiting on his behalf and had last been reported under attack from three armies at once. Sulla was not the man to question fortune's gifts. As soon as he had consolidated his position in Campania, he marched northwards to try to rescue his unlikely young supporter – and learnt of his victories on the way.

When Pompey heard that Sulla was approaching, he marched to meet him with pleasurable expectations. He could well imagine the incredulous delight with which the great man must have received the first reports of his successes over the Marian generals, and he was determined to make the most favourable possible impression at their first meeting. Accordingly he ordered his forces to be drawn up not in marching order but in full battle array, 'for he expected great honours from Sulla', says Plutarch, 'and received even greater'. When Sulla saw him advancing at the head of so formidable an army of young and vigorous soldiers, all immaculately turned out and elated by success, he actually dismounted from his horse and approached Pompey on foot. This itself was a mark of high distinction, but when Pompey saluted him *Imperator* – the coveted designation of a victorious Roman general – Sulla responded by greeting him in return with the same title. 'It was unthinkable,' says Plutarch, 'that so young a man, not even a senator, could receive from Sulla the title for which he himself was fighting with the greatest men in the state.' And this was not the last of the distinctions with which Sulla rewarded Pompey's enterprise, 'for ever after that time he would rise from his chair and uncover his head whenever Pompey approached' – two marks of distinction which Plutarch says he rarely conferred on anyone else, 'though there were many of high rank around around him'.

The rest of the summer of 83 was spent in consolidation by both sides – besieging hostile towns and cities that still held out in the districts otherwise under their control, recruiting new forces and sending agents to stir up disaffection in each other's armies. Carbo had returned to Rome in a fury and destroyed all possibility of a negotiated settlement by having all senators who had joined Sulla declared public enemies. He then had himself elected consul for the following year along with Marius the Younger, now in his late twenties – 'a son who showed his father's spirit though not destined to reach his years'. And for the most part the people of Rome were united with their consuls against Sulla, 'for they remembered the cruelty of his former attack on the city and took account of the decrees they had since proclaimed against him, the destruction of his house, the confiscation of his property, the killing of his friends and his own family's narrow escape'.

When the campaigning season re-opened in the spring of 82 there were two distinct theatres of war. The southern was Latium, where young Marius was preparing to block Sulla's advance on Rome from Campania. The northern was in Picenum and Umbria, where Carbo was directing operations against the Sullan forces under Metellus Pius and Pompey, the former as commander-in-chief, the latter now one of his legates along with another famous name, the future millionaire Marcus Crassus who had lost both his father and brother in the Marian massacres in Rome. That Metellus and not Pompey had been appointed commander-in-chief was not a recognition of superior ability – for Plutarch tells us that Pompey talked Sulla out of a decision to appoint him instead – but of superior rank, since Metellus as a proconsul was the highest ranking Roman to have joined Sulla, besides being his cousin by marriage. For a man like Metellus to hold the senior command lent a certain legitimacy to Sulla's cause, and Pompey, knowing that he would be allowed a fairly free hand with his own army, had tactfully endeared himself to the older man by formally writing to offer his services.

Plutarch tells us that the effect of Pompey on Metellus was like 'molten bronze poured round something that is cold and stiff with age', but unfortunately he gives no details of Pompey's activities beyond a general indication of continued success. 'Just as no account or record is taken of the boyish victories of great athletes who have become world-champions and carried off glorious prizes everywhere, so it is with the deeds of Pompey at this time: they were extraordinary in themselves but buried under the multitude and magnitude of his later wars and conquests.' But there are other sources from which we can piece together some of the exploits of Pompey's growing army, which eventually became three legions strong.

While the armies of Sulla and Marius were stalking each other like rival lions in Latium, Metellus was experiencing mixed fortunes in the north. After defeating one of Carbo's officers, the praetor named Carrinas, he was attacked in greater strength by Carbo himself, besieged in a friendly city, and relieved only by the news of a Marian disaster in the south. When Carbo heard that Marius had been routed at Sacriportus and put under siege in the town of Praeneste after being hoisted up the city-walls in a basket, he withdrew his disheartened army to Ariminum, the modern Rimini, with Pompey 'hanging on his tail and doing much damage'. Metellus then returned to the offensive, and while he was defeating another of Carbo's armies, Pompey overcame Gaius Marcius, one of Carbo's legates, at the town of Sena Gallica, some distance up the Adriatic coast from the mouth of the Aesis.

Sulla in the meantime was marching on Rome. After his defeat and siege of Marius, all the cities on his route threw open their gates to him and he entered the capital unopposed, though too late to prevent the wholesale execution of his sympathizers for which the beleaguered consul had sent orders from Praeneste. Among the victims was Pompey's father-in-law Antistius, who was cut down in the Senate House because he was thought to be a partisan of Sulla for Pompey's sake, and when she saw his body floating in the Tiber his grief-stricken wife Calpurnia committed suicide.

With the contraction of the southern front to little more than the siege of Praeneste, the heart of the war moved northwards into the Marian strongholds of Tuscany, Umbria and the Gallic lands south of the Po. After occupying Rome and confiscating the property of his enemies who had fled, Sulla now launched a three-pronged invasion of the Marian territory in which he and Pompey began to close in on the main concentration of Marian forces around Clusium while Metellus sailed up the Adriatic to by-pass the Marian base at Ariminum and land an army at Ravenna in support of the Sullan units already operating in the Po valley. Sulla himself, marching northwards from Rome, fought an indecisive, day-long battle against Carbo, who had been massing his troops at Lars Porsenna's famous city for an attempt to recapture Rome. Pompey in the meantime, marching south-west from Picenum, had joined forces with Crassus and met Carbo's officer Carrinas near the Umbrian town of Spoletium, where they killed three thousand of the enemy and put Carrinas under siege. Carbo sent a relieving force to Spoletium, but Sulla discovered its movements and arranged to have it ambushed on the way. Even so, Carrinas and his army took the opportunity of a stormy night to escape.

Angry with himself for losing Carrinas, Pompey soon made up for it by defeating a much larger force which Carbo had sent under his legate Gaius Marcius to relieve Marius at Praeneste. Marcius had eight legions, a force considerably larger than the entire army with which Sulla had landed in Italy in the previous year, but Pompey caught the enemy by surprise in a defile, killed a large number, and surrounded the rest when they took up a defensive position on a hill. Both sides then dug in for the night. The next morning Pompey was eager to renew the battle, but there was no one to fight. Marcius had decamped unobserved in the night by the simple expedient of leaving a lot of camp-fires burning. It was an ancient ruse and Pompey was furious with himself and his scouts for being taken in by it, but no further action from him was needed to complete the victory. For although Marcius had successfully extricated his army from the trap, his troops still blamed him for leading them into it, and mutinied. While one whole legion marched off without orders to Ariminum, most of the remaining men simply melted away, and their unhappy general was left with only seven cohorts out of his original eighty when he returned crestfallen to Carbo's camp.

By now the succession of Sullan victories and the capture of Rome were turning the odds against the Marians. Better generalship had told over superior numbers, and at least one Marian leader, the able Quintus Sertorius, had so far despaired of his party's cause in Italy that he had already left to prepare a base for the refugees in Spain. But the odds were suddenly reversed by the intervention of the Samnites. As this warlike tribe had not formally laid down its arms since the Italian War, Sulla had not included it in the general amnesty which he had proclaimed to the newly enfranchised Italians in the hope of undermining their support for the Marian regime. On the contrary, he had put to death all men of Samnite origin among the prisoners he had taken from the defeated Marian army outside Praeneste. The Samnites were well aware that the relative autonomy which they had enjoyed under the Marian regime would come to a bloody end if Sulla became master of Rome, and when they saw the continuing failure of all Carbo's attempts to relieve Marius, they decided to do it themselves and to avenge the massacre of their fellow-tribesmen at the same time.

When Sulla heard that seventy thousand Samnites were on their way to Praeneste, he marched to intercept them, entrenched his army on the heights of the only pass to the city, and repulsed their repeated attempts to force the pass and Marius' attempts to break out and join them. But Sulla's preoccupation with the Samnites gave Carbo his chance to deal with Metellus in the north. Leaving legates to hold Pompey in check and prevent his reinforcing either Sulla or Metellus, he marched up to his base at Ariminum, collected new forces, and made a surprise attack on Metellus' camp near Faventia, but he succeeded only in surprising himself by the scale of his failure. Of the seventeen thousand men he had brought with him no less than ten thousand were killed and a further six thousand deserted before the shattered remnants struggled back to their base.

Rattled by repeated failure, Carbo now made another attempt to rescue his fellow-consul by sending two legions to reinforce the Samnites, but he waited in vain for news that they had dislodged Sulla from the pass. Instead he heard that all the Gauls between Ravenna and the Alps had gone over to Metellus, and this new disaster finally broke his nerve. He despaired and fled to Africa. No doubt he justified this decision to himself by planning to recruit new forces among the Marian veterans there, but it was a shameful confession of his inability to use the still considerable forces at his disposal in Italy, where the war was far from over. Gaul might be lost, but Etruria and Umbria were still firm. At Clusium there was an army of thirty thousand threatening Pompey. And Sulla was still confronting the seventy thousand Samnites and two legions at the pass.

But suddenly there were no Samnites at the pass. They were marching on Rome, not for citizenship but for liberty, and it was civil war no longer. Their general was an ardent nationalist, and when he addressed his men before battle, he called for the utter destruction of the city. ' "These wolves," ' he cried, ' "that have made such ravages on Italian liberty will never vanish until we have cut down and destroyed the forest that harbours them." ' 'And truly,' writes Velleius Paterculus, 'the city of Rome had not faced a greater danger when Hannibal had pitched his camp within the third milestone' a hundred and thirty-five years before.

Sulla raced to Rome's defence with his entire army, arrived exhausted in the late afternoon, and fought at once with his back to the Colline Gate. By nightfall he was in despair. His left wing, which he had commanded in person, had been driven back so violently that only the dropping of the portcullis by the veterans on the wall had prevented the enemy pursuing his men through the city-gate. As for the right wing, which he had entrusted to Marcus Crassus, he had lost touch with it altogether and feared the worst. It was quite unexpected when messengers came from Crassus requesting him to send supper to the troops, but when Sulla seemed surprised that Crassus still had any troops to send supper to, he was informed that they were exceedingly hungry after routing the enemy. The victory was as good as won.

In the morning it was soon over. Fifty thousand men had lost their lives, and there was no shortage of Marian heads to display to the beleaguered citizens of Praeneste, whose sole remaining hope was the army which Carbo had deserted in Etruria. Then came Pompey's news, that he had met and defeated it in a great battle round Clusium in which he had killed twenty thousand and the rest had deserted. Praeneste surrendered and Marius committed suicide, denying Sulla the pleasure of his execution but providing him with a very satisfactory head to display in the Forum.

' "First learn to row before you try to take the helm," ' sneered Sulla when he saw the young consul's head being stuck on its spike – a tasteless quotation from Aristophanes that gives evidence of a classical education as well as a remarkable capacity for hypocrisy. For it was not only a cruel jest but an inappropriate one from a victor who owed so much of his own success to the even younger Pompey. But

Sulla did not approve of electing men in their twenties head of state, especially if they fought against him. It was quite different for twenty-two-year-olds who had held no public office whatever to raise private armies as long as they fought on his side, and now that he was master of Rome, he lost no time in rewarding Pompey and all his other supporters. But in Pompey's case he was prepared to offer more than the material rewards which he lavished on the rest. He saw in him a young man of great ability whom he could mould in his own image, and in his eagerness to reinforce the bond between them he insisted on a marriage alliance.

It was a thoroughly unsavoury proposition for all parties. It meant not only a divorce for poor Antistia, who had already lost both her parents, but an even more painful separation for the intended replacement, Sulla's stepdaughter Aemilia, who was already pregnant by her existing husband. Perhaps Pompey should have refused, as the young Julius Caesar did when Sulla ordered him to divorce Cinna's daughter. But their circumstances were very different at this time. Caesar, six years younger than Pompey, was a relative nonentity, one of a large number of young noblemen who had taken no part in the war and were almost beneath Sulla's notice. Pompey on the contrary was Sulla's protégé, dependent on continued favour for the promotion of a most unconventional career, and if we cannot applaud his compliance in what was undoubtedly a shabby affair, we can at least appreciate his dilemma. But no good came of the marriage. Soon after Aemilia was installed in Pompey's house she had a miscarriage and died, to the great distress of all parties except Sulla himself, whose feelings went no further than annoyance at the frustration of his plan.

Sulla's treatment of the defeated Marians shows that he was incapable of compassion, or indeed of any feeling finer than that of gratified self-interest. 'Down to the moment of his victory,' says Velleius Paterculus, referring to his attempts to undermine popular support for the Marian cause, 'he had shown himself more moderate than could have been expected; but when once he had conquered, his cruelty was unprecedented.' For a start Sulla ordered six thousand Samnite and other Italian prisoners of war to be herded together in the Circus Maximus and systematically butchered, with careful timing to create the maximum effect among his peers. It began just as he was starting to address a meeting of the Senate in the nearby Temple of Bellona, and when the terrified senators demanded to know what was happening, he was ready to rebuke them 'for letting themselves be distracted from important affairs of state by nothing more than the screaming of a few criminals paying the just penalty for their crimes'. Then came the notorious proscriptions. A list naming eighty outlaws appeared on public notice-boards in the city. All were prominent men supposedly of Marian sympathies, and all might be killed with impunity and with such financial advantage to their murderers that wealthy men became the victims of their own property. More lists followed as the days went by. Altogether some sixteen hundred prominent Romans perished by proscription, while Sulla sat daily in the Forum like an auctioneer knocking down the estates of his enemies at bargain prices to his friends.

But not all the proscribed were within reach. Many of the Marian leaders, like Carbo, had escaped from Italy before the final collapse and taken refuge in Spain, Africa and Sicily, where the governors were appointments of the Marian regime. From there they hoped to build up their shattered strength so that at worst they might maintain themselves safely in exile and at best organize a counter-invasion. And they were not without resources in those provinces, for while Spain was strong in men, Africa and Sicily were the two main sources of Rome's increasingly vital overseas corn-supply. It was therefore more than a matter of mere revenge when Sulla sent Pompey to Sicily with a large army in the autumn of 82.

After the unhappiness of his enforced divorce and remarriage Pompey was no doubt glad to have something more energetic and honourable to do than stay in Rome and watch Sulla enjoying his cold-blooded vengeance. He also had the satisfaction of obtaining his first formal, legal command, for though he had never held the praetorship or any of the more junior magistracies, the obedient Senate conferred praetorian authority on him for the purpose of his present assignment. He therefore had the same rank as Perperna, the Marian governor of Sicily whom he now set out to dispossess. But Perperna was so impressed by Pompey's reputation and the size of his army that he simply abandoned the island and fled. Carbo, who had just arrived in Sicily from Africa, did the same. He took his troops to the island of Cossyra, the present-day Pantellaria, which lies about three-quarters of the way between Sicily and the North African coast. From there he sent one of his companions in a fishing-boat to the port of Lilybaeum on the south-western corner of Sicily to see if Pompey had yet reached that part of the island. Pompey had sent a squadron of ships to patrol the south coast against this very eventuality. They picked up Carbo's lieutenant and soon afterwards Carbo himself, though exactly where and how the former consul was captured is not recorded. He may still have been on Cossyra or attempting to flee back to Africa, but wherever it was, he lacked his lieutenant's courage to fall on his sword. Perhaps he hoped that his rank would save him, but he survived the immediate execution of all his companions only because Pompey had ordered him to be spared for questioning.

To many it caused distress to see a man who had been three times consul grovelling in chains beneath the tribunal of a twenty-four-year-old who was not even a senator, and Plutarch says it would have been better if he had been put to death without seeing Pompey, 'so that the deed would have seemed his whose order it was', namely Sulla's. The best that can be said in defence of Pompey's conduct is that he may have felt it necessary to interrogate Carbo about the strengths and dispositions of the Marian forces in Africa; even so it cannot be denied that the young inquisitor relished his authority. Carbo made a pathetic spectacle as he was led away to the place of execution. No sooner had the sword been drawn than he begged a few moments and a private place to empty his bowels, and he died 'weeping like a woman', no doubt to the great satisfaction of Sulla when he read the detailed dispatch which accompanied the head to Rome.

A hostile tradition has it that this was not an isolated instance of cruelty on Pompey's part. There is a story that he delayed the execution of one of the prominent Marians who was a famous scholar purely in order to have time to pick his brains before removing his head, but Plutarch warns us to beware of such tales as the later fabrications of friends of Caesar. He argues that Pompey had no choice but to punish those enemies of Sulla who were so eminent that their capture could not be kept secret, but where less prominent men were involved, he tells us that Pompey allowed as many as possible to escape detection and even helped to smuggle some off the island. He also tells the story of Pompey's compassion on the city of Himera, which was high on the list for punishment but was saved by the selfless action of a leading citizen named Sthenius. This brave and honourable man begged an audience of Pompey and warned him that it would be very wrong to let the real culprit go and destroy those who were blameless. Amazed at this bold and extraordinary statement from a citizen who might have been expected to plead for pardon, Pompey demanded to know whom he meant by 'the real culprit' and was even more surprised when Sthenius replied that he meant himself, since he alone was responsible for persuading his fellow-citizens to follow their disastrous course. 'At that,' says Plutarch, 'Pompey was so admiring of the man's frankness and spirit that he pardoned not only him but the whole city.'

Although this story may have been dramatized by Plutarch to make the fate of a whole city depend on the self-sacrifice of one man, we do know from references in Cicero's Verrine orations that Pompey pardoned Sthenius at this time when he came before his court. Cicero says nothing about the proposed destruction of the city, only that Sthenius, a rich philanthropist, was denounced before Pompey by his enemies on a charge of having offered friendship and hospitality to the elder Gaius Marius, and that Pompey refused to consider the giving of hospitality to so distinguished a man a proof of disloyalty to Rome. But he does add that Pompey's handsome behaviour in this case won him 'the gratitude and friendship not only of the man he had saved but of the whole province'.

There seems no doubt that the young governor made himself generally popular in Sicily. If his executions of Marian leaders earned him the nickname of 'the apprentice butcher' from their sympathizers, the moderation which he showed in dealing with the Sicilian cities surprised all those who had expected the worst from a young man who was a protégé of the terrible Sulla and could so easily have let power go to his head. Where Sulla commanded obedience through fear and was indifferent to men's hatred, Pompey preferred to influence people by winning friends. But he was not to be trifled with. When the Mamertines of Messana refused his jurisdiction on the grounds of an obsolete piece of Roman legislation and began to argue their case instead of opening their gates, he cut them short by suggesting that they should ' "stop reading laws at men who have swords strapped to our sides" '. It was a typically Sullan reply, but where cities and individuals were prepared to co-operate with him, he treated them with a kindness that made a welcome change from the harshness of Perperna and revealed itself not least impressively in the strict control which he maintained over his troops. Already he was showing that flair for provincial administration that was to make him the great architect of Rome's empire in the East in the years to come.

Pompey's next assignment came in a decree from the Senate and a letter from Sulla ordering him to proceed from Sicily to Africa and make war against the Marian general Domitius Ahenobarbus, a bronze-bearded ancestor of the emperor Nero. Domitius, who was probably already in Africa when his name had been proscribed in the previous year, had assumed command of the province after the previous Marian governor had been burnt to death in an uprising at Utica. He had raised a powerful Roman army from the Marian veterans who had been settled there after the Jugurthine War, and he could count on the support of the new King Hiarbas of neighbouring Numidia in exchange for having supported his usurpation. Between them Domitius and King Hiarbas could field a formidable array, and Domitius was not the man to flee like Perperna at the first approach of danger.

Pompey's preparations were made as quickly as possible for so serious an undertaking. To govern Sicily in his absence he appointed his sister's husband Memmius, a man he could trust, and when everything was ready he set sail for Africa with six legions, a hundred and twenty warships and some eight hundred transports crammed with troops and their supplies of food, pay, weapons, armour and artillery. As he approached the North African coast he divided his armada and landed in two places, at Utica and Carthage, but this seems to have been an unnecessary precaution. Indeed, he not only landed unopposed but was immediately joined by seven thousand deserters from the enemy, which brought his total strength to something in excess of forty thousand men. It was a promising beginning, but just as he was ready to march inland in search of Domitius, he suffered the embarrassment of losing control of his troops for several days while they dug for buried treasure.

The trouble had started when some soldiers had unearthed a cache of buried coins. Soon the whole camp was buzzing with the story, and every soldier was convinced that he was sitting on a fabulous treasure which the Carthaginians must have buried before the destruction of their city some sixty-five years before. For days Pompey could do nothing with the men. Knowing that gold-fever is a disease best left to take its course, he simply waited for them to come to their senses and made fun of them for wasting their time digging in the ground with spades when they could be using their arms to win the spoils of war. And sure enough, as aching backs and blistered hands produced nothing more valuable than mounds of earth, they threw aside their shovels in disgust and bade Pompey to lead them where he pleased. They had, they assured him, been punished already for their folly and were more than ready to work off their frustrations on the enemy.

When Pompey came up with Domitius, he found the Marian army drawn up in a strong defensive position behind a wadi. The ground was rough and difficult to cross, and though Pompey had numerical superiority of two to one if Plutarch's figure of twenty thousand is correct for Domitius' army, he resigned himself to losing a lot of men in the attack which he was about to make. But as the two armies faced each other in order of battle, a desert storm intervened with such violence that Domitius gave up all idea of fighting that day and ordered his army to return to camp. Pompey seized his chance. As the enemy withdrew from line of battle into column of march, he ordered the bugles to sound the attack and was across the river-bed before Domitius could re-form to meet him.

Even so it was a desperate battle. Visibility was so bad that the troops could hardly recognize friend from foe and Pompey himself was nearly killed by one of his own men when he was slow giving the countersign after a challenge. But the enemy never recovered from the confusion of the surprise attack. As they turned in disorder to face the Pompeians, the wind drove the stinging rain into their faces, and they were gradually overwhelmed by superior numbers until only three thousand were left alive to take refuge in their fortified camp, which became Pompey's next objective. His victorious troops, elated by their success, had hailed him *Imperator* as soon as the battle was over, but Pompey refused to accept their salutation as long as the enemy fortress remained intact. Discarding his helmet for fear of not being recognized a second time, he set about storming the ramparts, and in a short time the camp was his, Domitius was dead, and the victorious general had accepted his title from his cheering army.

After this initial success Pompey received the immediate submission of many of the cities, and stormed the rest. He then set out against King Hiarbas of Numidia and found that unfortunate monarch already retreating before the advance of a Mauretanian army under Bogud, who was the son of Sulla's friend Bocchus and as ready as his father to ingratiate himself with Rome at the expense of a rival kingdom. The Roman pursuit was so fast and relentless that the king lost all his forces and fled for refuge to Bulla Regia, where he was put to death after the city had surrendered. Pompey then restored the throne of Numidia to the ousted Hiempsal, and marched his army through the country for many days 'until he had made terrible again the barbarians' fear of Rome, which had reached a low ebb'. He even declared that the wild animals of Africa should not be left without experience of the strength and courage of Romans, went on safari, and bagged a considerable number of lions and elephants. And all this, if Plutarch can be believed, was achieved in an amazingly short time, 'for it took him only forty days to make an end of his enemies, subdue the whole of Libya and adjust the relations of its kings, though he was but twenty-four years of age'.

Sulla's reaction to his protégé's extraordinary achievement was not one of unmixed delight. He knew from his own experience how fiercely loyal a successful army could become to its commander, and he thought it prudent to separate Pompey from his six legions as soon as possible. He therefore ordered him to send all his other troops back to Italy and to remain in Africa with only one legion until a replacement commander was sent out to relieve him. To Pompey this must have seemed a poor reward for his services. For his army to return home without him meant that he was to be deprived of the chance to celebrate a formal triumph in Rome, and this disappointment, coupled with resentment at Sulla's obvious doubts about his loyalty, made it all the more remarkable that he gave no sign of the deep distress which these instructions must have given him.

His troops on the other hand made no attempt to conceal their indignation when they received their orders to embark. When Pompey addressed them from the tribunal, they cried out that they would never forsake him, that Sulla was not to be trusted, and that they would go to Italy only if he would lead them there to secure his own safety. At first he tried to appease them with thanks for their loyalty and assurances about his safety which he may not have felt in his heart; but when he saw that they were adamant in their refusal to obey orders, he wept with emotion, stepped down from the tribunal and disappeared into his tent. They carried him out, and set him up again on the tribunal. Again he begged them not to raise a sedition, again they clamoured to be led by him to Rome, and all day long the camp was in uproar. Pompey pleaded, wept, cajoled and threatened, but nothing he said could persuade them to obey until he swore a solemn oath to commit suicide if they continued to try to force him into rebellion. Only then were they brought to some semblance of discipline, though their truculent clamour went on throughout the night.

The garbled reports which Sulla received of these events caused him some anxiety. At first he assumed that Pompey was already in revolt, and told his friends that 'it was evidently his fate, now that he was an old man, to have his contests with boys'. It was a good gibe at the youth of Pompey and the younger Marius, but it would have been no laughing matter for Sulla if Pompey had really turned against him and descended on Italy with so powerful a force. And when Sulla discovered that he had been wrong to judge his young protégé by the standards of his own behaviour, he showed his relief in the unprecedented warmth with which he greeted Pompey's eventual return to Rome. He went out to meet Pompey in great state, and after welcoming him he saluted him in a loud voice as 'Magnus' – 'the Great' – and ordered all those present to give him that surname. It was an honour that Pompey had not expected, but flattered as he was, he had the temerity to demand some more substantial reward for his services. He wanted a triumph, the formal celebration of his African victory by the whole city, the great procession through the city-gates which he would enter wearing on his head the *Imperator*'s crown of laurel and riding in a chariot drawn by the war-elephants which he had brought back with him especially for the purpose. But Sulla was adamant in his refusal. The law, he said, permitted only a consul or praetor to celebrate a triumph. Pompey had been given the authority *pro praetore*, it was true, but he had not been elected to even the lowest magistracy of the senatorial career, let alone the praetorship. If Sulla was now to grant a triumph to a young man who had scarcely grown a beard and was in fact too young to be a senator according to Sulla's rules, it would not only make the government ridiculous but also tarnish Pompey's own honour.

That was what Sulla said and it would have been enough to dissuade anyone else from further importunity, but Pompey refused to be cowed.

He was not impressed by arguments about the technicalities of his position, which he regarded as humbug coming from a man who had himself made war on Rome, however meticulously he had since sought to legalize his power. When Sulla had finished, the young man replied quietly, ' "You should reflect that more people worship the rising than the setting sun." ' At first Sulla did not catch his words and would probably have ignored them, but when he saw the looks of amazement on the faces around him, he demanded to know what had been said. The words were repeated, and for several moments Sulla was rendered speechless. Then suddenly he relaxed, grinned, and cried twice in a loud voice, ' "Let him triumph!" '

Thus Pompey had his way and his triumph, in which his only disappointment was finding the city-gates too narrow for his elephants and having to make do with a horse-drawn chariot instead. Otherwise everything was arranged on the grandest scale that could be conceived by the arrogance of youth to spite the many critics of Sulla's concession to his vanity. He had a little anxiety when some of his troops demonstrated for more pay and threatened to disrupt the great procession at the last minute, but the man who could stand up to Sulla was not the man to truckle to a bunch of demonstrators. He told them straight that he would rather give up the triumph than kow-tow to his troops, and when they saw that he meant what he said, they shut up and fell into line without further complaint. At the end of the day Pompey's prestige and popularity were higher than ever. He had even won the grudging admiration of some of his fiercest critics among the aristocracy for the firmness with which he had dealt with the demonstrating troops. Indeed, the very senator who had been most opposed to the triumph was now so impressed that he changed his mind completely and declared to all his friends that Pompey was ' "truly *the Great*, and worthy of the honour" '. As for the troops themselves, they admired him all the more for not letting them take advantage of him, and the common people too were wildly enthusiastic at the novelty of a *triumphator* who was so handsome and young, not even a senator.

Undoubtedly, says Plutarch, Pompey could have used his present popularity to become a senator before the legal age of thirty if he had so wished, but he preferred to remain in his equestrian rank in the same way that self-made men constantly vaunt their humble origins in order to exaggerate their success. If he had become a senator now, it would only have been by election to one of the lower magistracies, for Sulla was very strict about the age-limits for the senior offices of consul and praetor, which was the least that befitted his dignity. Better by far to stay as he was and add to the greatness of his new surname the singular distinction of being the first and last Roman knight ever to celebrate a triumph.

But the victory in Africa was not Pompey's only cause for celebration. Having lost the hapless Aemilia he needed a new wife to complete his re-establishment in the capital and provide an heir, and his return no doubt excited the hopes and prayers of many of Rome's noblest young ladies whose arranged marriages were more likely to satisfy their fathers' familial and financial criteria than their own more natural preferences. It was unusual to find so great a reputation combined with such youthful virility, and to judge from Plutarch's story of the courtesan who loved to boast that she never left his embrace without his teeth-marks in her neck, Pompey did not confine his prowess to the battlefield. The name of his new bride was Mucia, and through her he became allied to the distinguished families of the Mucii Scaevolae and the Caecilii Metelli, the latter of course being Sulla's most prominent supporters: Sulla had married a Metella and shared the consulship of 80 with Metellus Pius, who had been Pompey's nominal commander in the later stages of the Civil War in Italy. As for Mucia herself, she did not disappoint Pompey's hopes of an early family of his own, and in the next three years she bore him three children – a girl named Pompeia and the two boys Gnaeus and Sextus whose sad destiny was to fight in vain to avenge the lost greatness of their father's memory.

3

THE LEPIDUS AFFAIR

*'This is a fine policy of yours, young man, to use your
influence to get Lepidus elected instead of Catulus – the most
unstable instead of the best of men.'*
Plutarch, *Life of Sulla*, 34.5

While Pompey had been away fighting his enemies in Sicily and Africa,
Sulla had followed his own reprisals in Rome with a series of constitutional changes which revealed that his proscriptions had another,
higher motive than revenge. He had begun by legalizing his own position
by reviving the ancient office of dictator, which had last been held for
its proper purpose a hundred and thirty-five years ago in the emergency
of Hannibal's victories in Italy and had been completely obsolete since
the end of the third century. Traditionally the office was designed to meet
a specific crisis and tenable for six months only, but Sulla became 'Dictator for the Reconstitution of the State' – a task which had no time-limit.
He thus acquired supreme military and judicial authority for an indefinite
period, complete irresponsibility of action, and a more than consular
squad of twenty-four lictors to parade before him in the streets with their
bundles of rods and axes symbolizing his quasi-regal power.

It seemed to many that the Republic was doomed and one witty com-
mentator described his government as 'the official denial of monarchy',
but if Sulla's methods were irregular, his motives were conservative to
the point of naïvety. Far from seeking to perpetuate his autocracy, this
unusual dictator was a dedicated oligarch, endeavouring to turn the clock
back a hundred years to a more stable era when the aristocracy had been
content to observe the Aristotelian principle of 'taking turns in ruling
and being ruled' and before ambitious men had learnt to turn demagogue
in defiance of the collective will of their peers. A Marius must no longer
be able to appeal to the people to set aside the Senate's selection of a
Metellus or a Sulla to a coveted command. Ochlocracy and monarchy
were alike anathema to this peculiar tyrant, whose self-imposed mission
was to reinforce the aristocratic constitution and remove its likely
enemies before he retired. In short, he set out to do everything he could

in the way of legislation and liquidation to try to ensure that no one would ever again be able to do what he had done.

By 79 he had virtually completed his remodelling of the constitution according to his ideal of a settled aristocratic republic in which the Senate was the supreme authority. Diagnosing the cause of political instability as the power of the popular assemblies to legislate against the wishes of the Senate, and seeing the tribunate as a short cut to power for ambitious men, he restricted the legislative function of the people to voting on Bills already screened by the Senate and presented to them only by the senior magistrates. The ten tribunes of the *plebs* would no longer be able to veto legislation or, more importantly, initiate it. Their role for the future was to be the original one of looking after the interests of private citizens, and as if this was not enough to discourage ambitious men from standing for the tribunate, he passed a law debarring a tribune from holding any further office. No ambitious young nobleman would now be able to act constitutionally against the corporate will of the Senate because he could neither become nor use a tribune to short-cut the long senatorial path to power.

Under Sulla's regulations the career structure of a young man of senatorial family like Pompey was clearly defined. The various magistracies could be held only in a fixed order, with fixed intervals between them and at fixed minimum ages. A man must be thirty to become quaestor, forty-two to be consul, and a consul could be re-elected only after an interval of ten years. The people continued to elect the magistrates as they had always done, but they could no longer elect a favourite who failed to qualify in seniority, make the same man consul year after year, or vote a powerful command from a magistrate appointed to it by the Senate. Their only consolation was that the Senate would henceforth become an indirectly elected body to the extent that the most junior magistrates, the quaestors, would be automatically enrolled as members instead of having to wait to achieve the higher magistracies which would give them a better chance of being selected by the censors in their five-yearly review of the senatorial register.

To Pompey this new constitution had little to commend it. At the time when Sulla had completed his legislative programme in 79 he was barely twenty-seven, not old enough to offer himself for even the most junior magistracy. Indeed, it was probably by way of consolation that Sulla had given in to his demand to hold a triumph; but Pompey could not be reconciled so easily to a career structure which would keep him waiting fifteen years before he was eligible to offer himself for the consulship, the one office which seemed to him appropriate to his dignity and achievements. It was unthinkable that after commanding great armies against consuls he should have to start as a mere quaestor, and have to wait three years even for that. And he was not alone in his dissatisfaction with the Sullan constitution. When Sulla held the consular elections for the year 78 as a preliminary to his retirement from public life, only one of the successful candidates was a man he could trust. The other was known to be in favour of repealing much of Sulla's legislation, and it was to him that Pompey had lent the support of his very considerable prestige.

It seems surprising that Marcus Aemilius Lepidus was allowed to stand at all, when only the previous year Sulla had ordered a centurion to cut down a loyal officer of his own who had presumed on past services to offer himself for the consulship in disregard of the age-limit. But since Lepidus was of the right seniority and the constitution must be seen to be proof against such men if it was to survive, the dictator did nothing to interfere with his candidature beyond canvassing energetically for the other candidates, who were of proven loyalty to his ideals. All the same, he was highly displeased when Lepidus was not only successful but polled even more votes than Quintus Lutatius Catulus, his own favourite candidate who became the other consul-elect for 78.

Sulla put the blame on Pompey's influence with the electorate, and did not disguise his anger. When he caught sight of Pompey sweeping through the Forum with a crowd of friends to celebrate their candidate's victory at the polls, he called out to him, ' "I see, young man, that you rejoice in your victory, for you no doubt consider it a fine and noble thing that Lepidus, who is the worst of men, should have been proclaimed consul by a larger vote than Catulus, who is the best – and all because you used your influence with the people." ' And before Pompey could reply, he added prophetically, ' "But now it is time for you to wake yourself up and watch your own interests, for you have made a man who is really your enemy stronger than yourself." ' At the time Pompey thought this warning was just sour grapes and laughed it off, but he was not destined to remain friends for long with the consul he had helped to create.

As soon as he entered his year of office, Lepidus lost no time in proclaiming himself champion of all the anti-Sullan elements in Rome and Italy. If Sallust's version of a speech which he made to the people is reasonably authentic, he openly attacked Sulla's constitution even before the dictator had resigned. He even doubted that Sulla would or could safely resign, ' "unless you believe that he is now weary or ashamed of his tyranny, and that what he has stolen he will with greater peril relinquish" '. He called upon the people to reassert their rights to legislate and to the corn-dole which Sulla had stopped. ' "The Roman people," ' he scoffed, ' "lately rulers of nations, now stripped of power and reputation and rights, without the means to live and an object of contempt, retains not even the rations of slaves." ' He declared himself the champion of the Italians who had been disenfranchised and dispossessed of their lands for supporting the Marians. ' "A great part of the allies and the people of Latium," ' he thundered, ' "to whom you gave citizenship in return for many distinguished services, are robbed of it by one man, while a few of his henchmen, as reward for their crimes, have seized upon the ancestral homes of a blameless people." ' And he proposed the return of the Marians exiled by Sulla and the repeal of the iniquitous disenfranchisement of their sons, ' "for who else in the history of the human race has devised punishment for those yet unborn?" '

But Lepidus was not unaware of the reality of Sulla's power, and when he spoke of the victorious army, he tried to divorce the victory from its consequences and from its author. He appealed to the troops who had been pensioned off on farms taken from allied communities: ' "What have the victorious armies gained from their wounds and pains save a tyrant, unless perhaps they took the field to overthrow the power of the tribunes which was established by our ancestors, or to rob themselves with their own hands of their rights and jurisdiction – richly rewarded, no doubt, when banished to swamps and woods they find that insult and hatred are their portion while a handful of Sulla's favourites get all the prizes?" ' He knew that even among many of Sulla's most faithful supporters there was some sympathy with what he proposed, and when he asked ' "Who is there save his crime-stained cronies who does not wish everything else changed except only his victory?" ' it was a direct appeal to men like Pompey who saw the Sullan constitution as a block to their ambition.

Yet Sulla did nothing beyond making both consuls swear on oath that they would not resort to force of arms to settle any differences between them. Far from silencing Lepidus permanently, which he could easily have done, he preferred to demonstrate his confidence in the constitution by resigning the dictatorship, offering to submit his acts for public examination, and entertaining the whole city to a great banquet to celebrate his retirement. To the amazement of later Roman historians, who took autocracy for granted, he willingly gave up supreme power and proclaimed himself a private citizen, 'undaunted', says Appian, 'by the relatives of the proscribed or the exiles abroad or the cities whose towers and walls he had thrown down and whose lands, money and privileges he had swept away'.

It was certainly an impressive display of self-confidence for a man who had liquidated no less than ninety senators, fifteen men of consular rank and 2,600 knights to walk unguarded in the Forum with his friends, and when a few weeks later he retired from Rome to his seaside estate at

Cumae on the Bay of Naples, he had shown that it was not because he was afraid to live a private life in the capital. He knew where his strength was based. Whatever Lepidus might say, he had his 120,000 veterans throughout Italy and his 10,000 freed slaves in Rome, the so-called Cornelii, whose personal loyalty to their commander and benefactor was absolute. He needed no formal title to remain master of Rome. He had assumed the dictatorship in order to rewrite the constitution and deal with his enemies, and once this was done he was content to retire to the country and write his memoirs in full confidence that neither Lepidus nor anyone else could undermine his achievement as long as he remained alive.

But Sulla was not immortal, and as the year 78 advanced, Lepidus was greatly encouraged by reports of his deteriorating health. If Appian gives us a bucolic picture of the ex-dictator falling in love with the peace and quiet of the countryside and spending his days in healthy outdoor pursuits, the cynical Plutarch provides a very different impression of his lifestyle. For a man addicted to debauchery to a degree remarkable even for a Roman, Sulla's retirement from public life simply meant more time to indulge his excesses, with the result that he aggravated an internal abscess which had lain dormant for some years. To his horror he discovered that the ulcer had become infested with vermin, and as the foul corruption spread inexorably over his whole body during the spring of 78, he found himself racing against time to finish his memoirs before being literally eaten alive.

It was a hideous affliction, yet even in this extremity the old tyrant was ruthless in the defence of the law. If he left Lepidus unscathed as long as the consul remained within the law, it was very different when he heard that a magistrate of Puteoli was refusing to repay a debt to the treasury in expectation of Sulla's early death. He immediately summoned the unsuspecting offender to his sick-room and had him strangled to death at his bedside. But it was the last thing he did. The excitement proved too much for him, the abscess burst, and he lost so much blood during the night that he died the next morning with the consolation of having taken an enemy with him and having thus confirmed by his last act the epitaph which he had composed for himself – that no friend was ever more generous, no enemy more dangerous.

As soon as news of Sulla's death reached Rome, the fate of his half-eaten remains became the subject of a violent quarrel between the two consuls. Catulus proposed that he should be brought in procession to Rome for a state funeral, but Lepidus opposed any form of honour for the dead tyrant, and many shared his view. Pompey, however, was not among them. Although Pompey had reason to be offended with Sulla

– for he alone of all the dictator's friends was not mentioned in the will
– he was magnanimous enough to remember who had made him great,
and wise enough to realize that any slight to the memory of a benefactor
could only diminish the status of the beneficiary. He therefore put the
whole weight of his influence behind Catulus, won over the majority of
Lepidus' supporters by a combination of threats and entreaties, and took
upon himself the full responsibility for the funeral arrangements, which
were magnificent even by imperial standards.

A golden litter conveyed the body through Italy in a procession of regal
splendour. At the head rode trumpeters and a great number of horsemen,
who were followed by the standards under which Sulla had fought and
won so many victories. Then came the twenty-four lictors bearing the
bundles of rods and axes which had symbolized his dictatorial power
while he had ruled, and behind them came the golden litter itself, escorted
by regiment after regiment of Sulla's old soldiers who came together from
all over Italy to accompany their general on his last journey. As each
arrived, resplendent in his full-dress uniform, he was assigned his place
in the line until there was an enormous army following the bier. But magnificent as the march to Rome undoubtedly was, it was only a glimmer
of the splendour of the funeral proper.

The streets of the capital were lined with crowds of people more
numerous than had gathered for any such occasion in the past. They
gazed open-mouthed at the two thousand or more gold crowns which
had been made in haste at the order of cities, legions and individuals wishing to pay their respects, and these and other costly gifts were carried
along in the final procession. And for all Lepidus' brave words, neither
he nor any other prominent Roman dared to stay away for fear of the
assembled troops. All the priests and priestesses attended the remains,
richly attired in their finest vestments. The Senate turned out in full force,
as did the whole body of magistrates, each in his full regalia. Next came
the multitude of knights resplendent with decorations, and then the
legions, rank after rank of Sulla's veterans carrying gilded standards and
ceremonial silver-plated shields. When the cortège reached the Forum,
the bier was displayed on the rostra while the most eloquent Romans
of the day delivered the funeral orations which Sulla's own son was too
young to make. Then the procession formed up again, and several of
the younger senators carried the bier to the funeral pyre in the Campus
Martius, where the ashes were to be interred. As the pyre was lit and
the trumpeters sounded the last post, loud cries of farewell resounded
from all the vast assemblage, first from the Senate, then the knights, and
finally the people. Then came the great march-past by the whole army,
led by the knights among whom Pompey rode in what must have been

a state of high satisfaction at having secured so memorable a funeral for the man who had named him 'the Great'.

As soon as the funeral was over and Sulla's veterans had dispersed to their farms and villages, Lepidus lost no time in renewing his appeal to all the anti-Sullan elements in the state. He promised the people to restore the corn-doles and the powers of their tribunes; he promised the children of the proscribed freedom from the impositions laid on them by Sulla; and he recalled all the Marian exiles. But his greatest potential support was from the Italians whom Sulla had punished for opposing him by dispossessing whole communities of their lands and handing them over to his own veterans or friends. In promising to restore these lands, as in recalling the exiles, Lepidus was proposing something that was basically just, and Florus at least among the ancient historians admits it. But Florus also says that it was something that could be achieved only by another civil war.

Fate now played into Lepidus' hands. From Etruria came news that some Sullan colonists had been driven out of their farms by the previous owners, and the danger of a wholesale rising seemed so acute that the consuls were required to take the field with armies to pacify the district. But Lepidus had no intention of pacifying anyone. Leaving Catulus to do what he could in that direction, he began to recruit the dispossessed Marians into a large army in preparation for the following year when he would be free from his oath to abstain from civil war. Since he had been assigned the province of Transalpine Gaul for his proconsular governorship in the following year, he sent his legate Junius Brutus to take command there in his name and raise fresh forces from the local population. In the meantime he recruited in Italy itself, and was soon joined by a large number of exiled Marians, not least among them Perperna, the former governor of Sicily who had fled before Pompey's invasion of the island four years earlier. When the time came for the holding of the consular elections for the following year, at which the presence of both consuls was required, only Catulus returned. Lepidus did not come back until the new year, and when he did finally set out for Rome, it was with a large and menacing army at his back.

'It was a situation,' says Plutarch, 'which cried out for Pompey.' Catulus was ready to tackle Lepidus himself, but for the task of recovering northern Etruria and Gaul from the rebels he looked to Pompey not only for his military ability but for the intense personal loyalty which he could command from his former troops. Pompey accepted the command without hesitation. His former friendship with Lepidus had already been undermined by the consul's attitude to Sulla's funeral, and since it had been founded in the first place mainly on the hope of achieving constitutional reforms that would further his career, it was irrelevant now that the Senate had given him the rank of praetor and the command of a large army. Certainly there was no incentive to join a rebel of whose military ability he had a poor opinion, and while Catulus remained to organize the defence of Rome, Pompey quickly collected his troops and set out to deal with Brutus in the north.

As Lepidus drew nearer to the capital, the Senate proved typically indecisive, reluctant to give up hope of a peaceful solution until it was almost too late. After all, there were some senators who secretly favoured his cause, and many more were prepared to support his demand for an illegal second consulship if it meant avoiding another civil war. And since the consular elections had not been held, there were no new consuls to take the lead. Catulus as proconsul was ready to fight, as was Appius Claudius, the *interrex*, whose office was a vestige of the old monarchy that was resurrected for five-day periods whenever the state found itself without consuls. But it took Pompey's old friend Lucius Philippus to shake the Senate out of its paralysis. This was the eminent senator who nine years before had spoken on Pompey's behalf when the young man had been tried on a charge of misappropriating booty from the sack of Asculum in the Italian War. Now he turned the full force of his rhetoric to persuading the Senate to make its Ultimate Decree, the proclamation of a state of emergency which would authorize Catulus and Appius Claudius 'to see to it that no harm shall befall the Republic'.

If Sallust's version of this speech is authentic, it was certainly a fine piece of oratory and deserved its success, but perhaps the weaker members of the Senate were more influenced by a letter from Pompey declaring that the war was over. Pompey had laid siege to Brutus in Mutina, Brutus had surrendered, and Lepidus was cut off from reinforcements from the north. At once Pompey was the toast of Rome. As the news sped round the threatened city and its defending army, the citizens took heart and the troops were eager to be led against the enemy. The only hope for Lepidus now was to capture Rome, and he attacked with such desperate violence that he succeeded in driving Catulus back from his forward defensive position at the Mulvian Bridge; but when he reached the Campus Martius he was defeated, appropriately enough, over the ashes of Sulla. Lepidus despaired. He abandoned his troops and sailed for Sardinia, where he soon died of a despondency attributed more to stumbling across some evidence of his wife's infidelity than to the failure of his great enterprise. Perperna took command of the remnants of his army and went to join the last and greatest of the Marian leaders, the formidable Quintus Sertorius who was the virtual ruler of Spain.

Pompey in the meantime had slightly discredited his victory by putting Brutus to death. He had sent his distinguished prisoner under guard to a little town on the River Po and written his timely letter to the Senate, which was duly informed that the enemy commander had surrendered of his own accord. But the very next day he sent an agent to put Brutus to death and wrote again to the Senate to denounce him. Perhaps he had felt all along that Brutus was too dangerous a man to leave alive but had been able to secure his surrender only by promising to write to the Senate in agreed terms. Whatever the reason, this unauthorized execution earned Pompey considerable censure and suspicion from certain members of the Senate who recognized the same high-handedness that had put Carbo to death in Sicily five years ago. Even Catulus began to feel that Pompey was taking too much upon himself, and not without reason, for when he ordered the young general to disband his army and return to Rome, Pompey refused.

There was nothing overtly rebellious in Pompey's behaviour and he made plausible excuses about the need to keep his troops under arms, but it was clear to everyone what he wanted. His old friend Lucius Philippus acted on his behalf, proposing that the Senate should send Pompey with proconsular authority to assist the proconsul Metellus Pius against the unbeatable Sertorius in Spain; and since none of the senators could be prevailed upon to go instead, and Pompey's candidature for this formidable task was backed by the implicit threat of force, the Senate had little choice but to agree. For here lay the fatal weakness in the Sullan constitution. However restrictive the laws by which the dictator had sought to avoid the concentration and perpetuation of power in the hands of one man, there was no legislation that could provide that the right man of the right seniority would always be in the right position to deal with sudden crises like the Lepidus affair. And once a general had his army, he was in a position to blackmail the Senate into giving him yet another command at an even higher rank. And so it happened that Pompey, who was not eligible for the consulship for another fourteen years, gained the authority of proconsul at the age of twenty-eight.

' "But do you seriously propose to send this young man, who is merely a knight, to Spain *pro consule*?" ' asked one senator in surprise. ' "No indeed," ' replied Philippus, ' "but *pro consulibus*" ' – a piece of sarcasm that made the newly elected consuls wince with embarrassment at the implication that Pompey alone was worth both of them put together. But there was little they could say in reply, for Cicero makes it clear that they both refused to go in his place. Their only consolation was that by sending Pompey they would get rid of at least one possible danger to the state, for even among his supporters there were some who feared that this time he really had bitten off more than he could chew in taking on Quintus Sertorius, who was perhaps the most brilliant guerrilla leader of the ancient world.

4

WAR WITH SERTORIUS

'But as for that boy Pompey, if the old woman Metellus had
not come up, I should have given him a sound thrashing and
sent him back to Rome.'
Plutarch, *Life of Sertorius*, 19.6

Pompey's new opponent was a tragic figure of his generation, an intensely
patriotic Roman condemned to squander his enormous talent in civil war.
But for the incompetence of his superiors he might have taken Pompey's
place as one of the greatest empire-builders and administrators of the
Republic; as it was, he became the last and greatest supporter of one
of its lost causes.

Quintus Sertorius first made a name for himself as a young officer under
Marius in the Cimbric Wars, and in 97–93 he won fame for his exploits
against the Celtiberians in Spain. Three years later he was elected to his
first magistracy, the quaestorship, and when the Italian War broke out
he acquitted himself so well that he 'earned himself the reputation of a
man whose life would be one of great achievement'. In battle he always
led his men from the front, and when he lost an eye he prided himself
on having a mark of bravery to carry with him at all times.

By 88, when the greater number of the Italian allies had been pacified,
Sertorius had become a popular hero in Rome. Although he was only
thirty-five and had held only relatively junior commands in the war, his
reckless bravery and piratical appearance had so captured the popular
imagination that he was greeted with a standing ovation on his first visit
to the theatre after returning to the city. He decided to stand for the tribunate, but incurred the suspicions of Sulla who considered him a potentially dangerous demagogue and perhaps also a protégé of his old enemy
Marius. At any rate it did not suit Sulla to let an able young man of relatively unexalted birth become a tribune, and he saw to it that Sertorius
lost the election.

When Sulla had left for the East and trouble broke out between Cinna
and Octavius over the distribution of the new citizens among the electorate, Sertorius lent his support to the progressive Cinna and helped to

raise the armies with which they marched on Rome in 87. After playing a prominent part in the capture of Rome he exercised a moderating influence on the excesses of the victorious party. 'He was the one man,' says Plutarch, 'who resisted the opportunity to pay off old scores.' He even remonstrated with Marius, and when that embittered old man let loose his bodyguard of four thousand freed slaves amongst his real or fancied enemies in Rome, Sertorius rounded up the assassins and put them all to death.

In 83 he held the praetorship, and at the resumption of the Civil War he had the misfortune to serve under the general command of Scipio Asiaticus – the consul whose gross incompetence had prevented him from discovering until too late that his entire army had gone over to Sulla. Sertorius had repeatedly warned him of the danger, but Scipio was the kind of man to resent the advice almost more than the result of not taking it. By the end of 83 Sertorius had come to the conclusion that the Marian cause was as good as lost in Italy, and he sailed for the province of Nearer Spain which had been allotted to him for the following year. It was no cowardly decision. His superiors, and particularly the younger Marius, were only too glad to be rid of a critic who was always proved right, and in his province he could establish a refuge for the stream of exiles which would flow from Sulla's increasingly inevitable victory in Italy.

Once in Spain Sertorius found no difficulty in taking over his command. That long-misgoverned people responded enthusiastically to an incorruptible governor who remitted taxes, respected their notables, and made his soldiers build their own winter-quarters instead of billeting them in the cities. But he did not rely entirely on the natives. He armed the Roman settlers of military age and struck a fine balance between the demands of provincial administration and the need to prepare for the migration of the Civil War to Spain. When he heard late in 82 that Sulla was master of Rome and that Pompey was on his way to Sicily in pursuit of Carbo, he sent a legate to hold the passes of the Pyrenees against the possibility of an invasion of Spain by land. It was a timely precaution. A large Sullan army was at that moment marching through the south of France, and by the time it reached the Pyrenees the Sertorian forces were impregnably entrenched. But the treachery of one man achieved more than a whole army. Sertorius' legate was murdered by a bounty-hunter, his leaderless troops withdrew from their position, and the Sullan forces passed unopposed over the mountains before Sertorius was ready to receive them.

Sertorius withdrew to his naval base at New Carthage and sailed to Morocco with three thousand men, but when his first landing party was cut up by unfriendly natives, he decided that if he had to fight for a home he might as well fight for Spain as for Africa. He sailed back, seized Ibiza,

and waited to be attacked by the Sullan governor who was rapidly mobi-
lizing an overwhelming fleet against him. The ensuing battle would have
been the end of Sertorius but for a sudden storm which broke up the
pursuit and drove his remaining ships to some scattered and remote
islands. From here he made his escape through the Straits of Gibraltar
to a safe landing on the coast of Spain just above Cadiz, where he fell
in with some Cilician pirates and was tempted by their tales of the Isles
of the Blest to retire to a life of peace and leisure on Madeira or Porto
Santo; but when his informants departed to win wealth by restoring a
certain Ascalis to power in western Mauretania, he decided to involve
himself in the same cause but fight for the opposition.

The appointment of Sertorius to command Mauretanian forces soon
turned what had been a domestic squabble in an allied kingdom into an
extension of the Roman Civil War, for when Sulla heard that a Marian
general was supporting one side, he sent a general of his own to support
the other. Sertorius not only killed the Sullan general but won over his
troops and gained control of the whole country for interests which were
no doubt appropriately grateful. But he did not stay to enjoy the fruits
of his success in western Mauretania for long. He was anxious to continue
the war against Sulla, and responded at once to an invitation from the
Lusitanians asking him to champion their revolt against the Sullan governors of Spain.

Sertorius made it clear that he would accept command of the Lusitanians not as a rebel against the imperial power but as a Roman governor
leading loyal subjects against the nominees of an illegal regime. The Lusitanians seem to have accepted him as such, for they were fighting not
against Romanization but oppression, and if there were some who
secretly held the view that the only good Roman was a dead one, even
they appreciated that it would take a Roman to beat another. Their confidence in Sertorius was amply justified. At first the odds were overwhelm-
ingly against him. Only twenty cities offered him allegiance, and his
meagre forces numbered only 2,600 men whom he called Romans, a mot-
ley band of seven hundred Libyans whom he had picked up in Morocco,
four thousand light-armed Lusitanians and seven hundred horsemen.
Three years later he had defeated four Sullan governors commanding
between them countless cities, 120,000 infantry, six thousand horse and
two thousand archers and slingers. Even in his first year of operations
he defeated the governors of both the Spanish provinces, one by land
and the other by sea. The next year he faced two new governors, one
named Domitius, the other the same Metellus under whom Pompey had
served in Italy and who had shared the consulship with Sulla in the previous year. They fared no better than the last. While his quaestor Hirtu-

leius defeated and killed Domitius, Sertorius inflicted on Metellus a series of defeats so serious that the governor of Gaul came to help and suffered the same fate in the following year. By 77 Sertorius was virtually master of the whole peninsula. At Rome it was rumoured that he would soon be invading Italy from the West just as Sulla had done from the East, and there was no shortage of Marian sympathizers in the capital who would have been glad to see him try.

It is doubtful whether Pompey realized quite how superior this man was to the Marian generals who had failed so dismally in Italy. For Sertorius was more than a great soldier who had mastered the art of guerrilla warfare. By introducing Roman drill and signals he had turned bands of robbers into highly disciplined yet flexible fighting forces that could both outfight and outmanœuvre Roman legions under more conventional generals like Metellus. He also knew the value of fine array, and by providing his troops with beautiful cloaks and setting their shields and helmets ablaze with gold and silver decorations he developed an *esprit de corps* that was worthy of the best native regiments of the British Raj. The Indian parallel holds good in his administration too. While relying to a large extent on indirect rule through the existing aristocracies, he set up a school for the sons of native chieftains who became willing hostages for their fathers' loyalty in exchange for the chance of a Roman and Greek education that would fit them for an eventual share in the government. The fathers were proud to see their sons going to and from school in the purple-bordered togas worn by Roman schoolboys, and the lads themselves became devoted to Sertorius, whom they swore to protect with their lives. All the same, there was no question of anything but a purely Roman administration. Sertorius had set up what amounted to a Roman government in exile, and he had his own Senate composed of the most prominent of the refugees from the Sullan proscriptions. It is hardly surprising that the official Senate in Rome found its consuls of 77 unwilling to take up arms against such a formidable figure, or that it conveniently overlooked the lack of official qualifications in appointing as proconsul the ambitious young knight who was foolhardy enough to want to try.

Following his appointment, Pompey lost no time in setting out for his new province, but he spent the rest of 77 fighting a war in Gaul. Very little is known about these campaigns, but in Sallust's version of a letter which Pompey addressed to the Senate two years later he claimed 'to have raised and equipped an army within forty days of his appointment, to have assailed the enemy who were at the very throat of Italy, and to have driven them all the way back from the Alps into Spain'. He also claimed to have opened up another, more convenient route across the

Alps than the old Hannibalic one, and to have 'recovered Gaul'. Cicero confirms that he 'opened a path to Spain for our legions by the wholesale slaughter of the Gauls', and he speaks elsewhere of Pompey's 'war in Transalpine Gaul'. Lucan too mentions his 'Alpine War', and Pliny gives some idea of the scope of his achievement by describing the trophy which he erected on a pass in the Pyrenees on his return from Spain six years later. Apparently it recorded the reduction of no less than 876 cities between the Alps and the borders of Further Spain, and although it does not distinguish between the Gallic ones and those in Pompey's own province of Nearer Spain, it is likely enough that at least a third of them were between the Alps and the Pyrenees.

We have even less information on why the Transalpine Gauls showed such belligerence at this time. No doubt it had something to do with their governor's disastrous attempt to help Metellus in Spain, and there was probably some connection with Brutus' unfortunate attempt to stir up the Gauls of the Po valley in support of Lepidus. But whatever the cause of the upheavals, they clearly involved Pompey in a major campaign which had spectacular results, and it was the spring of 76 by the time he was ready to cross the Pyrenees and assert his position as proconsular governor of Nearer Spain.

Pompey's Gallic victories had the effect of both weakening and strengthening the power of Sertorius. On the one hand they lost him several of the cities of Pompey's province, which promptly changed their allegiance to the new governor; on the other they brought him a large reinforcement of Roman troops, the remnants of Lepidus' defeated forces which had been brought to Spain by Perperna in the previous year. At first that haughty incompetent had refused to join forces with Sertorius and had prepared to operate independently, but as soon as his troops heard that Pompey was on his way to fight them again, they 'seized their arms, caught up their standards, and demanded to be taken to the service of the one general who seemed able to save himself and his men'. Perperna was left with no choice but to do as they wanted, which meant bringing his fifty-three cohorts to Sertorius and putting both them and himself under his orders.

But Pompey was not of course Sertorius' only opponent. Metellus was still proconsul in Further Spain, and though he had been virtually paralysed there throughout 77, Pompey's approach had a heartening effect on his dispirited troops. For Plutarch tells us that poor Metellus was 'at his wits' end', having been constantly outmanœuvred and outfought by the more flexible Sertorius and his quaestor Hirtuleius. Indeed, he was so depressed that he had sought consolation in an excessively luxurious and intemperate style of living, and his troops looked to Pompey to provide the same invigorating effect that had rejuvenated their commander five years before when the two men had served together in Italy. And if Pompey's reputation put new heart into Metellus' army, it also dispirited some of the Sertorian tribes and cities whose only concern was to be on the winning side. A few disowned Sertorius at once, and many more began to temporize until the first clash between the two generals should give them a safer basis on which to calculate the odds.

Sertorius had done his utmost in 77 to demonstrate his power and confirm his alliances by a vigorous campaign in the interior of Pompey's province and the besieging of recalcitrant Celtiberian cities, which went on through the winter. Even so, the Berones of the upper Ebro and their north-western neighbours, the Autrigones, 'made frequent appeals for help to Pompey' in his winter-quarters on the Gallic side of the Pyrenees, 'sent guides to show him the roads, and even approached the staunchly Sertorian tribe of the Arevaci with an invitation to join them in changing sides'. Sertorius decided to nip this movement in the bud and 'to furnish a sample of his campaigning before making up his mind which of the two Roman provinces and generals to attack first in the coming year: whether to turn to the coastal region in order to keep Pompey away from the Ilercaones and Contestani, both staunch allies of his, or to march against Metellus in Lusitania'.

At the beginning of spring Sertorius marched up the Ebro valley to the disloyal cities, whose territory and crops he proceeded to devastate. In the meantime he sent Perperna with 20,000 infantry and 1,500 cavalry to defend the maritime territory of the Ilercaones, where his legate Herennius was already stationed to stiffen their resistance. He also wrote to Hirtuleius in Metellus' province, and to all he gave the same instructions: to defend the allied cities and wear down the Roman armies by skirmish and ambush, but on no account to engage in a pitched battle with either of the proconsuls. He then sent another officer to fetch troops and supplies from the Arevaci and collect them at Contrebia, which he intended to use as his base when he had finished punishing the Berones. It was up to Pompey and Metellus to make the first moves, and Contrebia was a useful centre from which he could march rapidly to reinforce any region when he saw what they had decided to do.

According to Livy, even Sertorius had no intention of meeting Pompey in a head-on collision if it could be avoided, and he did not believe that that was what Pompey would want either. He reasoned that it would be in Pompey's best interest to prolong the war. Sertorius' own accumulation of provisions had been largely used up in the vigorous campaigning of the previous year, whereas Pompey would be able to get unlimited supplies by sea, and it seemed unlikely to Sertorius that he would do much about the Berones and other interior tribes before he had tried to secure the coastal region of his province. And that is exactly what Pompey did, though not because he wanted to avoid a pitched battle.

At first it seemed to the new governor that his reconquest of Spain would be as swift and as sure as his recovery of Gaul. He seems to have met no opposition where it might have been most expected, in the passes of the Pyrenees, and after descending into Catalonia he advanced steadily down the coast of his province with apparently little effective resistance from the Indigetes, Lacetani and Ilercaones through whose territories he passed. Despite the appeals of the Berones he had no intention of letting himself be drawn into the mountainous regions where his legions would be prey to the guerrilla warfare in which his enemy excelled, and though he sent two legates into the interior further south, he was disappointed but not surprised when he heard of their defeats at Segovia and the Guadiana by Sertorius' legates. In the coastal plains he was confident of his superiority. Perperna was no more able to stop Pompey in Spain than in Sicily or Italy, and as Pompey advanced relentlessly down the coast, he expected that Sertorius would soon feel compelled to come down from the mountains and fight him on the plains unless he wanted to lose all his coastal cities. In the meantime he attempted to cut Sertorius' supply-lines from the enemy naval base at Dianium by sending his brother-in-law Memmius to New Carthage by sea, though he hoped that a war of attrition would not be necessary. He knew that if he could only defeat Sertorius himself in one great battle the war would be won, and he was greedy for the glory of another spectacular victory.

When Pompey heard that his rapid advance had succeeded in drawing Sertorius into the plains near Valencia, where he was personally conducting a siege of the loyal city of Lauron, he rushed to its assistance with his whole army, which Orosius puts at thirty thousand foot and one thousand horse. He arrived to find that Sertorius had twice as many infantry and eight thousand horse, and he was concerned to see the enemy advancing to take possession of a hill which dominated the town. Pompey attempted to reach it first, but when he arrived to find the Sertorian forces already in possession, he was glad that he had lost the race. It seemed to him that by digging in on the far side of the hill he would have Sertorius trapped neatly between his own lines and the city, and he was so confident of his superior position that he sent a messenger to Lauron to tell the citizens to take their seats on the walls to enjoy the spectacle of the great Sertorius undergoing a siege. But his confidence was premature. No sooner had he completed the entrenchments that were to besiege the besiegers than he discovered that Sertorius had left six thousand crack troops in reserve at his old camp, which was behind Pompey's own lines.

If Pompey now moved against the Sertorians on the hill, he would himself be attacked in the rear, and it was poor consolation to discover that the enemy had no intention of fighting a pitched battle when there was nothing he could do except either retreat or stay to watch the citizens of Lauron being slowly starved into surrender. Too ashamed to retreat and ever hopeful of some chance to relieve the town, Pompey chose to stay, and so learnt a second and bloodier lesson in the art of war from the man who disparaged him as 'Sulla's pupil'.

There were two main areas in which Pompey's army could forage relatively easily, one quite near to Lauron, the other much further away. Obviously the nearer area was preferable because it was easier to defend and less far to transport the forage back to camp, but when Sertorius began to raid it so frequently that the Pompeians found themselves doing more fighting than foraging, Pompey ordered them to concentrate on the more distant area which never seemed to be visited by enemy troops. It never occurred to him that this was exactly what Sertorius had hoped he would do. Indeed, he had almost stopped worrying about the problems of the commissariat as his foraging parties and their escorts returned day after day without so much as sighting an enemy patrol, and it came as a total surprise when a scout came galloping into camp one morning with alarming news.

A large task force had just finished loading the wagons and its sentries were doing a bit of foraging on their own account before joining the column for the return to camp when ten cohorts of light-armed Spaniards had suddenly rushed out on them from a nearby wood. The Romans fought back gamely and managed for a time to hold their own, but it soon became clear that this was no chance encounter with an enemy patrol. While the light-armed troops held the Romans in play and prevented them from getting into their proper formations, ten more Sertorian cohorts, heavy-armed this time, advanced swiftly to the attack along with two thousand cavalry which had been stationed further back in the woods where the neighing of their horses could not be heard. The Romans were soon in retreat, only to find that a detachment of enemy cavalry had ridden ahead to block their road back to camp.

Pompey immediately dispatched a rescuing force of one legion under his legate Laelius and prepared the rest of his army to follow up if it became necessary. When Laelius came on the Sertorian cavalry, who were cutting up the vanguard of the retreating Pompeians, he found no difficulty in forcing them back; but as he pushed forward to rescue the main body of the foragers, he failed to observe that the enemy which had fled so precipitately was in fact closing in behind him. Realizing too late that he had cut his way into a trap, Laelius sent urgently to Pompey for reinforcements. This time Pompey was taking no chances. He led out his whole army in battle array and marched to the rescue in apparently over-whelming strength; but before he could engage the enemy, he was brought up short by the sight of Sertorius' whole army drawn up on the side of the hill. Again he had been outmanœuvred. If he advanced, he would have to face a superior army on ground of its own choosing. He had no alternative but to stay where he was and watch the inexorable destruction of Laelius and ten thousand of his men.

Pompey was still smarting from this blow when he was dealt another yet more crushing to his pride. Lauron, the city he had come to save, finally capitulated, and Sertorius departed from his usual moderation to those who surrendered by razing it to the ground. The wavering tribes who heard how Pompey had stood warming his hands at the flames of an allied city thought twice about changing sides, and when Pompey retired to the Pyrenees at the end of the campaigning season of 76, he reflected miserably that he had achieved even less than old Metellus, who had at least managed to defeat Hirtuleius in Further Spain. His only con-solation was that Sertorius had not dared to engage him in a full-scale battle, though less because Sertorius feared losing battles than highly trained men. Pompey, it seemed, had finally met his match.

The following spring Pompey began with the same plan of campaign, and having descended from the Pyrenees into Catalonia he sought to retrace his steps down the east coast towards Valencia. Whether the Ser-torian generals Perperna and Herennius tried to oppose him further north as in the previous year is not known, but they were certainly prepared to make a stand in front of Valencia, where he found them waiting for him with the considerable strength of their combined armies. But Pompey was completely victorious, not only killing one of the enemy for every man he had lost in the previous year but capturing and destroying Valencia too.

This was a good start to the new season, but once again Pompey allowed himself to be misled by over-confidence. He had arranged to join forces with Metellus before attacking Sertorius himself, but now that he had tasted victory he was loath to share his laurels with his fellow-gov-ernor. Hearing that Sertorius was holding the line of the Sucro, he made haste to attack him before Metellus arrived. Sertorius was also eager to fight, preferring one enemy to two, and late in the day the two great armies closed. Both generals were commanding on the right wing, and each soon succeeded in pushing back the enemy left. Hearing that his own left wing was in trouble, Sertorius handed over command of the right and led his reserves to support the crumbling left, where Pompey was now conspicuous in the pursuit on a great white horse magnificently caparisoned in gold. Sertorius immediately counter-attacked with such violence that as Pompey strove to rally his troops he found himself almost surrounded by the Libyans of Sertorius' bodyguard, one of whom rushed at Pompey on foot. Pompey hacked off the man's hand with his sword, but he too was wounded and saved himself only by leaping from his horse and fleeing on foot while his assailants fought each other for the booty of his beautiful saddle and its golden trappings.

But while the Pompeians were being driven back on the right, Afranius, commanding their left wing, had taken such advantage of Sertorius' absence that he had not only routed the enemy right but carried the pursuit as far as the enemy camp, which his troops were now plundering. They were beyond control, and when Sertorius suddenly returned in force, a considerable number were caught unawares and cut down as they struggled to carry away great heaps of spoils. This incident took some of the lustre from Afranius' success, and when Pompey sat down with his commanders in his tent that night to assess the day's work, he had to admit that taking things all round they had had the worst of it. All the same, there was reassurance in the fact that the main part of his army had slugged it out with the enemy without advantage to either side.

The next morning both generals began drawing their lines of battle as soon as it was light, but before they were ready to engage, their scouts reported that Metellus was rapidly approaching with his whole army. Sertorius immediately sounded the withdrawal, broke camp, and marched off, commenting sourly that he 'would have given that boy Pompey a sound thrashing and sent him packing to Rome if his old woman had not arrived'. Pompey then marched to join Metellus, and as a mark of respect for the older man he ordered his lictors to lower their fasces in salute when the two proconsuls approached each other. But Metellus so respected Pompey that he refused to accept this honour and assumed no other marks of superiority, except that when the two armies camped together the watchword for both was given from his tent.

The two governors now operated together in the coastal region round Valencia, but they found it as hard fighting hunger as their elusive enemy, who constantly harassed them in this largely devastated area without offering them the pitched battle which they now had a chance of winning. At last, as both armies were out foraging in the plains of Saguntum, their scouts reported that Sertorius and Perperna were advancing in full force from the River Turia, which gave its name to the ensuing battle that lasted from noon till nightfall. Pompey himself fought furiously and his brother-in-law Memmius lost his life, but his army was gradually driven back by Sertorius, who cut down six thousand of his men for the loss of half that number. Metellus on the other hand was getting the better of

Perperna and had killed some five thousand of the enemy when Sertorius returned from his pursuit of Pompey to assist his less competent colleague. Metellus now found himself in Pompey's predicament at the Sucro, fighting to rally his troops to stand firm against the enemy's counter-attack. He too received several wounds, but unlike Pompey he was fighting on foot and had no golden trappings to cover his retreat. But the sight of this valiant old man hacking away at the enemy and being gradually overwhelmed had an invigorating effect on his troops. They rallied at once to protect him, and having carried him back to safety under a roof of shields, they returned to the attack with such fury that they emerged victorious at the end of the day.

The next morning Sertorius was sufficiently unsure of himself to decline another pitched battle. He decided instead to withdraw his forces inland where the difficult terrain would be more in his favour, but as a Parthian shot he attempted a surprise attack on Metellus' camp which was neatly frustrated by Pompey. Pompey and Metellus then set out in pursuit, dogging his steps as he retreated north-westwards up the valley of the Turia and deep into the mountain fastnesses of the Celtiberians. In the hope that they would lose heart Sertorius did not disperse his army as he had so often done before but marched it across the watershed to the sources of the River Douro. But still the Roman armies followed until finally he locked himself in the city of Clunia and stood at bay like a stag among a pack of exhausted hounds.

Pompey and Metellus began to draw siege-lines round the fortified city in the confident expectation of being able to reduce it without difficulty in a matter of weeks. But Sertorius was far from beaten. The barbarians whom the Romans allowed to escape from the city to spread alarm and despondency among the enemy tribes were in fact taking orders and instructions to his allies, who eventually turned up in enormous strength to threaten the Roman position. In the chaos that followed Sertorius promptly marched out of Clunia, cut his way through the siege-lines, and joined the relieving army, which he used so effectively that Pompey and Metellus found themselves in an untenable position. They had no choice but to make their way back to the coastal plains as best they could against constant ambushes and skirmishes with the Sertorian guerrillas. But even there their hard-pressed commissariat found no relief. The once rich coastal plains had been virtually denuded by the foraging of so many armies earlier in the year, and there was no chance of bringing in supplies by sea since Sertorius' pirate-allies had closed all the ports. Clearly there was nothing more that could be done that year, and as the campaigning season was nearly over in any case, the two governors decided to separate, Metellus to cross the Pyrenees to more comfortable winter-quarters in

Gaul, Pompey to march inland and spend his second Spanish winter in the territory of the Vaccaei of the Douro valley.

The behaviour of the two governors during the winter of 75–4 shows interesting differences of character. Metellus sank back into a luxurious way of life and held a lavish celebration of his success at the Turia, but his despair of ever beating Sertorius in battle betrayed itself in a proclamation putting a price on his head of one hundred silver talents, twenty thousand acres of land and a free pardon. Pompey, in contrast, lived rough among his men, swallowed his pride, and wrote for reinforcements to the Senate in Rome. He had written before, but his requests had always been ignored by a Senate which had conveniently found itself too preoccupied with political and financial difficulties at home to worry about the problems of a troublesome young general in Spain. But this time there was a note of bitterness in his letter, and a threat. This, according to Sallust, is what he wrote:

If, instead of seeking your safety and destroying your most criminal enemies, I had undertaken all the dangers and hardships of my youth in making war against you, my country and our ancestral gods, you could not have treated me worse in my absence, Fathers of Rome, than you are now doing. Having exposed me in spite of my youth to this most savage war, you have done everything in your power to destroy me and an army that deserved well of you by starvation, that most wretched of all deaths. Is this the expectation with which the People of Rome send their sons to war? Are these the rewards of our wounds and the shedding of so much blood for our country? Worn out with writing you letters and sending envoys, I have exhausted all my personal resources and my credit, while you have given me barely enough for one year's expenses in the last three. Ye Gods, do you think I am a substitute for your Treasury so that I can maintain an army without provisions or pay?

For my own part I freely admit that I embarked upon this war with more zeal than sense, seeing that it took me less than forty days from receiving your empty command to raise and equip my own army at my own expense. Your enemies were then at the throat of Italy. I drove them back from the Alps into Spain. In the process I opened for you another and more convenient route across those mountains than the one Hannibal had taken. I recovered Gaul, the Pyrenees, Lacetania and the Indigetes. With raw soldiers and far inferior numbers I withstood the first assaults of the unconquered Sertorius, and I spent the winter in camp among the most savage of enemies, not in the towns nor with any concern to increase my personal power.

But why should I enumerate my battles and winter-campaigns, the towns I destroyed or recovered? Deeds speak louder than words: the camp of the enemy captured at Sucro, the battle at the River Turia, the destruction of the enemy general Herennius together with his army and the city of Valentia. All this you know already, and in return, grateful Fathers, you have given me want and hunger. The result is that the condition of my army and the enemy's is the same, for neither is paid and both can march victorious into Italy. Now this is the true situation, and I beg you to take notice and not try to force me into private remedies for our necessities. My province of Nearer Spain, so far as it is not in enemy hands, either we or Sertorius have devastated to the point of desolation, so that with the exception of the coastal cities it is actually a burden and expense to me rather than an asset. Last year Gaul provided the army of Metellus with pay and provisions, but now it can barely feed its own population after the bad harvests. As for me, I have not only exhausted my private means but even my credit. You are our only resource: unless you give us assistance, I warn you that, unwilling as I am that such a thing should happen, my army will return to Italy, and with it will come the whole of this war in Spain.

The sting was in the tail, and when this letter was read out in the Senate at the beginning of 74, the last sentence had the desired effect. If the outgoing consuls of 75 did not care whether Pompey was reinforced or not since they were taking up provincial governorships of their own, the two new consuls for 74 would do anything rather than have their year of office marred by the return of Pompey the Great. They may not have believed that the war would really come back with him, but the prospect of virtually surrendering Spain to Sertorius and having an unpredictable and vindictive Pompey once again sitting with an army outside the gates of Rome was sufficiently unattractive to convince them of the wisdom of sending him two legions and fresh supplies of money.

Sertorius too received external support about this time from Rome's inveterate enemy on the other side of her empire, the irrepressible King Mithridates of Pontus. Either late in 75 or (more probably) early in 74 King Nicomedes died in neighbouring Bithynia, and in the absence of legitimate heirs his kingdom devised to the Roman People, who promptly annexed it as a province. Mithridates was furious. Undaunted by the memory of his defeats at the hands of Sulla, he was not prepared to see control of the Bosporus passing into Roman hands, and he immediately began to assemble his forces for an invasion of Bithynia in support of an alleged son of its former ruler. At the same time he cast about for allies, and hearing of a Roman general who had fought his old enemy Sulla in civil war and was still tying down Rome's best generals in a seemingly endless war in Spain, he sent envoys to Sertorius to suggest co-operation. There were those who even spoke of Mithridates and Sertorius as a modern Pyrrhus and Hannibal and saw Rome gradually being crushed between the powers of East and West; but the king had more modest and realistic strategical objectives in view when he offered Sertorius money and ships in return for a Roman commander and recognition of his claim to the whole of Asia Minor, including the old Roman province known simply as 'Asia'.

The rebel Senate which Sertorius called to debate the proposals was delighted to be asked to bestow a title to what was not theirs to give in exchange for the means to continue the war, and it was amazed when Sertorius insisted on a partition of Asia Minor. Mithridates, he said, was welcome to Cappadocia and Bithynia, 'countries used to kings and of no value to Rome', but the old Roman province was sacrosanct. ' "Ye Gods," ' cried the king when he heard Sertorius' reply, ' "what terms will the man demand when he is back in Rome if now that he has been driven to the shores of the Atlantic he seeks to set limits to our kingdom and threatens us with war if we try to get hold of Asia?" ' All the same, he sent Sertorius the enormous sum of three thousand talents and forty ships in return for a Roman officer and drill-masters for his army: it was worth a good deal to the king to keep Pompey and his legions in Spain.

When the campaigning season opened in 74, Pompey marched from his winter-quarters among the Vaccaei to the Pyrenees, to rendezvous with Metellus on his return from Gaul and also possibly to meet the two new legions which had been sent from Rome. The two governors again agreed on joint operations, not in the devastated eastern seaboard this time but in the Ebro valley and the headwaters of the Douro. It was abundantly clear by now that this was not a war to be won by death-or-glory tactics, the Hannibalic march and the great pitched battle. Against Sertorius' guerrilla warfare their tactics had to be slower, less spectacular but ruthlessly efficient: steady progress area by area, the reduction of one stronghold after another, the painstaking consolidation of one region before advancing to the next. It was not the most exciting kind of warfare and our sources give it scant attention, but we do at least have one or two glimpses of the more interesting battles and sieges.

Frontinus, the insatiable collector of stratagems, mentions one of Pompey's at this time, the effective if dishonourable method by which he took possession of Cauca, a city of the southern Vaccaei. Pompey suspected this strongly fortified town of Sertorian sympathies and knew that a formal request to put in a garrison might lead to a lengthy siege. Accordingly he merely asked the citizens to do him the kindness of allowing his sick and wounded to rest and recover there. Anxious to oblige him in anything that would avoid having to refuse a garrison, they agreed at once and opened their gates to a long and pathetic procession of limping men and stretcher-bearers. Indeed it seemed that Pompey's casualties had been far heavier than anyone had imagined, and the Sertorian sympathizers were secretly pleased as they counted their numbers. But no sooner had the gates closed again than the lame took up their beds and fought. It was a neat variation on the Trojan Horse, and similarly successful.

But this was not the sort of trick that could be used twice in the same war, and Pompey was not always so successful in his more regular sieges. The seemingly ubiquitous Sertorius was usually at hand to defend the cities that remained loyal to him. At Pallantia, for example, Pompey was piling faggots against the city-walls when Sertorius suddenly appeared with a large army and forced him to withdraw. Admittedly Pompey managed to set fire to the walls first, but Sertorius quickly rebuilt the damaged fortifications before marching to the relief of another city to which Pompey and Metellus had turned their attention. This was Calagurris in the upper reaches of the Ebro, and it witnessed a major battle in which Pompey lost three thousand men and the chance to reduce the city before the onset of winter forced him back across the Pyrenees to less uncomfortable quarters in Gaul.

The past year had not been notably successful for Pompey, to judge from his failures at Pallantia and Calagurris, but it had also been less successful for Sertorius than might appear from Livy's brief acknowledgement that he was once more 'a match for his opponents in all the arts of war and strategy'. Sertorius was becoming very worried by the increasing friction between the native and Roman elements of his own army. At the highest level of his general staff, men like Perperna were puffed up with their own importance and failed to realize how singularly their continued success depended on the genius of their commander-in-chief. In the ranks the Roman soldiers were increasingly resentful of their equality of treatment with the native troops. A particular grievance was Sertorius' reliance on his Celtiberian bodyguard, which was utterly devoted to him, and there was general resentment against the strictness of his discipline, for he had been known to decimate a whole cohort as punishment for the rape of a woman in a captured city.

There was in addition a growing feeling that the pretext of fighting a purely Roman civil war was wearing rather thin. To Sertorius himself it was still real enough, and he is credited with saying even in a moment of victory that he would prefer to be allowed to live in Rome as the meanest of her citizens than in exile as supreme ruler of all the rest of the world; but the Celtiberians were already calling him 'Hannibal' and beginning to despise their Roman comrades, some of whom started to desert to the army of Metellus, who was clearly not against offering them a free pardon. At first the number of desertions was small, but Sertorius fuelled the very disaffection that he was trying to suppress by the extraordinary severity of his punishments, and Appian indicates that by the end of 74 this growing problem had enabled Metellus 'to overrun many of the enemy towns and bring the men belonging to them under subjection'.

Of the events of the following year, which was Pompey's fourth in Spain, we know almost nothing beyond Appian's bald statement that 'both governors plucked up more courage and advanced boldly against the cities that adhered to Sertorius'. Some they won over, others they assaulted with varying results, but there is no mention of any great battles. All the same, they are said to have been 'elated by success' after a campaign in which Pompey seems to have played the major part. Livy's epitomator tells us tantalizingly that the missing ninety-fourth book of the *History* contained an account of 'the successful campaign of Gnaeus Pompeius in Spain against Sertorius', and clearly his achievement in 73 was solid if not spectacular.

By 72 the constant pressure to which Sertorius had been subjected in the previous two years had widened the cracks in his army's unity. Whether Sertorius himself was cracking up under the strain and giving himself up to wine, women and song, as reported by the biased Appian, is open to question, but certainly there was increasing resentment among his Roman troops against the Spaniards and among his senior colleagues against his leadership. Chief among the latter was the worthless Perperna, who bitterly resented playing second fiddle to an abler man who was his social inferior. As long as Sertorius had been successful, there was nothing he could do to undermine his leadership, especially since he himself had signally failed to win any of the engagements which Sertorius had so generously entrusted to his incompetence. But now that things were not going so well, Perperna saw his chance to use his rival's increasing difficulties to secure the command for himself. He worked on the pride of the other Marian leaders by asking if they had rejected Sulla's tyranny only to become Sertorius' slaves, and he persuaded the more responsive ones to undermine the loyalty of allied tribes by harsh treatment supposedly ordered by his commander. When Sertorius sent these officers to suppress the ensuing revolts, they stirred up still more trouble until Sertorius himself began to lose patience and took reprisals on the Iberian chieftains' sons whom he had been educating at his school at Osca. He was thus cruelly misled into destroying much that was most enlightened in his administration.

But all these methods of discrediting Sertorius were essentially long-term. Perperna was impatient, and as he was also beginning to fear that his intended victim might learn the truth, he started to conspire directly against Sertorius' life. The principal problem was that Sertorius was constantly attended by his large and incorruptible bodyguard, and it was not until one conspiracy had been betrayed except for the identity of its ringleader that Perperna's dull intellect was sufficiently stimulated by danger to discover a solution. It was the oldest trick in the world, but it worked against the still unsuspecting Sertorius, who graciously accepted Perperna's invitation to a lavish dinner-party. As the evening wore on, the wine flowed so freely that both Sertorius and his bodyguard were unusually relaxed when the host suddenly dropped his goblet on the floor. This was the signal for Perperna's accomplices to draw their hidden swords, and in a few seconds it was all over: Quintus Sertorius, unconquered by the enemy, lay dead at the hands of his friends.

Perperna and his colleagues had prepared the ground well enough to enable him to take supreme command without significant opposition, but his satisfaction was rapidly eroded by the harsh reality of continuing the war with a depleted and demoralized army. It was not just that many of the Iberians, sensibly lacking confidence in his ability, simply gave up and sent messages of submission to Pompey's camp. As the days went by even the Roman troops, formerly so resentful of Sertorius' reliance on the Spaniards, found their resentment turning to regret, especially when his will was read and the chief assassin turned out to have been left a most generous bequest. As for the Roman governors' estimate of the new enemy supremo, it is adequately expressed in Metellus' decision to return to his own province and leave Pompey to finish him off on his own.

Pompey could scarcely believe his good fortune when it became clear that Perperna was preparing to stake everything on a pitched battle. But Perperna had little choice, for he had neither Sertorius' ability to fight a guerrilla war nor confidence in the continuing loyalty of his rapidly dwindling army. For ten days the two generals made trial of each other with skirmishes and raids until Pompey was convinced that his adversary had no set plan of campaign. He then used his superior generalship to bring about a battle on ground most favourable to himself by means of a stratagem which appealed to Frontinus for its simplicity. He sent out ten cohorts as a decoy, and when Perperna obediently attacked them, they retreated and led the pursuing army into the place of ambush, where Pompey himself appeared in force and won a complete victory. As Perperna's troops gave way all along the line, their craven commander tried to save his own skin by hiding in a wood, but Pompey's horsemen soon flushed him out and dragged him to their general's tent. Pursued by the curses of his own men, the captured and the wounded, he tried to bargain for his life by shouting aloud that he had all Sertorius' secret correspondence. He claimed to possess signed letters from men of consular rank in Rome inviting Sertorius to return to Italy and promising their support if he could rekindle the Civil War: in exchange for his life he would happily betray the most prominent Marian sympathizers still in Rome.

But Pompey refused to listen. With a discretion beyond his thirty-three years he ordered Perperna to hand over the papers, which he promptly burnt without either reading them himself or allowing anyone else to do so. He then had Perperna put to death before he could reveal their contents or the names of any of the correspondents. It was a wise and honourable decision, rightly praised by all our sources. Rome had had more than enough of civil war, and Pompey was not going to allow another witch-hunt of Sertorian sympathizers whose only defence would be to take up arms. Nor did he yield to the temptation to use the information to his own advantage, though he could easily have used the letters to blackmail leading men in Rome to support his career. Pompey was, if anything, too decent, and in the end it would be his undoing.

There now remained the vast tidying-up operation of a disordered province. For eight years Spain had been punished for the quarrels of Rome at the hands of Roman generals, and now that Sertorius was dead and his assassin defeated, most of the rebel tribes and cities surrendered of their own accord. Only Uxama and Calagurris held out for any length of time before they were reduced – the former by Pompey, the latter by one of his legates. After that it was a matter of painstaking reorganization and resettlement, a task which engaged Pompey's energies until an urgent summons from the Senate late in 72 sent him marching back to Italy to deal with a new emergency: the revolt of Spartacus and his seemingly unconquerable army of ex-gladiators and slaves.

5

SPARTACUS AND CRASSUS

'I think I do nothing demeaning or unworthy, fellow-citizens,
in making the first move to good will and friendship with
Pompey, to whom you gave the name *the Great* when he was
still beardless and voted a triumph before he was even a
member of the Senate.'
Plutarch, Life of Crassus, 12.4

In the five years since Pompey had left for Spain, Rome had been engaged
in wars elsewhere in her sprawling empire, notably in the East where
Mithridates' designs on Bithynia had been frustrated by the consul Lucius
Lucullus. He not only cleared the king out of Bithynia in 73 but began
an invasion of Pontus itself which eventually compelled Mithridates to
seek asylum with his son-in-law, the King of Armenia. In the meantime
Lucius' brother Marcus had gone out to govern Macedonia and carried
Roman arms victoriously to the Danube. But not all Rome's wars were
so successful or so comfortably far away. In 73 Italy had become a battlefield once again as the imperial capital was suddenly called upon to face
a danger no less formidable than the rebellion of her allies, and from
enemies even closer to home.

They were slaves, those useful chattels whose labour was the basis of
most ancient economies and whose easy availability made it unnecessary
for the otherwise ingenious Roman engineers to bother inventing any
labour-saving devices. Their lot was not always a bad one. The more
intelligent and fortunate taught the children of the aristocracy, acted as
their secretaries, ran their homes and estates and had the hope of freedom
one day, granted perhaps in their masters' wills. But for many more there
was the hard grind of the factories, the mines, or the large-scale agriculture which had developed since the rapid expansion of the empire in
the second century had brought slaves in their hundreds of thousands
to work the fields and tend the flocks of the great estates of Italy and
Sicily. The system was generally protected by the mixture of nationalities,
the severity of punishment, and the fact that bred slaves had no homes
to return to. But Sicily had already been the scene of two major Servile

Wars: the first had started in 135, the second in 104, and both had proved difficult to suppress.

The present rebellion in Italy had begun with an outbreak of gladiators from their training school in Capua. Their leader was the famous Spartacus, a Thracian by birth, who had once served as a mercenary with the Romans but deserted to become a highwayman until this period of lucrative self-employment had ended in the slave-market. In a rare compliment to a slave Plutarch says that he was not only courageous and strong but also intelligent and 'culturally superior to his fortune, for he was more Hellenic than Thracian'. Some seventy or eighty gladiators had overpowered their guards, made their escape, and killed the Roman troops which pursued them. Then arming themselves properly with the soldiers' weapons they sought refuge on the heights of Mt Vesuvius, where they were joined by shepherds and other fugitive slaves.

As soon as this news reached Rome the Senate sent the praetor Claudius Glaber to deal with the rebels. Glaber cornered Spartacus on part of the mountain where sheer cliffs surrounded a single steep approach, which the praetor now cut off with siege-lines. But Spartacus made rope-ladders from wild vines, and he and his men descended the cliffs out of sight of the Romans. They then crept round the back of the siege-lines and attacked with such devastating effect that Glaber's troops panicked and fled, leaving the gladiators in possession of his camp.

The prestige of this success soon attracted large numbers to the rebel army, mainly slaves from the great estates but some of the free poor too. And the army was formidable in quality as well as quantity, for many of its recruits were survivors of the great battles against the Cimbri and Teutones whom Marius had sold into slavery. As their numbers multiplied they began to terrorize Campania, not only sacking country houses and villages but attacking towns like Nola and Nuceria, which they all but destroyed.

The next force sent against them, under the praetor Varinius, proved as unsuccessful as the first, and when the praetor Cossinius was sent to his colleague's aid, Spartacus defeated them both in a pitched battle, killed Cossinius, and captured their camp. Revenge was sweet. Spartacus dressed himself up in the regalia of a praetor and made four hundred of his Roman captives fight to the death for the amusement of his slaves. He then marched south into Lucania, sacked Metapontum and Thurii in the arch of Italy's foot, and reached the Bruttian town of Consentia, the modern Cosenza, before deciding that it was time to return home. For these rebels, unlike the Sicilian slaves, had homes to go to. Most were Thracians, Gauls or Germans, and Spartacus prepared to lead them up the Apennines to the Alps and thence to their various countries. He now had some seventy thousand men for whom he had found or manufactured arms, but he was not so blinded by his recent successes that he failed to see the impossibility of holding out forever against all the legions which Rome could in time either raise in Italy or recall from abroad. And Rome was beginning to take Spartacus very seriously. 'It was no longer the indignity and disgrace of a revolt by slaves that worried the Senate,' says Plutarch, 'but fear; and because they now realized the extent of the danger, they sent both consuls into the field, as though to one of the greatest and most difficult of wars.'

Unfortunately for Rome the consuls of 72 were not very good soldiers, and Spartacus found little difficulty in defeating them first separately and then together when they joined forces and met him in a great pitched battle in Picenum. He then continued his march northwards up the Aemilian Way, and at Mutina defeated the governor of Cisalpine Gaul who, with a relatively small force, had made a brave attempt to stop him. If Rome was aghast at the failure of the consuls, her citizens were terrified by the next piece of news. It seemed that after demolishing the last obstacle that barred his way to the Alps Spartacus no longer wanted to take it: instead he was reported to be considering an attack on Rome itself. Why he should have changed his mind when his plan of escape had all but succeeded is not clear. Perhaps his men, many of whom had come to Italy thirty years before to seek new homes, simply refused to follow him further north. Or perhaps he had come to believe that Rome was not invincible at all, and that he could succeed where Hannibal had failed. After all, Hannibal's failure had been due to his lack of support among Rome's allies in Italy, but there was no shortage of slaves either in the country or in the city itself, and perhaps Spartacus hoped to find the streets of Rome already flowing with citizen blood when he arrived before the gates. At any rate he began to move menacingly southwards again towards Picenum, where there was nothing to stop him but the two demoralized legions of the consuls whom the Senate had recalled in disgust to Rome and relieved of their commands in favour of Marcus Crassus, a praetor of the previous year who in Pompey's absence seemed to offer the only chance of salvation.

Crassus was about nine years older than Pompey, towards whom he had always entertained a sense of rivalry. Like Pompey he had joined the Sullan army which invaded Italy from Greece in 83, with a burning desire to avenge the deaths of his father and elder brother who had perished under the Marian regime, but with few if any troops. Although he later performed great services in the war, he was always conscious of holding a lower place in Sulla's estimation than the younger Pompey, whose arrival with a large and victorious force of his own had won such immediate acclaim. He never forgot how he had once asked Sulla for an escort on a dangerous mission only to be told 'to take his dead father and brother and the other brave men whom the enemy had destroyed'; and despite his joint victory with Pompey at Spoletium, it was not until his successful command of the right wing had secured Sulla's critical defeat of the Samnites outside the walls of Rome that he really achieved military fame and the gratitude of his commander-in-chief.

For the next nine years he had hardly been involved in military activities. While Pompey went in pursuit of the Marian fugitives in Sicily and Africa, Crassus concentrated on exploiting the situation at home and using his brilliant business-brain to turn his modest inheritance into one of the richest fortunes in Rome. The proscriptions were a godsend to the astute speculator. When Sulla was busy auctioning off the estates of the proscribed at knock-down prices, Crassus was a privileged bidder in a buyer's market; and when Sulla replenished the depleted Senate by elevating three hundred knights, Crassus became a ready seller in a seller's market as the new senators sought to acquire estates and properties appropriate to their status. And property dealing was only one of his many interests. He had organized a fire-brigade and teams of builders and architects from the vast numbers of slaves which he had acquired cheap with the estates of Sulla's victims. A fire never broke out in Rome without the rapid appearance on the scene of one of Crassus' agents, offering to buy endangered properties at bargain prices or negotiating terms for rebuilding before calling up the firemen and putting out the blaze. There was also his banking business. Advancement up the senatorial ladder of office could not be achieved without money, and when a desperate candidate needed ready cash to bribe the electorate or put on a show, Crassus was always ready to lend a sympathetic ear and an appropriate sum. From most he would demand a high rate of interest and be prompt in collecting repayment. To others he would lend for nothing but a speculation in a promising career and the knowledge that he was weaving potentially powerful men in a web of obligation, and no doubt there were many grateful or fearful supporters of his own advancement to the praetorship in 73.

Crassus had watched the progress of the Servile War with increasing interest, and when the consuls of 72 were defeated and recalled, he was ready to make the biggest and boldest speculation of his career. It was not just that his own extensive estates were suffering from the depredations of the slaves: he saw the chance to achieve a military reputation that would bear comparison with the achievements of Pompey in Spain or the Luculli in the East, to win the eternal gratitude of his fellow-landowners, and to ensure himself a consulship from a grateful people. He therefore came forward with an offer to raise six legions at his own expense on the condition that he was appointed to supreme command of the war with the rank of proconsul, the same rank which Pompey held as governor of Nearer Spain.

The Senate agreed with alacrity, and Crassus began to raise his six new legions and the necessary auxiliary forces – a task which was not as difficult as might be supposed. Italy was full of Sulla's veterans who had been pensioned off on little farms, and when they were offered the chance of serving one of their old commanders who was a more certain source of pay than the near-bankrupt Treasury, there was a rush of volunteers to enlist in his army. Crassus then sent his legate Mummius ahead to take command of the two legions which had been defeated in Picenum, with instructions to use them to keep in touch with Spartacus' army but on no account to engage or even skirmish with the slaves. But Mummius, unable to resist the chance to win all the glory for himself, ignored these orders, attacked Spartacus in what appeared a promising situation, and was severely trounced. Crassus was furious. When Mummius returned, he not only gave the disobedient legate the dressing-down of his life but ruthlessly punished his defeated legionaries by decimating the five hundred most cowardly. Then, 'when he had demonstrated to his men that he was more to be feared than the enemy', he led them against a detachment of Spartacus' army and won his first victory. Spartacus now gave up all hope of an attack on Rome against so powerful a force of legions, and led his men southward again through Lucania into Bruttium, the toe of Italy, from where he planned to cross to Sicily and 'rekindle the Servile War there, which had not been long extinguished and needed only a little additional fuel'.

While Spartacus was negotiating with the captain of a pirate fleet to ferry his army across the straits, Crassus employed his soldiers in drawing siege-lines across the whole of Italy's toe – a ditch, wall and paling some thirty-five miles long from coast to coast. It was an enormous undertaking, but Crassus drove his men hard and completed the work in a remarkably short time despite all the gladiators' ingenious attempts to stop him. He then sat down to starve Spartacus out, but when the Senate heard that the war was promising to be a long one and there was a danger of Spartacus' escaping to Sicily, they voted to recall Pompey from Spain and Marcus Lucullus from Macedonia. Crassus himself actually wrote advising this precaution, but probably only because he knew that the Senate would do it anyway and he wished to avoid appearing small-minded. The very last thing he wanted was to share his glory with his rival, and now that Pompey was on his way home he did all he could to bring Spartacus to a decisive battle.

Spartacus' position was becoming untenable. The pirate captain who had accepted his gifts had let him down, and as the winter drew on his supplies of food were running short in the little triangle of Italy in which he was now confined. He even tried to come to terms with Crassus, but when his approaches were scornfully rejected, he first crucified a Roman prisoner in the ditch between the two camps to remind his men what would happen to them if they lost and then tried to break out of Crassus' siege-lines. Choosing a wintry night when blizzards made observation almost impossible, he filled part of the ditch with branches and corpses and got thirty thousand of his men safely across before the Romans could stop them.

Crassus soon realized that this was a blessing in disguise. It had not only divided Spartacus' army, but the detachment which had escaped now chose new leaders in the same spirit of dissension which had undermined the Sertorian cause in Spain. Crassus attacked this separate force in Lucania and would have annihilated it if his pursuit had not been stopped short by the appearance of Spartacus himself, who had meanwhile also managed to escape the siege. But with the depressingly familiar reaction of the second-rate the new leaders of the detachment which Spartacus had saved were more resentful than grateful, and they continued to operate independently until Crassus attacked them again and stopped them operating altogether.

Desperate to escape from Italy before Pompey's arrival, Spartacus now made for Brundisium in the hope of finding some pirates who would take him to Sicily, but he was pulled up short by the news that Marcus Lucullus had just landed there from Greece. He then retreated into the mountains of Petelia with an advance guard of Crassus' army hanging on his tail. But he was not beaten yet. He suddenly turned and defeated the pursuing Romans so completely that the success quite turned his men's heads, and they demanded to be led against Crassus himself. It was exactly what Crassus wanted. Seizing the chance of finishing the war without the help of Pompey or Lucullus, he attacked and won his final victory, in which the indomitable Spartacus was cut down trying to reach him through the thickest of the fighting.

'Yet even in this success,' says Plutarch, 'Fortune somehow managed to include Pompey.' As Pompey marched rapidly southwards he ran into five thousand of the fugitives from Crassus' victory, cut them to pieces, and promptly wrote to the Senate that 'while Crassus had conquered the gladiators in pitched battle, it was he who had extirpated the war entirely'. With so many victories of his own to boast about it seems somewhat small-minded of Pompey to try to steal Crassus' glory too; but there is no need to feel too sorry for Crassus. If it was a failing in Pompey to resent the success of a rival, it showed a less unpleasant character than the pleasure which Crassus could not help taking in the disasters of others, even of a young friend like Julius Caesar whose first words on being captured by pirates in 74 had been, ' "How Crassus will rejoice to hear of this!" '

Plutarch tells us that it was agreeable to the Romans to believe that Pompey had ended the Servile War. For as our sources clearly show by referring constantly to the indignity of a war against slaves and making some ridiculous exaggerations of the numbers killed in the final battles, the Romans wished to forget that the lowest and most despised of mankind had defeated their consuls, terrorized Italy as effectively as Hannibal, and needed eight legions to put them down. They preferred to think of it as a minor affair brushed aside by the return of a victorious general who had been fighting respectable enemies abroad, and if it was Crassus who erected an impressively macabre monument to his victory by crucifying six thousand captives along the Appian Way from Capua to Rome, it was Pompey who was the hero of the day.

As Pompey approached Rome with his army, citizens of all classes streamed out to greet him, some in sheer delight at his victorious return, some to ingratiate themselves, and not a few in fear that he knew their secret Marian sympathies and might not yet have ceased his revenge. There was also, says Plutarch, 'mingled with the great honour shown him and the great expectations cherished of his return, a certain apprehensiveness that he might not disband his army but do what Sulla had done and seize absolute power by force of arms'. But Pompey soon removed any such suspicions by announcing that he would disband his army as soon as he had held his triumph. As for the prominent Marian sympathizers who feared that he might have discovered their treasonable correspondence with Sertorius, they were soon reassured when they heard how he had burnt all the letters unread and had put Perperna to death before he could reveal any names. For Pompey made it quite clear that he had returned in a spirit of reconciliation, and not revenge. Besides treating the defeated Sertorians with clemency in Spain he had showed a rare sensitivity by omitting the name of Sertorius himself from the trophy which he had set up in the Pyrenees on his way home, and his sole concern now was to receive the two rewards which he considered his just deserts – a triumph for his victory in Spain and the consulship for the following year.

The triumph was easy enough to achieve. The grateful Senate voted it at once, and with a great deal more enthusiasm than it voted Crassus an *ovatio*, the second-class triumph which was held on foot and was the highest honour that could be awarded for a victory against mere slaves.

But the consulship was a matter of election by the people, and though Pompey had many friends in the Senate who were prepared to waive the law governing the stages of the senatorial career, he wisely sought to reinforce the popularity of his victories by promising the electorate what they most desired. For the plebeians this was the restoration of the powers of the tribunate, which Sulla had emasculated. For the knights, whose votes carried more weight in the timocratic electoral system for the higher magistracies, it was the restoration of their control of the jury-courts which Sulla had transferred to the Senate. And when Pompey addressed the vast assembly which gathered to hear him outside the city-walls, he made both these promises amid terrific applause.

The restoration of the tribunes' power to present Bills to the plebeian assemblies was not a new cause for Pompey. He had seen its value as a means of advancing his own career in defiance of the established ladder of office even before Sulla was dead, and this was one of the reasons why he had supported the reformist Lepidus for the consulship of 78. Although events had conspired to give him a series of exceptional commands from the Senate rather than the people, there is no reason to suppose that he had ceased to see the possible usefulness of tribunician legislation in the future, quite apart from the more immediate advantages of giving the people what they most desired. 'For there was nothing,' says Plutarch, 'for which the Roman people had lusted more frantically or yearned more ardently than to behold that power again, and Pompey regarded it as a great piece of luck that he had the opportunity for this political measure, as he could have found no other favour with which to repay the good will of the citizens if anyone else had anticipated him in this.' And certainly many had tried. There had been constant agitation for this reform ever since he had left Rome, and the whole campaign had come to focus on his return for the final victory.

Even Sulla's law preventing a tribune of the people from holding any other magistracy had not discouraged capable men from seeking that virtually impotent office and daring to demand the restoration of its powers. One of the first had been the tribune Sicinius in 76, a formidable orator and agitator who was not afraid to attack anyone in the city, with the significant exception of Marcus Crassus who already had the sinister reputation of having 'a straw tied to his horn' – the sign of a dangerous bull. Sicinius was eventually silenced by the consul Curio, but his agitation had not been without effect since C. Aurelius Cotta, one of the consuls of the following year and a dyed-in-the-wool aristocrat, actually passed a law removing the career-killing prohibition that a tribune could seek no further public office. No doubt he hoped that this minor concession would act as a placebo, but the people were less appeased than excited at this first taste of victory, which meant they would now find fewer nonentities standing for election as their tribunes.

In 74 the tribune Quinctius was the terror of the establishment, and though he was effectively silenced by the consul Lucius Lucullus, the tribune Macer took up his torch in the following year and made some inflammatory speeches, one of which is given by Sallust. Macer knew that Pompey had been starved of funds and reinforcements by the Senate, and he was shrewd enough to associate Pompey with the popular cause:

'Just wait till Pompey gets back, the man they bore on their necks like slaves when they feared him but tear to shreds now their fear is removed. Nor are those self-styled defenders of liberty, many as they are, ashamed to need one man before they dare to right a wrong or can defend a right. For my own part I am convinced that Gnaeus Pompeius, a young man of such great renown, prefers to be the leading man in the state with your consent rather than to share in your mastery, and that when he returns he will be your friend and champion in restoring your tribunes' power.'

Pompey's appeal to the knights has a more complicated history. It was not based on his own equestrian status. Every young man of senatorial family was a knight until he had been elected to his first magistracy and entered the Senate, and it was an extraordinary chapter of accidents that had brought Pompey within reach of the highest office of the senatorial career while he was still one of them. The knights to whom Pompey was appealing were the businessmen of Rome, equestrians who rarely became, or sought to become, senators. Not that all knights were businessmen of course. A great number were gentlemen farmers not far removed in style of life from the senatorial aristocracy, but there was a hard core of big businessmen: merchants and bankers, contractors of supplies to the army, mine-owners, slave-traders and, most significantly in this instance, the tax-farmers who formed the great companies that competed for the contracts to collect revenues from the provinces and made sure that they reimbursed themselves at a handsome profit. It was here that the interests of the senatorial and equestrian classes diverged. Men of the senatorial order became governors of provinces with a responsibility to protect their subjects. Men of the equestrian order were the farmers of taxes whose only interest was their harvest of profit; and since some governors were as bad as the publicans in bleeding their provinces white, the composition of the juries of the extortion courts at Rome was the deciding factor in almost every case brought by, or on behalf of, hardpressed provincials against one of their senatorial governors.

When these permanent courts had first been formed in the mid-second century, they had been a standing commission of the Senate, and as such predisposed to acquit rather than condemn fellow-senators who considered their provincial governorships wasted if they failed to replenish the family fortunes which had so often been depleted by the costs of getting themselves elected. But in 123–2 the tribune Gaius Gracchus, seeking electoral support against the senatorial regime which had opposed his reforms and clubbed his brother to death in the streets, supported a law transferring these courts to equestrian juries, which were naturally predisposed to condemn. The result was a number of appallingly cynical convictions of model governors whose only crime was to have been too scrupulous in protecting their subjects against the exactions of the *publicani*; and despite several attempts at reform and partial compromise in the early years of the first century, the courts had remained more or less in the hands of the knights for over forty years until Sulla had handed them back to the Senate in 81–80.

But Pompey was not alone in wanting the consulship for 70. Crassus wanted it too, and when he returned to Rome after a journey delayed by his time-consuming crucifixions he approached Pompey with the suggestion that they should stand for election together. It was a natural community of interests. Pompey had the popularity and Crassus the cash. Pompey was the darling of the people and the knights, and Crassus had a large number of senators nicely caught in his extensive financial web, quite apart from their obligations to him for saving their estates from the slaves. All the same, Plutarch says that men thought it a remarkable tribute to Pompey's distinction that Crassus, 'the richest Roman of his time, the ablest orator and the greatest man, who looked down upon Pompey and everybody else, had not the courage to sue for the consulship until he had asked for Pompey's support'. But it is not really so surprising, for Crassus was a sufficiently hard-headed businessman not to let a spot of rivalry spoil a good deal. As for Pompey, his reaction was equally realistic. Plutarch says that he was 'delighted' with Crassus' approach, and 'having long wanted the opportunity of doing this great financier some service and kindness, he readily solicited the people on his behalf by announcing that he would be no less grateful to them for such a colleague than for his own consulship'.

Once agreed, it was as good as done. The Senate voted to waive the legal objections to Pompey's candidature, and while he began preparing for his triumphal entry to the city, Crassus began spending money like water to try to catch up in popularity with the people and make sure that his *ovatio* was as grand as a second-class triumph could be. Because the generals could not enter the city until the day of their triumphs, they were elected consuls *in absentia*, and on 29 December 71 Pompey entered the city in his triumphal chariot followed by the cavalry and infantry of his victorious army. It was the day before he formally entered his year's office as consul, and this was the second triumph which he celebrated while still a mere knight.

As Pompey had become head of state without any experience whatever of public office or senatorial procedures he took the precaution of getting the scholarly Terentius Varro to write him a commentary 'from which he might learn what he ought to do and say when he was counselling the Senate'; but he was not short of self-confidence, and was soon redeeming his promise to the people by introducing a Bill to restore the full powers of the tribunes. When it went through, the people were overjoyed, and to cap his popularity he reminded them how recently he had been a knight with a flamboyant gesture. It was the year of the censorship, and among the duties of the two ex-consuls appointed to fulfil this august function every five years were a revision of the list of senators, a census of the various classes of citizens, and an examination of the young knights on their military service. As they sat in state on their ivory chairs in the Forum, the knights paraded before them one by one and were solemnly asked to recite the campaigns in which they had fought and the names of their generals. The censors then awarded honours or penalties accordingly, while the citizens packed the Forum to enjoy the pageant and cheer or hiss as the mood took them.

On this occasion the examination of the knights was proceeding normally when suddenly the crowds became curiously silent as all eyes turned in amazement to watch a small procession descending with great magnificence into the Forum. It was Pompey, preceded by his twelve lictors and wearing all the insignia of the head of state but leading his horse as all the other knights were doing. As he approached, he ordered his lictors to make way for him through the dense crowds and led his horse up to the tribunal on which the astonished censors were sitting. When the senior censor eventually found his voice, he formally put the question: ' "Pompeius Magnus, I ask you whether you have performed all the military services required by law?" ' Pompey paused for a moment to gain maximum effect, and while the crowds held their breath to catch his words he replied in a loud voice, ' "I have performed them all, and all under my own command as *Imperator*." ' The people gave a great shout of approval and continued cheering so enthusiastically that it was quite impossible to command silence. Business was effectively over for the day, and the delighted censors rose from their seats and accompanied Pompey home, to the immense satisfaction of the people who followed in a great throng and made the streets ring with their applause.

But Pompey could not remain forever at this zenith of popularity. He was a military rather than political animal, and though he at first made frequent appearances in court as an advocate for his friends besides carrying out his consular duties, he gradually retired from the public eye as the year progressed. He had restored the tribunate, but he was no democrat by nature or inclination, and wisely he did not pretend to be. When his other electoral promise was fulfilled some time after August, it was not under his own name that the Bill to reconstitute the jury-courts was promulgated but under that of the praetor L. Aurelius Cotta, whose statesmanlike measure did not give the courts entirely to the control of the knights but drew the jurors in equal numbers from three classes: senators, knights and a slightly lower timocratic class known as the *tribuni aerarii*. Pompey's only role in this reform was the negative one of 'letting it go forward'. This was in line with the general spirit of reconciliation with which he had brought the Civil War to an end by burning Sertorius' correspondence, and which showed itself again in his willingness to let a tribunician Bill go through for the recall of the exiled supporters of Lepidus, among whom was Lucius Cinna, son of the former consul and brother-in-law of the young Julius Caesar who was now campaigning ardently for the restoration of his wife's family.

For the rest of his term of office, Pompey continued to perform his consular duties but otherwise tended to avoid the Forum. He rarely showed himself in public, and when he did, it was always with so great a retinue of followers that it was hardly possible to see him. 'He encompassed his presence with majesty and pomp,' says Plutarch, 'in the belief that he should keep his dignity free from contact and familiarity with the masses.' For as the biographer shrewdly observed, he knew that

life in the robes of peace has a dangerous tendency to diminish the reputation of those whom war has made great and ill-suited to democratic equality. Such men claim the precedence in the city which they held in the field, while those who achieve less distinction in the field feel it intolerable if in the city at any rate they have no advantage. Therefore when the people find a man active in the Forum who has shone in camps and triumphs, they depress and humiliate him, but when he renounces and withdraws from such activity, they preserve his military reputation and authority untouched by their envy.

Crassus was Plutarch's second kind of man, the lesser general who seeks to make up for it by achieving precedence in the city, and there was great rivalry between the two consuls who each sought to be *princeps* – leading citizen – in his different way. Once Pompey's great triumph was over and the tribunician Bill passed, he lacked the financial resources to keep up with Crassus. It is true that he gave some votive games in August and possibly some other public entertainments, but Crassus carried on fêting the populace in the most stupendous fashion, even after his *ovatio*. At the feast of Hercules he gave a banquet for the whole city at ten thousand tables set up in the streets. He made the people a free allowance of grain for three months, and to keep his prestige intact at higher levels he was constantly appearing at court, where he used his oratorical ability as effectively as his money in the defence of his friends. And in the Senate too there were many who regarded Pompey as a dangerous upstart and looked more favourably upon Crassus, not only as the saviour of their landed interests but as an older man who had reached the consulship after passing through the appropriate grades of the senatorial career.

Inevitably there was a rapid deterioration of relations between the two consuls, and 'as they quarrelled with each other about everything', says Plutarch, 'they rendered their consulship politically barren and virtually without achievement'. Plutarch's political judgement may be rather harsh, but there is no reason to doubt the reality of their rivalry. By the end of the year they were scarcely on speaking terms, and when they addressed the assembly before laying down their office, it seemed that they were irreconcilable. In this atmosphere of tension a Roman knight named Aurelius suddenly ascended the rostra and asked permission to address the assembly with the plea that he had something of grave importance to communicate The consuls granted his request, curious to know what was troubling this rough country squire who had never before meddled in public affairs.

' "You must all wonder what a man like me is doing addressing you," ' he began in a state of some embarrassment, ' "but I must speak out. I had a vision in my sleep. Jupiter himself appeared to me in a dream and ordered me to declare in public that you should not allow your consuls to lay down their office until they have become friends." ' He then got down from the rostra as quickly as he could, and all eyes turned to the two consuls sitting in their chairs of state. For a while neither moved, until suddenly Crassus came forward towards Pompey, clasped his hand, and said in a loud voice, ' "Fellow-citizens, I think there is nothing unworthy in my yielding first to Pompey, whom you were pleased to call *the Great* while he was still beardless and to whom you decreed two triumphs before he was a senator." ' And with that, says Plutarch, they were reconciled, and laid down their office.

The truth of this story may be open to question, but it is not improbable that an attempt was made to sweeten the embittered relationship of these two powerful men before their consulship expired, and likely enough that some political nonentity provided the occasion. He may even have been put up to it by Crassus himself, whose business instincts made him think better of continuing a vendetta against an abler general who had temporarily had his day. He had nothing to lose by appealing to Pompey's vanity. It made him look magnanimous in the eyes of the people, and he knew well enough that once they had resigned public office, his greater experience in city affairs would ensure him the position of leading citizen until another military crisis arose to bring Pompey out of retirement and make him more useful as a friend than an enemy.

6
PIRATES AND POTENTATES

Since the price of provisions fell immediately, the delighted
populace exclaimed that the very name of Pompey had been
enough to end the war.
Plutarch, *Life of Pompey*, 26.2

When their year of office expired it was usual for consuls to take up proconsular governorships of provinces assigned to them by the Senate, but
neither Pompey nor Crassus wished to do this. Crassus was anxious to
get back to business and the general life of the city in which he was so
successful not only as a manipulator of men and money but as an orator
in the courts. As for Pompey, who might have been thought eager for
further military exploits, he wins the praise of the historian Velleius for
showing himself a good republican, content to rest on his many laurels
instead of seeking to be permanently in command of armies and provinces. And it is no doubt true that one year in Rome after so many years
of campaigning abroad had not exhausted his enjoyment of comfortable
domesticity with a wife whom he had not seen for six years and with
his three young children, the youngest of whom he had probably never
seen – not to mention the task of caring for his considerable estates and
the daily round of early morning levees, afternoon baths and evening din-
ner-parties which occupied so much of the time of the nobility in Rome.
All the same, it is also the case that there was only one provincial command worth having at the time, that against Mithridates, which was
already in the capable hands of Lucius Lucullus. And while Pompey continued to maintain his posture of magnificent aloofness from everyday
political life, he probably could not help envying Lucullus who was near-
ing the zenith of his success in the East.

With an army less than a quarter of the size of the king's – and despite
the incompetence of his fellow-consul Cotta whose immediate contribution to the war-effort had been to lose the entire Roman fleet – Lucullus
had managed in the space of three years to starve Mithridates out of
Roman Asia, recover Bithynia, raise a new fleet that destroyed the king's
mastery of the sea, rescue Cotta from the siege of Chalcedon, invade

Pontus, capture the royal capital, and enjoy the enormous satisfaction of writing to the Senate to request the appointment of the usual ten commissioners to help him organize the king's own country as a new province of Rome. By the time Pompey returned to Rome in 71 the only thing lacking to complete this spectacular series of victories was the capture of Mithridates himself, who had fled for refuge to the court of his elderly son-in-law, King Tigranes of Armenia. Lucullus had sent an envoy to the Armenian court to demand the surrender of the arch-enemy, and while waiting for a reply, he had returned to the Roman province of Asia to prove himself as able in administration as in war. But if Lucullus made the year of Pompey's consulship the best that had ever been known in the old Pergamene kingdom since it had fallen under the rule of Rome, it also marked the beginning of the end of an exemplary governor's own career.

Lucullus' reforms in Asia during late 71 and in 70 show only too clearly why the inhabitants of that unhappy province had welcomed Mithridates almost as eagerly in 74 as in 88, when after forty years of exploitation by Rome they had not hesitated to carry out the king's order to massacre every Italian man, woman and child east of the Aegean. Sulla had perpetuated the problem by punishing the massacre with the imposition of a war-indemnity of twenty thousand talents in addition to the usual tax-farming and usury, with the result that potentially the richest and happiest province of the empire had sunk even deeper into poverty, degradation and despair. 'Already,' says Plutarch, 'twice the amount of the indemnity had been paid to the money-lenders, yet the compounding of usurious interest had brought the capital sum up to the staggering figure of 120,000 talents.' As Roman bankers rubbed their hands in their counting-houses, whole cities were forced to borrow vast sums against the security of their public buildings, their harbour-dues and even their works of art. And the personal suffering was even more appalling. 'While cities were selling their votive offerings and sacred statues,' Plutarch continues, 'individual families were forced to sell their comely sons and virgin daughters, until at last the citizens had no security left but their own persons, and no choice but to surrender themselves to their creditors to serve them as slaves.'

Lucullus began by limiting interest rates to twelve per cent per annum, cutting off all interest that exceeded the principal, and ordaining not only that the lender should receive no more than a quarter of the borrower's income but that any creditor who compounded interest was to be deprived of the whole. These measures proved so effective that within four years the province had been able to pay off its entire debt, and all the countless mortgaged properties had returned unencumbered to their owners. But if the governor won the admiration of the whole province and the commemoration of his justice in the annual festivals named Lucullea which grateful cities instituted in his honour, their enthusiasm was not shared by the business interests in Rome. Being devoid of ideals more elevated than their vaults the equestrian financiers, whose power as a political pressure-group had been increased by the law which had restored their influence in the extortion courts, made no secret of their intention to destroy him. And Pompey, amused by their anger, began wondering how and when they would take their revenge, and how it might be turned to his own advantage.

But for the present Lucullus appeared to be going from strength to strength. King Tigranes refused point-blank to hand over his father-in-law, despite the fact that he had not even granted Mithridates an interview until the Roman envoy had demanded his surrender. Tigranes, now nearly seventy, had become the most powerful potentate in the Near East. Building on his inherited kingdom he had expanded his empire westwards over Sophene, southwards over the whole of northern Mesopotamia from the Euphrates to the borders of Media Atropatene, and still further to the south and west into Syria and Cilicia Campestris, whose cities he had depopulated to fill a vast new capital, modestly named Tigranocerta, in the hill-country between Taurus and the Upper Tigris. For so mighty a monarch to surrender his own father-in-law would have been tantamount to accepting a vassalage, and when the Roman envoy returned with the expected reply, Lucullus began his preparations for an invasion of Armenia that would make him the first Roman to cross the Euphrates with an army.

News of this projected expedition caused Lucullus' enemies in Rome to begin their own campaign to discredit him through the popular tribunes. These useful servants of wealthy pressure-groups 'raised a great outcry and accused him of seeking one war after another, not because the city had need of them but solely in order that he might be in perpetual command and never have to lay down his arms or cease enriching himself out of the public dangers'. There was also an ominous murmuring from Lucullus' troops against a further advance into unknown country, but in the spring of 69 he marched them through Sophene and made straight for Tigranocerta.

The first messenger to bring Tigranes news of the Roman advance had his head cut off, so dissuading anyone else from enlightening him until it was too late. The king was forced to withdraw to the Taurus to muster his troops, while Lucullus laid siege to the capital in the hope that its vast stores of treasure would encourage Tigranes to come to its defence and fight a pitched battle. Tigranes duly arrived with an enormous army of 150,000 infantry, 55,000 cavalry and 20,000 bowmen. Against this massive host Lucullus had a mere ten thousand legionaries and one thousand auxiliaries in the form of horsemen and archers, but he advanced undaunted to meet the king, and by the end of the day Tigranes was in headlong flight after losing even his diadem in the rout.

The result of this spectacular victory on 6 October 69 was that the Greeks whom Tigranes had transported from their own cities to people his new capital rose up against the barbarians and helped Lucullus to capture Tigranocerta. In gratitude he sent them back to their homes, and as news of his great victory spread throughout the Armenian empire Lucullus found himself courted by suppliant kings who had been Tigranes' vassals. According to Plutarch, even the King of Parthia sent envoys, but only because he hoped to persuade Lucullus to give him Mesopotamia in return for an alliance against Armenia, and Lucullus sent them politely away.

The following spring he set out on his most ambitious scheme, to advance into the heart of the Armenian plateau where Tigranes had taken refuge. Tigranes and Mithridates had used the winter to muster a new army consisting of picked men organized in the Roman fashion, with which they sought to win a war of attrition: refusing pitched battles and sallying out to attack foragers and advance parties, whose casualties soon became uncomfortably high. But by feinting a march on the old capital, Artaxata, Lucullus succeeded in drawing the royal armies into the pitched battle he so urgently required, and the result was all that he could have wished: the kings fled and the road to Artaxata was open.

With success so nearly in his grasp Lucullus was defeated by the weather and the temper of his troops. However much booty they had amassed and however much more they could expect to find at Artaxata, there was little consolation in carrying it further and further from home into unknown country beset by the ice and snow of autumn. They refused to advance further, and Lucullus had no option but to turn south again. He led his army back across the Taurus by a route which brought him down into Mygdonia, an area of northern Mesopotamia, where he captured the city of Nisibis, the last of Tigranes' possessions south of the mountains.

Only Lucullus was disappointed. Great as his achievements had been, he had failed to capture the enemy kings, and he was worried by the disturbing reports which had been filtering through to him from Rome. In 70 Lucullus had been proconsul in Asia, Cilicia, Bithynia and Pontus, but as a result of tribunician agitation Asia had been taken from his control in 69. And now news reached him in Nisibis that Cilicia had been transferred to the command of his brother-in-law and rival, the consul

Quintus Marcius Rex. Meanwhile the morale of his army was being further undermined by another brother-in-law, the militarily inept P. Clodius Pulcher, whom Lucullus had refused to promote and who had almost certainly been promised a better commission under Marcius Rex. Clodius worked up the grievances of the troops, particularly the Valerian legions which had seen continuous service in the East since Valerius Flaccus had taken them to Greece against Sulla and Mithridates in 86, and when the campaigning season opened in 67, the men at first refused to move. It was only when news came that Mithridates had reinvaded Pontus that Lucullus was able to go to the aid of his legates there, who had already suffered several defeats.

In Pontus he found the king well entrenched in his old strongholds and refusing to fight until the arrival of Tigranes, who was on his way to help his father-in-law after using him as a diversion while he had regained his own kingdom. Lucullus sought to avoid the conjunction of the two kings by marching against Tigranes, but word now came that a plebiscite in Rome had not only deprived him of the last of his commands but also ordered the discharge of his Valerian legions. On a motion of the tribune Gabinius the consul Acilius Glabrio had been invested with sole command of the war in both Bithynia and Pontus, which meant that Lucullus would become a private citizen once his successor arrived.

Desperate to salvage something from the wreck of his brilliant achievements and conscious of the danger to Asia if Mithridates and Tigranes were to remain unchecked, Lucullus even sent messages for assistance to his brother-in-law Marcius Rex who was then proceeding through Lycaonia on his way to take up his command in Cilicia. But Marcius refused, and when Lucullus begged his men to defend Cappadocia from an invasion by Tigranes, the most he could persuade them to do was to advance to its borders and fortify a camp. Beyond that they refused to move until their new commander arrived, and there was nothing Lucullus could do but 'look on helplessly while Tigranes ravaged Cappadocia and Mithridates resumed all his old insolence'. And as the last bitter irony it was now that the ten commissioners arrived to help him organize a new province which no longer existed.

These events were of great interest to Pompey as he wondered what sort of mess Lucullus' replacements would make of a rapidly deteriorating situation, but he had scarcely had time to consider the possibilities of engineering his own appointment to the East when the Roman people became preoccupied with a crisis much nearer to their hearts. An unprecedented growth in the practice of piracy throughout the whole of the Mediterranean was so affecting merchant-shipping that vital imports of corn had almost ceased, and the soaring price was further inflated by profiteering warehousemen who locked up their granaries.

Piracy had always been a popular pastime in the East, especially for the inhabitants of Rugged Cilicia, that mountainous and barren part of the southern Turkish coast between Alanya and Silifke, the ancient Coracesium and Seleuceia. From their mountain fortresses and look-outs the sea-raiders could keep watch on the rich shipping-lanes that passed north of Cyprus to and from the Levant, and they had been a menace to commerce even in the days when great Hellenistic kingdoms had been able to police the seas. But when the Romans had emasculated the Seleucid empire in the second century, they left a power vacuum in the eastern Mediterranean which allowed piracy to become the biggest growth-industry and protection-racket in the ancient world.

When King Mithridates swept over Roman Asia in 88 he took the pirates into his service in much the same way that the Ottoman sultans were to make use of the Barbary corsairs in the sixteenth century AD. He fitted them out with new and better ships, and by the time he had been temporarily defeated by Sulla they had become a formidable power in their own right, and one that was singularly difficult to come to grips with: as Dio points out, their ships were so fast and their naval stations so widespread and numerous that even if they were defeated at sea they usually made good their escape and returned at their leisure to take revenge. Moreover, 'from attacking ships at sea they began to assail harbours, castles and whole cities', says Appian, who gives the following account of the growth of the pirates' power down to 67:

In the beginning the pirates sailed about like robbers harassing the inhabitants of Asia Minor with a few small boats, but as the war against Mithridates lengthened, their numbers grew and they went to sea in larger ships. Then having once tasted great profits, they did not cease their activities even when Mithridates made peace [with Sulla in 85] and returned to his own kingdom. For having lost both livelihood and country by reason of war and fallen into utter penury, men took to harvesting the sea instead of the land, at first with pinnaces and small galleys with only one and a half banks of oars but later with great biremes and triremes which sailed under the command of pirate-captains who were more like generals of an army than mere robbers. By sudden attacks on unfortified cities, by undermining or battering down the walls of others and even subjecting some to regular sieges, they took great piles of plunder and carried off the wealthier citizens to hold for ransom in their secret havens. They now scorned the name of pirates, and called their plunder the spoils of war. They had workmen chained to their tasks in their shipyards, they were continually bringing in materials of timber, bronze and iron, and being elated by their profits, they gave up all thought of changing their way of life but likened themselves to kings, rulers and great armies in the belief that if they should all unite, they would be invincible. They built more and more ships and made all kinds of arms, mainly in their bases in that part of Cilicia which is called 'Rugged' and which they had established as their common anchorage and encampment, for though they had fortresses and look-out points and desert islands all over the place, they chose for the principal rendezvous this part of the Cilician coast which was particularly mountainous and harbourless and rose sheer from the sea in great cliffs. And for this reason they were all called Cilicians, though the original pirates of Rugged Cilicia had been joined by Syrians, Cyprians, Pamphylians, Ponticans and men from almost all the Eastern nations who, on account of the length and severity of the war, preferred to do wrong rather than suffer it, and for this purpose chose the sea instead of the land.

Before long their numbers had grown into tens of thousands, and they no longer dominated only the Eastern waters but the whole Mediterranean to the Pillars of Hercules. Indeed, they were now even fighting and winning naval engagements with Roman generals, among them the praetor of Sicily on the coast of his own province. No sea could be navigated in safety, the land remained uncultivated for want of commerce, and even the city of Rome itself felt this evil most keenly, not only because of the distress of her subjects but because her own population began suffering from hunger on account of its large size. But it seemed such a great and difficult undertaking to destroy so large a force of seafarers who were scattered abroad in every land and sea, who had no fixed possessions to encumber their flight, no single homeland from which they sallied forth, no property nor anything else to call their own save only what they came upon by chance. It was such an unprecedented type of war, subject to none of the rules and with nothing clear-cut or certain about it, that it caused a sense of helplessness and fear in the capital. Murena had attacked them and accomplished next to nothing, likewise Servilius who succeeded him. And now the pirates were contemptuously attacking the very coasts of Italy itself, particularly round Brundisium and Etruria, where they succeeded in carrying off not only some Roman ladies of noble family who were travelling, but a couple of praetors too, complete with their entourages and their full insignia of office.

It was as though the whole Mediterranean contained a vast piratical hydra sprouting innumerable heads everywhere at once. We need only remember how the 'Cilician' allies of Sertorius blocked the Spanish ports against Pompey and Metellus in the mid-seventies to realize the scope of their operations and the Herculean nature of the task of destroying them. Moreover there was a kind of freemasonry operating among the various pirate-captains, for they would willingly send money and assistance to any of their fellow-tradesmen who sought it, even if they did not know each other. 'And this,' says Dio, 'was one of their main strengths, because it meant that those who paid court to any one of them were honoured by all while those who came into collision with them were despoiled by all.' Clearly this was not a monster to be killed by cutting off only one head at a time, and it was unfortunate that when the Romans finally realized this and conferred an ocean-wide command on one generalissimo, they picked not a Hercules but a man whose abject failure was the fault of his own incompetence.

This was Marcus Antonius, praetor for 74, who was invested with an *imperium infinitum*, almost certainly with proconsular authority, over all the coasts over which Rome claimed empire. It was a vast amount of power to put into the hands of one man, but as the sarcastic Velleius rightly observed, the worthlessness of its recipient ensured that it constituted no more of a danger to the Republic than to the pirates. Antonius began operations in the western Mediterranean, presumably in an attempt to do something about Sertorius' pirate-allies who were cutting off all sea-borne supplies to Pompey and Metellus in Spain, but having achieved little or nothing there he turned his attention to Sicily, which suffered from his exactions almost as much as it had done under the infamous Verres, if Cicero can be believed. He then set sail for the pirate strongholds of Crete with so great an assurance of success that his ships contained more fetters than arms. The result was a shameful episode inadequately summarized by Livy's terse epitomator: 'He undertook a campaign against the Cretans with minimal success and closed it with his death.' The Cretans had cut off most of his ships, defeated them without difficulty, and then hung the bodies of their prisoners to the yard-arms before returning in triumph to their secret harbours. The best Antonius could think of was to make a disgraceful treaty with his victors and then claim a triumph of his own and the surname Creticus, which a Senate loath to admit his failure was hypocritical enough to grant him before death prevented him from doing any more harm.

But the Senate could not let Crete go unpunished. It broke Antonius' treaty on the grounds that the islanders were still sheltering Mithridates' pirate-allies, and sent the more militarily competent of the two consuls of 69, Quintus Metellus, to deal with them. Although Metellus proved extremely effective against Crete, he was still only hacking at one of the hydra's many heads. Elsewhere they sprouted more vigorously than ever, and piracy went from strength to strength in the following two years which also witnessed the gradual destruction of all that Lucullus had achieved against Mithridates by land. It became unsafe for Roman citizens to travel by land in their own country, let alone to others by sea. Even Rome's own port of Ostia came under attack, and as the year 67 advanced, the pirates' stranglehold on maritime commerce became so tight that the city was threatened with starvation, and its people thronged the Forum demanding that something should be done.

This was the opportunity that Pompey had been waiting for. His friend the tribune Aulus Gabinius had already dismantled the last of Lucullus' powers, and now that a new crisis had arisen over the corn-supply this same demagogue was ready to make the most of it. Pompey and Gabinius were certainly hand in glove, whatever the exact nature of their relationship. Dio is not sure whether Gabinius was actually prompted by Pompey to do what he did 'or wished in any case to do the great man a favour'. Plutarch simply describes him as 'one of Pompey's intimates', but Cicero hinted at a financial arrangement in the bitter speech which he made to the Senate after his return from exile ten years later: 'If Gabinius had not as a tribune succeeded in carrying the Bill concerning the war against the pirates, there is no doubting that the stress of his own poverty and profligacy would have forced him to turn pirate himself – a calling which he would have pursued with less damage to the state than he inflicted when he remained, vile traitor and robber that he was, within the city walls!' At any rate it could do neither Pompey nor Gabinus anything but good in 67 to give the people what they would be sure to want as soon as it was suggested to them. But there was also the Senate to consider, and because Gabinius knew that most of its members would be aghast at the prospect of entrusting the capable Pompey with such vast powers, he tried to pre-empt their opposition by making his proposal without mentioning the name of the man he had in mind for the command.

Gabinius began by suggesting to the Senate that it should choose from ex-consuls one supreme commander against all pirates everywhere, give him a three-year command, and put at his disposal sufficient forces and lieutenants to enable him to cover the whole Mediterranean simultaneously. It was the obvious solution, virtually the same command which had been given to Antonius in 74, but if Gabinius had thought that by omitting the name of the obvious candidate for the job he would be able to persuade the Senate to approve his proposal in principle, he was sadly mistaken. Even the most stupid senator realized what he was up to, and almost all opposed him, particularly the consul Piso and the ex-consul Hortensius, who was especially sensitive about the issue since he had been offered Metellus' command against Crete in 69 and refused, considering it safer to fight his battles against Cicero in the lawcourts at Rome than against the Cretans in warships at sea. Piso became so incensed that he attacked Gabinius physically, and in the undignified fracas which followed the tribune was lucky to escape with his life.

The conflicting evidence of our sources makes it difficult to reconstruct the exact order of events, but it seems most likely that Gabinius then called an assembly of the people and put his measure before them, perhaps with certain elaborations on the scale of the command which he envisaged but still without naming the commander. Predictably the people cried out for Pompey, and when they heard that his friend, their favourite tribune, had nearly been killed by the Senate, they rushed into the Senate House with such violence that the Fathers threw dignity to the winds and ran for their lives; all of them successfully save Piso, who was caught and dragged out into the Forum to suffer the further indignity of owing his preservation to the intercession of Gabinius himself. Dio says that this was the end of the Senate's attempts to oppose the Bill by argument and that it resorted instead to the old remedy of getting other tribunes to veto it, but Cicero mentions that Hortensius also spoke against the proposals in an assembly as well as the Senate House; and since Plutarch further indicates that other senators made similar speeches against them to the assembled people – with the significant exception of the young Julius Caesar who 'cared nothing for Pompey but sought always to ingratiate himself with the populace' – it is not unlikely that another assembly was held to discuss the proposals before Gabinius finalized the Bill, put in Pompey's name, and fixed the day for the formal vote. After all, tribunes or senior magistrates could call any number of assemblies at very short notice to deliberate all manner of things, and it would be strange in such a crisis if the voluble Romans were limited to two. The senators who opposed the Bill had no difficulty in finding two amenable tribunes, Roscius and Trebellius by name, and Trebellius rashly swore to let the motion go through only over his dead body.

Before beginning the formal reading of his Bill on the day of the vote, Gabinius called upon Pompey to address the people with a carefully prepared speech designed to defuse the opposition of his peers and increase his own glory by making it appear that he was being forced to accept the command against his will. 'For it was always Pompey's way,' comments Dio, 'to pretend as far as possible not to desire the things he wanted most, and on this occasion he did so more than ever because of the jealousy that would follow if of his own accord he laid claim to the leadership, and because of the increased honour which he would enjoy if he should be appointed against his will as the man most worthy of command.' And this, according to Dio, is what Pompey said:

'I rejoice, citizens of Rome, in being honoured by you. For all men naturally take pride in the benefits conferred on them by their fellow-citizens, and I, who have often enjoyed honours at your hands, hardly know how to be adequately pleased on the present occasion. Nevertheless I do not think it right for you to be so insatiable for my services any more than I think it right for me to be constantly in some position of command. For I have been toiling since childhood, and you should share your attentions with others. Or have you perhaps forgotten the hardships I suffered in the war against Cinna – yes, and I was only a boy then? Or the labours I endured in Sicily and Africa before I was properly of age? Or the dangers I ran in Spain when I was not yet even a senator? I am not saying that you have shown yourselves ungrateful for all those labours. How could I? Far from it, for in addition to the many other important tasks of which you have thought me worthy my appointment to the command against Sertorius, when no one else was either willing or able to undertake it, and the triumph which I celebrated contrary to custom on my return are two things which have brought me the greatest honour. The plain fact is that having borne the weight of so many responsibilities and dangers I am worn out in body and wearied in soul. And do not go thinking that I am still a young man or start counting up that I am only however many years old. For if you count up instead the number of campaigns that I have fought and the dangers I have faced, you will find that they far exceed my years, and that will make you more ready to believe me when I say that I am not yet able to endure any more labours and anxieties.

'But if any of you should persist in this business in spite of all I have said, just consider for a moment the jealousy and hatred that such positions bring. I know it is a point that you consider unimportant – and you are right not to pretend to do so – but to me it would be a heavy burden, and I freely confess to you that there is no terror in war that could cause me more distress or grief than this. For who in his right mind could live happily among men who are jealous of him? And what man is there who would be eager to carry out any state business in the knowledge that to fail would mean standing trial while success would only succeed in making him the object of envy? For this reason then, and for the reasons I gave earlier, I beg you to leave me in peace to mind my own business, so that now at last I can give some attention to my private affairs and not die prematurely from sheer exhaustion. Elect someone else against the pirates. There are many who are both willing and able to serve as admirals, both younger and older men, so that your choice from among so many becomes easy. For surely I am not the only one who loves you, nor do I have a monopoly in the skills of war. Several suitable candidates spring immediately to mind, and if I do not name them, it is only because I do not wish to appear to be favouring any particular individual.'

It was altogether a very subtle speech, and it soon became clear how carefully concerted it had been to allow Gabinius to portray his candidate in the most favourable possible light when the tribune made his reply:

'The attitude of Gnaeus Pompeius in this matter, fellow-citizens, is worthy of his character; he neither seeks command for himself, nor accepts it the moment it is offered him. For it is not the part of a good man to be eager for office and to lust after public business. In the present case, moreover, it is right and proper for a man not to undertake all the tasks that are imposed upon him until he has given them careful consideration, in order that he may carry them out with similar circumspection. Rashness in making promises merely turns to untimely haste in trying to carry them out, and this has been the downfall of many. Certainty before one begins, on the other hand, remains the same in action, and that is to everyone's advantage. But having said that, fellow-citizens, I still maintain that it is your duty to choose not what is pleasing to Pompey but what is most advantageous to the Republic. The right men to put in charge of your affairs are not those who are eager for office but those who can do the job, and while you will find many of the first sort, you will not find another Pompey.

'Recall for a moment how many serious defeats we suffered in the war against Sertorius through lack of a general, how we found no one else either among the young or old but Pompey, and how we sent him out in place of both consuls when he had neither reached the proper age nor yet was even a senator. I only wish you had a great many good men like him, and if I thought it would do any good to pray for them, I should do so. But the special kind of ability which we seek is not a matter of prayer, nor does it come to anyone automatically. A man must be born with a natural bent for it, must learn what is useful, practise the right things, and above all enjoy the favour of Fortune. And since all these attributes rarely coincide in one man, you must all with one accord, whenever such a rarity is found, both support him and make full use of him whether he likes it or not. For such compulsion is the best possible thing both for them that apply it and for him who suffers it – to the former because they may be saved by it, and to the latter because he may thus save the fellow-citizens on whose behalf an honourable and patriotic man will most readily sacrifice body and soul.'

With this impassioned appeal to Pompey's patriotism we might have expected Gabinius' panegyric to have come to an end, but he now exploded into a dazzling display of oratical fireworks of which the principal constituent was the rhetorical question:

'Or do you think that Pompey here, this man who in his youth was capable of being both a soldier and a general, of increasing your possessions, of preserving those of your allies and acquiring those of your adversaries – do you think that such a man could not be of the greatest service to you now that he is in the prime of life and possesses the accumulated experience of all his former wars? Will you reject as an adult the man you chose to take command in his youth? Will you not entrust this campaign to the senator to whom you committed all those wars when he was still only a knight? Remembering what you demanded him in so many dire emergencies when he had not been properly tested, will you not put these no less pressing affairs into the hands of the same man now that you have made such ample trial of his ability? Will you not send against the pirates the ex-consul whom you chose to fight Sertorius before he was even eligible to hold the most junior public office? Do not even think of doing otherwise, fellow-citizens! And as for you, Gnaeus Pompeius, be persuaded by me and by your country. For her you were born. For her good you were reared. Your duty is to serve her interests, to shrink neither from toil nor danger to secure them, and if it becomes necessary to lose your life in her service, do not wait for nature's appointed span but go to meet whatever death chances to cross the path of duty!'

The people, already keen for Pompey before the speech-making had begun, had been dismayed by his apparent reluctance to accept the command. And now that Gabinius had reminded them again of his past glories, their enthusiasm for the hero of Sicily, Africa and Spain was burning so fiercely that they became alarmed as the tribune began to question their favourite's patriotism and they saw Pompey himself sitting with a thunderous frown of mock-anger at Gabinius' side. But Gabinius had not finished. Handling his audience with all the skill of an accomplished angler sure of his fish, he now turned to Pompey and coaxed him in conciliatory tones:

'But I am clearly a fool to offer this advice to you, Gnaeus Pompeius – a man who has proved his bravery and his love for his country in so many great wars. Heed me, therefore, and these good citizens here, and do not be afraid because some are envious of you. Rather press on the harder for this very reason, and scorn your detractors as nothing compared with the love of the vast majority of your fellow-citizens and the common advantage to us all. And if you are willing to upset a little those who are jealous of you, this is another good reason for taking command – in order that you may vex them by conducting the war and winning great glory contrary to their hopes, while at the same time setting a seal worthy of yourself on your former achievements by ridding us of so many great evils.'

Gabinius sat down amid thunderous applause, but when he stood up in preparation for the formal reading of his Bill, his fellow-tribune Trebellius suddenly jumped to his feet and demanded the right to speak – a right established by custom rather than law, since Gabinius as convenor of the assembly had the power to command both silence or speech from whomsoever he pleased. Gabinius, caring nothing for precedent where an opponent was concerned, refused his permission with the help of some raucous catcalls from the angry mob. He then began the reading of the Bill preparatory to calling upon the citizens to form up in their tribes and vote, but he had scarcely opened his mouth when Trebellius was on his feet again and using his tribunician prerogative to forbid his colleague to proceed.

This was something over which Gabinius had no control. Any one of the ten tribunes could veto the proposed legislation of any of his colleagues, and though Gabinius had known that Trebellius and Roscius had pledged their support for the senatorial opposition, he had doubted that when the day came they would find the nerve to impose their veto on a motion that clearly had the support of nearly the whole assembly. But he had prepared himself all the same, and as soon as Trebellius stopped him, he promptly pulled another scroll from under his toga and began the reading of a second Bill which Trebellius could not forbid, for it concerned Trebellius himself and proposed his deposition from the tribunate as a man unfit for office. It was, in effect, a vote of no confidence in Trebellius in the best Gracchan tradition, and there was nothing the unhappy victim could do but listen in dismay as the motion was read out and the citizens jostled and pushed each other in their eagerness to get into their tribal divisions for the vote. All that was needed for the passing of a Bill was a majority of the votes cast by each of the thirty-five tribes, and when the custodians of the ballot-boxes began reporting the results to the president, the affirmations came one after another: *ut rogas* – 'as you ask'. After the first seventeen tribes had voted for Trebellius' deposition and only one more was needed for the majority, Gabinius paused and looked at Trebellius, whose nerve finally broke. Jumping to his feet, the dissident tribune called out that he withdrew his veto on Gabinius' original Bill, and Gabinius then refrained from asking the eighteenth tribe for its vote, which was a foregone conclusion. And so the voting procedure finished and Trebellius remained a tribune, a little white in the face perhaps but remarkably healthy-looking for a man who had promised to let Gabinius' Bill become law only over his dead body.

By now the assembly was eager to vote on the original Bill and in no mood for further opposition, so that Roscius, the other tribune who had promised to stop Gabinius, despaired of being allowed to make his prepared speech even if he could have made himself heard over the noise of the angry crowd. But if there was no hope of preventing Pompey's appointment, it would be something if he could succeed in diluting his power, and he therefore gestured frantically with his hand in an attempt to persuade the people to choose two commanders instead of one. 'At that,' says Dio, 'the crowd gave a threatening shout that so startled a crow which was flying peacefully overhead that the poor bird fell down dead as though struck by lightning.' Roscius then kept quiet, says Dio drily, 'both with his tongue and his arm', leaving few who dared to continue the opposition.

But Gabinius himself now called upon one of the latter, the old and universally respected Quintus Lutatius Catulus whom he expected to speak in support of Pompey and, if he did so, to carry a large part of the Senate with him, for Gabinius and Pompey were still anxious to win over as many of the peers as they possibly could. Unfortunately Gabinius had guessed wrongly that the popular admiration for Pompey would have changed Catulus' mind, and though Catulus had been prepared to remain quiet, when invited to address the assembly he maintained his original position in a speech cleverly designed to dilute Pompey's power without saying anything derogatory about Pompey himself. And such was the people's respect for this venerable elder statesman that they were prepared to listen to paternalistic admonitions from him that they would have shouted down from any other man.

'That I have always been extremely anxious to achieve the greatest benefit for the greatest number [he began] you all know well enough. All I need do therefore is to say simply and frankly what I believe to be for the good of the state, and it is only right that you should hear me out quietly and keep discussion among yourselves for after I have finished. For if you make an uproar, you may well fail to catch some useful suggestion which you would otherwise have heard, but if you pay attention to the speakers you will surely find something to your advantage.

'To begin with then, I declare first and foremost that it is wrong to entrust to any one man so many commands one after another. This has not only been forbidden by the laws but has been found by experience to be dangerous. That Marius ended up as he did was attributable entirely to his having been entrusted with so many wars in so short a time and to your making him consul six times in seven years. And what made Sulla what he became if not his continual command of armies for so many years in succession, and his subsequent appointment as dictator and then consul? You see, it is not in human nature – and this is equally true of the young and the old – for men who have held great power for long periods of time to be willing to abide by our ancestral customs. Now I do not say this in disparagement of Pompey, but because it never appears to have done you any good and because it is against the laws. After all, if a command brings honour to those who deserve it, it should belong to all whom it concerns, for that is democracy; similarly if it brings labour and effort, all ought to have a share in it, for that is equality.

'Then again there is the consideration that entrusting the war to one man deprives many individuals of the opportunity to gain the practical experience that will make your choice of men who can be trusted with any future business an easy one since you will have made trial of their abilities. If on the other hand you persist in your intention, there will inevitably be a shortage of those who will give themselves the necessary training and be available for command. This is the principal reason why you were at a loss for a general in the war against Sertorius, for you had previously kept employing the same men for long periods. Therefore even though in all other respects Gnaeus Pompeius deserves to be elected to command against the pirates, I maintain that in so far as he would be chosen contrary to the principles of both law and experience it is not right either for you or for him that this should be done.

'That then is the first and most important point I have to make. The second is this, that as long as the consuls and praetors and promagistrates are receiving their offices and commands in conformity with the laws, it cannot be right or advantageous for you to overlook them and create some new office. After all, for what purpose do you elect annual magistrates if you are going to make no use of them for such occasions? Surely not that they may just strut about in their purple-edged togas, or that they should enjoy only the name of their office without its duties? How then can you fail to arouse the enmity of these and all the rest who choose to enter public life if you overthrow the ancestral offices, entrust nothing to those who are elected according to the laws, and assign some outlandish and unprecedented command to a private individual? There is only one ancient precedent for electing one man in addition to the annual officials, namely the dictatorship, and even that was an appointment strictly limited by law to a tenure of six months and to operations in Italy alone. But if there is no such emergency in Italy to require such a person, how could it be right for you to create a new type of supreme command lasting three years and encompassing practically all our affairs both in Italy and over-seas? You are all aware what terrible disasters have befallen our cities from such things – how often an unlawful lust for office has led so many men to disturb our state and bring countless calamities upon their heads. But I shall say no more about this, for who does not know that it is neither right nor advantageous to entrust affairs to one man, or for one man to have control over all the good things that we enjoy, however excellent that man may be? Great honours and excessive powers excite and ruin even the best of men.

'Let us turn now to consider the practicalities of the situation. It is simply not possible for one man to control the whole sea and manage the whole war properly. If you are going to achieve what is necessary, you must wage war on the pirates everywhere at once, so that they may not become hard to capture either by uniting in great numbers or by finding refuge amongst those not in-volved in the war. You know as well as I do that there is no way for a single commander to do this. For how could one man be fighting on the same day in Italy and in Cilicia, Egypt and Syria, Greece and Spain, the Ionian Sea and the islands? It therefore stands to reason that you must have many soldiers and many commanders if they are going to be of any use to you. And if anyone urges that even if you entrust the entire war to one man he will in any case have many admirals and lieutenants under him, I should answer that argument with this question: is it not more just and advantageous that these men who are destined to be subsidiary commanders should be chosen instead by you and receive independent authority from you, the people of Rome? What is there to prevent this? It has the overwhelming advantage that they will pay much more attention to the war if each is entrusted with his own command, for he will not then be able to lay the responsibility for neglecting it on anyone else, and there will be much keener rivalry between them because as indepen-dent commanders they will each get the glory for what they achieve. What subordinate is there who will show the same zeal when he is going to win vic-tories not for himself but for another? Gabinius himself admits that one man could not wage so great a war alone, and that is why he is asking for so many subordinates to be given to the supremo who is chosen. The question is simply whether those who are sent should be independent commanders or assistants, generals or legates, men commissioned with full authority by the people of Rome or favourites selected by a single commander-in-chief. Surely every one of you must admit that my proposal is more in accordance with the laws and more likely to be effective against the pirates, as well as being better in all other respects too. Besides, just consider for a moment how it would look to the rest of the world for your regular offices to be overthrown merely on the pretext of a war against pirates – it would be a sheer disgrace!

'Then finally I beg you to spare a thought for Pompey himself. His task as virtual monarch over all your possessions will not be free from envy, as he himself admitted. And have you considered what would happen if he failed in this enterprise? Do you wish to risk his life in a war against pirates? Great as he is, he *could* fail, especially in sea-battles which are notoriously unpredictable, and if he did, what other man would you find to take his place for any more urgent tasks which may arise?'

But Catulus had no sooner put his final question when the people disarmed him with a thunderous cry of '"*You*, Quintus Catulus, we shall have *you*!"' It was a tribute which left no more to be said.

Flattered in his failure, Catulus made no further attempt to stop the people having their way. And for once the people were right. Catulus' words about equality of opportunity would be all very well in a world of equal ability, but he was talking as if he were in the Republic of Plato rather than the Sink of Romulus. For what would have happened if the laws against re-election to the same magistracy had been rigorously applied to the Cimbric and Teutonic Wars? Without the continued re-appointment of Marius there might have been no Sullan dictatorship, it is true, but only because there would have been no more Rome. As to the argument that rivalry between independent commanders produces greater effectiveness, there was no single fact that had contributed more generously to Rome's military failures in the past and to the unnecessary prolongation of so many of her wars. We need only think of the early stages of the Cimbric Wars when the refusal of two rival commanders to co-operate at Arausio in 105 caused one of the worst disasters in Roman military history – the virtual annihilation of two Roman armies with a loss of eighty thousand men. Or turning to the East, we have the irony of the constant wars against Mithridates, who could have been captured and killed as long ago as 86 if Sulla's legate Lucullus had not refused to co-operate with his commander's rival, Fimbria. For Fimbria's army had utterly defeated the king at the Rhyndacus and the war could have been ended forever if only Lucullus had agreed to use his fleet to cut off the king's escape by sea – or, as Orosius has it, 'if he had put the considerations of the state's welfare above those of the Civil Wars'. As it was, Mithridates lived to fight again, and though Lucullus in the present war had fought with the greatest success as long as he had been in sole command, the recent appointment of equals in authority to separate parts of a formerly unified command was rapidly losing all the gains he had made. In Pompey's Spanish War his rivalry with his fellow-pro-consul Metellus had prompted him more than once to take on Sertorius single-handed with near-fatal results; and Sertorius had himself fallen victim to the rivalry of an incompetent snob whose jealousy had been allowed to override their common cause.

But Catulus was right to point out the possible dangers to the republican constitution in appointing Pompey to this powerful command. His words were prophetic to the extent that the establishment of a single, permanent commander-in-chief of all the armed forces was one of the two bases of the imperial system with which Octavian ended the Republic without resorting to the overtly autocratic position of Caesar, for his compromise owed as much to the more constitutional supremacy of Pompey as to the naked totalitarianism of his adoptive father. The very arguments which Dio makes Catulus put forward explain the increasing inability of the old republican system to govern an empire. For if the safety of the republican system was to be ensured, there were only two ways in which the pirates could be dealt with. One was to appoint an incompetent supremo, which had already been tried without success; the other, to appoint a multiplicity of rival co-equals, had repeatedly proved a failure in the past.

Dio's account, which I have been following so far, suggests that Gabinius put his Bill to the vote immediately after Catulus' speech, but Plutarch's order of events is rather different. He puts Roscius' attempt to speak after Catulus' speech, though he tells the same story of the despairing tribune's gesture which evoked so loud a cry of 'No!' from the people that it concussed the hapless bird flying overhead. Then after a brief digression into the physics of such phenomena he goes on to say that the assembly broke up at that point, that Gabinius fixed another day for the vote, and that Pompey withdrew to the country before then, presumably in order to avoid exacerbating the jealousy of his peers by being present to receive the acclamation of the people after the passing of the Bill, which was now a foregone conclusion. Plutarch also says that even after he had heard the result the new commander-in-chief was careful to enter the city unnoticed at night, again to avoid an envy-provoking reception by the mob, and that he made his first public appearance the next day at a sacrifice. Gabinius in the meantime had summoned yet another assembly for him, and on this occasion, now he had been given the job, Pompey made quite sure that he would have the means to carry it out successfully.

Already he had been voted supreme commander of the sea, the islands and all the mainland to a distance of fifty miles inland. He had also been empowered to select fifteen legates from the Senate for his several areas of command, to take from public treasuries and tax-collectors as much money as he needed, to raise two hundred ships and to levy as many soldiers and rowers as he wished. All these had been provisions in the original *lex Gabinia*. But Pompey was not a man for half-measures, and by the end of the day Plutarch tells us he had secured 'many things besides those already voted and almost doubled his forces, for he was to have 500 ships, 120,000 troops and 5,000 horse: he was also voted twenty-four legates instead of fifteen, all men who had held previous command or had served as praetors, and each of these was to have the assistance of two quaestors'.

It was an enormous force, and the general expectation of its success under Pompey's command had the immediate effect of making the price of corn drop so sharply that it was commonly maintained that 'the very name of Pompey had been enough to end the war'. And the Senate too, if not reconciled to the principle of Pompey's appointment, was for the most part sufficiently resigned to a *fait accompli* not to try to undermine his efforts. In their own interests, if not in his, a large enough number of his peers were sensible enough to 'support these measures and pass others which from time to time were necessary for their effectiveness', for as Dio suggests, they realized that there was little to gain and much danger in deliberately alienating a man who had the power to do what Sulla had done and who was, after all, 'Sulla's pupil'.

7
VICTORY AT SEA

'And when I bore the Roman standards high
And shining bright across the whole great sea,
Ere twice the Moon's fair orb could wax and wane
The pirate force turned fearful of the wave,
Abandoned every creek and humbly begged
A home in some small corner of dry land.'
Lucan, *Pharsalia*, 2.576–9

Attacking his new task with an energy that belied his pretended reluctance to undertake it, Pompey organized his vast armament so rapidly that his legates were sailing to their operational areas at the first signs of spring, despite the dangers of navigation so early in the year, in the hope of catching the pirates relatively unprepared. His strategy was masterly in its comprehensive simplicity. He had divided the Mediterranean area into thirteen districts, to each of which he assigned a legate with a powerful force of ships and troops and with strict instructions not to move outside the boundaries of his particular command even in close pursuit. It was essential that every part of the coast should be constantly patrolled, and if hunted pirates managed to escape from one operational area into another, the pursuing squadron must retire and leave the enemy to take its chance with the neighbouring Roman commander or with the commander-in-chief himself, who was preparing to tour the whole Mediterranean with his sixty best warships and either engage any large concentrations of pirates on the high seas or drive them back into the clutches of his lieutenants.

Of the thirteen operational areas six were in Western waters and seven in the East. Beginning at the Straits of Gibraltar Pompey assigned the east coast of Spain and the Balearic islands to Manlius Torquatus, while the Straits themselves, together with the whole of the North African coast as far as Libya, became the heavy responsibility of Tiberius Claudius Nero, who was also required to patrol the Atlantic coast of Spain round Cadiz. He then divided the north-western Mediterranean east of the Balearics among three legates, of whom Marcus Pomponius was

assigned to the south of France and the Ligurian Sea, Publius Atilius to
Sardinia and Corsica, and Lucius Gellius to the west coast of Italy itself.
That left only Sicily, important as the nearest source of the corn which
fed Pompey's electorate, and it was clearly a tribute to Aulus Plotius when
the proconsul selected him for what was probably the most immediately
critical of the six Western commands.

Of the seven legates appointed to the Eastern commands, it was Lentulus Marcellinus who took over responsibility for the North African
coastline south of Sicily and patrolled the whole area from Libya eastwards to Egypt. The Adriatic coast of Italy down to the heel most probably went to Lentulus Clodianus, whose authority then yielded to that
of Terentius Varro, commander in the Ionian Sea and the west coast of
Greece. This was the same scholarly friend who had written Pompey a
beginner's guide to consulship and was now about to disprove the theory
that those who teach cannot do, for according to Pliny he performed so
well in the war that he was decorated with the naval crown. Further east
we find the critical region of the Levant assigned to Metellus Nepos,
whose district is given by Appian as 'Lycia, Pamphylia, Cyprus and
Phoenicia' – a list from which the omission of Cilicia may suggest that
he had instructions not to interfere with the hornets' nest until the
commander-in-chief was ready to come and smoke it out in person.

The remaining three commands were all in the Aegean area, where
piracy had survived the expulsion of Mithridates. The three commanders
were Lucius Sisenna, Lucius Lollius and Publius Piso, who patrolled the
west, the east and the north respectively. To Sisenna went the whole of
the Greek coast, including the Peloponnese, Attica, Euboea, Boeotia,
Thessaly and Macedonia, though not the vast complexity of islands in
the central Aegean which were assigned to Lollius along with the whole
of the Aegean coast of present-day Turkey as far as the Hellespont. There
Piso took over from both Sisenna and Lollius, and his arrangements to
seal the entrance to the Black Sea were so thorough that his ships are
said to have formed a gate across the mouth of the Propontis.

By this disposition of the thirteen lieutenants with their own fleets and
armies Pompey exercised his supreme command over virtually the whole
of the Mediterranean basin from the Pillars of Hercules to the Levant
and from the Hellespont to Cyrenaica. Only in Crete was there a commander of equal rank engaging in the same operation, but for the present
Pompey had more than enough to occupy his mind without worrying
about his status in the one small island where Quintus Metellus was
pirate-hunting in accordance with the commission assigned to him during
his consulship two years earlier. Pompey's priority was to restore the
supply of grain to the capital. He therefore sailed in succession to Sicily,

Africa and Sardinia, where 'by means of strong garrisons of fleets', says
Cicero, 'he made secure those three sources of Rome's corn-supply'. Then
having swept the Tyrrhenian and Libyan Seas clear of pirates, he beat
the seas off Spain and Gaul and drove the corsairs like pheasants against
the butts of his legates and their coastal patrols. And while it was not
of course possible for these patrols to watch every stretch of coast simultaneously, it was not only Roman forces with which the pirates had to contend. Now that powerful assistance was near at hand, the long-suffering
cities and native communities could no longer be coerced or blackmailed.
Even those which had profited from harbouring pirates in the past were
now anything but anxious to share their punishment, and soon only the
most remote and secret hideaways availed to postpone the day when
starvation or despair would force the enemy to brave the Roman fleets
on the horizon or the cavalry or informers of more accessible shores.

Not surprisingly a feeling of helplessness began to overtake the pirates.
In the past there had usually been the possibility of uniting to meet a policing operation with formidable resistance, or if discretion had prevailed
there had always been the option of a change of seas. But now it was
every group for itself. Any large concentration of pirates, even if the different groups had been able to unite, would be met by superior force,
and there was nowhere in the West left to flee to. Pursued by Atilius off
Corsica, the pirates would find no refuge in a Sicily beset by the patrols
of Plotius or in a Gaul where Pomponius was watching the Ligurian Sea.
Nor was there greater security in the bays of Africa or Spain, even if they
avoided Pompey's own battle-fleet which might be anywhere at any time.
And escape to the Atlantic through the Straits of Gibraltar would mean
running the gauntlet of Tiberius Nero, who also had more ships patrolling Spain's south-western coast. The pirates' only chance was in the East.
There was a fair width of sea between Sicily and Tunisia, and once
through into Eastern waters it should be possible to reach the fastnesses
of Rugged Cilicia. And thus Cilicia became the goal of those frightened
shoals that managed to escape being driven into the net which Pompey
had cast about the western Mediterranean.

According to Plutarch and Appian it took Pompey only forty days to
clear the West of pirates, and though this same length of time has been
attributed to too many other campaigns of his to carry any independent
validity, he cannot have spent much more than six weeks in the West
because a contemporary speech of Cicero refers to the subsequent, Eastern phase of his operations as taking forty-nine days – an apparently exact
number – and to the whole campaign as lasting from early spring to the
mid-summer of 67. And between the two phases Pompey had to find time
to return to Rome in order to deal with the consul Piso who, according to

Plutarch, was 'interfering with Pompey's equipment and discharging his crews out of envy and hatred'.

It is hard to understand how Piso could have expected to get away with such petty subversion of a successful campaign only weeks after he had narrowly escaped a lynching merely for attacking its proposer. Gabinius had already written out a Bill to depose the consul by plebiscite, and with the markets of Rome overflowing with cut-price provisions he could easily have secured its passage by the thousands of cheering people who now streamed out of the city to welcome the returning hero. But Pompey proved himself at once superior to revenge and averse to political extremism. Observing no enhancement of his own glory in the prospect of Piso's degradation and anxious to avoid what might have become a constitutional crisis, he refused to let Gabinius proceed with either the deposition or any of the other unspecified actions which Plutarch says the tribune had prepared against the consul. Instead we are told that he 'arranged everything in a reasonable manner', and whatever the exact nature of Piso's interference with Pompey's logistics – for while Dio mentions only an attempt to prevent enlistments in his designated province of Transalpine Gaul, it seems probable that Piso was also using his consular authority to demobilize crews already raised and ready for action in Italy itself – we can be sure that it did not happen again.

In order to waste as little time as possible Pompey had ordered his fleet to round the peninsula while he was visiting Rome, and he now marched south-east to Brundisium to re-embark. But eager as he was to begin operations in the Eastern waters he could not resist the lure of Athens, that ancient city whose self-conscious culture would never cease to captivate her crude conquerors. After all, the business of war was uncertain as well as urgent, and Pompey felt it would be a pity to die without seeing so famous a city and giving its effete citizens a chance to reciprocate his gratification of their vanity. Moreover, Athens had a fine harbour, which made a suitable rendezvous for the squadrons which Rome had ordered her allied states and kings to contribute to the war-effort.

By the time Pompey sailed from Piraeus his legates' fleets had been operating in their designated areas for several weeks, and he made it his first task to inspect them before striking at Cilicia itself. According to Appian he 'amazed and terrified the pirates by the rapidity of his movement, the scale of his preparations and his formidable reputation'. He also amazed his delighted allies, and when long-suffering friends like the Rhodians scented success in the wind, they co-operated wholeheartedly in 'forcing the enemy from every harbour, bay, hideaway, creek, promontory, strait and peninsula in every sea'. Equally importantly, he was a wise enough huntsman to leave one of the earths unstopped. By allowing the surviving enemy to take refuge in Cilicia he not only saved himself the time and trouble of a much more protracted and extensive hunt but reserved for himself the glory of the final kill.

Turning at bay in Cilicia the demoralized pirates found courage in desperation. They deposited their families and possessions in strongholds, and when Pompey's battle-fleet appeared off the promontory of Coracesium, they sailed out to meet him in an engagement which promised to turn the seas incarnadine but turned out instead to be one of the most satisfactory anticlimaxes in Roman military history. Appian indeed denies that there was an engagement at all, and although he is contradicted by Velleius, Florus and Plutarch, what fighting there was does seem to have been short-lived. Perhaps Florus' account is the most reliable. Whereas Velleius refers vaguely to 'a scattering and putting to flight' and Plutarch to 'a defeat' of the enemy, Florus gives a degree of detail which could have derived from an eye witness account. 'The pirates,' he says, 'did no more than meet the first attack: as soon as they saw the beaks of our ships all round them, they immediately threw down their weapons and oars, and with a great clapping of hands – which was their sign of supplication – they begged for their lives.' Nor were there any of the treacherous reprisals which might have been expected of Sulla's pupil. 'This was not just our least bloody victory,' continues the approving Florus, 'but we never found any conquered people afterwards more loyal to us.' And if the details of the battle are in doubt, the reason which Florus gives for the bloodlessness and the permanence of Pompey's victory has the unequivocal support of all our sources.

It took Pompey only three months to end a war to which he had been appointed for three years because he had shown the pirates the two things which they had least expected. The first was a really effective Roman naval commander capable of planning and executing a strategy sufficiently grand to prevent them from uniting to oppose a policing action or escaping to avoid it. The second was his clemency to his captives. Where Sulla massacred and Crassus crucified, Pompey pardoned. 'When he caught pirate bands,' says Plutarch, 'he treated them kindly, and after seizing their ships and persons he did them no harm.' This un-Roman policy was as wise as it was humane. By treating his early captives well he encouraged others not only to surrender themselves but to betray the whereabouts of some of the more notorious criminals whose black deeds had put them beyond all hope of pardon. And that in turn helped to reduce both the numbers and the resolution of those who were preparing to resist him in Cilicia and risk what he had shown to be an unnecessary death.

Pompey's combination of superior force and the readiness not to use

it was as effective as it was unusual. His fleets were equipped not only
to fight at sea but with transports full of siege-engines and all the other
paraphernalia necessary for what would have been a long and bloody
campaign to reduce the pirate strongholds in Rugged Cilicia. His leniency
meant that they were hardly used. One after another the strongholds were
surrendered with little or no compulsion, and what came out of them
revealed the amazing scale and profitability which international piracy
had been allowed to achieve. There were cargoes of all kinds, from raw
materials to luxury goods, from corn, oil and wine to rare delicacies,
treasure and gold; and there were quantities of human booty, the richer
captives being held for ransom, the poorer chained to their tasks, but
all owing their rescue to Pompey's clemency which had spared them the
reprisals which their captors might have taken if refused all hope of survival for themselves. Nor was it only the profits of piracy that were surrendered. Such big international business had not thrived for so long
without plant and equipment, and Pompey's troops were now faced with
the task of removing or destroying not only vast quantities of ships and
armaments but also the factories which produced them, stockpiles of
timber and metals, and shipyards full of vessels in various stages of
construction.

But great as Pompey's achievement had been in ending the war so
rapidly, his greater achievement was in securing the peace. By allowing
thousands of pirates and their families to keep their lives but not their
means of livelihood he was presented with a dilemma which could have
been resolved in two ways. Either he could simply revoke his promise
and eliminate the pirates; or he could eliminate the cause of their crimes.
To his eternal credit he chose to do the latter. 'He reflected,' says Plutarch,
'that it is not natural for man to be or to become a wild and unsocial
creature, and since even naturally wild animals can be tamed by offering
them a gentler way of life, it should be all the easier to reform naturally
social man by a change of environment.' In modern terminology Pompey
belonged to the environmental school of social studies, but unlike so
many modern theorists he had both the courage and the ability to put
his convictions to the test.

'With remarkable wisdom,' says Florus justly, 'he removed those maritime people far from the sight of the sea, and by tying them down to
the cultivation of fertile areas of the interior he at once restored the land
to its proper inhabitants and recovered the use of the sea for trade.' From
other sources we have the names of some of the cities to which Pompey
transplanted the pirates, and while we find that not all were inland as
Florus implies, we also discover that his main coastal settlement was well
to the more hospitable east of Rugged Cilicia and away from the precipi-

tous cliffs of the pirates' former haunts. This was Soli, a city more or
less on the borders between Rugged and Level Cilicia and greatly in need
of new citizens since most of its former inhabitants had been carried off
by King Tigranes to populate his new capital at Tigranocerta. But Pompey was not so carried away with idealism that he transplanted the pirates
indiscriminately Strabo makes it clear that he not only destroyed all those
towns in Rugged Cilicia for which piracy was the sole possible means
of support, but that he was very careful in his selection of the families
who were to be given the opportunity to revitalize this potentially important maritime city, which became a lasting monument to the greatness
of his faith in human nature. Renamed Pompeiopolis and adorned with
impressive buildings appropriate to its benefactor, it became a rich and
thriving city in which there was no temptation for the new citizens to
use their magnificent harbour other than for the promotion of peaceful
commerce.

No honest assessment of Pompey's achievement in the war against the
pirates can be too favourable, for all that his success attracted some small-
minded and jealous criticism from lesser men. In no more than three
months the maritime commerce of the Mediterranean world had been
freed from near-paralysis by a remedy that was as permanent as it was
immediate. There would be pirates again of course, and it was one of
the ironies of fate that Pompey's own younger son, now probably about
nine years old, would one day be responsible for promoting piracy
again in his attempt to avenge his father's defeat in civil war; but even
so the problem never again approached the magnitude to which it had
grown in the decades before 67. The military statistics give an idea of
the vast scale of the pirates' operations, even when the figures are treated
with the greatest reserve. According to Appian the numbers of pirate-
ships taken were seventy-one captured and 306 surrendered, of which
Plutarch tells us that ninety were first-rate warships with bronze beaks.
The number of enemy dead was put at ten thousand, and twice that
number are said to have surrendered, though it is not clear whether
Appian is referring to the whole war or only to the final campaign in
Cilicia. Certainly the official figures for the whole war were much higher,
and even though they probably included every enemy vessel from the
largest warship down to the smallest fishing-boat, Pliny maintains that
the inscriptions from Pompey's triumph claimed the enormous number
of 846 ships captured. But even if we take the official claim with a
generous pinch of salt and accept Appian's figures as a likely estimate
for the whole war, it was clearly an undertaking that would not have
been brought to so rapid and permanent an end but for the enlightened
clemency of the commander-in-chief. Unfortunately, however, it was not

a policy that commended itself to Quintus Metellus in Crete, and this independent commander's more traditionally ruthless prosecution of his own two-year campaign against the Cretan pirates now almost precipitated a minor civil war.

The trouble began when Cretan envoys came to Pompey in Cilicia and begged him to accept their island's surrender. Despairing of any fate but death or enslavement from the merciless old proconsul who had already devastated their lands and was now besieging their cities, the Cretans can hardly be blamed for trying to surrender to Pompey in the hope of sharing the same leniency which he was reported to have shown to the pirates of all the rest of the Mediterranean. And Pompey, being the man he was, felt that it would be a confession of inferiority to Metellus if he refused, even though the exact legality of his acceptance is open to question.

For the purpose of making war against the pirates he had been granted an infinite proconsular *imperium* over the seas and all the land to a distance of some fifty miles from the coast, within which it appears that his authority was to be equal but not superior to that of the various provincial governors. That much is stated by Velleius and supported both by Piso's attempt to frustrate Pompey's enlistment of troops in Transalpine Gaul and indeed by Metellus' present refusal to accept his interference in Crete, even though the whole of that island lies within fifty miles of the sea. Legally, therefore, it appears that as co-equal in authority with Metellus in Crete Pompey was within his rights to accept the Cretans' surrender, but by the same argument Metellus was equally justified in ignoring a surrender made to another official who was only of equal rank and in continuing the war under his own authority and with his own forces. Whether it was statesmanlike or wise or just to do so is of course another question, and a sadly irrelevant one once a nobleman's *dignitas* was at stake.

Pompey and Metellus were victims of their society's overriding obsession with personal honour and of the *lex Gabinia*'s tactful avoidance of an issue which it had been easier to ignore in the hope that it would not arise than to try to solve in advance. If Gabinius had proposed for Pompey an authority superior to all other provincial governors of the highest rank, it would have raised a very serious constitutional crisis at home. It was after all the *maius imperium* which would become one of the two bases of the Augustan principate, and already there was a sufficient number of real and would-be autocrats to make many genuine republicans ready to sacrifice efficiency on the altar of aristocratic equality. On the other hand it was part of the Republic's failure that it could not accommodate itself satisfactorily to exceptional situations, and the miserable fiasco which now took place in the one part of the Mediterranean where co-equals had been charged with the same task shows how impossible it would have been to achieve anything at all against the pirates if Catulus had had his way and Pompey's command had been made collegiate instead of individual.

After accepting the Cretans' surrender Pompey wrote to Metellus to cease operations, and he sent Lucius Octavius, one of his own legates, to take command of the Cretan cities on his behalf. Metellus replied by ignoring Octavius, beginning what became an increasingly acrimonious correspondence with Pompey, and increasing his pressure on the Cretan cities in an attempt to secure the glory of a personal victory before Pompey could steal it from him. Octavius was left in a dilemma. He could not accept the rebuff to his own commander-in-chief, and yet he had no forces with which to defend the pirates who were now claiming his protection if Metellus continued to wage war on them. In an attempt to resolve this ludicrous situation a would-be peacemaker appeared in the person of Lucius Sisenna, the legate commanding Pompey's forces in the western Aegean, but when he found the proud Metellus adamant against all requests that he should spare the Cretan towns, he returned to Greece without taking the final step which would have meant beginning a civil war in support of Rome's enemies.

Left to his own devices Octavius then tried to shame Metellus into compliance by visiting the besieged cities and putting his own life at risk from the Roman artillery, but Metellus simply continued to ignore him. One night Metellus even stormed a city in which Octavius was asleep, and when on the next morning he proceeded to put to death all the citizens who were supposedly under Octavius' protection, it was no longer just Pompey's honour which was at stake. Octavius was furious in defence of his own honour, and as Sisenna had died shortly after returning to Greece, he took over his forces and began to use them in limited operations designed to stiffen the Cretan resistance and 'aid the victims of oppression'. There followed what was probably a protracted chess-match with the unfortunate Cretan cities as pieces until Octavius was overtaken by a natural disaster as he and a pirate-king were making a tactical withdrawal by sea from the town of Hierapydna which they could no longer hold. They were caught in a storm, and their losses were so heavy that Metellus was able to press home his advantage and complete the subjugation of the whole island, from which he earned a triumph and the surname Creticus.

Whether Pompey himself would have been prepared to take direct military action against Metellus if the Cretan war had gone on much longer is not certain. Dio maintains that he was actually making preparations to sail to Crete against Metellus early in 66, when he was probably getting on top of his arrangements for the pacification of Cilicia, the resettlement of the pirates, the foundation of new cities and all the other time-consuming details of the administration of peace. On the other hand Crete was only one island in his vast maritime *provincia*, and it must be doubted if he was willing to embroil himself in a confrontation with Metellus that went beyond acrimonious correspondence and his tacit encouragement of the semi-official efforts of a legate to protract the Cretan war into stalemate. But what is certain is that the Cretan affair now shrank into insignificance as Pompey received word from Rome that he had been granted what he had most desired. For though he made his usual pretence of unwillingness to be loaded with yet heavier burdens of command, there was nothing for which he had yearned more ardently than what he now achieved – the supreme command of the war against Mithridates and the governorship of almost all the provinces which his fallen rival Lucullus had held at the height of his success.

8

GENERALISSIMO
IN THE EAST

'Alas for my endless labours! How
much better to have been a nobody if
I am never to cease leading armies,
lay aside this load of envy and spend my
time in the country with my wife.'
Plutarch, *Life of Pompey*, 30.6

The Bill by which the tribune Gaius Manilius provided for the transfer
of the Mithridatic War and the Asiatic provinces to Pompey also provided
the occasion for the first political speech before the popular assembly
by that rising politician Marcus Tullius Cicero, Pompey's exact contemporary. Cicero was hardly convincing in his conventional plea of being
'unaccustomed to public speaking', for his recent election to the praetorship at the head of the poll had been the reward of many years of skilful
oratory in the lawcourts. Thanks to this excellence at the bar he had
gradually bound an influential clientele to his interest, and the only
naïvety in this first political speech is one that reveals his dependence
on the business interests of Rome – men of the class into which he had
been born, whose votes carried great weight in the timocratic election
procedure, and whose continued support was indispensable to a man
seeking to advance a career as a first-generation senatorial.

Addressing himself to the people from 'the fairest stage of eloquence',
from which he had been kept for so long by his desire to gain an
appropriately high standard of eloquence by practice in the courts,
Cicero proceeded to congratulate himself on having for his first political
speech so noble a subject as Pompey, 'a topic harder to end than to begin,
requiring not a search for material but restraint and moderation'. Then
having flattered the audience and their favourite, he mentioned the
impending financial disaster to 'my good friends, the Roman knights,
who are concerned for the great sums they have invested in the farming
of your revenues, and have asked me to represent to you the case of the

public interest and their private fortunes'. And if it was not likely to bring tears to the eyes of the ordinary man in the Forum to hear that a few financiers were going to lose the odd million from an unwise investment in Asia, what Cicero had to say about the danger to the whole Roman economy from the collapse of the great finance-houses was sound enough, even if it went over the heads of most of his listeners. Finance was an area in which it was necessary to anticipate the crossing of bridges, and the Roman people must act at once to remove the fear of a recurrence of what had happened in 88, when Mithridates had overrun Rome's richest province and put to death every Italian east of the Aegean. Indeed, it was only the fortuitous presence of Pompey in the East on other affairs that was preventing a collapse of confidence even now, and he was the obvious man to take over formal command against Mithridates and vindicate the honour of Rome that had been so shamefully stained by the unavenged blood of so many of her citizens and allies.

Warming to his rhetoric in Palmerstonian tones, Cicero now turned to jingoism to rouse the emotions of those to whom international finance was a closed book. He reminded them how their forefathers had extirpated Corinth, the glory of Greece, for little more than an insult to a Roman Don Pacifico, and he contrasted such magnificent retributions of the good old days with the present disgrace of a nation that allowed a cold-blooded butcher of its citizens to remain alive and on his throne over twenty years after the Asiatic vespers. Although Lucullus had defeated Mithridates and driven him from his kingdom, the general's successors had proved inadequate to conduct so great a war. Mithridates was again lording it in his ancestral realm and fearing no man but the one the Roman people were now being asked to send against him. Who then could possibly object to the appointment of Gnaeus Pompeius to this great war?

But a few did object, several tacitly, according to Plutarch, and two who spoke most heatedly against the Bill. One was Hortensius, Cicero's failing rival at the bar and therefore predisposed to oppose anything which Cicero advocated, although it is only fair to remember that he had also spoken against Pompey's appointment to his command against the pirates. The other was that sturdy reactionary Quintus Catulus, so determined to oppose all democratic legislation that if he had been the inventor of chariots they would almost certainly have run backwards. Theoretically, of course, his objection was valid: it *was* dangerous to appoint one man to 'almost all the powers which Sulla had had', especially when that man was Sulla's pupil and had the armies with which to do what many a would-be revolutionary in Rome had tried and would try and fail to do without them. In practice however he was not only wasting his time in opposing Pompey's appointment but was mistaken in his estimate of the man and his autocratic pretensions, as time would tell. Moreover he had made himself so ridiculous by calling on the Senate to imitate the plebeian secession of 449 and 'seek out some mountain or lofty crag whither they might flee for refuge and preserve their threatened freedom' that it scarcely needed Cicero's logic to refute objections that were based on little more than suspicion of the unprecedented. 'Our forefathers always bowed to precedent in peace,' agreed Cicero, 'but to expediency in war', and having already hinted that the mindless following of precedent had been responsible for the disastrous replacement of Lucullus by Glabrio, he now set Pompey's extraordinary command alongside Scipio's in the war against Carthage or that of Marius in the Cimbric Wars – generals whose brilliant successes proved that precedents were made to be broken when Fortune provided one of her favourites at a time of national crisis.

Pompey undoubtedly enjoyed that same good fortune, declared Cicero, just as he possessed those three other prerequisites of a great general, experience, ability and prestige. But there was also a quintessence in Pompey's qualifications, the old Delphic virtue of self-control, that made him a particularly desirable appointment from the point of view of those whose opinion was usually disregarded except where, as here, it happened to coincide with Rome's selfish interest. These were the provincials themselves, whose peculiar affection for Pompey made a damning indictment of the usual standard of Rome's provincial administration and the conduct of her generals in the field. 'Words cannot express,' said Cicero, 'how bitterly we are hated among foreign nations on account of the outrages and injustice committed by those whom we have sent out to them in recent years.... Remembering therefore that Pompey owes his greatness not only to his own virtues but also to the vices of others, you must not hesitate to entrust everything to this one man – the only general found in all these years whose allies actually rejoice to receive him and his army into their cities.' It was a point that overlooked the exemplary administration of Lucullus, but it was valid in so far as he too had been an exception to the rule of the Roman rapacity that had been responsible for the massacre of 88, when the debt-ridden Asians had reached the degree of despair that could welcome even so unlikely a deliverer as Mithridates. And no Roman wanted to risk a repetition of that.

It was a good speech – as good as it was unnecessary. Cicero catalogued Pompey's remarkable career. His audience all knew it. He reminded them that Pompey's very name had been enough to bring the price of corn crashing down. Their wives all knew it. He encountered the fusty old arguments of Hortensius and Catulus. The people had already ignored them, and in any case there was a group of equally distinguished nobles who realized the necessity of securing Asia and the folly of opposing the appointment of the one general who happened to be on the spot with sufficient forces and ability. As for Cicero's capitalist friends, who had been chiefly responsible for eroding Lucullus' command because he had restrained their excessive profiteering, it was ironic that they now needed no encouragement to seek the services of another exemplary provincial administrator to repair the failures of Lucullus' successors. Nor was it only equestrian fortunes that were endangered. There was many a senator, though technically debarred from trade, who nevertheless had vast sums tied up in the tax-farming companies through agents and intermediaries. There were many more, like Cicero himself, who foresaw personal advancement in supporting the greatest Roman of the day. And there was at least one, a mere quaestor newly returned from Spain, who was eager to support the democratic process which might one day give him a similar command, just as Pompey himself had invested in his own future by supporting the restoration of the tribunes' legislative powers which had been abolished under the Sullan constitution. This was Julius Caesar, still low on the ladder of office, a roué apparently devoid of ambition until he had discovered a latent military potential in Spain and had burst into tears at the sight of a statue of Alexander the Great in Cadiz – a man who had conquered the Persian Empire and died by Caesar's age.

To what extent Pompey himself engineered the granting of his new commission is unknown. He had certainly envied Lucullus the Eastern commands and there is no doubt that he was on excellent terms with Gabinius, who was himself in close liaison with Manilius, Pompey's new tribunician supporter now that Gabinius' own year of office had come to an end. And Plutarch maintains that Pompey's mock annoyance at having been burdened with yet more envy-provoking tasks went down badly even with his closest friends. But while it may reasonably be assumed that the campaign to win this command for Pompey was not carried through without his knowledge and connivance, it is far from certain that he masterminded it himself. What is certain is that he once again hurled himself into a new task with a degree of energy that belied his pretended reluctance, though not to the detriment of his maritime responsibilities as Dio alleges. It is true that he took no further notice of Metellus' operations in Crete and left that proconsul in peace to pursue the regulation of the island as a Roman province, but Plutarch makes it clear that he was extremely careful in his disposition of the fleet to guard the whole sea between Phoenicia and the Bosporus. And it was no doubt the continued patrolling of the Eastern waters by Pompey's fleets during the next four years that prevented a revival of even small-scale piracy by former buccaneers who might otherwise have proved reluctant to turn themselves into peace-loving farmers, particularly if they had been able to look to the support of a resurgent Mithridates with none but incompetents to oppose him.

As soon as Pompey received the official dispatches containing his new commission, he made a careful analysis of the tasks which faced him and the resources available. His instructions under the Manilian law were both specific and general. The specific ones were to prosecute the war against Kings Mithridates and Tigranes and to assume the governorships of Bithynia, Pontus and Cilicia, provinces which their inept proconsuls were ordered to hand over to him at once without waiting for the expiry of their terms of office. The more general provisions authorized him to make war and peace with whomsoever he wished, and it was this un-limited authority, so terrifying to some of his peers, that formed the basis for one of the most comprehensive, statesmanlike, beneficial and endur-ing exercises in empire-building that Rome ever experienced. But how-ever ambitious the imperial schemes which may already have been taking shape at the back of Pompey's mind, he now focused his whole attention on his immediate objectives.

Mithridates was again in possession of the supposed Roman province of Pontus, and was reported to have an efficient army of thirty thousand foot and three thousand horse ready to defend his western frontier. Tigranes was again in possession of his own kingdom of Armenia and was overruning Cappadocia, from which he had expelled the pro-Roman King Ariobarzanes. And Cicero had been right in saying that only Pom-pey's powerful presence on the south coast of Turkey had restrained Mithridates from marching westwards again into Roman Asia. The in-competent Acilius Glabrio, who had succeeded Lucullus in Bithynia and Pontus, was now cowering in the relative safety of Bithynia. He was not only incapable of recovering Pontus but even seems to have feared to go and collect the few troops who were still with Lucullus as the latter stood doggedly on guard against Mithridates in the wilds of Galatia. As for Cilicia and the southern front, Lucullus' successor there had been Gla-brio's rival in inadequacy, and while Pompey had taken over from him a military force which he would have liked to bring into the field against Mithridates at once, with Tigranes on the rampage in neighbouring Cap-padocia he could not leave defenceless to Armenian imperialism the richer part of a potential province which he had just been resettling with Mithri-dates' former pirate-allies. Not that Pompey lacked military as well as naval forces of his own. His commission against the pirates was still operative under the Gabinian law, and though his troops had been divided among operational areas throughout the Mediterranean, he no doubt had with him a force sufficiently large to have effected the siege and capture of the pirate-strongholds of Rugged Cilicia if it had proved necessary. All the same, the eyes of his political enemies in Rome were watching him as closely as those of his military enemies in the East, and he was determined not to rush in where fools had feared even to tread.

Plutarch tells us that Pompey's headquarters in Cilicia now became a hive of activity as he sent out streams of edicts to allied cities, commands to friendly kings, instructions for the redeployment of the fleet that would deny Mithridates the use of the seas, memoranda to Lucullus that he was no longer in command even of the remnant of his troops, legates to take over the legions of his new provinces, and recruiting-officers to re-enlist the superannuated Valerian legions who were keen to serve under the charismatic new supremo. He also sent a certain Metrophanes with what Dio calls 'friendly proposals' to the arch-enemy himself, and although Dio puts this down to 'a desire to test the disposition of Mithridates', the real reason can only have been to get first-hand information of the king's strength and to gain time while he completed his own extensive preparations. It is inconceivable that Mithridates could have been expected to agree to any treaty of peace which would have satisfied the Roman people's desire for his utter humiliation, and the king's scornful reply revealed his confidence not only in the effectiveness of his new model army but in the support of a new prospective ally, King Phraates III of Parthia. But Mithridates had underestimated his opponent, and when he eventually sent envoys of his own to request help from Phraates, he was dismayed to find that monarch far too busy expanding his own empire in league with Pompey at the expense of Mithridates' old ally Tigranes, who now had no thought for the fate of Pontus when his own Armenian possessions were under attack.

In the meantime Lucullus played the last, unhappy scene in the drama in which he had held the stage for so long. The setting was the town of Danala, a remote fortress among the eastern Galatians whose barons had originally supported Mithridates' profitable invasions of Roman Asia and Greece in the eighties. But they had soon come to resent the brutal megalomania with which he had then tried to coerce them into his empire, and they were now for the most part pro-Roman – sufficiently so, at any rate, for Lucullus to have been able to maintain his dwindling army on the border between Galatia and Pontus during the latter part of 67 until his meeting with Pompey, who had marched north from Cilicia to take over his troops and begin the eastward offensive. For Lucullus it was a moment of bitter humiliation, for Pompey the gratification of his dearest ambition, but it was to the credit of both that they at least began with the dignified restraint of true gentlemen. Their first interview, says Plutarch, was conducted 'with the greatest cordiality', and Pompey obviously tried to make it as easy as possible for Lucullus to retire gracefully by making a point of congratulating him on his former victories. But it had been symbolic when the lictors bearing Lucullus' proconsular fasces had offered some of their own green laurels to Pompey's rod-bearers whose signs of victory had withered in his long march through a hot and barren country. No amount of civility could eradicate the sense of embittered hatred which Lucullus entertained towards the man who seemed to have come only 'to take over a triumph rather than a war', and soon mutual congratulation gave way to such acrimonious recrimination that the two generals had to be separated by their friends.

It was an occasion well suited to sensational embroidery by our sources, and while Dio maintains that Pompey ignored the abuse which Lucullus heaped upon him, Plutarch and Velleius depict a vigorous exchange of insults in which each gave as good as he received. According to Plutarch, Lucullus accused Pompey of 'going to fight the image and shadow of a war', and said he was no better than 'a lazy carrion-crow, alighting on bodies that others have killed and tearing to pieces the shattered remnants of wars'. And he belittled all Pompey's past triumphs: ' "Having seen how you appropriated to yourself the victories over Sertorius, Lepidus and the followers of Spartacus – victories won by Metellus, Catulus and Crassus – I am not in the least surprised to find the glory of the Pontic and Armenian wars being usurped by a man who contrived even to insinuate himself somehow or other into the honour of a triumph for defeating mere runaway slaves." ' But if this no doubt cathartic broadside was not altogether unjustified, especially in its last salvo, its recipient had no shortage of effective ammunition of his own. ' "It was you who were shadow-boxing and play-acting all this time," ' retorted Pompey, ' "and it is thanks to your failure to finish what was originally an easy war that I am now faced with a struggle against military forces disciplined by the defeat of a king who has now learnt the use of shields and swords and horses and has modelled his new army on our own." ' And though there is more than an element of truth in all these accusations and in Velleius' remark that Pompey's lust for authority was as insatiable as Lucullus' greed for gain, it is Plutarch who puts his finger on the essential military superiority of the younger of these two great generals. If Lucullus had been honest with himself, he would have recognized that it was not the jealous senators or profiteering knights in Rome who were responsible for his present replacement by Pompey but his own inability to inspire the devotion of his troops. Both were excessively proud men, and Pompey is justly criticized by Velleius for wanting to be not only the first but the sole hero in any undertaking; but when it came to dealing with the troops, Pompey possessed that common touch which Lucullus lacked. Where Pompey's imperatorial magnificence did not exclude a comradeship with the troops in the field, Lucullus was 'by nature incapable of courting the affection of the rank-and-file and thought that anything that was done to please his men only dishonoured and undermined his authority'. For this reason the same soldiers who had repeatedly mutinied against following Lucullus further east, even in the moments of his greatest victories in Armenia, were prepared to follow Pompey to what seemed the ends of the earth in the next three years.

For a time it appears that Lucullus remained where he was, stubbornly issuing edicts which Pompey immediately countermanded and making a pathetic pretence of organizing Mithridates' kingdom as a Roman province, no doubt to the great embarrassment of the ten commissioners who had been sent out to assist him when there had been a province to organize. But it is questionable if Plutarch is right in suggesting that this refusal to yield gracefully caused Pompey to cut down the number of troops which Lucullus wanted to take home to march in the triumphal procession which he could still claim for his past victories. Pompey clearly needed as large and efficient an army as possible for the invasion of Pontus, and it was only in the retrospect of peacetime that his refusal to leave Lucullus more than 1,600 men to take back to Rome seemed unnecessarily mean. As for Plutarch's further sympathizing with Lucullus' complaint that Pompey left him not only so few troops but 'all the most mutinous, who were the least useful to himself and most hostile to Lucullus', it would surely have been as great a criticism of Pompey's common sense to have left good troops as it was an indictment of Lucullus' leadership to have had as many as 1,600 troops so mutinous that Pompey felt safer without them. And if Lucullus was short of men for his triumphal procession, he was certainly not short of treasures and spoils with which to impress the people of Rome.

By the time Lucullus finally departed Pompey had virtually completed his own preparations for the invasion of Pontus, whose king was now in a less confident mood. His fear was not so much that Pompey's military forces were greater, for though the Roman infantry was more numerous the king enjoyed an undoubted superiority in cavalry. It sprang from the realization that traditionally stolid Roman diplomacy had for once surpassed the intrigues of a Hellenized Oriental Gentleman. His hopes of assistance from his fellow-potentates had been shattered, partly by a rebellion of Tigranes' disloyal son but mainly by Pompey's rapid liaison with the new King of Parthia, who saw no advantage in risking the stability of his own throne by supporting Rome's enemies when with her connivance he could safely extend his own empire at their expense. Consequently Mithridates sent envoys to Pompey's camp with friendly overtures of his own, but Pompey no longer had any interest in playing for time and would have been a fool to give Mithridates the chance to recover from his predicament. Mithridates' only choice was to fight or lay down his arms, hand over all deserters, and surrender himself unconditionally to the discretion of Rome.

With the second alternative clearly unacceptable Mithridates prepared to fight for his kingdom, but not in his present position on his western borders. He was having great difficulty provisioning his troops in an area already devastated by Lucullus, and as word of Pompey's clemency to enemies who surrendered passed through the Pontic army, the king found himself losing quantities of deserters to the Romans instead of receiving them from Lucullus as he had been doing so short a time ago – a fact which incidentally reinforces the criticisms of Lucullus' qualities of leadership. Mithridates' best chance was a strategic withdrawal to the interior of his kingdom, where he would not only be able to provision his own forces more easily from new territory but employ his superiority in cavalry to its best advantage in harassing Pompey's foraging parties. Psychologically, too, he might benefit, for though a retreat can often be a demoralizing experience, the will to resist can also grow stronger as a defending force is withdrawn closer to the heart of a nation; and he had the recurrent mutinies among Lucullus' troops as evidence that even a successful army's morale can be undermined by drawing it further and further from home into increasingly remote and hostile regions.

As the hunt began, Pompey could not but admire his adversary's tactics, and though it is clear that he had anticipated them by providing for supplies to be sent after him, he still suffered from the attentions of Mithridates' cavalry, especially as his supply-lines lengthened. He therefore set his mind to devising a way of getting the better of the enemy cavalry, but it was not until he had been led a long and weary chase right through Pontus into Lesser Armenia that he was able to employ to his advantage a tactic he had learnt to his cost from Sertorius in Spain. By this time the Roman forces were becoming so seriously short of provisions that Pompey decided to follow the scorched trail of Mithridates no longer but to blaze one of his own into the most fertile lands of Lesser Armenia. There he could forage plentifully and without much fear of losing the king, for he calculated that Mithridates would be unlikely to abandon so attractive a part of his empire which also happened to contain the bulk of his treasure in a series of fortified cities. And he was right. Mithridates now felt that he was getting the better of the Roman army. According to Dio he was also beginning to receive deserters from Pompey's side (though whether Romans or only allies is not stated), and having recovered his confidence he took up a powerful and well-watered position on a hill-top not far from where Pompey had established a fortified camp as a base for foraging in open country. It was not yet his intention to commit himself to a full-scale pitched battle which Pompey would be sure to win, but he very effectively launched a more limited offensive by making the most of his cavalry and archers to attack Pompey's foraging parties. Pompey's position became untenable, and when the king saw the Romans moving camp to a more wooded area where the terrain neutralized the superiority of his cavalry, he unsuspectingly began pressing home his attacks.

At daybreak the next morning the Roman cavalry rode out as though in desperation to challenge Mithridates' horsemen, who were only too delighted to reply in superior force and were not the least surprised when the Romans fell back in apparent dismay through the more wooded country that lay between the two camps. What did surprise them was the sudden appearance of mixed squadrons of Roman cavalry and light-armed infantry on either side and to their rear. Too late they realized they were in an ambush. As soon as the encircling forces had burst out of cover, the main body of Pompey's horse stopped its orderly retreat, wheeled round, and counter-attacked, re-enacting the same stratagem that had been used against the Romans by Hannibal at Trebia in 218. Although they were superior in classical cavalry warfare in open country, Mithridates' huzzars were hard pressed to defend themselves, hemmed in by an extraordinarily hybrid swarm of Roman cavalry and Epaminondic infantry who rushed in and out stabbing furiously at their horses, and if their king had not quickly sent in some heavy infantry, it could have been the end of them. As it was they retired so badly mauled that Frontinus tells us how Mithridates 'lost all confidence in his cavalry', and Pompey was now able to forage freely and prepare for his next move.

It was probably about this time that Pompey's military superiority was increased still further by the arrival of the three legions which he had taken from Marcius but had not summoned to join him until he was sure that Tigranes had been forced to withdraw from Cappadocia and was no longer a threat to Cilicia. With these reinforcements he could probably field an army of between forty and fifty thousand legionaries against Mithridates' now dwindling thirty thousand, and he decided to give the king a taste of his own medicine by cutting supplies to his troops and starving him either into surrender or into some rash and fatal move. With his larger number of infantry and a cavalry force that was now more than a match for what had been the enemy's strongest arm, he surrounded Mithridates' impregnable position with a ring of fortified camps some eighteen miles in circumference. While the besieging army was comfortably supplied from Acilisene, a rich part of the upper Euphrates valley which Pompey now had enough troops to bring under Roman control, the besieged started eating their pack-animals, and it would not have been surprising if the king had begun to despair. But despite the weakening of his forces by hunger and desertions and their demoralization by the knowledge that Pompey had no intention of attacking them in their impregnable position, Mithridates showed himself far from the 'mental paralysis' which Appian attributed to him, as to all men, on the approach of calamity. To get vital supplies he sent out foraging parties regardless of loss of life; and lest he should be suspected of preparing for flight Frontinus tells us that he sent messengers to arrange conferences with 'several of his foes' (presumably lesser kings who were in alliance with Rome as well as Pompey himself), and gave every indication that he was trying to hold on in that defensible position in order to try to negotiate some sort of terms short of unconditional surrender. Thus it was Pompey's turn to be surprised when he woke up one morning to discover that Mithridates and his whole army had passed through his cordon during the night with the assistance of that classic ruse of leaving camp-fires burning.

Pompey immediately set out in pursuit. His scouts reported that Mithridates was moving still further eastwards through his own Lesser Armenia to the realm of Tigranes, and though the latter king had been distracted by the Parthian threat to his own southern borders, he might nevertheless be persuaded to join forces again with his father-in-law against a Roman whose expedition was directed as much against the one as the other. But try as he would to overtake the fleeing Mithridates, Pompey found himself lagging behind a force whose smallness was advantageous in flight, especially as it was travelling by night over familiar terrain. During the day Mithridates pitched camp in a naturally defensible position, which Pompey would have found difficult to assault even if he had arrived before nightfall with an army unwearied by a long pursuit in the heat of the day. But just as Pompey had won his cavalry battle by copying the Hannibalic tactics at Trebia in 218, so now he caught Mithridates by the same method which the great Carthaginian had used to annihilate a Roman army the next year at Trasimene.

Determined to bring the enemy to battle on ground of his own choosing before the king reached the Euphrates, Pompey sent his scouts forward to report on the route ahead, which lay through mountainous terrain. He then set out to overtake Mithridates by a circuitous route in order to prepare an ambush, and it is a great tribute to Pompey's generalship that he could get his men to follow him in the heat of day on such a

long detour. There is no good reason to doubt Dio's account and join those
modern historians who favour the rather different versions of Plutarch
and Appian, the former simply making Pompey catch up Mithridates and
fight a night battle against a strongly fortified camp, the latter postponing
what all the other sources say was a night battle to the next day when
Mithridates had unaccountably put himself in a position from which he
had no escape. Even if Dio's account were to lack the support of a detailed
discussion of the stratagem by Frontinus (a practical military man who
was clearly happy to accept a version which probably came from the lost
books of Livy), it is entirely feasible that Pompey could march as fast
in Armenia as Scipio had done in Spain, or that he could use the same
tactics against Mithridates that Hannibal had used against the Romans
in Italy. Nor is it a problem that Dio's account has the Romans fighting
exhausted at night. For if an exhausted army would be incapable of fighting a fresh enemy encamped in a superior position, it is quite another
matter if the general has arranged for the weary attackers to have the
advantage of a charge downhill on an enemy whom they have taken completely by surprise.

Since the king had never been pursued after dark and also thought that
the Romans might have given up the pursuit altogether – for he had been
saved more than once before by the Roman troops' refusal to follow
Lucullus – he had no reason to feel insecure as he marched through a
defile between some steep hills that night. On the contrary, his forces were
feeling more relaxed than at any time since the cavalry battle, and the
last thing they expected to hear was a sudden blast of Roman trumpets
from the heights above. But it is best to let Dio tell the story in his own
way:

First all the trumpeters sounded the attack simultaneously at a signal, then
the soldiers and all the rest of the multitude shouted war-cries, the troops clash-
ing spears against shields, the rest beating stones against bronze utensils and
anything metal they could find. Then the hollow mountains took up the din
and gave back such a hair-raising echo that it scared the wits out of the barbarians, who, hearing it suddenly in the wilderness at night, thought they had
fallen upon some supernatural catastrophe. In the meantime the Romans on
the heights began raining down stones, arrows and javelins from every side,
and they could not miss wounding large numbers of the close-packed enemy,
who were reduced to extremities in the valley-bottom. For the barbarians were
not arrayed for battle but for the march, their men and women all moving
about in the same place with the horses, camels and all sorts of baggage. Some
were riding on horseback, others on chariots or in carriages and waggons, all
in a hopeless confusion which was only increased as those who were not yet
wounded huddled together still closer in their fear, and were thus the more
easily slain.

But if it was bad enough while the Romans were assailing them from a distance, it was worse still when the attackers ran out of missile-weapons and charged down upon them in armoured waves. The outermost of the barbarians were slaughtered at once – a single blow usually sufficed, since the majority were unarmed. Then the centre was crushed together still more tightly as they all tried to get away from a danger that was all about them, and thus they perished, pushed and trampled by one another without ever having the chance to defend themselves properly or show any daring against the Romans. Moreover their strength was in their cavalry and archers, and these troops were unable to deploy themselves in the narrow space even if they had been able to see what they were doing in the darkness. For a brief space when the moon rose they took courage in the hope that they might beat back some of their assailants in the moonlight, and indeed they might well have benefited if the Romans had not contrived to have the moon behind them so that it cast long shadows that baffled their clearly defined opponents before they could even get to close quarters. The barbarians, thinking the Romans nearer than they really were, would strike vainly in the air, and when they did get to close quarters in the shadows, they would themselves be wounded when not expecting it. Thus many of them were killed and as many taken prisoner, though a considerable number managed to escape, including Mithridates himself.

Exactly how many were killed and captured, and how 'considerable' the number who escaped with the elusive king, Dio does not specify, but the estimates of Plutarch and Appian at ten thousand for the slain seem more credible than the obviously exaggerated forty thousand of some other sources. As for the numbers who fled, Plutarch tells us that the king cut his way through the Romans with eight hundred horsemen, and adds somewhat sensationally that these soon dispersed, leaving him with only two companions besides his brave concubine Hypsicrateia, 'who rode and fought' – though presumably did not look – 'like an Amazon'. Appian on the other hand has Mithridates escaping 'with only his body-guard' but then 'falling in with a troop of mercenary cavalry and about three thousand infantry, who followed him in his flight'. All these figures may be without foundation, but if we take the eight hundred horse mentioned by Plutarch and Appian's three thousand infantry as making up Dio's 'considerable number' with which Mithridates escaped, and if we accept their ten thousand as Dio's 'many slain', we have credible statistics for the battle: ten thousand killed, ten thousand captured, and nearly four thousand escaping with Mithridates, whose army would therefore have been some 24,000 strong before the battle – a figure which is in line with the 32,000–33,000 with which he is said to have begun the campaign and allows for deaths, captures and desertions of 8,000–9,000 in the meantime. But whatever the exact statistics of Pompey's victory, Florus rightly tells us that the night's work had been 'the final defeat of Mithridates, who never again effected anything although he continued to try every expedient, just as a snake whose head has been crushed still threatens to the very last with its tail.'

The king's immediate reaction was to continue his flight into Armenia where he had found refuge with his son-in-law when he had last been driven out of his kingdom by Lucullus four years before, but first he made for his fortress at Sinora, 'full of money and treasure'. There he distributed rewards and inducements to the troops still with him (together with phials of poison for senior people in case suicide became preferable to capture), and having helped himself to six thousand talents for travelling expenses he sped on eastwards to a bitter disappointment. If he had been bringing his once powerful army with him he might have found Tigranes more inclined to join forces with him again, but as things now stood his son-in-law was in no mood to accept a powerless refugee whose presence might ruin whatever chance he had of seeking some personal accommodation with the seemingly invincible Roman general. He had problems enough of his own. He was not only embroiled with the Parthian invasion of Gordyene connived at by Pompey but with a rebellion by his own son, Prince Tigranes, who had married a daughter of the Parthian king and was now following his father-in-law's example in seeking to turn Rome's war of revenge to his own advantage at his own father's expense. And if, as Dio tells us, the elder Tigranes suspected Mithridates of complicity in his son's rebellion, he can hardly be blamed for reacting less than enthusiastically to the appearance of Pontic envoys begging refuge for his treacherous father-in-law: he simply threw them in prison and put a price on Mithridates' head.

In this seemingly hopeless situation a lesser man might have been tempted to surrender, but Mithridates is nicely characterized by Florus as 'the sort of man whose misfortunes served only to stiffen his determination'. There was still one part of his once far-flung empire left to him, his principality in the Crimea, and though Pompey's naval patrols meant that it could be reached only by marching up the east coast of the Black Sea through difficult and largely hostile terrain, Mithridates did not hesitate. Once there he might raise his fallen fortunes, and he saw himself not only holding onto a remote corner of his kingdom but recruiting new armies from the friendly tribes of southern Russia and descending like another Hannibal into Italy while the Romans were still occupied in the East.

Although he was somewhat disappointed that Mithridates had not been taken in by Tigranes so that he could proceed to kill two birds with his next stone, Pompey was not unduly worried by the king's reported flight to the north, and it is doubtful if he would have set out in pursuit even if he had been aware of the grandiose global strategies that were exercising the imagination of his hyper-thyroidal fugitive. Having crushed though not captured the first of the two kings against whom the Roman people had commissioned him to make war, he recognized his immediate priority as the crushing of the second, and he therefore contented himself with sending a flying column after Mithridates while he prepared his main forces for an invasion of Armenia. For even if Mithridates evaded his pursuers, his chances of reaching his Crimean principality by land seemed slim, and his chances of being welcomed there by its ruler, his unfilial, pro-Roman son, seemed even slimmer. Moreover, even if Mithridates were to succeed in regaining his kingdom there, Pompey felt confident that with the Black Sea under the control of a powerful Roman fleet he had the means either to blockade the king into submission or to mount a military expedition against him if it really became necessary. The important thing was to make sure that Mithridates had fled far enough not to be likely to re-enter Pontus and try to recover his power in the wake of Pompey's proposed invasion of Armenia.

While he waited for news of Mithridates' movements and prepared for his Armenian expedition, Pompey put in hand the construction of a monument to his victory that would be both far grander and more useful than the usual trophy. It was to be a new city, and the victory over Mithridates was to be perpetuated in its name, Nicopolis – the City of Victory. It was near the site of the battle in an area described by Strabo as 'well-watered and well-wooded', and if, as we are told, it was good enough to have been the favourite region of the discriminating Mithridates, Pompey considered it suitable for a new city whose nucleus was to be his own wounded and veteran troops who would secure at once both their own interests and those of Rome in the area. And like maritime Pompeiopolis, inland Nicopolis became a flourishing and important city which bore witness to the constructive side of Pompey's greatness without distracting him from his destructive responsibilities.

After crossing the Euphrates and reaching the headwaters of the Araxes, Pompey was met by the rebellious Prince Tigranes and learnt to his immense satisfaction how the Parthian king had unwittingly proved a more valuable Roman ally than his original diplomatic initiative had led him to hope. For the young prince, seeing his Parthian father-in-law invading his father's province of Gordyene in accordance with Pompey's arrangements, had gone to join him with a group of other Armenian notables 'equally displeased with the old king's rule', and together they had urged Phraates not to content himself with Gordyene but to march right on to the Armenian capital of Artaxata. At first Phraates had hesitated, so Dio tells us, because it went far beyond what he had agreed with Pompey, and he was not eager to become embroiled with Rome; but it had not been long before the temptation to share the wealth of Armenia and put a grateful son-in-law on its throne had overcome such inhibitions. Soon Parthian armies had advanced into Armenia in such force that the old Tigranes had taken to the mountains at the appearance of his son and Phraates before the walls of his capital. If the defenders had opened the gates of Artaxata to the young prince, Pompey could now have been facing a formidable power-bloc, but Artaxata's garrison had been loyal to the old king, and the failure of repeated assaults on its massive walls had convinced Phraates that the city could never be taken except by a protracted siege. He was not prepared to stay so long so far from his own kingdom, where there was always the possibility of a *coup d'état* in his absence, and he soon returned to Parthia with the greater part of his army, though he did leave some of his troops to help Prince Tigranes. But the old monarch had not been wasting his time in the mountains. He had been busily collecting loyal forces, and as soon as Phraates had disappeared over the horizon, he swept down on his son and trounced him so effectively that the fleeing prince was soon casting about for other allies. Ironically enough his first thought had been his grandfather in Pontus, but when he discovered that Mithridates' plight was even more desperate than his own, he decided to appeal to his grandfather's conqueror instead. And so it was that Pompey was greeted by an excessively friendly and helpful Armenian prince as soon as he reached the Araxes.

It was probably about this time that the Roman flying column returned to report that Mithridates had disappeared across the River Phasis up in Colchis, and with this reassurance that the first enemy had completely fled his kingdom, Pompey advanced against the second in the company of the young Tigranes, for whom all the cities on the royal road to the old Armenian capital obligingly opened their gates. But the best was yet to come. Despairing of armed resistance to the Romans but determined that his unfilial son should not win by diplomacy what he had lost in battle, the old king also made overtures to Pompey, 'whose disposition he had ascertained to be mild and gentle in contrast to Lucullus'. He could argue with conviction that he had dissociated himself completely from Rome's principal enemy: indeed, he had helped Mithridates earlier only from familial obligations, and to show his present good faith he now sent Pompey Mithridates' recent emissaries loaded with chains. But when none of this prevailed against the counter-diplomacy of the son, who may have flattered himself that Pompey's rejection of his father's overtures was due to a personal preference that went beyond pure pragmatism, King Tigranes swallowed the last bitter fragments of his once massive pride and showed the highest degree of political wisdom by a sudden metamorphosis into the most abject humility. If he could not rule despite the Romans, he was ready to rule by their leave – and even to out-grovel his son if only he could save his throne.

There were then two pleasant surprises waiting for Pompey when he had advanced to within sixteen miles of Artaxata, that mighty fortress which he expected to be defended with the same resolution against him as against Phraates. The first was an invitation from the old king to send a Roman garrison into his capital. The second was the reason why Pompey himself had not been included in the first invitation. No sooner had the Roman garrison entered the city than Tigranes left, not fleeing to his customary mountains but riding straight to Pompey's camp with a retinue of family and friends in order to surrender himself in a manner which the accounts of Dio and Plutarch show to have been most carefully contrived for maximum effect.

Believing that first and second impressions should be equally favourable, the old king had dressed himself 'as far as possible midway between his former dignity and his present degradation, in order', says Dio, 'that he might seem to Pompey to be worthy both of respect and pity'. In selecting his ensemble he had rejected his full-dress uniform of white tunic with a sleeved jacket of imperial purple, but he kept his diadem, tiara and sword – to create a favourable first impression by wearing them and an even more favourable second by casting them aside. Thus attired he mounted his charger and rode in modest state to Pompey's camp, which he would have entered on horseback if Pompey had not sent a lictor to bid him dismount and enter on foot. Tigranes' *chef de protocol* had obviously not discovered that the Armenian custom of riding into friendly cities was anathema to Roman etiquette, but it did not matter. By dismounting at once and showing every willingness to do as Romans did in Roman camps, the king turned what was nearly a major social solecism into a handsome gesture of submissiveness, which he promptly reinforced by handing the lictor his sword without waiting to be asked.

It was as true then as it is today that there is nothing an upper-class republican loves more than a king who flatters his vanity, and Tigranes played his part magnificently. The Roman general, pavilioned in splendour, was sitting to receive him with the young Tigranes at his side, but when Pompey saw this dignified old man not only walk towards him but tear off his diadem and fling himself and his tiara on the ground, it was too much. Before Tigranes could kiss them Pompey had leapt to his feet and was gently helping the king to a chair, to the obvious annoyance of the prince who neither rose nor greeted his father in any way. Pompey then with his own hands carefully retied the discarded tiara on Tigranes' head and spoke what Dio describes as 'words of encouragement' in what must have been an extraordinary scene.

The exchange of civilities which followed is given by Velleius and Plutarch, perhaps a little more graphically than reliably but certainly not incredibly. According to Velleius the king explained that he would have submitted himself and his kingdom 'to no man but Pompey, whether Roman or otherwise; that he would be ready to bear any condition, favourable or otherwise, upon which Pompey may decide; and that he felt as little disgrace in being beaten by one whom it would be a crime against the gods to defeat as he felt dishonour in submitting to one whom Fortune had elevated above all others.' But flattered and delighted as he was by this appeal to his vanity, Pompey was not only businesslike in his reply but took the opportunity to contrast his own magnanimity with his predecessor's uncompromising severity. '"You must lay the rest of your losses to Lucullus,"' he told the king according to Plutarch. '"It was he who took from you Syria, Phoenicia, Cilicia, Galatia and Sophene, but what you still have, you may hold – provided that you pay the sum of six thousand talents to the Roman people as a penalty for your crimes, and that your son becomes King of Sophene."'

This solution had much to commend it to all parties. For Rome it meant victory, honour and financial gain without the effusion of blood, and if Plutarch complains that in throwing away his diadem Tigranes had been flattering Pompey with the victories of Lucullus, the fact remains that Pompey's prestige had secured peace for the future as well as victory for the present: Rome had no desire to annex Armenia, and now that honour had been satisfied it was far better that the government should remain in the hands of the old royal house which could claim the loyalty of the people yet was too weak to pose a serious threat to Rome's provinces and was satisfactorily at loggerheads with the other great power of the East, namely Parthia. For Tigranes it meant the retention of his ancestral kingdom which he would surely have lost by any other policy. It was of course disappointing to have won and lost so much extra territory during his long reign, but Oriental monarchs tended to take a somewhat speculative view of imperialism, and it was not unsatisfactory to have ended an exciting lifetime of imperial investments with his original stake intact and only the broker's costs to pay. And Strabo tells us that Armenia was well able to pay not only the six thousand talents which Pompey demanded (and which Velleius tells us were duly handed over to the quaestors) but also a generous bounty to all the Roman troops, for the old man had been so delighted when Pompey had made the army hail him as king that he had offered half a mina to each private, ten minas to every centurion, and a whole talent for a military tribune.

But these cheers for the father jarred unhappily on the ears of the out-manoeuvred son, who was unwise enough not to disguise his disappointment at being fobbed off with a little kingdom when he had wanted a whole empire.

Even allowing for the fact that it was quite usual for sons of Oriental potentates to hate their fathers, Pompey found it a useful rather than an endearing trait. As a particularly filial son himself he had disliked Prince Tigranes' refusal to be reconciled with his father almost as much as he resented the young man's scorn at the inadequacy of Sophene. Admittedly the prince may have wondered how long his father would let him keep even Sophene once the Romans had departed, but however justifiable he may have considered his resentment, he was very foolish to insult the Roman general not only by refusing his invitation to dinner that night but by adding that he would soon find another Roman to give him what he wanted. But even then Pompey was tolerantly disposed to overlook these indiscretions until the young man went too far and forfeited his kingdom by making difficulties about the one sacrosanct subject – money.

Just as Mithridates had kept most of his treasures in Lesser Armenia, so Tigranes seems to have favoured Sophene for his, and presumably because there was not enough ready cash at Artaxata to provide the agreed war-indemnity and the soldiers' promised bounty, the king needed to draw on those treasures in what was now to be his son's kingdom. But the prince took the line that he was not responsible for his father's debts and made plans to leave Pompey's camp, presumably to lay his hands on the money himself. Pompey now became extremely angry, and having put the prince in honourable confinement he sent messengers to the guardians of the son's fortresses with instructions to hand over the necessary sums to the father. But they refused to hand over anything to anyone except their new ruler. Pompey then sent the young Tigranes under guard to fetch the money himself, but when those sturdy guardians still refused to open their vaults because they could see that their new king was acting under duress, Pompey's temper finally snapped and he clapped the prince in irons to be reserved for his triumph. He then added Sophene to the father's kingdom, and once the elder Tigranes was again their formal king, he apparently had no difficulty in getting all the money he wanted from those strange treasurers whose strict sense of propriety would do credit to many a Swiss banker today.

By now the year was well advanced, and though there was still a mopping-up operation to be completed both in Pontus and in Armenia (where it was necessary to bring the son's rebellious adherents into line behind a king whom he had declared a Friend and Ally of the Roman People),

Pompey was anxious to settle his troops comfortably in winter-camps before the cold weather set in. For this purpose he chose northern Armenia, not perhaps the obvious choice from a purely climatic point of view but strategically desirable for the defence of Armenia against Caucasian insurgents and for his proposed spring advance into the territory into which Mithridates had vanished several weeks before. And there were no problems with supplies. With the grateful Tigranes all eagerness to provide his benefactors with creature comforts the Roman commissariat had only to ask, and everything soon seemed settled for a peaceful winter. But before the year ended Pompey was provided with one more opportunity to increase his fame.

This last success of 66 was by way of a Christmas present, for it occurred when the Romans were celebrating their mid-December festival of Saturnalia from which so many of our traditional celebrations derive. Perhaps for ease of supply as well as strategic reasons Pompey had divided his army into three camps, the other two under the command of his legates Metellus Celer and Valerius Flaccus. Exactly where they were located is not known, but it seems likely to have been somewhere north of Lake Sevan but south of the River Cyrus, the present-day Kura, beyond which lay the wild Caucasian tribes of Iberians and Albanians. And it was a king of the latter who now decided to attack Pompey's divided forces at the time of their maximum unpreparedness. According to Dio the motive of King Oroeses was twofold: friendship for Prince Tigranes combined with the desire to make a pre-emptive strike against the Romans, whom he rightly believed to be considering an invasion of his kingdom in the following year. But though his plan and sense of timing were sound enough, he made the usually fatal mistake of underestimating his enemy as he launched his three divisions simultaneously against the three Roman camps.

It was only against Flaccus' camp that the Albanians achieved even temporary success by overrunning the outer line of entrenchments. In their excitement they failed to realize that Flaccus had not abandoned his outer perimeter until he had constructed an inner and more easily defensible one, and they had no sooner poured into the intervening space than he counter-attacked with a controlled precision that made mincemeat of their disorganized hordes. Elsewhere Metellus Celer had repelled King Oroeses himself at the first attack, while Pompey, hearing of the assaults on his other camps, marched out to defeat the would-be destroyers of his own. He then hurried in pursuit of the fleeing enemy, and though he failed to overtake the king himself, he caught up with the rear of his retreating armies and cut up large numbers as they struggled to recross the Cyrus. Altogether it was a most satisfactory diversion from the usual Saturnalian activities, and Pompey was pleased to have given the Albanians their first taste of the Roman military banquet with which he was now determined to regale them more sumptuously as soon as possible. But it could wait until next year. He was ready but reluctant to lead his army into the Caucasian winter, and when King Oroeses sent envoys requesting a cessation of hostilities, he agreed on a truce that would postpone his retribution to the spring.

9

THE NEW ALEXANDER

But it is as relevant to the glory of the Roman Empire as of
one man to mention at this point all the names and triumphs
of the victories of Pompey the Great, for they equalled in
brilliance the exploits of Alexander the Great and virtually of
Hercules himself.

Pliny, *Natural History*, 7.95

In reaching the old Armenian capital of Artaxata in 66 Pompey had
carried Roman arms further east than any man before him, but this was
merely the prelude to a much grander imperial performance which he
was already orchestrating for the remoter regions of Transcaucasia in
the following year. It appears that he intended to conquer the Transcaucasian tribes methodically from east to west, beginning with the
Albanians, whose territory extended to the Caspian in what is now Soviet
Azerbaijan, and then marching westwards through modern Georgia to
the coast of the Black Sea. But when spring came he discovered that
King Artoces of Iberia intended to make a pre-emptive strike against
him, and since the Iberians inhabited mainly that part of eastern Georgia
lying due north of central Armenia, it was here that Pompey had to begin
his new campaign.

According to Plutarch the king's decision was prompted by a desire
to gratify Mithridates, but this seems a singularly improbable motive in
view of Appian's careful statement that the Chorzeneans and Iberians
had tried to stop Mithridates' flight through their territory. More likely
is Dio's explanation that Artoces was rightly 'afraid that Pompey intended to march against him too', and in choosing to attack first he was
acting as befitted the monarch of a kingdom for whom submission must
have been unthinkable if we can believe Plutarch's expression of the immense pride of a people 'who had never been subject to either the Medes
or the Persians' and from whom 'even Alexander the Great had departed
in haste'. But Pompey the Great was not so easily distracted. When King
Artoces sent ambassadors with friendly overtures he recognized at once
the same ploy which he himself had used to gain time against Mithridates

only a year before, and his suspicions were soon confirmed by intelligence reports of a mobilization of the Iberian forces, mostly mountain-peoples from the southern Caucasus. He therefore left legates to continue the reduction of the fortresses of Pontus and Armenia that were still holding out, and marched rapidly northwards to recover the initiative from his new and far from contemptible adversary.

According to Strabo the way into Iberia from the south was by the valleys of the Cyrus and its tributary the Aragus. Each of the passes was guarded by a great fortress, Harmozica on the Cyrus, Seusamora on the Aragus, and Dio indicates that their narrowness could make the frontier virtually impregnable if they were occupied in sufficient strength. But Pompey advanced with such speed that the Romans were within sight of Harmozica before Artoces even realized they were on their way, and as his own forces were not yet ready to fight a pitched battle, there was little the king could do but re-cross the river, burn down the bridge behind him, and leave the men of his city's garrison to do their unaided best to oppose the invaders. Bravely they sallied forth against the legions, but after a sharp defeat they resented their king's desertion so much that they promptly surrendered the fortress to Pompey, who then secured control of the pass by putting in a garrison of his own.

Beyond Harmozica the narrow valley opened out into a broad and fertile plain, full of prosperous farming settlements and naturally peace-loving people. All these Pompey overawed into submission as he continued marching upstream until he reached the next major bridge across the Cyrus. There Artoces was waiting for him on the northern bank, and as Pompey approached, he sent a further set of envoys requesting peace. Pompey's reply was that Artoces must first demonstrate his good faith by yielding the bridge and furnishing provisions for the army. Without hesitation the king complied, but 'when he saw Pompey actually across the river', says Dio, 'he grew afraid and fled away to the River Pelorus', his next natural line of defence.

Although Dio criticizes the king for first drawing on and then running away from an enemy whom he might have hindered from crossing the Cyrus, it seems likely that Artoces was deliberately drawing Pompey further and further into the remoter and more mountainous regions of his most warlike peoples. Pompey's reaction was to deal with the retreating Iberians just as he had dealt with the retreating Mithridates in the previous year. By one of his now famous forced marches he overtook and confronted Artoces, who then prepared to fight relying on his formidable bowmen to decimate the Romans before they could come to close quarters with his own infantry. But Pompey charged so fast that the Iberian archers had no time to show their skill, and once the armies were fighting hand-to-hand the Roman legionary rapidly proved his disciplined superiority. Soon Artoces was leading the retreat across the Pelorus, and once he got himself safely across he fired the bridge and left the remnants of his defeated army the choice between the sword, the river or surrender. Of those who took the first two options the majority perished, and though a few brave diehards tried to prolong the struggle by scattering into the forests and practising sharp-shooting from the tree-tops, Dio tells us that they did not hold out for long after Pompey had had the trees chopped down under some of them.

It was all over in a few days. Artoces had lost nine thousand men dead and ten thousand captured, and he now sent yet more envoys with more proposals for peace, though obviously more seriously intended this time because they were accompanied by handsome gifts. These Pompey accepted in the hope that a show of good will would encourage the king to conclude a reliable truce and not compel him to continue the pursuit even further into increasingly remote and difficult country, but he was not prepared to agree to bail without a surety. He demanded Artoces' children as hostages for his good conduct, and though the prevalence of unfilial sons among Oriental potentates might suggest that the king would be only too glad to get rid of them, the Iberian royal family was clearly an exception to the rule. Anxious for peace but fearful for his children's safety, the king temporized until Pompey discovered that the river was now low enough to be forded in places and suddenly sent his army across. And that was the end of the Iberian campaign. Artoces sent his children, a peace was concluded, and Pompey enjoyed the double satisfaction of adding another kingdom to his list of conquests and ensuring that its monarch would not interfere in either Pontus or Armenia.

Since he had been forced by the Iberians to start his Transcaucasian expedition in the middle Pompey now had to decide whether to turn east into Albania, where he had planned to begin it, or to march westwards into Colchis, where he had proposed to end it. To turn east at this stage would have been perverse. The Albanians had already experienced the efficiency of the Roman war-machine, and once they heard of his victory in Iberia it seemed unlikely that they would break the truce which they had made the previous winter or make any further provocative incursions into Armenia. The priority now must be to invade Colchis and follow the retreat of the king who was the chief object of his commission from the Roman people, for it would make Pompey ridiculous if he allowed himself to become embroiled in Albania only to discover too late that Mithridates was reinvading Pontus by the same way that he had fled. And if Pompey was disappointed at having to postpone the glory of carrying the Roman eagles to the Caspian, there was the attraction of seeing

Pompey the Great (106–48)

Sulla (*c.* 138–78), commemorated on coins minted in 54 (*left*) and 56 (*right*), the latter by his son Faustus who depicted him sitting and receiving the bound King Jugurtha in 105 from King Bocchus, who kneels and offers the olive branch.

ABOVE LEFT King Hiarbas of Numidia, who supported the Marians in Africa and was defeated and killed in Pompey's invasion of 81.

ABOVE RIGHT Pompey's African triumph, celebrated probably in 79, was commemorated on this coin of 71 as a subject less politically sensitive than his recent victory over Sertorius in Spain. He enters the city in a four-horsed chariot with Victory flying above him. The rider probably represents his son Gnaeus.

Pompey's naval victories are recalled on this coin minted in 44–3 by his son Sextus, who maintained his independence with a large fleet. On the obverse (*left*) Pompey's portrait appears with the name Neptune and a trident. On the reverse a Roman warship sails to the right.

TOP King Mithridates VI of Pontus (120–63), wearing a lion's head in imitation of Alexander the Great.

ABOVE LEFT King Tigranes I of Armenia (c. 97–56), Mithridates' ally defeated by Pompey who made him a client-king of Rome. This coin was minted in Antioch while Syria was part of Tigranes' empire (83–69).

ABOVE RIGHT King Phraates III of Parthia (70–57), the self-styled 'King of Kings' whom Pompey ceased to treat with respect once he had got the better of Tigranes and Mithridates.

ABOVE LEFT King Ariobarzanes I Philoromaios of Cappadocia (*c.* 95–62) whose unswerving loyalty to Rome justified his cognomen and earned great rewards from Pompey, who also continued to keep his successors solvent with huge private loans on which he waived capital repayments.

ABOVE RIGHT King Antiochus I of Commagene (69–*c.* 31), wearing the Armenian tiara, was reduced to submission by Pompey: a glance at the map shows the strategic importance of this buffer-kingdom.

ABOVE LEFT Tarcondimotus I of Cilicia (64–31), to whom Pompey granted the wilder parts of north-eastern Cilicia with access to the sea as part of his defensive arrangements for the new province (compare Deiotarus *vis-à-vis* Pontus). He assisted Pompey in the Civil War, and was made King by Antony.

ABOVE RIGHT King Antiochus XIII (69–65), the last of the degenerate Seleucids before Pompey annexed Syria as a Roman province.

King Aretas III of the Nabataeans with a splendidly Arabic profile on one of his own coins. His submission was commemorated on a coin minted by Scaurus as aedile in 58: Aretas kneels by his camel and offers the olive branch.

the Land of the Golden Fleece to enhance the purely military reasons for an advance westwards to the shores of the Black Sea.

The border between Iberia and Colchis was that southern spur of the Caucasus now known as the Suram or Meschian range, the watershed between the Cyrus, which there begins its eastward journey of some eight hundred miles to the Caspian, and the headwaters of the Phasis, now the Rioni, which empties itself into the Black Sea port of Poti. Today an impressive piece of modern engineering could take an army from Baku on the Caspian to the Black Sea port of Poti in the relative comfort of railway carriages along a track that climbs with the Kura and descends with the Rioni, but for Pompey's legions it was a formidable enterprise to negotiate the pass through the Meschian mountains into the precipitous ravines of the upper Phasis. According to Strabo there was only this one pass between Iberia and Colchis, but though he adds that it was guarded on the Colchian side by the fortress of Sarapana, the modern Sharapani, we are told of none but natural hazards on Pompey's journey. No doubt the news of his Iberian victory had preceded him, and he seems to have met no military opposition as he descended the valley with the help of the 120 bridges which Strabo tells us were necessary to cross the winding river as it followed its tortuous course through narrow gorges. On the way he may have seen what Appian considered to be the origin of the golden fleece which brought the Argonauts to Colchis, 'for the many streams which issue from the Caucasus bear invisibly small particles of gold, and the inhabitants put shaggy sheepskins into the stream to collect them'. As he advanced still further down the river's two-hundred-mile journey to the sea, he would have marked a pleasant contrast between the high plateaux of Iberia and the more Mediterranean climate of the Colchian plains before he arrived at Poti, the ancient city of Phasis, where he had arranged a rendezvous with his prefect Servilius, the officer commanding his Black Sea fleet.

After reviewing the naval forces and holding a council of war with Servilius, Pompey decided to march up the Black Sea coast in pursuit of Mithridates in a combined operation with his fleet. To have made no attempt to follow the arch-enemy to his Crimean principality a whole year after defeating him in Lesser Armenia might have exposed him to criticism at home; and even if it proved true that the land-route was virtually impassable for a large army and there were no rich pickings to be had on the way, he would at least turn back with the confidence of knowledge rather than hearsay. Moreover, a useful demonstration of Roman strength might deter the Colchians and their northern neighbours from accepting any approaches from the unpredictable Mithridates. But if it is fairly clear that these were the flexible objectives with which Pompey crossed the Phasis and marched northwards, how far he advanced and how much opposition he encountered are questions less easy to answer. From his later claims to have subdued the western Caucasian tribes of the Heniochi and Achaei he must have gone considerably beyond the maritime city of Dioscurias where Mithridates had passed the previous winter, and presumably he was involved in some fighting with these remote and belligerent mountaineers before deciding that to advance further would be more trouble than it was worth. Both Dio and Plutarch stress the difficulty of the terrain, especially the lack of harbours which were essential to effective co-operation with the fleet. They also mention the extreme hostility of the tribes, and while it is hard to believe that these wilder peoples could field armies on anything approaching the scale of the more sophisticated kingdoms of Iberia and Albania, Pompey was undoubtedly right if he felt that there was no point in losing good men in guerrilla warfare. To go still further from his prime responsibilities of Pontus and Armenia in pursuit of a defeated king whose last refuge could be blockaded by a powerful fleet was pointless. It seemed equally pointless to expend effort on relatively impoverished tribes when there were rich kingdoms waiting to be punished in his rear, quite apart from the further consideration that Mithridates free but impotent was temporarily more useful to him than Mithridates dead or in chains. It was sufficient for the present to have made an effort to reach the Crimea by land and to have assured himself of the difficulties which the king would have to face if he attempted a counter-invasion of his old kingdom by that route. To capture and kill the arch-enemy would virtually complete his commission under the Manilian law, and there was much that he wanted to do before then to prove that his youthful resemblance to Alexander the Great was much more than superficial.

Accordingly Pompey instructed Servilius to intensify the blockade of Mithridates and then marched back to Colchis with the intention of reaching Albania before the end of the campaigning season. But though the year was getting on, Dio tells us that he did not take the most direct route, which would have been to retrace his steps more or less due east up the valley of the Phasis and straight across Iberia. He decided instead to take a more circuitous route via Lesser Armenia, perhaps, as Dio says, in order to throw the Albanians off their guard but also perhaps because he knew the difficulties of the two ways from Iberia into Albania, the one 'following the River Alazonius from its headwaters in the Caucasus through great marshes into a narrow, rock-hewn gorge', the other providing the very opposite hazard of 'a rugged and waterless waste' after emerging from the gorge of the infant Cambyses. Besides, it would do no harm to visit Lesser Armenia en route and make sure that his legates were getting on with their job of subduing the more stubborn fortresses of the wealthiest part of Pontus.

When Pompey finally began his invasion of southern Albania, probably more or less in the same region where he had pursued King Oroeses across the Cyrus after repulsing the attacks on his camps in the previous winter, he found that after his long detour at the end of summer the volume of water had reduced sufficiently for his army to be able to ford the river at several points. Even so it was a difficult operation, but by sending his unencumbered cavalry across higher up he used the horses' bodies to help break the force of the current and make it easier for the pack-animals and infantry to cross below – the infantry lowest of all so that the men had the chance of catching any pack-animal that lost its footing and was in danger of being swept away. According to Plutarch the army also had to face a line of palisades erected by the enemy on the far bank, but there is no mention of this in Dio, whose careful account says specifically that the Romans encountered no enemy action at that point. As before, the most formidable forward defences were natural, and despite the fact that the army marched in the cool of the night from the Cyrus to the Cambyses, the troops still suffered greatly from heat and thirst on an arduous journey that was deliberately lengthened by untrustworthy guides.

Crossing the Cambyses without opposition they marched on to the Abas, this time with a precautionary supply of water carried in ten thousand skins. It was a heavy additional burden but a necessity compensated for by the ready availability of provisions from the local communities, which were themselves well provided with food and only too ready to share it with an invader who promised no depredations. Thus Pompey led his army to the Abas without great discomfort, and it was only after he had crossed this river that he was informed of the approach of King Oroeses, who had indeed been surprised by the invasion and had been too busy collecting forces in the mountainous north of his country to try to halt it at any of the natural lines of defence further south. But now the king was advancing in force for a decisive battle, and Pompey set his mind to devising a stratagem to ensure that the decision went his way. It was not that he doubted the capacity of his legionaries to outfight at close quarters the relatively undisciplined crowds of Oriental infantry with their miscellaneous assortment of arms and armour – some heavy-armed with breastplates and great oblong shields but many others jave-lineers and archers who were clad in the skins of wild beasts and armed with little more than their courage once the hand-to-hand fighting began. The problem was that before the legions could show their superiority it was necessary to neutralize the enemy cavalry, an arm in which Oroeses was even more formidable than Mithridates had been. According to

Strabo there were both light and heavy cavalry, the latter as heavy as
Medieval cavalry with both horse and rider almost completely encased
in impenetrable armour except, of course, where the riders' thighs
gripped the horses' flanks. (It is a common fallacy that the development
of heavily armoured knights had to wait for the invention of stirrups:
the stirrupless lancers of Albania, Armenia and Parthia were so heavily
armoured and mailed that they were virtually helpless if once unseated,
and the weight of their charge was irresistible by infantry regiments that
tried to keep their line.) It was thus essential for Pompey to outmanœuvre
the enemy horse at the first opportunity, and he achieved this by a variation of the same Hannibalic stratagem which he had employed so successfully against Mithridates in the previous year – a feinting cavalry attack
followed by a controlled retreat and the encirclement of the enemy's over-
confident pursuit.

The battle, as reconstructed from a careful combination of the accounts
of Dio and Frontinus, began with Pompey's advance into a plain flanked
by hills. He placed his cavalry conspicuously in front, but he cleverly concealed both the size and dispositions of his infantry. Some he concealed
in defiles in the neighbouring hills with orders to cover their helmets and
other gleaming armour to prevent the sun's reflection giving away their
position to enemy scouts, but the greater part he placed in the plain itself,
behind the cavalry and kneeling motionless behind their shields so that
they were invisible to the enemy until they came to close quarters. As
Oroeses advanced, Pompey ordered the cavalry to attack and watched
with satisfaction as his tactical plan came to life with the precision of
a parade-ground exercise. When the cavalry engaged, it was no surprise
to the Albanian knights that the apparently contemptible Roman squadrons were soon fleeing before them like chaff before the wind, and their
delighted king obligingly sent his infantry forward in confident anticipa-
tion of victory. Too late he saw the regiments of Roman infantry materia-
lizing from an apparently empty plain, parting to let their own cavalry
through, then closing in on their now disorganized pursuers. Too late
he noticed further Roman cohorts making flanking attacks on his advancing infantry from the cover of the hills, and he watched in dismay as the
apparently routed Roman cavalry re-formed behind their own lines,
wheeled about, and attacked that rear part of his army which was not
already being submitted to the methodical butchery of the encircling
legions. But even when so hopelessly outmanœuvred the proud Albanians
did not give in without a struggle. The king's own brother fought
valiantly to rally his men until he came into personal combat with Pompey, who ran him through in the best heroic tradition. Pompey was
always to be found where the fighting was thickest, and it was this per-

sonal gallantry as much as his generalship that earned him the almost fanatical devotion of his men.

If our two main sources more or less agree on the stratagem by which Pompey defeated the Albanians in this one great battle in the later part of 65, their complete disagreement on its purpose gives very different evaluations of his achievement. In Dio's account Pompey concealed his infantry 'because he was anxious to bring Oroeses into battle, and feared that if the king learnt the true numbers of the Roman army, he would retreat'. Frontinus, in contrast, says that Pompey needed to gain a tactical advantage to offset the numerical superiority of the enemy, and if the figures which Plutarch and Strabo assign to the Albanian forces are trustworthy, Frontinus' explanation must be preferred. According to Strabo the Albanians, militarily more powerful than the Iberians, 'fielded 60,000 foot and 22,000 cavalry when they risked everything against Pompey', and even if we accept Plutarch's lower figure of twelve thousand for the cavalry, an army of well over seventy thousand men and strong in cavalry was surely larger than Pompey's expeditionary force. Admittedly Plutarch adds that the Albanian troops were for the most part 'poorly armed' (in flat contradiction of Strabo), but even if the quality of the Albanian infantry is questionable, the number of Pompey's troops will scarcely have been larger than the fifty thousand with which he had faced Mithridates in the previous year, and was probably considerably smaller since he must have left adequate forces with his legates in Pontus and Armenia. On balance, therefore, it seems reasonable to credit Pompey with a major victory over a formidable enemy. At any rate it was a battle without a morrow. The king sued for peace, Pompey 'overran the whole country', and the Roman troops looked forward to boasting to their friends how they had avenged an attack on their winter-camps by making a Saturnalian bonfire out of a wood in which some of the Albanian diehards had sought refuge from utter defeat the next autumn.

By the time Pompey had arranged affairs in Albania to his satisfaction he should have been thinking of returning to more suitable winter-quarters in the area of his main responsibility, but the call of the Caspian was irresistible. He turned eastwards, eager to set foot on the shores of a sea which was believed to be connected with the world-encircling Ocean; but when only a tantalizing three days' journey from his destination, he was turned back, so Plutarch tells us, by armies of poisonous reptiles. It is not inconceivable that the undaunted hero of the human battlefield was undermined by the thought of losing his laurels to the tail of a scorpion, a viper's fang or the literally ridiculous bite of one of the loathsome tarantulas which according to Strabo caused their victims to die laughing uproariously at their fate. What is certain is that

Pompey marched rapidly back to the comfort of Lesser Armenia, where he was anxious to see how much further his legates had progressed towards completing the capture of all seventy-five of the strongholds in which Strabo tells us that Mithridates had deposited most of his treasures. At some stage on this march or soon after his arrival Pompey received ambassadors from two more distant peoples, the Medes and the Elymaeans, who dwelt east of the Tigris and to the south-west and south of the Caspian. Velleius speaks of a Roman 'invasion' of Media but this, together with Appian's mention of 'fighting' and 'battles' against the Medes and his inclusion of 'Darius the Mede' in the list of 'kings conquered' which was displayed at Pompey's triumph, is usually interpreted as imaginative elaboration. But it is difficult to claim 'conquest' without some military contact, even if it amounts to little more than a show of force at the frontier, and it seems more probable that the arrival of a friendly Median embassy at this time was connected with an expedition to the Tigris which Dio says Pompey's friend Aulus Gabinius carried out during the year. At any rate the arrival of these distant ambassadors provided gratifying evidence of the success of Pompey's policy of instilling into all the Near Eastern kingdoms a sufficiently healthy respect for Roman power to make them think very seriously before interfering in the arrangements which he was planning for the security of Rome's interests in Asia Minor and the Levant. Pompey returned friendly replies to the Median and Elymaean kings, and these were doubtless received with a greater degree of satisfaction than was experienced by King Phraates when he read the messages which Pompey now sent in reply to a Parthian embassy which had arrived with a whole catalogue of complaints.

The 'King of Kings' had watched with increasing anxiety the succession of Roman victories during the year, which were not confined to the spectacular successes of Pompey himself. According to Dio he was equally worried about events nearer home, which included not only the systematic subjugation of Lesser Armenia and Pontus by Pompey's other legates but also Gabinius' provocative advance to the Tigris. He therefore sent to Pompey a list of grievances and a request for a renewal of the diplomatic understanding which they had reached at the beginning of the campaign when King Tigranes had been their common enemy. But Pompey no longer needed Phraates. Mithridates was vanquished, Pontus was on its way to becoming a Roman province, and Tigranes' kingdom was to be supported as a useful buffer against more powerful potential imperialists like Parthia. Far from renewing the diplomatic understanding with Phraates, Pompey now faced the Parthian ambassadors with a demand for the return of the formerly Armenian territory of Gordyene which less than a year ago he had actually encouraged Phraates to invade.

And when the wretched envoys pleaded that they had been given no instructions in this matter, he not only packed them off home with a curt
note to their king but sent his legate Afranius with sufficient troops to
secure Gordyene by force if necessary, and then hand it over to Tigranes.

This was not the first disagreement between Pompey and Phraates. The
Parthian had already been refused a request to be sent Prince Tigranes,
now languishing under heavy guard in the Roman camp. And if it is hard
to believe that Phraates had really expected Pompey to send him a potential Parthian puppet-ruler for neighbouring Armenia on the plea that the
young man was his son-in-law, Pompey had at least been diplomatic
enough to reply that on consideration he 'felt that the boy belonged more
to his father than to his father-in-law'. But now Pompey added insult
to injury by addressing his latest letter simply to 'King Phraates' instead
of 'Phraates, King of Kings', the title by which Romans had always hitherto humoured the Parthian vanity, and the recipient was thus left in no
doubt that the end of his usefulness to Pompey was the end of any special
relationship.

It was a sound object lesson in power-politics. As Dio pointed out,
'this treatment of Phraates by Pompey in the fullness of his power indicated very clearly to anyone desiring to indulge his greed that everything
depends on force of arms, and that he who is victorious by that means
earns the right to lay down whatever law he pleases'. Phraates had no
choice but to evacuate Gordyene nor any recourse save further diplomatic
reproaches, which Afranius proceeded to ignore by marching straight
across Mesopotamia on his way back from there. But if news of Pompey's
continuing successes in the East made many a senator nervous that he
would also prove to be Sulla's pupil in Rome, they were mistaken. However much Pompey enjoyed knocking the heads of kings and princes
together overseas, at home he had no desire for any sort of autocracy
that went beyond a general recognition of his position as the first citizen
in an aristocratic Republic.

But the internal politics of Rome could not have been further from
Pompey's mind as he began to receive the contents of Mithridates' strongholds, some of which were reduced by force while others surrendered
of their own accord. Among the latter was Sinora, the place where Mithridates had put himself in funds before beginning his long flight northwards
to the Crimea. It was surrendered by his mistress Stratonice who felt
understandably resentful at having been abandoned, and though she had
been raised from rags to riches by the whim of that impulsive king she
now took the pleasurable revenge of handing over his priceless treasures,
including herself, to the Roman conqueror. But Pompey took neither her
nor any of the countless concubines who were found in all the castles.

The others he restored to their parents or husbands, who were all princes and generals worth conciliating, and he left Stratonice with ample wealth after selecting from her vast hordes of treasure only the finest pieces 'to adorn the temples of Rome and add splendour to his triumph'. And while it is impossible to believe that no wealth at all found its way into Pompey's personal coffers (especially when Appian tells us that it took all of thirty days to remove all the gold and jewel-encrusted furniture from only one of Mithridates' depositories), Plutarch is insistent that he handed everything over to the quaestors, even a throne-room suite of solid gold which the Iberian king now sent him as a personal present.

From Sinora Pompey moved gradually north-westwards down the Lycus valley from one Aladdin's cave to another, but of all the wonders which he inspected in Pontus proper the most fascinating and precious haul came naturally enough from the least accessible, a stronghold called Caenum which Strabo describes as a massively fortified acropolis perched high above a sheer ravine. Whether it was taken or surrendered we are not told, but the sources are anything but silent about its contents. For the scandal-loving Plutarch the most exciting were Mithridates' lists of poisoned sons and officials, torrid correspondence with the objects of his remarkable passion, and interpretations of dreams, both his own and those of his wives who were no doubt very careful to dream judiciously. For Strabo they were the valuable treasures which he saw in his own day in the great Temple of Jupiter on the Roman Capitol, 'where they had been dedicated by Pompey the Great'. But what compelled the admiration of the scholarly Pliny was the king's collection of biological treatises and specimens and the amazing breadth of scientific knowledge which they revealed. 'He was,' says Pliny, 'a more assiduous investigator of biological science than any man before him', and while Pompey was no great intellectual himself, he had the wit to appreciate the value of what he had found and promptly ordered his scholarly freedman Lenaeus to translate the whole library into Latin. 'And so,' comments Pliny, 'Pompey's great victory over Mithridates was as beneficial to science as to the state.'

Where Pompey went next is not known, but on his journey down the Lycus towards the sea he must surely have sojourned at Cabeira and Eupatoria. The former is described by Strabo with an estate-agent's precision as 'a most desirable palace, whose amenities included zoological gardens and hunting parks conveniently near to mines and a water-mill'. All it lacked was a name more appropriate to its new owners, and Pompey was for once modest or cautious enough to defer to Higher Authority and rename it Diospolis – the City of Zeus. But having placated providence at Cabeira, he indulged his passion for self-glorification when he arrived at the vast city that lay half-finished at the confluence of the Lycus and the Iris in the middle of a broad and fertile valley. As Mithridates had planned to call this new city after his own cognomen, Pompey followed his example with the result that Eupatoria became Magnopolis and benefited from its second founder's desire to complete the construction on a scale appropriate to its new name.

After following the river to the sea Pompey established his headquarters for the rest of the winter at the great maritime city of Amisus. From here he could keep in touch with his Black Sea fleet and be ready to take any action that might prove necessary against Mithridates while getting on with the formidable administrative task of turning a kingdom into a province, supervising the continuing subjugation both of Pontus and of those parts of Armenia which had not yet acknowledged Tigranes, and deciding what to do about the rest of that king's once vast empire, the greater part of which had already been taken from him by Lucullus. But there was more in Pompey's mind than a grand confirmation or redistribution of kingdoms, principalities and cities to the 'many kings, princes and leaders who came to pay court to him at Amisus'. There was one of Tigranes' former possessions which its wealth, strategic importance and chronic instability combined to mark out as a candidate for direct annexation by Rome, and when the campaigning season opened again in 64 Pompey proposed to invade Syria and carry his victorious arms to the Red Sea.

His motives for this new campaign have been variously interpreted by our ancient sources. According to Plutarch it was largely a matter of personal ambition which involved a dereliction of a primary duty to destroy Mithridates. At Amisus, he says, 'Pompey's ambition had already led him into obnoxious behaviour, for having himself criticized Lucullus for issuing edicts, distributing honours and doing while the enemy was still alive all such other things as victors are entitled to do once a war is finished, he was now acting in exactly the same way and starting to regulate the Pontic province regardless of the fact that Mithridates was still ruling in the Crimea and had collected a battle-worthy force'. And he goes on to describe Pompey as 'a man possessed with an overwhelming ambition to recover Syria and march through Arabia to the Red Sea in order that he might bring his victorious career in touch with the Ocean which surrounds the world on all sides: for in Africa he had been the first to carry his conquests to the Outer Sea, in Spain he had made the Atlantic the frontier of Rome's empire, and in his recent pursuit of the Albanians he had narrowly missed reaching the Caspian'. But while there was certainly a strong element of self-glorification in Pompey's motivation, Plutarch allows his admitted preoccupation with the psychology of his biographical subjects to blind him to the less personal considerations. Appian is more realistic when he says that Pompey's large army gave him an irresistible opportunity 'to annex a large and defenceless empire on the pretext that it was unnatural for the government of Syria to be returned to the Seleucid dynasty, which Tigranes had dethroned, rather than to pass to the Romans, who had conquered Tigranes'. But Appian fails to explain why it was Syria that Pompey chose to annex in preference to any of the other defenceless kingdoms such as Cappadocia. The answers are basically four: that Syria's great wealth had made her ripe for further exploitation by the Roman commercial interests which were already there; that she already possessed a highly organized governmental substructure of Hellenized cities that was readily adaptable to Roman provincial administration; that the very defencelessness and instability which made her such an easy conquest for Rome would have left her no less easy a prey to a renascent Armenia or expansionist Parthia without the establishment of a permanent Roman military presence; and that such a presence was equally necessary to guard against a revival of piracy in the eastern Mediterranean.

The sad fact was that the last representative of the proud Seleucid dynasty was unrecognizable as an heir to what had been the greatest empire to have been carved out of Alexander's conquests by his warring successors. By the end of the second century BC that empire had shrunk to little more than eastern Cilicia and Syria, with a more or less nominal authority over Palestine's Judaic core which Kings Antiochus IV and VII had failed to Hellenize despite the success of their arms. Throughout Pompey's youth the kingdom was tossed like an over-ripe plum among a bewildering succession of rival claimants until it was squashed altogether under the heel of the Armenian imperialism which Tigranes began in the East at the same time as Mithridates was expanding the Pontic empire westwards into Asia Minor and Greece. Tigranes ruled Cilicia and Syria for fourteen years until Lucullus' invasion of Armenia in 69 forced him to recall his viceroy and army of occupation from Antioch and incidentally gave the Seleucids their last chance to disprove their total degeneracy. King Antiochus XIII returned to the throne, propped up by Lucullus and considerable popularity from his subjects whose initial enthusiasm for the Armenian 'liberation' of 83 had long since dissolved into disillusionment as they had watched Tigranes metamorphose from his original tactful impersonation of a Hellenistic monarch back to the more natural Oriental despotism which he enjoyed at home. But the Seleucids were still a house divided against itself, and they suffered the usual consequences. After internal battles between their subjects Antiochus XIII and his rival Philip II became the puppets of rival Arab sheikhs, who first sought to rule Syria through the Seleucid kings and eventually, according to Diodorus, decided to dispense with indirect rule altogether, join forces, and divide Syria between them. At any rate, though Philip received some moral support and a new theatre from Marcius Rex, Lucullus' incompetent replacement as governor of Cilicia, in return for a contribution to Pompey's war-chest in the campaign against the pirates in 67, he was soon ousted in his turn and his slippery throne reoccupied by Antiochus for a precarious year in 65–4. But even this was achieved only by courtesy of a foreign ruler, the Arab sheikh Sampsiceramus who had previously been keeping Antiochus under lock and key in Emesa and probably released him now only in the hope of staying out of trouble in what promised to be a more serious Roman intervention in the area by a supremo of a very different calibre from Marcius.

That such intervention was being planned must have been clear to far less shrewd observers than this subtle sheikh long before Pompey himself arrived at Antioch, which was probably in the early summer of 64. Josephus suggests that his quaestor Aemilius Scaurus was already involving himself in Jewish affairs by then, and since Scaurus is said to have hurried on to Jerusalem only because he found Damascus already taken by the legates Metellus Nepos and Lucius Lollius, it is clear that Pompey's lieutenants were active well down in Syria at least as early as the spring of 64. Josephus also mentions Gabinius as another of Pompey's legates who became involved in Jewish squabbles, perhaps soon after returning from the expedition to the Tigris, and from Plutarch we know that Afranius was detailed to subdue the Arabs of the Amanus range in preparation for Pompey's own invasion of Syria. Nor was this merely a clearing of the route into Syria from the north for an army which could well look after itself. The Amanus mountains provided refuge for bands of robbers whose livelihood came from attacking the lucrative trade-route from Syria into Level Cilicia, and their suppression was clearly a prerequisite for the settled prosperity of the whole region which Pompey was now proposing to bring under the direct rule of Rome. How much more extensive the preliminaries were we do not know, but from what little we can glean from stray references to the activities of officers like Afranius, Metellus, Lollius, Scaurus and Gabinius, it would have been a singularly sanguine or stupid Seleucid who could persuade himself that Pompey had organized all this preparatory effort merely so that he could come and give his blessing to a virtually defunct dynasty that had proved so utterly incapable of stable government.

It was probably well into the spring of 64 by the time Pompey was ready to leave Amisus. His final instructions to the fleet to continue the

Crimean blockade were underlined by a proclamation of the death-penalty for any merchant caught breaking the embargo, and though it is unlikely that he really believed his supposed statement that he was 'leaving famine as a mightier enemy than himself' against a king whose principality backed onto the cornlands of the steppes, the fact remains that the Crimea was an isolated refuge when completely cut off from maritime communication. And while Pompey had no doubt been informed that Mithridates had succeeded in re-establishing himself there against his unfilial son and was recruiting new forces, even Plutarch approves his observation that Mithridates was a difficult quarry to run down and much easier to deal with when he was strong enough to fight. In the meantime it was not as if he was losing contact with naval intelligence in the Black Sea. If proper arrangements were made a message could travel any distance at the speed of a ship or a galloping horse, and as Pompey marched south from Amisus, he took good care to set up an effective courier service to relay by land any intelligence about Mithridates' movements that might arrive at Amisus by sea.

It seems unlikely that Pompey was in a hurry to reach Syria, but his first protracted stop would have been a necessity anyway. Only some eighty miles south of Amisus lay the gleaming bones and skulls of over seven thousand Roman troops whose bodies had been left unburied after their defeat by Mithridates when Lucullus' legate Triarius had fought him alone in 67. And if in the urgency of a desperate situation Lucullus had been justified in giving the correct disposition of the living a higher priority than the decent disposal of the dead, Plutarch maintains that his failure to bury his soldiers with the proper honours did more than anything to complete the alienation of an already demoralized and mutinous army. Pompey now visited the battlefield near Gaziura on the River Iris, and however sincere he might have been in wanting to do the right thing for its own sake, he would doubtless have reflected on the favourable contrast which would be drawn between himself and his predecessor as he spared no effort or expense to give the skeletons 'an honourable and splendid burial'.

From there his route continued southwards by the borders of Galatia and on through eastern Cappadocia, two vast and relatively primitive inland areas which he had destined not for annexation but stabilization under rulers who would be Friends and Allies of the Roman People. Inevitably he must have become involved in arbitration, negotiation, persuasion and entertainment with the rulers and tribal leaders, all of which would have further delayed a journey from which the forwarding of competent legates to Syria had fortunately removed the urgency. And then there was a king to be 'conquered' in Commagene, which lay between the Taurus mountains and the River Euphrates. At least that is what Appian suggests by including Antiochus I of Commagene alongside 'Tigranes the Armenian, Artoces the Iberian, Oroezes the Albanian, Darius the Mede and Aretas the Nabataean' in his list of 'kings conquered', and though his reference elsewhere to Pompey's having 'made war' on Antiochus at this stage could be nothing more than an inference from the name's appearance in the official list, those modern scholars who discount a military operation against Commagene as against Media may well be mistaken. Just as the expedition of Gabinius to the Tigris may have been aimed at the submission of Darius, so too the arrival of Pompey in Commagene could have been the occasion for teaching its king a short, sharp and salutary lesson in the rightness of might 'until', as Appian says, 'Antiochus came into friendly relations with Rome'. Or even if there was no actual fighting involved in the 'conquest' of either Commagene or Media, the fact that Dio tells us that Antiochus surrendered voluntarily to Lucullus after the fall of Tigranocerta does not mean that a similar submission now occurred without the help of at least a show of aggressive force from Pompey that would account for his inclusion of these kings among others whom he had definitely conquered in major campaigns.

While Pompey was crossing the Taurus and doing whatever he had to do to settle Commagene, his legate Afranius was putting the finishing touches to his campaign against the Arabs of the Amanus, and there was probably not an enemy to be seen by the time the new Alexander reached the area of his model's great battle with the Persians in northern Syria two hundred and seventy years before. Certainly there was no opposition from the unhappy Antiochus of Antioch, and once Pompey had installed himself in the Seleucid capital it took only a few words to depose the last king of the dynasty that had ruled there for nearly two and a half centuries. Pompey then proclaimed the annexation of the kingdom as a possession of the Roman People: a roughly triangular province bounded by the Amanus range and the kingdoms of Commagene and Osroene in the north and then narrowing to incorporate Phoenicia in the south, the western part of present-day Lebanon. Significantly it did not include the kingdoms of the Jews or the Nabataean Arabs that lay to the south and east, but their avoidance of direct Roman rule did not excuse these frontier realms from a salutary exposure to Roman might that would make them realize their responsibilities to safeguard the interests of the power by whose courtesy they were to be allowed to retain their autonomy. And for the Jews at least this meant a rude awakening from the complacency which they had enjoyed when it had been to Rome's advantage to support their independence against the Seleucid empire, for now that the Seleucids were no more and Syria had become a prized possession of Rome, the last thing Pompey wanted was a strong and aggressive Judaea threatening the new frontier.

As a result of the aggressive imperialism of its late King Alexander Jannaeus his widow Salome had in 76 become queen of a kingdom which had never been so great since the time of David and now rivalled that of the Nabataean Arabs for the title of the strongest military power between the Lebanon and Egypt. From Galilee and Gaulanitis in the north down to Idumaea and Moab in the south Jannaeus had brought the greater part of the lands on both sides of the Jordan under Jewish rule, and by conquering almost all the Graeco-Syrian cities south of Phoenicia he had opened his western empire to the sea. But the King of Judaea had not possessed the sole imperialist appetite eager to devour the Seleucid corpse, and Jannaeus' death left his widow watching Tigranes' southward advance with increasing anxiety. When he captured Ptolemais on the coast of Galilee, Salome sent him a large bribe in the hope of dissuading him from moving still further south, but it was the Roman invasion of Armenia in 69 that sucked Tigranes' armies back from Syria. If the Jews gave thanks for the timely appearance of this distant deliverer, they would soon be cursing the Romans as they had once cursed Antiochus IV for assaulting their Holy of Holies. Nor did they realize how the Greeks would welcome more tolerant conquerors who were as little concerned to Judaize Hellenism as to Hellenize the Jews. The destruction of Hellenistic Pella by a Judaizing Jannaeus had offended Graeco-Syrian sentiment as much as the sack of their Temple by a Hellenizing Antiochus had outraged the Jews, and it said much for Roman imperialism that it was ready to respect all manner of alien cultures and religions as long as they did not interfere with the basic requirements of submission, namely stability and a steady income.

What Josephus describes as a 'god-sent opportunity' for Roman intervention in Jewish affairs was provided by the revival of a civil war which had broken out between the two sons of Jannaeus and Salome when the ailing queen had died in 67. Its origin had been the resentment of their younger son Aristobulus, who had been excluded from his mother's Pharisee-dominated regime and had seized a large number of fortresses in the Lebanon and Trachonitis even before his mother's death. For there were many of his father's friends who either shared his leanings to the Sadducees or simply looked for personal advantage from the gratitude of a successful usurper, and by the time his elder brother Hyrcanus came to the throne, Aristobulus was powerful enough to outfight him at Jericho and blockade him into abdication in Jerusalem. Hyrcanus then enlisted the aid of the King of the Nabataean Arabs, Aretas III, and in 64 returned from the Nabataean capital of Petra with his new patron and

an army of fifty thousand men. This time it was Aristobulus' turn to be besieged in Jerusalem, and he would no doubt have succumbed in time but
for the arrival of Aemilius Scaurus and a Roman army from Damascus.

At once both brothers sent him envoys bearing bribes, which he
accepted with alacrity. But having enriched himself to the tune of some
eight hundred talents and listened with total indifference to the claims and
counter-claims of the two rivals, Scaurus naturally lent his support
where it would clearly be most profitable to himself, to Pompey and to
Rome. And in the court of Roman advantage the case of Aristobulus was
unanswerable. For if Scaurus were to support Hyrcanus and Aretas, he
would be strengthening a coalition of the two most formidable powers in
southern Syria and be involving himself and his army in an extremely
difficult attack on a powerfully fortified city. If, on the other hand, he
sided with the beleaguered younger son, he would not only set a large
number of vengeful Jews at the throat of the Arabs and other Jews but
would monopolize the gratitude of the Jewish king. Scaurus therefore
raised the siege and marched back to Damascus, while Aristobulus
pursued his retreating enemies and cut up large numbers of them near
the site of his former defeat.

Pompey was no doubt as pleased with the results of Scaurus' intervention in Jerusalem as with the capture of Damascus by two other
legates, but these were only two out of the myriad situations which
claimed his attention at his headquarters in Antioch, where he probably
remained for the rest of 64 and the following winter. While we lack the
wealth of detail for Syrian affairs that we enjoy for those of Judaea, it
would be surprising if less than six months sufficed for so complicated
a task as the organization of a new province even if it had been able to
monopolize the energy and efficiency of its administrator. As it was, Pompey's responsibilities were not restricted to Syria, and if it is right that
he remained in or near the old Seleucid capital for the rest of the year,
it was no idle whim, for he would have found himself ideally placed there
to keep in touch with every part of his vast maritime and territorial
provincia.

It was to Antioch, for example, that envoys arrived from Kings
Tigranes and Phraates, the former seeking further military assistance
against the latter, the latter complaining bitterly about Armenia's continuing claim to the northern part of Mesopotamia, and Dio tells us that
there were many around Pompey who urged him to take this opportunity
to invade Parthia. But Pompey wisely feared to tread where Crassus
would one day rush in all too disastrously. Ironically enough it had been
the Macedonian colonists of ill-omened Carrhae who had saved Afranius'
army from starvation when he had decided to cut across Mesopotamia

in a straight line from Gordyene. But it was not so much consideration of the practical difficulties of a Parthian campaign that deterred Pompey: he was simply not prepared to jeopardize his organization of Asia Minor and the Levant by allowing himself to be lured into a full-scale invasion of a sprawling inland empire whose conquest could have brought Rome no wealth worth the labour and would undeniably have overstretched his mandate under the *lex Manilia*, particularly while Mithridates was still alive. To have Tigranes and Phraates at loggerheads beyond the frontiers of Rome's sphere of interest was all that Pompey wanted from them, and flattering as it would have been to Rome's vanity to make Phraates accept his diadem from her general as Tigranes had done, it was no small tribute to the prestige of her arms that the 'King of Kings', already insulted by Pompey's curtailment of his title in all correspondence, was now willing to submit his boundary dispute with Tigranes to Roman arbitration. Pompey replied by sending a commission of three members of his staff to settle the frontier, and both kings seem to have acquiesced in their decision.

By the spring of 63 Pompey was ready to move south into the areas where his legates had begun operations in the previous year while he had remained in Antioch. According to Strabo he now suppressed the Arabs of the Libanus mountains who used their bases there and on the coast to harry the trade of the Phoenician ports such as Byblus and Beirut, but this work could well have been entrusted to legates just as the similar operation in the Amanus range had been undertaken by Afranius. By Josephus' brief account of his journey to Judaea he is brought south up the Orontes via Lysias and Apamea and thence between the Libanus and Anti-Libanus ranges, where he crossed the watershed between the Orontes and Leontes and visited the Ituraean cities of Heliopolis and Chalcis before turning east to Damascus through the gap between Anti-Libanus and Hermon. At Lysias he destroyed the fortress of an evidently unaccommodating character called Silas the Jew and he did the same to Apamea, but the wiser and possibly worthier Ituraean dynast Ptolemy of Chalcis bought himself out of a beheading with the timely payment of a thousand talents which Pompey found useful for paying the army. But such tantalizingly few allusions in Josephus are only drops in the administrative ocean through which Pompey made his way to the south, and we shall never know how many more fortresses were destroyed and petty potentates deposed in the interests of the security of the new province. No doubt there were many more executions than that of the Tripolitan tyrant Dionysius and many more amicable understandings reached with worthier characters like Sampsiceramus, the Sheikh of Emesa, who had once hoped to master Syria by the manipulation of a Seleucid puppet

but whose realistically rapid acceptance of the new situation earned him
not only Pompey's respect but a reputation at Rome that allowed Cicero
to use 'Sampsiceramus' as a synonym for 'Pasha' in snide references to
Pompey in letters to Atticus. But Josephus is interested only in the Jews,
and in the absence of any comparable narrative for Syrian affairs we have
little more evidence for Pompey's southward journey until he reached
Damascus and found the place full of ambassadors 'from all Syria and
Egypt and Judaea'.

To find envoys from all over Syria waiting for him was not a novel
experience. They were waiting for him everywhere and overwhelming
him with the 'judicial business' in which Plutarch says he spent most of
his time, 'settling the disputes of cities and kings, and sending friends
to deal with those to which he could not attend in person'. But the appearance of ambassadors from King Ptolemy Auletes of Egypt was both a
new and interesting development, for that once formidable dynasty had
not yet quite reached the degree of degeneracy of the Seleucids with whom
in their greater days they had fought many times for possession of Palestine. It was not an attempt on Ptolemy's part to obtain as a gift from
Pompey what he had been unable to win from others by force of arms, and
he was under no illusions that the Palestinian cities Ptolemais and Philadelphia could ever be more than the gravestones of a dead claim to the
area which Pompey was now entering. His sending of envoys to Pompey
with a crown worth four thousand gold pieces was no more than the
payment of a first premium on an insurance policy which he hoped would
guarantee him the friendship of a formidable empire-builder who could
easily find a pretext for intervention in Egyptian affairs if he so desired.
Not that Ptolemy was altogether averse to Roman intervention in his
kingdom. The important thing was that any such intervention should
be in support of his own shaky regime, and in the meantime there could
only be advantage in assisting any operations against the Nabataean
Arabs who were always a danger to Egypt. But Ptolemy's fears and hopes
for the security of his throne were alike groundless. Pompey had no more
intention of embroiling himself in the internal affairs of Egypt than of
Parthia, though he obviously did not say as much to Ptolemy's envoys
because we find him receiving further gifts of gold for himself and clothing
for his army as he moved further south.

About the Jewish ambassadors and their representations we know very
much more because of Josephus' highly detailed histories, *Jewish Antiquities* and *Jewish War*, but it is important to remember that Pompey
did not share their author's preoccupation with that nation. For Pompey
the Jews were just one of the many kingdoms throughout the East which
had to be dealt with in a way conducive to Rome's interests, and even

when Hyrcanus and Aristobulus both appeared before him to argue their rival claims to the Jewish throne, he was far more interested in his projected Arabian campaign than with the tiresomely repetitive disputations of a people whose religious observances were as incomprehensible as their dissensions were satisfactorily weakening. Hyrcanus, supported by a dignified deputation of a thousand suitably respectable and deferential Jews, pleaded the claims of primogeniture and meritocracy, and though Pompey had his doubts about the validity of the second, he was more favourably disposed to Hyrcanus' supporters than to the gaggle of bejewelled and swaggering magnificoes who accompanied Aristobulus. Pompey criticized the latter for his violence and told both claimants to keep the peace 'until he had time to come to their country and settle their affairs after seeing how things stood with the Arabs'; but Aristobulus felt so affronted that he rushed back to Judaea and began rousing his kingdom to oppose Pompey's passage further south.

Pompey's reaction was as swift as it was angry. Summoning further legions and auxiliaries to augment the already powerful expeditionary force which he had prepared against the Nabataeans, he marched rapidly down the Jordan valley via Scythopolis and Pella to a few miles past the confluence of the Rivers Jabbok and Jordan, where Aristobulus was holding the formidable acropolis of Alexandrion. Pompey ordered the king to come down and discuss the situation sensibly, and since there were many among the king's supporters who urged the futility of making war against the Romans, it was not long before a somewhat crestfallen and worried Aristobulus was once more arguing about his rights under a flag of truce. For a while Pompey was patient with the young man and his constant returns to the acropolis, supposedly to discuss the negotiations with his friends but in reality because he was 'torn between hope and fear, hopeful that Pompey would confirm his kingship but fearful of losing his military position if not'. But Aristobulus was naïve if he thought the admitted nuisance of assaulting Alexandrion could be used as a bargaining-counter with Rome's greatest general, and when he had come down for the third or fourth time Pompey told him either to order the immediate surrender of his garrison or prepare for a suicidal defence. Aristobulus hesitated no longer but wrote the necessary instructions to the garrison of Alexandrion. He then left for his capital with a sense of relief that Pompey had not declared for Hyrcanus but deeply disgusted at the thought that the all-important question of his future must apparently be shelved until the Romans had dealt with the Arabs.

Once away from the glare of the Roman eagles and back behind the reassuring solidity of Jerusalem's massive fortifications Aristobulus let injured pride get the better of him and resumed preparations for war.

But as the Roman army approached through the groves of palm and balsam his bravado diminished until it disappeared completely when he heard that Pompey was encamped at Jericho. At last he had learnt the belated wisdom of Tigranes. He now approached Pompey no longer as an insolent magnifico but as a humble suppliant, displaying extravagance only in his promises of gifts, offering to throw open the city of his own free will and requesting nothing for himself but only peace for his nation. At once Pompey forgave him, and if only Aristobulus had been able to keep his promises he would have kept his kingdom too, for Pompey was no more enthusiastic than Scaurus had been to make a client-king out of an ally of the Arabs, and he was pleased to be spared a siege of Jerusalem. But Aristobulus lacked Tigranes' absolute control over his officers, and when Gabinius returned from the city to say that the king's over-zealous partisans had refused either to hand over the promised funds or admit a Roman garrison, his fate was sealed. Without further ado Pompey clapped him in irons and prepared to assault Jerusalem, which closer inspection revealed as falling short of impregnability on the northern side. As dissension broke out among the inhabitants, the diehards found themselves in the minority, seized the fortified Temple, and destroyed the bridge which joined it to the upper city. The upper and lower cities and the palace were left to Hyrcanus' supporters, and they now hastened to open the gates to Pompey.

Even so an assault on the heavily fortified Temple-enclosure was a formidable undertaking, and while Pompey sent to Tyre for artillery (probably part of the equipment which he had brought out with him for the war against the pirates), he still hoped to reach a peaceful settlement by making conciliatory proposals to the defenders. Little as he understood of their religion, he must have doubted that so obviously devout a people would risk the unnecessary destruction of their greatest sanctuary, and it no doubt surprised and perplexed him when his overtures were rejected with immediate scorn. If it was patriotism that motivated the diehards, it was evidently not shared by Hyrcanus and the Pharisees who were falling over themselves in their eagerness to assist the invader. And it must have seemed particularly odd to anyone not acquainted with the history of Jannaeus' persecution of the Pharisees that the more politically liberal and pro-Hellenic Sadducees were the ones now preparing to defend the citadel of Judaism to the point of suicide rather than live under a restored Pharisaic regime. Perhaps there were some among the defenders who thought that the Temple's defences would hold out long enough to make the Romans give up and go away, leaving the rival factions to fight it out among themselves. Perhaps there were others who trusted to divine intervention to prevent 'proud foreign nations trampling the altar without removing their shoes'. But if so, the former underestimated Pompey's determination as dangerously as the latter overestimated Jehovah's concern.

To guard against possible counter-attacks by the defenders or changes of heart among his collaborators Pompey ordered his legate Piso to occupy the upper and lower cities and fortify the palace and all the houses surrounding the Temple. He then applied his mind to the central problem of the assault, and having made a careful evaluation of both the natural and artificial fortifications with the help of Hyrcanus, he concluded that the Temple, like the whole city, was weakest to the north. He therefore pitched camp on that side and began the earthworks which were necessary to fill the vast fosse that joined the parallel Tyropoeon and Kidron valleys which protected the western and eastern sides.

It was a gigantic undertaking against a determined enemy able to rain missiles and make sallies from their high walls and towers, but the same religious devotion that made the Jews such obstinate enemies also had its weekly compensations, for Pompey discovered to his amazement that they refused to fight on the Sabbath against anything but a direct attack. Consequently he worked overtime on fosse-filling on the days when the defenders were doing no manner of counter-offensive work, and eventually his earthworks were high enough to allow the newly arrived siege-engines to be moved forward, and the bombardment began. It took a great deal of battering to produce the breach that was needed for the infantry assault, but at last one of the towers collapsed and the Romans poured through the gap. First across was Faustus Cornelius, Sulla's son who was now Pompey's apt pupil. Behind him came an army eager to work off the frustrations of a three-month siege, and while the priests impressively continued their rituals as though nothing untoward were happening, some twelve thousand Jews were sacrificed around them, and Pompey became 'the first Roman to subdue that nation and set foot in their Temple by right of conquest'.

Naturally curious to see what manner of deity motivated this virtually theocratic people he was at a loss to understand the dreadful sacrilege which he was supposed to be committing by inspecting an inner sanctuary that turned out to be an empty room. But having satisfied his curiosity, he proved a singularly considerate conqueror compared with Nebuchadnezzar or Antiochus IV. To have looted the Temple-treasures would have incurred a hatred unconducive to the docility which he sought from this conquered nation, and while there were some pieces that would have looked well in his triumphal procession and the temples of Rome, the Jews could always be made to pay their value many times over. The ritual furniture and even the two thousand talents deposited there were thus spared – the cash for a decade until Crassus took it for his Parthian campaign, the more sacred things until Titus sacked the city in AD 70 and carried them off to Rome – and Pompey ordered the Temple attendants to clean up the mess and resume all their usual rituals without fear of further interference.

Now that the fighting was over it was a relatively quick matter to put into effect the political and territorial arrangements which he had had plenty of time to plan during the three months of the siege. He installed Hyrcanus as High Priest and ruler of a Jewish state that was now a shadow of its former greatness and excluded in particular most of the Hellenistic cities which had been forcibly Judaized by Jannaeus. As a further insurance against renascent Jewish militarism he razed the fortifications of Jerusalem and carried off not only the ambitious Aristobulus but several other members of his family and a thousand of his most prominent partisans. He then imposed the taxation which would soon make the term 'publican' synonymous with 'sinner', but if Josephus complains that the Romans 'extorted as much as ten thousand talents in a short space of time', he is objective enough to place the blame where it rightfully lay, on the internal dissensions of his nation. But Pompey's mind was no longer on the Jewish campaign. It was just one more chapter satisfactorily concluded in the history of his Eastern conquests, and he was glad to shake the dust of Jerusalem off his feet as he marched towards his next objective, 'a rose-red city half as old as Time'.

This was Petra, the already fabled capital of the Nabataean Arabs whose king, Aretas III, was next on the list for submission or subjugation. 'Hitherto,' says Plutarch, 'this powerful nation had made no account of Roman power', but having seen the effect of Rome's iron hand on Jerusalem, the king now sent unsolicited assurances in advance 'that he was willing to obey and perform all Pompey's commands'. But if he hoped that this submission by letter would be enough to stop Pompey's advance on his capital, he was mistaken. While never a general to fight for the sake of fighting, Pompey rightly wished to confirm Aretas in his good intentions by visiting his capital with an appropriate show of force and an open hand that was always ready to clasp another in friendship once its palm had been crossed with gold. Besides, he was eager to see for himself the rock-hewn city that lay in his path to the Ocean, and if, as Plutarch maintains, there were murmurings in his camp against marching even further from Mithridates, he could still argue that it would be time enough to chase Mithridates when there was something worth fighting and that in the meantime the security of the Syrian province demanded the submission of the Arabs no less than of the Jews.

But Pompey was not destined either to reach Petra or fight again with

Mithridates. As he marched steadily southwards from Jerusalem, his line of communication from Amisus was expressing important dispatches from the fleet by relays of messengers bearing spears tipped with laurel. This was a sure sign of good news, and it was unfortunate that when the last of scores of relays thundered into Pompey's camp somewhere on the way to Petra, the commander-in-chief happened to be out exercising his horse and missed the excitement of their arrival. At first he was annoyed when the troops came rushing out to him, but when he saw their wild excitement and the couriers' spears, he dismounted at once, seized the dispatches, and led the way into the camp. For a moment he was at a loss where to go to address the troops. They had brought no regular tribunal with them, and this news was too urgent to wait for the soldiers to construct the military substitute by piling up clods of earth. But someone had the bright idea of piling up pack-saddles instead, and it was from this improbable eminence that Pompey delivered the formal vindication of his conduct of the war: there had been a *coup d'état* in the Crimea, the new king was devoted to the Roman people, and Mithridates himself was dead.

10
THE GREAT SETTLEMENT

Thus he won many battles, brought into subjection many
potentates and kings both by war and treaty, colonized eight
cities, opened up many lands and sources of revenue to the
Romans, and established and organized most of the nations of
the continent of Asia with their own laws and constitutions,
so that even to this day they still use Pompey's laws.
Dio Cassius, *Roman History*, 37.20.2

After he had received the now familiar acclamation of *Imperator* from
wildly cheering troops 'who felt that in the person of Mithridates ten
thousand enemies had died', Pompey ordered the army to prepare
appropriately lavish sacrifices and celebrations while he dictated his
victorious dispatches to Rome. Reaction to his news in the capital was
as rapturous as in his own desert camp. The consul Cicero immediately
proposed a ten-day public thanksgiving, and if there were kill-joys who
questioned why this victory should be celebrated for twice as long as
Marius' defeat of the Cimbri, they kept their sour grapes to themselves.
The proposal was accepted by the Senate, and as Rome took on a
carnival atmosphere to celebrate 'the termination of all wars both on land
and sea', Pompey relegated the one minor exception to that sweeping
claim to Scaurus, whom he left in charge of Syria and the Arabian
campaign while he hastened to Amisus to satisfy himself about affairs in
the Crimean principality and accelerate the organization of the Pontic
kingdom as a province.

We do not know how much detail was given in the dispatches which
Pompey received in Syria, but he no doubt heard a full if not necessarily
accurate account from the representatives of the hopeful usurper
Pharnaces who were waiting for him with gifts when he reached the
Black Sea. After Mithridates had succeeded in re-establishing himself in
the Crimea against his pro-Roman son Machares, he had devoted his
undiminished energies to raising new armies for vast new enterprises of
reconquest and revenge. By 63 he had formed the nucleus of a powerful
striking force on Roman lines, an army of 36,000 picked men formed in

sixty cohorts and supported by larger numbers of irregulars. But the raising and maintenance of an army of this size was achieved only with the cruellest exactions. Since the king was cut off from the treasures of his Pontic strongholds he had been reduced to levying the most brutal taxes and virtually devastating the whole principality by commandeering everything that could be used for the war-effort. Neither the suffering of his subjects nor his own unpopularity were of the least concern to him, for 'he felt there was nothing that might not be ventured or hoped for', writes Dio, 'and if he were to fail he preferred to perish along with his kingdom but with his pride unhumbled than to live on without it in humility and disgrace'.

But as the year progressed not all his officers and men shared his enthusiasm for death or glory in what seemed an increasingly hopeless cause. The resources of the Bosporan cities would never be sufficient to build a naval force that could take on Pompey's Black Sea fleet, and as Mithridates toyed with his fantastic schemes for invading Italy by land while the Romans were preoccupied in the East, he failed to observe how rapidly he was losing the confidence of his soldiers, 'now shrinking from the prospect of prolonged service in a foreign land against men whom they had not been able to overcome even in their own'. As long as Mithridates remained alive there could be no hope of reconciliation with Rome, but without him perhaps something might be salvaged from the ruins of his megalomania, and what his favourite son Pharnaces had in mind was the chance to live and rule at least part of the ancestral kingdom as a client-prince of Rome.

Hatred of Mithridates grew so widespread that the king thought it a wise precaution to send a considerable part of his army from his own capital at Panticapaeum to secure Phanagoreia on the opposite side of the straits. But the officer commanding Phanagoreia found it intolerable to yield his authority to the hated eunuch who led the reinforcements. He killed him, won over the troops, and proceeded to defy the king from the very city which had been the first to open its gates to him two years before.

From Phanagoreia the rebellion quickly spread. Pharnaces conspired against his father, and when Mithridates sent guards to arrest him they preferred to join the troops with which Pharnaces was already marching against the king at Panticapaeum. In vain Mithridates tried to bargain with his son, and when he found himself all but deserted by his guards in a palace surrounded by enemies, he tried to anticipate parricide by suicide. While the troops outside were shouting for the young king, the cornered monarch was cursing himself 'for having taken such careful precautions against all the poisons that are administered in food but failing to provide against that most deadly variety that is to be found in the house of every king – the disloyalty of armies and children and friends'.

At least that is the story which Appian tells, and as famous last words go, they are better than many. Unfortunately for Mithridates, the precautions which he had taken against being poisoned had made him proof against the massive doses which he now administered successfully to wives and daughters. He then tried to stab himself, but the blow was too weak to be fatal and it appears that he failed to end his life without help, though whether it was a loyal and compassionate guard who administered the *coup de grâce* or the troops who had been battering down the palace-gates will never be known. The former is the widespread version in our sources and it has tended to be regarded by modern historians as the official version compiled by Pharnaces to free himself from the taint of parricide, but it seems doubtful that this was what Pompey read in the dispatches of a young king wishing to gain Roman recognition. It would be remarkable if Pharnaces had tried to evade personal responsibility for the annihilation of Rome's arch-enemy, and the story of the faithful bodyguard's compassionate blow smacks of romanticism among our ancient historians. At any rate, to prove beyond doubt that Mithridates was dead Pharnaces had his father's body embalmed and forwarded for Pompey's inspection along with the many more attractive gifts which were waiting for the proconsul when he reached Amisus.

Pompey's refusal even to look at the corpse was probably due to more subtle reasons than the incompetence of the amateurish embalmers whose failure to remove the brain had rendered the face almost unrecognizable. No doubt he felt that it was neither honourable nor dignified to gloat over the pathetic remains of his once great adversary, still less to humiliate them. And if, as Plutarch suggests, there was an element of superstition in his attitude and he was anxious 'to propitiate divine jealousy', Appian is correct in stressing Pompey's genuine admiration for this formidable enemy of Rome. Since the reputation of a conqueror stands in direct proportion to the stature of the conquered, it was also politic of Pompey to arrange a magnificent funeral at his own expense and have the body laid honourably to rest in the royal tombs of his ancestors at Sinope. As for Pharnaces' request to be allowed to rule 'either his paternal kingdom or the Bosporus alone', Pompey was happy to grant him the latter with the significant exception of Phanagoreia, 'whose inhabitants he proclaimed free and independent because they had been the first to resist Mithridates when he was recovering his strength, and because their having given the lead to others had been the cause of the final collapse'. But this was not the only reason. Undoubtedly Pompey was grateful to

Phanagoreia just as he was obliged to Pharnaces, whom he now rewarded with the title of 'Friend and Ally of the Roman People', but with a foresight which time would vindicate he was not prepared to place absolute trust in any son of Mithridates, even in the confinement of that Crimean kingdom. Even if Pharnaces had taken the initiative instead of waiting for Phanagoreia to show him the way, Pompey would still have looked for some local counterbalance to his power, and the establishment of a free city like Phanagoreia in the middle of a client kingdom was one of the subtleties of the extremely skilful settlement of the East which Pompey completed in the year following Mithridates' death.

Looked at on its merits, Pompey's organization of the East was no mere tying-up of loose ends from a patchwork of military adventures designed for self-glorification at the expense of the achievements of other generals whom he superseded. It was the culmination of a carefully planned and coherent exercise in empire-building which not only acquired the three new provinces of Pontus, Cilicia and Syria but also stabilized Rome's interests through the far greater area which had fallen under the sway of Kings Mithridates and Tigranes at the height of their powers. For the annexation of the three areas that combined most satisfactorily the criteria of wealth, accessibility by sea and organizational practicality could not be achieved in isolation from the vast regions of the interior, which also had commercial as well as strategical importance for Rome. Everywhere Pompey had to adapt his dispositions to a bewildering variety of local conditions and personalities ranging from the highly sophisticated urban communities of the Hellenistic cities to barbarian despots, who might be great feudal monarchs like Tigranes or petty chieftains of savage tribes that lacked even a semblance of civilization. All these multicoloured threads had somehow to be woven into one coherent web on the loom of Roman interest, and if the result was a work of administrative art quite amazing in its intricacy, it was no less remarkable for the speed with which it was completed.

After the ravages of two thousand years it is impossible to reconstruct every detail and subtlety of so vast a tapestry, but for Pontus at least we are fortunate in having the interested account of Strabo, who was born in the old royal capital of Amaseia and outlines the basic pattern which we can supplement with the fragments provided by other sources. But to appreciate the size of the problem which Pompey faced in Pontus it is best to begin with the size of the physical area. In so far as it is possible to attribute any degree of stability to the realm of a man like Mithridates, the basic kingdom stretched along the south coast of the Black Sea from Heracleia in the west to Colchis in the east and extended inland as far as Galatia, Cappadocia and Tigranes' Armenia. Its six-hundred-mile coastline was as long as Great Britain is tall (measured as the energetic crow flies from Land's End to John o'Groats), and its total area must have been well over forty thousand square miles, not all of which was suited to annexation by Rome on either economic or administrative criteria. Economically the most attractive regions for direct rule were the rich and fertile lowlands of the coastal plains and river valleys, which also carried the lucrative trade-routes which crossed the kingdom east–west from Armenia to Bithynia and more or less north–south from the Black Sea ports down through eastern Cappadocia to the Euphrates. Administratively it would have been impossible to annex the whole kingdom without revolutionizing the sacrosanct system of Roman provincial government: Rome's annually changing governors could be expected to supervise an existing substructure of local government but not to discharge the functions of a hereditary monarchy which had naturally discouraged local autonomy and kept the reins of government firmly in the royal hands through a centralized bureaucracy. What was needed was a flexible combination of direct and indirect rule of the sort which was to characterize the British Raj in India, and it says much for Pompey that he not only saw the need but possessed the ingenuity to interweave his planned urbanization of the economically attractive areas with an almost infinite variety of indirect rule elsewhere to produce an administrative pattern that was new to Roman imperialism.

To judge from Strabo's brief summary this was as easily done as said: 'When Pompey took over the kingdom after overthrowing Mithridates, he distributed the parts towards Colchis to the potentates who had fought on his side but divided the remainder into eleven city-states, which he added to the existing province of Bithynia. He then gave over to the descendants of Pylaemenes the position of king over certain of the Paphlagonians inhabiting the interior between Pontus and Bithynia, just as he gave over the Galatians to their hereditary tetrarchs.' But Strabo was not a historian, still less a biographer of Pompey. He was a geographer, and it is only by collecting his numerous other references to Pompey's dispositions as he proceeds with his travelogue and by adding to them the evidence of other sources both literary and non-literary that we can even begin to appreciate what lay behind his bald statement.

The giving of 'the parts towards Colchis' to potentates who had fought on Pompey's side was an administrative necessity explained by Strabo's account of the inhabitants of the maritime regions east of Sidene, tribes like the Tibareni, Chaldaei, Samni and Heptacometae. 'All were utterly savage,' he says, but evidently the degree of barbarism increased with orientation since he describes the most easterly, the Heptacometae, as 'even worse than the rest, dwellers in trees and towers who lived off the

flesh of wild animals and nuts and attacked all travellers, including three
maniples of Pompey's army which were once unfortunate enough to
enter their territory'. Such savage regions were obviously uncontrollable
by urban centres, and there was therefore no inducement to try to revive
the defunct coastal cities of Pharnacia and Trapezus as city-states.
Pompey's solution was to tie these regions down to local potentates who
were themselves made subject not to a Roman governor but to a reliable
client-king. This was the Galatian Deiotarus, to whom Pompey most
probably also gave Lesser Armenia once he had emptied it of its treasures
and destroyed its fortresses, for though Pompey had given Colchis to a
potentate named Aristarchus, just as he had restored Armenia to Tigranes,
he was not putting all his precious Pontic eggs in a basket with such
unreliable Eastern sides. Having found in Deiotarus a man whose personal
loyalty and obligations to himself made him a more trustworthy Friend
and Ally of the Roman People, he had no hesitation in handing over to
him the coastal regions of Pharnacia and Trapezusia along with Lesser
Armenia in order to interpose another cushion that would protect the
heart of the new province not only from the unruliness of local tribes
but against possible revivals of imperial ambitions among the more
powerful kingdoms further east. But if Pompey was happy to discard the
intractable coastal regions of north-east Turkey east of Sidene, he felt
very differently about the parallel regions of the interior which lay
behind the Paryadres mountains, particularly the valleys of the westward-
flowing Lycus and Iris rivers and the first hundred miles or so of the River
Halys. These rich and fertile regions were far too valuable both intrinsically
and as trade-routes for anything but direct rule, and since they lacked
the prerequisite urban centres of local government, Pompey created them.

Thinking back to the campaigns of 66 and 65 we can appreciate the
foresight with which Pompey had been preparing for the annexation of
Pontus from the moment he had driven Mithridates out of it. When he
had ordered the construction of Nicopolis on the border of Lesser
Armenia before advancing against Tigranes, it had seemed amply justified
as a monument to his victory over Mithridates and a useful place to
settle superannuated and wounded troops on his line of communication
with the coast. But set in the context of the organization of the new
Roman province, the foundation of Nicopolis assumes a much deeper
significance. Besides the obvious economic and strategic importance of
its situation in fertile lands on a lucrative trade-route at the eastern
border of the new province, it is now seen to be the most easterly of
Strabo's 'eleven city-states' among which Pompey divided the territory
which he had selected as suitable for direct rule. It was in fact the first
link in a chain of urban centres controlling the Lycus and Iris valleys,

and when he returned to the coast down the Lycus valley after his Albanian campaign of the following year, he forged two more out of Cabeira and Eupatoria, which he renamed Diospolis and Magnopolis. Between these three inland cities and the coastal Amisus he now parcelled out the whole of the Lycus valley throughout the river's hundred-mile course north-westwards, from Lesser Armenia to where it joins and becomes the Iris at Magnopolis and turns sharply north for another forty miles before reaching the sea.

For the rest of the Iris basin with its myriad other tributaries above Magnopolis the most obvious candidate for a local authority was the old royal capital of Amaseia, the birthplace both of Mithridates and of Strabo, who describes it in endearingly enthusiastic detail. As the hub of Mithridates' completely centralized administration it would have been the one place with a sufficiency of trained administrators; and if its con-version from a seat of royal bureaucracy to a city-state would have entailed something of a revolution in the administrative mentality, there was at least the administrative capacity to control much more than the surrounding plains. Consequently Pompey incorporated in its territory the whole of the Scylax valley to the river's origins on the borders of the Galatian Trocmi.

There remained a large wedge of attractive land east of the Scylax, south of the Lycus and down to the upper Halys to complete the eastern part of the new province. To administer those parts of this extensive area that were out of reach of Amaseia or the three cities of the Lycus valley Pompey established two more local authorities, one at Zela nearly thirty miles south of Amaseia, the other at Megalopolis which was to the south of the Halys, some sixty miles south-east of Zela and about the same distance south of Diospolis and south-west of Nicopolis. Zela was already established as a temple-city sacred to the goddess Anaitis and 'belonging for the most part to temple-slaves', and 'when Pompey organized it as one of his city-states after the overthrow of Mithridates', says Strabo, 'he urbanized it, settled the inhabitants within the walls, and added considerable territory to it'. Megalopolis on the other hand (whose name is an all-Greek version of Magnopolis as one might substitute *teleorama* for the hybrid *television*) sounds as though it was a completely new foundation like Nicopolis, which it also resembled in combining the functions of a centre of local government with the role of a frontier post guarding a valuable trade-route. A glance at the map shows its strategic importance on the main north–south line of trade and com-munication between Amisus and Tomisa on the Upper Euphrates, and its administrative area incorporated the whole of the old Pontic eparchies of Colopene and Camisene.

But having decided on a neat clockwise division of the eastern part of Roman Pontus between the seven city-states of Amisus, Magnopolis, Diospolis, Nicopolis, Megalopolis, Zela and Amaseia, Pompey showed his administrative flexibility by leaving virtually independent a tiny theocracy in the middle. This was Comana, a temple-city like Zela but sacred to the goddess Ma under whose High Priest the 'luxurious inhabitants waxed fat' from rich domains tilled by her six thousand slaves and from a lively trade in tourism and pilgrims. According to Strabo's account it sounds to have had more in common with Las Vegas than Lourdes, with the added attraction of sanctified prostitution which rapidly emptied the purses of merchants and off-duty soldiers who proved insatiably devout in religious observances until their money ran out. Pompey rapidly concluded that to deprive the many devotees of this easy path to virtue would have been no more sensible than to deprive Rome of a tithe of its revenues. He therefore made his own gift to the goddess of an extra piece of land some seven miles in perimeter but took care to appoint his own man as both high priest and governor. This arrangement had the further advantage of finding a rewarding role for Archelaus, the son of Mithridates' former general of that name who had begun as one of Rome's most formidable enemies and ended as her most stalwart friend. But the services of the father who had been 'greatly honoured both by Sulla and the Senate' were not Pompey's sole consideration in giving Comana to the son. The young Archelaus had also been helped by his friendship with Gabinius, and it was ironic that his present sponsor was destined to be his executioner less than a decade later when the luxurious theocracy had become too small for his growing ambition and he had sought a marriage alliance with Cleopatra of Egypt in defiance of the Syrian governor's wishes.

These were Pompey's arrangements for the eastern part of the new province, which was confined to the interior until it touched the sea beyond the Paryadres range in the region of the Jasonian promontory. Westwards from there the new province incorporated virtually the whole of the coast as far as Heracleia, beyond which the existing province of Bithynia continued Roman rule of the Black Sea coast as far as the Thracian Bosporus. But despite its great length, the annexation of the coastal region between Point Jasonium and Heracleia was made considerably easier by the existence of three great Hellenistic cities, Amisus, Sinope and Amastris. To each of these Pompey assigned large and contiguous territories except where he gave the Galatian king Deiotarus a western access to the sea through a strip of land in the lower part of the Halys valley, just as he had given him the coastal regions of Pharnacia and Trapezusia further east. Apart from this narrow Galatian strip

separating the Sinopian and Amisenian territories Pompey thus incorporated in his province an uninterrupted stretch of some 350 miles of the
Black Sea coast, and though we lack information on the allocation to
Amastris and Sinope, the detail which we have for Amisus reveals the
scale of these re-established republics.

Amisus now administered not only the Mithridatic eparchy of
Saramene in which it stood but extended westwards into that part of
Gazelonitis which it shared with Deiotarus and eastwards to incorporate
both Themiscyra and Sidene, beyond which Deiotarus again took over
with Pharnacia and Trapezusia. Taken together these new territories gave
Amisus a coastal plain some hundred miles in length, and when Strabo
described them in his *Geography* he might have been producing a
prospectus for the Promised Land, which indeed is how it must have
appeared to the eager investors in the great tax-farming companies of
Rome. Gazelonitis, for example, Strabo describes as 'everywhere level
and productive of everything, with a particularly fine woollen industry'.
And when he comes to Themiscyra, he is almost lost for superlatives with
which to portray this 'beautiful country ... so well-watered and well-
wooded ... its plain always lush and verdant, supporting great herds
of cattle and horses ... its arable land providing unlimited crops of
millet and sorghum ... its foothills yielding fruit all year round ... a
stranger alike to drought and famine'. It was not surprising that Pompey
was anxious to annex such an earthly paradise, and since these were
settled farmlands which did not have to contend with the savage tribes
of the more easterly coastal regions of Pharnacia and Trapezusia, he
could safely put them under the local authority of a revived city-state like
Amisus.

Although the coastal regions were Pompey's chief attraction among
the formerly Mithridatic possessions east of Amisus and he was happy to
leave the greater part of inland Paphlagonia under a client-king, there
was one interior region which he wished to bring under direct Roman rule,
and since its distance from the coast and the interposition of mountains
made it difficult to incorporate in the territories of the maritime states,
he divided it between two new cities. The first, appropriately named
Neapolis, was some forty miles north-west of Amaseia, and Pompey
made it the administrative centre for the rich area of Phazemonitis,
which was bounded on the west by the Halys and on the north by the
former eparchy of Gazelonitis (now shared between Amisus and King
Deiotarus). The second was another Pompeiopolis, founded some sixty
miles south of Sinope and about fifty miles up the valley of the Amnias
which flows due east into the Halys from its origins in the Olgassys
mountains of central Paphlagonia. The mountains themselves were left

to the Paphlagonians, but the fertile Amnias valley, bounded on the east by the Halys and by the territory of Sinope to the north, was not only intrinsically valuable but important as a continuation of the direct line of communication and trade which stretched overland from Bithynia in the west to Armenia in the east via Pompeiopolis, Neapolis, Magnopolis, Diospolis and Nicopolis.

But this is only part of the story. We may have pieced together the pattern of the political geography of the new province, but we have yet to discover how the city-states were themselves organized. With the exception of coastal Amisus and Sinope, which had gained a limited recent experience in self-government since 71 and 70 when Lucullus had reconstituted them as 'free and independent' states after long years of subjection to Mithridates, Pompey's new cities had to be taught not only self-government but the government of the large territories for which they were now to be responsible. Pompey gave them a constitution similar to that of the Republic but in a way that blended agreeably with the old Hellenic traditions. He admitted into the citizen-body not only the free inhabitants of the towns but all the free men in the territories assigned to them. The executive he entrusted to magistrates annually elected by the citizens from candidates who had to be at least thirty years of age, and he established a permanent council composed of ex-magistrates but subject to revision, as at Rome, by censors on carefully specified grounds. The whole legal apparatus down to the most minute detail he set out in an ordinance known as the *lex Pompeia*, which he proceeded to establish as the uniform constitution of all the cities of the combined province of Bithynia and Pontus that were to form the administrative substructure through which a Roman proconsul might be enabled to govern so vast an area. And if durability is a criterion of legislative success, we have the evidence of Dio that Pompeian constitutions were still in force at least as late as the early third century AD, by which time they were nearly a century older than the present constitution of the United States of America.

We have little information about Pompey's arrangements in Bithynia itself beyond the fact that he imposed the same constitutions on the city-states there as in Pontus and the possibility that while he divided the formerly royal lands among the cities for administrative purposes he kept them in the formal ownership of the Roman People and left the collection of their revenues to the *publicani*, who certainly seem to have been active there already. For Bithynia, unlike Pontus, had come into the possession of the Roman People in 74 by bequest of the last king, Nicomedes III, and existing provincial arrangements had only to be modified. All the same there was more to provincial organization than internal administration, and if existing Bithynia presented Pompey with less problems in this respect than new Pontus, their combination provided an enormous inland frontier to be safeguarded. Eastwards from the point where western Bithynia left the protective northern flank of the Roman province of Asia we find an amazing complexity of client-kingdoms which Pompey organized with a versatility that proved equal to the almost infinite variety of local conditions.

With the Paphlagonians, for example, he had been presented with the problem of large numbers of tribal chieftains with no central authority, and while the principle of division is all very well if you wish to rule, the stability of a peripheral area is often better secured by an agreement with one man than with a committee of equals who are as like as not to be opposites. In Paphlagonia therefore Pompey united all the petty principalities under a King Attalus of the Pylaemenid house which claimed descent from the leader of the Homeric Paphlagonians, and having created this throne he could reasonably expect its first grateful occupant to look after the interests of his patron. Similarly in Galatia he made Deiotarus king over a very much larger region, but here there was an even greater need for delicacy than in Paphlagonia. The man he had chosen was technically only a tetrarch of one of the three proud clans into which this Gallo-Grecian people was divided, namely the Tolistobogii, the Tectosages and the Trocmi. In other words Deiotarus was one of twelve equal princes who stood at the head of their incoherent nation, and while his distinguished services to Rome in the long struggle against Mithridates had marked him out as the obvious candidate for a client-kingship of the whole, Pompey would probably have found great difficulty in imposing his proposed unification on the three clans without the help of an unintended legacy from Mithridates himself. This was the weakening effect of a treacherous massacre of a large number of Galatian nobles, including several tetrarchs, which had taken place at Pergamum in 86. By leaving fewer sensitive dignities to be offended it had considerably eased Pompey's present abolition of the tetrarchate in all but name, for he now appointed a paradoxically single tetrarch to each of the three clans and acknowledged one of them, Deiotarus, as *primus inter pares* by giving him the title of king over large new territories. It was one of those situations where a little delicacy in the matter of title can preserve sufficient of the semblance of equality to reconcile supposed peers to their otherwise obvious inferiority.

To the south of the strip of southern Pontus which formed the corridor between Deiotarus' ancestral tetrarchate and his new eastern territories lay the sprawling and mangled mass of Cappadocia, a large inland kingdom which had deserved well of Rome and now received rewards appropriate to its exceptional loyalty. Cappadocia had been a united kingdom for some two centuries, and the present monarch had ruled as the Friend and Ally of the Roman People in more than name ever since his accession in 95. Where even the Galatian princes had collaborated with the seemingly unconquerable Mithridates in his westward imperialism, Ariobarzanes had preferred to lose his throne than his honour when he could resist no longer, and though he had seen his kingdom overrun by Mithridates and ravaged by Tigranes he had remained faithful to his independence and to his alliance with Rome. It was therefore a pleasant and easy duty for Pompey to reward him with not only the restoration of his ruined capital but valuable additions to his kingdom both to the east and west. To the east Ariobarzanes acquired the whole of Sophene, the kingdom on the far side of the Euphrates which Prince Tigranes had scorned in his anger at his father's restoration to Armenia: an area of great strategic and commercial importance on the trade-route that led south-east from Amisus via Zela, Megalopolis and Tomisa into Upper Mesopotamia. To the west Pompey extended the Cappadocian kingdom to incorporate the richest part of Lycaonia. The uncivilized southern portion he gave to a local chieftain who promised to control the Isaurian bandits in return for Roman recognition, but the more valuable region round Cybistra with its rich cornlands and valuable mines he also presented to Ariobarzanes. Here again he combined the demands of gratitude with Rome's own strategical and commercial interests, for this area incorporated the Cilician Gates, the pass by which trade and troops travelled between the old province of Asia and the new provinces of Cilicia and Syria through the mountain range known as the Cilician Taurus.

Cappadocia therefore protected the whole of the northern boundary of Level Cilicia, the richest and most valuable part of the second of the three new Pompeian provinces which combined with 'Asia' and Bithynia to bring nearly the whole of the coasts of Asia Minor and the Levant under the direct rule of Rome. As for Pompey's formal annexation of Cilicia, this had been a natural consequence of his war against the pirates, and its organization as a province had begun as early as 67, even earlier than the organization of Pontus which started with the foundation of Nicopolis late in 66. It was also much easier to organize than Pontus, at least in the Level part for which we have some evidence, because it already possessed a number of Hellenistic cities which had a tradition of self-government, and Pompey's task was one of renovation rather than origination. He had repopulated the urban centres with reformed pirates, pre-eminently of course the coastal city of Soli which he had renamed Pompeiopolis and refurbished on a scale appropriate to its new greatness.

But Soli had suffered so disastrously from Tigranes' ruthless deportation of its citizens to people Tigranocerta that it was over a year before Pompeiopolis could take its place as a new city, at least to judge from its coins which show that it adopted the year 65 as its new era in honour of its new founder. Other cities were re-established more quickly, and on the evidence of coins with eras dating from 67 we can add to Appian's list of Adana, Epiphaneia and Mallus at least three others, namely Zephyrium, Mopsuhestia and Alexandria. And there were others too, notably Tarsus which Pompey seems to have honoured by making it the provincial capital but evidently annoyed so much more by his glorification of Soli that it became an eager adherent of Caesar in the future Civil War.

But if the organization of Level Cilicia can be reconstructed at least in outline, it is impossible to say how Pompey organized Rugged Cilicia once he had dislodged all the pirates from their strongholds there. His destruction of all its fortresses and resettlement of many of its former inhabitants in the revived city-states to the east no doubt reduced the scale of the problem, but its abundant timber remained a valuable attraction, and it must have been provided with a governmental apparatus sufficiently effective both for the administration of its remaining inhabitants and to ensure against a relapse into its old evils. Then just as he had combined his new Pontus with the existing Bithynia to the west to make a continuous maritime province along some six hundred miles of the Black Sea coastline, so too he combined the two real Cilicias with the westward districts which had borne the quite unjustifiable name of 'Cilicia' before, a province which had been fairly fluid but basically seems to have included Pamphylia-Isauria, the Milyas, Pisidia and possibly Lycia too.

There were other similarities between the new coastal provinces of Bithynia-Pontus on the Black Sea coast and the enlarged Cilicia on the Mediterranean. Their eastern boundaries were similarly unsuitable for direct rule because of the intractability of their tribes, and in the same way that Pompey had secured eastern Pontus by giving it to the client-king Deiotarus, he likewise found a reliable local dynasty to take control of the area of the Amanus mountains which separated Cilicia from Syria and carried the equivalent east–west trade-route of southern Turkey through the so-called Syrian Gates. So important a line of communication could not be left unguarded any more than the eastern plains of the Cilician province could be left open to the raids of the mountain-robbers whose suppression by Afranius was an effective but temporary measure preparatory to Pompey's long-term solution of the problem. This he achieved by appointing a certain Tarcondimotus as toparch of this critical area, and as in the case of the Galatian Deiotarus the choice was a good one to judge from Cicero's description of him in 51 as 'our most loyal ally and the dearest friend of the Roman People beyond the Taurus'. While the full extent of Tarcondimotus' principality is not known, it is certain that it included the region of Castabala-Hieropolis, very probable that it stretched to the sea as far as Aegae, and likely that it also incorporated part of the territory of Rugged Cilicia, which would have given him a westerly coastal region analogous to that of Deiotarus in Pontic Gazelonitis and would help to explain how at least part of Rugged Cilicia was controlled.

By appointing a reliable guardian for the eastern borders of Cilicia Pompey had also ensured the north-west frontier of Syria, but he still needed other client-kingdoms for the northern and north-eastern borders of his third new province. For this reason he had let King Antiochus of Commagene feel the weight of Rome's heavy heel when he had first marched into Syria in 64, and having thus inculcated a healthy respect he now changed tactics and presented Antiochus with the city of Seleuceia on the eastern bank of the Euphrates to seal the new bond of friendship and alliance with Rome. It was a valuable gift because the city was opposite the royal capital of Samosata, which therefore secured for Antiochus (and thus indirectly for Rome) both sides of a river crossing that was as important strategically and commercially as Cappadocian Tomisa further north. And just as Pompey contrived to protect the eastern flank of his Pontic province with more than one layer of client-kingdoms, he similarly brought into his network of alliances King Abgarus of Osroene, a kingdom east of the Euphrates that would help to reinforce the eastern flank of Cilicia as well as the north-east corner of Syria in that vulnerable area before the river swings south-east and puts a useful barrier of desert between Parthian Mesopotamia and the heart of the third new Roman province.

In the Levant, as in Pontus, Pompey's concern had been to mould provinces out of those areas which conformed most satisfactorily to the criteria of wealth, ease of administration, accessibility and security. Although he had carried his conquest of Syria down into Judaea and was prevented from reaching Petra and the Red Sea only by the arrival of the news of Mithridates' death, he had had no more intention of bringing the whole area from Commagene to Egypt under direct Roman rule than of annexing the whole of the Mithridatic kingdom. Since so many of his arrangements were necessarily made *ad hoc* from personal experience, it is perhaps best to try to follow his march southwards through the eyes of Pompey the administrator just as we followed Pompey the general in the last chapter, though again we must beware of overemphasizing his concern with Judaea simply because of the greater amount of information provided by Josephus.

By the time he reached Antioch Pompey would have appreciated the administrative possibilities for northern Syria, which, unlike Pontus, already possessed large numbers of Hellenistic cities with a long enough tradition of civic organization and governmental experience to have survived the fourteen years of Armenian domination. One indeed, the city of Seleuceia-in-Pieria near the mouth of the Orontes, had actually held out against all Tigranes' efforts to reduce it during the whole of that time, and Pompey was so impressed that he declared it independent, not only in recognition of its heroic resistance but as a swift indication that Rome was as ready to reward as to punish. But if the decline of the Seleucid dynasty had encouraged the autonomy of the city-republics, it had also permitted the growth of petty dynasts elsewhere, and while Pompey was naturally predisposed to republican constitutions, he did not impose them everywhere. In the less ruly areas where a tough dynast was better suited to control an uncivilized population he would some-times confirm a local ruler in possession of a city or group of cities according to his assessment of the individual's ability and reliability. This was almost certainly what he did in the most northerly area of Cyrrhestice, and certainly what he did further south at Emesa and Arethusa, where he confirmed the rule of the Arab sheikh Sampsiceramus. At Lysias, on the other hand, he destroyed both the city and its ruler, Silas the Jew. Lysias was much too near to the heart of the old Seleucid kingdom to be left under a local dynast regardless of personal merits, and if Pompey was prepared to surround the old tetrapolis of Seleuceia, Antioch, Laodicea and Apamea with suitably reliable principalities on its inland sides, the tetrapolis itself was strictly reserved for republican city-states. And that was why he also destroyed the citadel of Apamea on his way up the Orontes.

South of the tetrapolis it was the coastal regions which invited annexa-tion by conforming most attractively to the four criteria. In the interior he noted the emergence of the great tribal kingdoms of the Ituraeans, Judaeans and Nabataeans as the three strongest powers from the Lebanon down to Egypt, but he began with no fixed designs on them beyond a little clipping of wings and an initially cordial invitation to their heads to tie themselves to the Roman interest as client-kings. How they were treated would depend on how they behaved, and when he advanced into the Ituraean territory between Libanus and Anti-Libanus he was gratified to find the High Priest of the Sun more than happy to face westwards in temporal affairs. This was Ptolemy, a Hellenized Arab who ruled his nation in two capacities from two capitals, the sacred city of Baalbek-

Heliopolis and the administrative centre of Chalcis further south down the valley of the Leontes. Being favourably disposed to this dynasty by Ptolemy's ready compliance with all his demands and the prompt payment of a thousand talents, Pompey confirmed him in almost all his possessions, which extended very considerably to the east of Anti-Libanus and therefore provided another usefully protective layer between the coveted coastal region and the Parthian empire beyond the Euphrates. And indeed it was fortunate for Ptolemy that he had so few possessions on the coast, for Pompey proceeded to behead his relation by marriage who ruled Tripolis and to destroy Botrys, Gigartus and various other Ituraean strongholds which had interfered with the peaceful commerce of prosperous Byblus, Beirut and the other great trading cities further south.

But taken all round the Ituraean kingdom suffered very little from Pompey's visitation, and it is interesting to speculate on what would have happened to the Jewish kingdom if it had been blessed with a similarly stable and compliant ruler. Almost certainly Pompey would still have forced the Jews to disgorge at least the coastal cities of the Maccabaean conquests south of Phoenicia and possibly several of their more recent acquisitions inland, if only to break up the formidable unity of this powerful kingdom. As it was, he was forced into a military conquest by right of which he did much more. He not only freed all the coastal cities from Dora down to Raphia for incorporation in his new province but did the same to an important group of cities between the Ituraean and the now shrunken Jewish kingdoms, notably Scythopolis, Pella, Dium, Gadara and Hippos. To these he added five others, possibly Canatha (formerly Ituraean), Philadelphia and Gerasa (formerly under a tyrant), and probably Abila and Capitolias, and thus he formed a decapolis which still existed in a modified form in the second century AD. For however much he might trust a local dynast, he recognized much advantage in 'free' communities which would tend to be good republican watch-dogs against the imperialist revivals of strong dynasties while avoiding the instability of weaker ones whose internal squabbles would require tiresome interventions by the nearest Roman governor. He also recognized that there was even more security if those city-states could be grouped into a block, and while it was not practical to make a whole Syrian province out of contiguous city-states as in Pontus, at least nine of the cities of the decapolis had adjoining territories. The exception was Canatha, which, like Damascus further north, was a more easterly city of great strategical and commercial importance, and it is significant that both these two, the former previously Ituraean, the latter taken from the Nabataean Arabs by Pompey's legates early in 64, were kept separate from the Ituraean kingdom despite the fact that Pompey was ready to entrust Ptolemy with part of formerly Jewish Gaulanitis to the north of Hippos. As for the rest of the pruning of the once great Jewish kingdom, he left intact only Judaea itself, Peraea, Galilaea and Samareitis, and having re-established free city-states to the north, east and west, he also liberated Marisa on its south-western boundary in what had been Jewish Idumaea.

But if the Ituraeans had come off fairly well and the Jews very badly from Pompey's rearrangements, the third and most southerly of the kingdoms, that of the Nabataean Arabs, came off best of all, not least because Pompey himself was recalled to Pontus before he could reach Petra. Again it is interesting to speculate on what would have happened if he had been able to complete his projected journey to the Red Sea, and the probability is that the Nabataean Aretas would have followed the conciliatory example of the Ituraean Ptolemy, especially after seeing how effectively the Romans had dealt with the Jewish opposition. But when King Aretas saw that it was only the legate Scaurus who was coming against him, he seems to have assumed a defiant attitude in reliance on the formidable natural defences of his rock-hewn capital, which could be entered only through a narrow gorge. It was only a matter of time before the Roman army was suffering so severely in that desolate and inhospitable terrain that Scaurus was forced to send back to Jerusalem for supplies. These the sycophantic Hyrcanus sent at once, but even more usefully he sent them under the command of his friend and adviser Antipater, for Antipater was also a close personal friend of Aretas and had secured his help for the restoration of Hyrcanus before the Romans had arrived on the Jewish scene in 64. Here then was the ideal intermediary to extricate Scaurus and Aretas from a mess that was embarrassing to both and advantageous to neither. Scaurus had no more desire to see the secrets of impregnable rose-red cities than to reach the Red Sea, but since the Romans could not be seen to lose face he sent Antipater to talk Aretas into a gesture of submission that would save everyone a great deal of trouble and keep the Nabataean kingdom intact. After all, if Aretas had proved able to defend his capital indefinitely, he could not have saved his northern possessions, and Antipater soon persuaded him to request the Friendship and Alliance of the Roman People and pay a modest indemnity of three hundred talents, which was cheap as the price of retaining even the cities east of the Dead Sea which he had recently acquired from Hyrcanus.

These were the arrangements for the southern part of Pompey's third new province, the whole of which basically comprised most of the Mediterranean littoral from the Egyptian border to the Gulf of Issus, a batch of city-states between the Jewish and Ituraean kingdoms, and a

wider area in the north of Syria beyond Phoenicia. They were mainly
networks of cities which Pompey had 'freed' from the various kingdoms,
though of course there were as many *de facto* degrees of freedom for
cities as there were of independence for client-kings. Even complete
exclusion from the Roman province did not necessarily entail exclusion
from Roman taxation as the Jews discovered to their cost, and similarly
the often considerable local autonomy of a city-republic within the
province did not mean that it could keep all its revenues any more than
that it could legislate in important matters against the will of the Roman
governor. True freedom was a privilege enjoyed only by a very few
special cases such as Seleuceia near the mouth of the Orontes, the
Phoenician cities of Tyre and Sidon, or Ascalon in the far south, all of
which remained completely outside formal Roman authority. But even
the circumscribed freedom of the cities incorporated in the Roman province was not without its blessings. For many it meant a new lease of
life, and if Pompey's hurried departure from Syria meant that he put in
hand the reconstruction of only one city, Gadara, it was his achievement
to have organized and authorized a general programme of urban
restoration which was left to successive governors of Syria, notably
Gabinius, to put into operation.

Before we leave Syria and follow Pompey back to Amisus where he
spent the winter of 63-2 completing his organization of the Pontic
province and its periphery, it is worth pausing to ask why he chose to
restore Gadara before all other Syrian cities. The answer is that Gadara
was the birthplace of Pompey's freedman Demetrius, who was a proto-
type of the rich and powerful freedmen of the early Roman emperors.
He was the invaluable personal assistant of a proconsul temporarily
responsible for the whole of the East, and not surprisingly this put him
in a position of great power. It was Demetrius who would arrange the
day's programme of visits and audiences, organize the streams of visitors
and suppliants, screen the piles of correspondence, and act as Pompey's
memory when information was required at a moment's notice. And
however devoted he might be to his patron's interest, his position of
confidence with the arbiter of so many Eastern destinies made him the
recipient of generous gifts, whether he chose to allow himself to be
influenced by them or not. Consequently Demetrius returned to Italy a
great deal richer than he had left it, and whereas Pompey himself continued to maintain a relatively modest town-house, his freedman fore-
shadowed the extravagances of Pallas, Narcissus and Polyclitus by
purchasing 'the very pleasantest suburbs of Rome, the finest places of
entertainment, and the enormously luxurious gardens which were called
"Demetrian" after him'.

But Demetrius was not the only employee to have done well from the rapid growth of the Eastern branch of Rome's imperial business. While key-executives like Gabinius, Scaurus, Metellus and Afranius will also have received gifts from grateful clients, the official profit-sharing scheme was not confined to top management and Pompey's private secretaries. By the time Pompey was ready to begin the long journey home from Amisus in 62 his accountants had prepared the financial results for the last five years and a balance-sheet which showed an enormous and immediately distributable cash surplus of some 584 million sesterces or 24,333 talents. Of this he decided to take back 200 million sesterces to Rome but he distributed the whole of the remaining sixteen thousand talents to his army, not as back-pay but as a profit-sharing bonus on top of the regular wages and previous incidental gratuities such as Tigranes' lavish distribution. Each private soldier received six thousand sesterces with appropriately higher sums for the higher ranks, and if the total of 384 million sesterces seems an excessively large distribution com-pared with the 200 million remitted to Rome, we must remember that this was only a distribution of cash-in-hand. The Roman Senate was presented with income projections showing enormous increases in yearly revenues from tribute and taxes, and if forward cash-flow from inter-national operations was a closed book to the average Roman citizen, even the humblest appreciated the imminent increase in bread and circuses, while the more business-minded equestrians could look forward to handsome profits from farming the taxes of the rich new areas which Pompey had opened up to them.

As Pompey began to march slowly westwards through Asia Minor to the Aegean coast in the spring of 62, Plutarch tells us that he 'proceeded with increasing pomp and magnificence'. Exactly what route he followed is not known, but the probability is that he travelled through Bithynia, to which he had now joined Pontus, and entered the province of 'Asia' in Mysia, probably via Miletoupolis where an inscription names him 'Saviour and Benefactor'. From there he will have entered the Troad, where another inscription seems to confirm what we might have guessed, that he visited Ilium on the Hellespont to enjoy the sensation of satisfac-tion which Agamemnon had felt after the fall of Troy. But if Pompey also reflected on the dire results of Agamemnon's hubristic pride, he showed no signs of humility as he continued his victorious progress down the Aegean coast. We next hear of him at Mytilene on the island of Lesbos, where Plutarch tells us that he attended a contest of poets whose sole theme was the greatness of his exploits. He was also greatly taken with the theatre there, and since he had in mind to adorn the imperial capital with a permanent monument to his greatness, 'he ordered sketches and plans of it to be made in order that he might build one like it in Rome, only much larger and grander'. He also granted Mytilene its freedom for no better reason than to please Theophanes, the official historian of his campaigns, who had been born there. How many other cities he visited we cannot be sure, but although Appian tells us that he embarked for Greece at Ephesus, Plutarch's reference to his visit to Rhodes suggests that he travelled down the whole of the coast of Asia Minor from north to south before crossing the Aegean. Rhodes was already a free city in recognition of its indomitable resistance to Mithridates' invasion of Roman Asia, but there were no doubt many other benefactions which Pompey could confer on the town besides giving a talent to each of its philosophers, whose wordy disputations gave him a cultural experience that he would probably have paid twice as much to be excused.

Whether Pompey sailed straight to mainland Greece from Ephesus or stopped at any of the Cycladic islands on the way is again unknown, nor do we have any information for his activities on the mainland beyond Plutarch's statement that he sojourned once more at Athens, where he gave fifty talents towards the restoration of the city. All we can be sure of is that he must have visited far more cities than we hear about on a journey from Pontus to Italy that began in the spring and ended only in December, though there is at least one reason to believe that by far the greater part of that time was spent east of the Aegean. For it was probably in Greece that Pompey finally became certain of a personal calamity which 'that divine agency whose concern is always to mingle a portion of evil with Fortune's most great and splendid gifts had long been secretly planning in order to make his homecoming a bitter one'. He had hoped, says Plutarch, to set foot in Italy 'not only with a reputation more glorious than any other man but also to find his family as eager to see him as he was to see them'. As it was, he returned as a cuckold.

Although he had treated all rumours of Mucia's infidelity with contempt while he had been far away, he could now no longer ignore the conclusive evidence which he received when he was 'nearer Italy', which probably means in Greece. What this evidence was we do not know, for while Plutarch says that it is all stated in Cicero's correspondence, the relevant letters have not survived except for one which mentions to his friend Atticus that everyone heartily approved the divorce. As for Pompey's own feelings on the subject, Plutarch tells us that he threw a blanket of silence over the whole affair and 'neither wrote at the time nor afterwards declared the reasons why he put Mucia aside'.

But it was not Pompey's divorce that was the principal talking-point in Rome when news arrived in December that he was about to cross the Adriatic with his victorious army. 'All sorts of rumours had travelled to Rome before him,' says Plutarch, 'and there was much commotion there as though he was certain to lead his army on the capital and establish a monarchy.' Such was the legacy of his pupillage to Sulla, and Crassus is unlikely to have been the only prominent senator to scuttle out of Rome with his children and money, though Plutarch suggests that the latter's action may have been prompted 'less by a real fear than as a means of lending credence to the calumny and making men's hatred and envy of Pompey more acute'. But Pompey had no sooner set foot on Italian soil at Brundisium than he dispelled all anxieties by the immediate disbanding of his army, an action which Dio regarded as the crowning glory of his career of achievements in the East, 'the greatness of which was unrivalled by any earlier Roman':

For here was a man who possessed enormous power both by land and sea. He had furnished himself with vast wealth from his captives. He had secured the firm friendship of large numbers of kings and potentates, and nearly all the states which he had governed were devoted to him by reason of his benefactions. In short, he had all the means at his disposal to take possession of Italy and make himself sole master of Rome. But he chose not to do it. Instead he dismissed his forces at once and on his own initiative, without waiting for any law to be passed by the Senate or people, because he understood that men held the careers of Marius and Sulla in abomination and he did not wish the Romans to fear even for a few days that they should undergo any of the same experiences.

The wave of relief and delight which swept over Italy with this news brought Pompey to Rome on the very crest of popularity. 'When the cities saw Pompey the Great travelling along unarmed and with only a few close friends as though returning from a foreign holiday,' says Plutarch, 'the people everywhere streamed forth to show their good will and escorted him back to Rome in such huge numbers that if he had entertained any revolutionary designs, he would have had no need of the army which he had disbanded.' But of course Pompey entertained no revolutionary intentions whatever. He had never sought an autocracy, and if his early career had been highly irregular and he had once used an army to blackmail the Senate into awarding him the command against Sertorius, even then his ambitions had never compromised his republicanism. If he wanted to be the greatest man in the state, he never wanted to be above the state, and the manner of his return to Rome in December 62 should have been sufficient proof of his constitutional *bona fides* to earn his acceptance among even the most conservative and cautious of the senatorial nobility. That it did not mark a further deterioration in the incurably diseased condition of a governmental system that was sickening rapidly towards another series of convulsions that would be the death of the Republic.

11
TRIUMPH AND
ANTICLIMAX

How happy it would have been for Pompey to have ended his
life at this point, up to which he had enjoyed the good
fortune of Alexander; for the future brought him only success
that made him hateful and failure that was irreparable.
Plutarch, *Life of Pompey*, 46.1

On 28 September 61, the day before his forty-fifth birthday, Pompey
began to celebrate the most magnificent triumph ever witnessed by Rome,
in happy ignorance of the change of fortune through which exactly
thirteen years later, on the eve of his fifty-eighth birthday, 'the man who
had found no more land to conquer would find none to bury him'. Ever
since he had returned from the East in the previous December the preparations had been in hand for a spectacle so grand that it lasted two
days, though Plutarch insists that 'even this was insufficient time to display
much of what had been prepared, and there was enough left over to
dignify a second triumph'. For Pompey was no ordinary *triumphator*.
'Others may have celebrated three triumphs before him,' says Plutarch,
'but Pompey was the first to celebrate his third triumph over the third
continent, for having celebrated his first over Africa and his second over
Europe, he was now triumphing over Asia' – with the result, adds
Velleius, 'that the three divisions of the world had become so many monuments to his greatness'. Moreover the third division of the world was
incomparably the richest. Pompey's conquests in the East had not only
trebled the annual income of the Roman empire but brought him a
personal haul of money and valuables which made even the wealth of
Crassus seem a very modest competence by comparison. Ten years ago,
when Pompey had returned from Spain, it had been Crassus who had had
the money to make his *ovatio* and other celebrations for his victory over
Spartacus a more lavish series of entertainments than Pompey's proper
triumph over Gaul and Spain. Now it was Pompey to whom money was
no object, and he was determined to give Rome a spectacle that would

eclipse anything in living memory and reflect a personal *dignitas* so dazzling that it would blind all beholders to the claims of lesser rivals for the role of first citizen of the Republic.

Long before dawn on the great day the triumphal route was packed with citizens who had been up all night to secure the best positions. Many will have chosen the slopes of the Capitoline Hill up which the procession climbed to its goal, the Temple of Jupiter Best and Greatest where the *triumphator* sacrificed and dedicated appropriate spoils to the guardian of Rome's empire. Others will have preferred to see the ceremonial entry to the city through the Triumphal Gate, which had proved too narrow for the elephants which Pompey had brought back from Africa to pull his chariot in his first triumph in 79. And these were only two of the best places on the route along which the magistrates and Senate led the great procession from the Campus Martius to the Capitol round the Circus Maximus, through the Velabrum, and up the Sacred Way.

After the magistrates and senators came the vast array of spoils and captives preceded by great placards proclaiming all the nations over which Pompey was triumphing, any one of which would have been enough to deserve a triumph of its own. According to Plutarch they listed 'Pontus, Armenia, Cappadocia, Paphlagonia, Media, Colchis, Iberia, Albania, Syria, Cilicia, Mesopotamia, the regions of Phoenicia and Palestine, Judaea, Arabia, and all the power of the pirates which he had overthrown both by sea and land', and the fourteen nations named were possibly the ones that were represented by allegorical statues when he opened his great theatre five years later. Then came impressive statistics, both military and financial: 'Among these peoples there were taken not less than a thousand strongholds, nearly nine hundred cities and eight hundred pirate-ships, while thirty-nine new cities were founded'; 'Whereas public revenues from taxes had been 200 million sesterces, a further 340 million sesterces would accrue from the new additions to the city's empire, and Pompey was also bringing into the Treasury in coined money and vessels of gold and silver 20,000 talents [480 million sesterces] besides the money which he had given to his troops, of which even the lowest received six thousand sesterces.' But even for those who could read them these gigantic figures were meaningless. Everyone wanted to see the tangible evidence of captives and spoils, and while the statistics had produced exclamations of admiration from those who wished to show off their superior education to illiterate neighbours, there was open-mouthed astonishment all round at the glittering spectacle which now unfolded before them.

The stage-management of the show was masterly. Every nation listed in the triumph was represented by distinguished captives or hostages, none of them bound and all most gorgeously arrayed in their national costumes. Placards identified them, sculptured trophies and paintings depicted all the main incidents in Pompey's campaigns against them, and great heaps of plunder and arms bore witness to their wealth and power. From the pirate campaigns came wagon-loads of the bronze beaks and figure-heads of the captured ships, piles of captured weapons and an impressive selection of the pirate-kings, including the two Cretan leaders Panares and Lasthenes. Their presence showed that no degree of superiority in Pompey's achievements was great enough to prevent his resenting even the relatively minor victories of others, for though Panares and Lasthenes had formerly surrendered to him, they had been captured by Metellus. But just as Pompey had been unable to resist claiming an unmerited share in the glory of Crassus' victory over Spartacus ten years before, so he had used a tribune to prevent these two Cretans from marching in the belated Cretan triumph which Metellus had at last been allowed to celebrate in the previous year. Their appearance in his own procession gave Pompey an excuse to include the wretched island of Crete on at least one of the inscriptions listing his infinitely greater and more genuine achievements, which would have been impressive enough if they had been limited to 'the liberation of all coasts from the pirates and the restoration of the command of the seas to the Roman People'. And yet the trophies of the Pirate War of 67, splendid though they were, formed only one small constellation among the galaxy of spoils and potentates which represented the Eastern campaigns of the following four years.

According to Appian there were 324 captives or hostages representing the nations 'conquered or subjugated' by Pompey, before whose chariot 'there now marched the satraps, sons and generals of the kings he had fought'. From the Transcaucasian expedition there came leaders of the chastened Heniochi and Achaeans, three Scythian queens, three chiefs of the Iberians, others from Albania, and Prince Olthaces of Colchis, who was perhaps an ousted predecessor or hostage of King Aristarchus whom Pompey had set on the throne of the Land of the Golden Fleece. From the client-kingdoms south of Pontus there were representatives of Cappadocia and Commagene, and from the Syrian campaign marched the wretched Aristobulus, former King of the Jews. But the most glittering prizes in the collection were naturally the exhibits from the conquests of the two arch-enemies Mithridates and Tigranes. As neither of these defeated monarchs could be present in person, the former because he was dead, the latter because he was now ruling the core of his conquered kingdom as a client of Rome, they were represented by statues of them-

selves and by living relatives. From Armenia Tigranes' unhappy son
strode forward with as much arrogance as he could muster from the
sense of desperation which he shared with the equally irredeemable
Aristobulus, and behind him came one of his father's wives, a bejewelled
Oriental queen whose brighter prospects meant that she no doubt
enjoyed the admiration of the gaping crowds a great deal more than the
humiliated and hopeless prince. But splendid as the Armenian contingent
undoubtedly was with its prince and queen and generals in their grandest
ceremonial uniforms, even this was eclipsed by the brilliance of the display
of Pontic royalty and treasures that had been so painstakingly prepared
to magnify the conqueror of the king who had been Rome's most powerful and persistent enemy in the East for the last thirty years.

The centre-piece of the Pontic exhibition was a gigantic statue of
Mithridates himself, eight cubits high and made of solid gold. Even on
the minimum measure for the cubit it was well over double life-size, and
as it gleamed in the sun it reflected all the pride of a monarch who had
been larger than life in the minds of a whole generation of Romans.
With it came Mithridates' throne and sceptre and, to point the comparison which was the theme of the whole display, the couch of King
Darius I, the greater ancestor of the Persian monarch whose empire had
been conquered by Alexander. There were also two silver statues, one
of Mithridates, the other of his ancestor Pharnaces I who had ruled
Pontus in the earlier part of the second century, and all manner of rich
treasures, chariots and litters heavily ornamented with silver and gold,
palatial furniture, exquisite jewellery and arms of every conceivable
description, not to mention a gleaming heap of 75 million drachmas in
silver coin. And amid all this flotsam and jetsam from the wreck of their
family fortunes were paraded the living representatives of the mighty
fallen – five sons of Mithridates bearing the evocative names of
Artaphernes, Cyrus, Oxathres, Darius and Xerxes, two daughters named
Orsabaris and Eupatra, and a great many governors and generals
including the famous Menander, commander of the formidable Pontic
cavalry.

By the time the jostling crowds had gaped in amazement at this seemingly endless parade of wealth and power complete with sculptured and
pictorial representations of the kings in battle, flight and surrender, they
were in a suitable frame of mind to adore the conquering hero himself,
whose last and most splendid trophy had reminded them of his previous
conquests by an allegorical representation of the three continents of the
inhabited world. This was the supreme moment, the appearance of the
Roman Alexander whose conquests in the East had now justified the
surname of 'Great' which he had been given in civil war at a time when

his only resemblance to the great Macedonian had been facial. Even the cloak which Pompey was wearing was said to have belonged to Alexander, 'if anyone can believe it', says the sceptical Appian. His chariot, pulled by four white horses, was studded with gems and precious stones, and as he stood erect in his triumphal regalia a slave came behind, holding over his laurelled head the *triumphator*'s crown of gold. So magnificent was his appearance and so skilful the stagecraft which had preceded it that even a blind man would have had no difficulty in following Pompey's progress. The cheers of the crowd, increasingly wild with excitement at the increasing splendour of the procession, now rose to a terrific crescendo of applause at the approach of the *triumphator*, and behind him came his victorious army, reassembled especially for the occasion and providing a demonstration of military power as awe-inspiring as it was spectacular. First came the chief commanders, some mounted, others on foot, and then regiment after regiment of cavalry and infantry, their arms and armour resplendent in the autumn sunshine as they followed the eagles which they had carried further East than any Romans before them. Having seen the harvest, the Roman people were now seeing the war-machine which had reaped it for them, and it was clear how helpless Rome would have been if Pompey had not outgrown his schooling as Sulla's pupil.

Although Velleius, Plutarch, Pliny and Appian all mention that the triumph lasted two days they do not tell us how it was divided, and it is frequently assumed that the procession itself was split between 28 and 29 September. It has been argued, for example, that the Senate and magistrates could have processed to the Capitol with the placards, trophies and spoils on the first day but that Pompey himself did not enter the city until the second, his own birthday, with the parade of captives and the army. But there is absolutely no evidence for such a division in our sources. On the contrary, Pliny's reference to 'the triumph which Pompey led on 28 September' indicates his personal presence on the first of the two days just as clearly as his other reference to the occasion mentions the carrying of spoils on the second, 'which was Pompey's own birth-day, 29 September'. And while it is true that Pliny could well have been writing loosely because his interest was that of a natural historian, it remains *a priori* improbable that the procession itself was spread over two days. A triumphal procession was by nature coherent, and a *triumphator* who so obviously wished to show himself a pillar of the republican establishment would scarcely have insulted the Senate and magistrates by letting them lead no one to the Temple on the first day any more than he would have offended his army by leaving the military parade to the second day. Nor is it easy to believe that he would have separated himself from the spoils any more than from the captives. After all, the tangible profits, which were to be kept, were more important than the captives and hostages, most of whom were to be returned. Moreover there is one unusually compelling intuitive reason for supposing that Pompey marched in formal triumph on 28 rather than 29 September. His whole career had been one of unprecedented greatness at an early age. He had celebrated two triumphs before he had even become a senator, one in his mid-twenties, the other in his mid-thirties, and when he had become consul at the age of thirty-five it was seven years before the legal minimum age and after holding none of the more junior magistracies of the official senatorial career. All this had been stressed to great effect by Cicero in his speech supporting the Manilian Law which had given Pompey his Eastern command in 66, and though a hero who was now in his mid-forties was scarcely an infant prodigy, the desired comparison with Alexander the Great clearly required him to be as young as possible when his comparable achievements were celebrated. Plutarch indeed criticizes other writers for trying to force the Alexandrian comparison by claiming that Pompey was still less than thirty-four, 'though in fact', he adds erroneously, 'he was nearly forty'. In fact if Pompey entered the city in triumph on 28 September 61 he was forty-four when he celebrated his third triumph over the third continent of the inhabited world; if he waited until the following day he was forty-five, and thus one year further from the tender age of thirty-two at which Alexander had died at the zenith of his greatness.

On the assumption that the whole procession was completed on 28 September, the second day of the celebration was most probably given over to festivities, sacrifices and a great exhibition. It was the Roman people's opportunity to absorb the magnitude of their general's achievement before the valuables were dispersed to the various temples and treasuries, and while there were probably fresh diversions in the way of military parades and entertainments, there had been so many things to see on the first day and so many more which had not found room in the procession that a static display on the second day would have been a very suitable way of consolidating the memory of the first. Apart from the major exhibits there were all the trophies which Plutarch says were 'as numerous as all the battles in which Pompey had been victorious in person or through his legates'. According to Dio each one was a work of art in itself, 'all most beautifully arranged to represent all his achievements down to the smallest detail', and among them stood the greatest trophy of all, 'decked out in the most costly fashion and bearing the inscription that it was the trophy of the whole world'. By means of these trophies with their statues, pictures and inscriptions the people in whose name all this had been done could trace the whole course of events from the Pirate War down to the death of Mithridates. They could experience for themselves something of the reality behind the official dispatches and cold statistics. They could look again at the brazen beaks of the pirate-ships and the piles of captured arms, or if they wanted an even better impression of the scale of the enemy's armament, they could go down to the harbour and see for themselves some of the seven hundred undamaged warships which Pompey had had brought into port and moored there for public inspection. They could follow in pictures and tableaux every detail of the campaigns against Mithridates and Tigranes, not only the great battles but such episodes as the siege of Mithridates and his flight by night. They could even take vicarious pleasure in the end of the arch-enemy himself, 'depicted', says Appian, in all the ghoulish detail of his last moments, 'surrounded by representations of the daughters who chose to die with him and by figures of the sons and daughters who had died before him'. And when they had had their fill of vicarious pleasure in following the failing fortunes of their foes in war, they could glut their curiosity about the distant peoples who were now more or less subservient to the empire of Rome.

Like the Great Exhibition of AD 1851 the second day of Pompey's triumph could well have been designed to bring an appreciation of their empire to its rulers, the bulk of whom would never be able to go and see it for themselves. Nations which had been nothing but names to the vast majority of the people of Rome were now brought to life in the imperial capital by statues of their gods in barbaric array, their arms and armour, their national costumes, the rare and precious treasures of their royal courts, the costly merchandise and strange products of their lands. From one fortress alone Appian tells us that Pompey had taken so great a store of palatial furniture that it had taken a whole month to remove – an inventory including 'some two thousand goblets of onyx welded with gold, complete imbibers' sets of cups, wine-coolers and drinking-horns, elegant couches and chairs, bridles for horses and trappings for their breasts and shoulders, all encrusted with precious stones and gleaming with gold'. There was ebony from India and balsam trees from the royal gardens of Judaea, both new to Roman triumphs according to Pliny. The former had ranked with ivory in the tribute which the Sudanese had paid to the kings of Persia, the latter produced 'a scent so exquisite that all other perfumes were as nothing compared'.

Jewelled rings were another innovation in a Roman triumph, for though Sulla's stepson Scaurus had possessed a collection of gemstones, Pliny tells us that it was Pompey who first made them fashionable in Rome by bringing home the ring-cabinet of Mithridates and dedicating it to Jupiter on the Capitol. And he did the same for pearls, which also appear in lavish quantities among the other luxuries which Pliny selects from the official records of the triumph. There was a gaming-board complete with a set of pieces, the board measuring two feet by three, made out of two types of precious mineral and carrying on top a gold moon of thirty pounds' weight. There were three gold dining-couches, enough gold vessels inlaid with gems to fill nine display-stands, gold figures of Minerva, Mars and Apollo, and no less than thirty-three pearl crowns. For the king who preferred a more substantial hedge against inflation there was a square mountain of gold entwined by a golden vine and supporting deer, lions and every variety of fruit; and for the queen who had everything there was a beautiful sundial sitting on top of a grotto of the finest pearls. Pompey also brought the first murrhine ware to Rome, elegant bowls and cups made out of fluorspar which became so highly prized in Pliny's own day that a single murrhine cup of only three pints' capacity changed hands for 70,000 sesterces. Petronius paid 300,000 sesterces for one ladle, and Nero outdid everyone else by paying a million for a single bowl. But it was the introduction of pearls for which the far from puritanical Pliny so roundly condemns Pompey, who exhibited in his triumph a portrait of his own head rendered entirely in pearls. 'There it was,' scorns Pliny, 'that portrait so pleasing with its curl of hair swept back from the forehead, that noble head revered through all the nations of the earth – that portrait, I say, was rendered in pearls! Truly it was austerity that had been defeated and extravagance that celebrated its triumph that day!' And as he continues to splutter in indignation at what he obviously considered as disgraceful an excess as Agamemnon's fatal trampling of the purple with which Clytaemnestra tempted Providence, he could not help seeing it as an unhappy omen of Pompey's own fate: 'that head,' he wrote, 'so ominously displayed without its body in Oriental wealth, bore a meaning that could not be mistaken' – a macabre reference to the beheading of Pompey in Egypt exactly thirteen years later.

But it is a curious fact about omens that they are recognized after the event, and if anyone at the triumph of September 61 had suggested that the conqueror of the inhabited world could ever suffer so wretched a fate, he would have been laughed to scorn by the witnesses of a display of greatness that seemed as unassailable as it was unparalleled. And after the triumph, when the treasures had been dispersed and all the hostages and captives except Aristobulus and Tigranes were being sent home in happy disregard of the usual custom of putting them to death, Pompey had the satisfaction of knowing that Rome would have more permanent reminders of his achievements. Greatest among these was to be a new theatre which he was planning for the Campus Martius, a palace of entertainment which would associate his name permanently with pleasure and detract from the glory of whoever happened to put on a show there. For the beauty of a theatre was that it could bear his own name, and though he was planning other public works to the glory of the gods, he could not help congratulating himself on the happy thought of making his biggest gift to Rome a building more secular than sacred. All the same, the gods did very well out of Pompey. Besides the magnificent dedications to the temple of Jupiter on the Capitol, he planned a temple to Venus the Victorious to attach to his theatre, one of Hercules to house a magnificent statue, and one to Minerva, where his offerings would not have to appear alongside those of any other *triumphator*. This last was also the fulfilment of a vow which he had made before he began his campaigns, and it was probably in this temple that he set up the following dedication, which comes from Diodorus and appears to be one of the more authentic in detail of all the inscriptions and claims which our sources preserve:

Pompey the Great, son of Gnaeus, Imperator, having freed the coasts of all the inhabited world and all islands within the bounds of Ocean from the war with the pirates – being the same who delivered the besieged kingdom of Ariobarzanes, Galatia and all the lands and eparchies lying beyond it, Asia and Bithynia; who gave protection to Paphlagonia and Pontus, Armenia and Achaea, also Iberia, Colchis, Mesopotamia, Sophene and Gordyene; who brought into subjection Darius, king of the Medes, Artoles [sic], king of the Iberians, Aristobulus, king of the Jews, Aretas, king of the Nabataean Arabs, Syria bordering on Cilicia, Judaea, Arabia, the province of Cyrene, the Achaeans, the Jozygi, the Soani, the Heniochi and the rest of the tribes along the sea-coast between Colchis and the Maeotic Lake and their kings to the number of nine, and all the nations that dwell between the Black and the Red Seas; who extended the boundaries of the empire to the boundaries of the earth; who secured and in some cases increased the revenues of the Roman People – he, by confiscation of the statues and the rest of the images set up to their gods, as well as taking other treasures from the enemy, has dedicated to the goddess 12,060 pieces of gold and 307 talents of silver.

Once the glorious two days of the triumph were over it was the dreary debris littering the streets that more accurately reflected the political anti-climax which followed Pompey's victorious return. The military genius who had conquered the three divisions of the world now found himself still something of an amateur in the petty political battles of Rome. On campaign he had been his own master, in full control of the means to achieve his clearly defined ends. In Rome he was one of a committee of peers, either stifling in their mediocrity or active in personal enmities which held the highest priority in their attitude to any proposal. And it must have been more than a little deflating for the Roman Alexander to find that other men had profited more by his prestige while he had been away than he was able to do himself now that he was back.

Perhaps the prize example of what had been achieved by a clever manipulation of Pompey's absent prestige was Marcus Cicero's elevation to the headship of state in the elections of 64. By his successful defence of many influential senators in court and by promoting the business interests of his own equestrian class Cicero had reached the praetorship in 66, but this was the highest magistracy to which a non-noble could reasonably hope to aspire. The consulship had long been regarded as the hereditary prerogative of the *nobiles*, the inner aristocracy of men who could already claim a consul in the family, and as Quintus Cicero wrote in the *Short Guide to Electioneering* which he addressed to his brother in 64, 'men of consular rank who have not risen to the position of their ancestors will not wish to be surpassed by you, and even among the people there is a widespread aversion to ennobling a self-made man'. But if Quintus' little handbook (whether authentic or not) gives us an invaluable insight into the foul tactics of Rome's typically dirty political game, it taught our aspiring Cicero nothing that he did not already know. He had thrown the full weight of his advocacy behind the plebiscite that had given Pompey his command in the East; he had undertaken the defence of the Bill's promoter when he had been brought to trial; and with his continuing glorification of Pompey in the next two years he had followed Quintus' advice 'to give everyone the impression that Pompey is a strong supporter of your candidature, and that your success will suit Pompey very well'.

To have done otherwise would have been foolish, for while Pompey had many enemies there was no doubt whose name weighed most heavily in the scale of political patronage. As far as the aristocracy was concerned, a glance at the list of legates whom Pompey had chosen for his Pirate War and Eastern campaigns is enough to show how many prominent senators had been only too glad to take lucrative commissions on his staff, and if Pompey's interest could be secured for Cicero's candidature, some of these men might be looked to for political backing among the group which Quintus calls 'the highest personages, without whose good graces much powerful support could never be mobilized'. As for the equestrian order, Pompey's conquests in the East which provided them with so many new fields for profitable tax-farming made him as natural a favourite with the business lobby as Cicero himself, who had always championed their interests. And if the timocratic voting system made the ballots of the 'urban mob' less weighty in elections than in legislation (and there were likely to be influxes of country citizens brought into the city by their noble patrons to vote for the election of family or friends), it remained an important fact, as Quintus observed, that Cicero's ardent support for Pompey had endeared him to the 'urban mob and its political managers'. For Pompey, by vindicating the people's faith in him, was the living embodiment of popular wisdom against the arrogance of an aristocracy which claimed to monopolize that rare commodity.

This does not mean that the popular hero was aware of much of what was said or done in his name until long after the event. Historians too often speak as though Pompey was manipulating the political scene in Rome by remote control, but while he might reasonably expect men who had served on his staff to feel some obligation towards him at home, his military and administrative preoccupations and the slowness of communications with the capital meant that he lacked both the interest and the ability to interfere in more than a very general way in the petty political manœuvres in Rome. And that is why it was a far from confident Cicero who began his canvass for the consulship of 63 by writing to his influential banker-friend Atticus in Greece in July 65 and asking him to intercede with Pompey's friends on his behalf in an attempt to put some substance behind the claim that Pompey supported his candidacy.

But Cicero was favoured by an extremely fortunate set of political circumstances at the elections of 64. Of the six candidates who stood for the two consulships of 63 Cicero had only two really formidable opponents, Antonius Hybrida and Sergius Catilina, both protégés of Pompey's enemy Crassus, who was busily bribing them into power as part of the rearguard action which he had been fighting and losing against the menacing growth of Pompey's power and wealth in the East. As censor in 65 Crassus had sought to strengthen his own political and financial position by working for the enfranchisement of the Gauls beyond the Po and by proposing either the annexation of Egypt or at least the regularization of that rich kingdom's relationship with Rome. But he had failed in both attempts. The enfranchisement of the Transpadane Gauls had been blocked by his colleague Catulus, anxious that Crassus should not increase his influence in an electorate enlarged by an influx of new citizens who would be outside the hereditary patronage of the rest of the *nobiles*. And Cicero had been prominent among the Pompeian interests that had helped to squash the Egyptian proposals, which were clearly designed to provide Crassus with a lucrative personal commission through which he might divert a large cash-flow in his own direction. But Crassus did not give up so easily. If he could not achieve his object by direct means, he could invest in the skills of the more able, ambitious and indigent of the nobility. And when Julius Caesar secured the praetorship and the High Priesthood of the state religion in 63, the Midas-touch of Crassus was as surely behind the corrupt pontifical elections as it had been behind the magnificent games which Caesar had given as aedile in 65, the year in which he had spoken in favour of his promoter's Egyptian proposals. But popular as Caesar was, not least for trading on his connection with the now legendary Marius, he was still too young to be more than a medium-term speculation in high politics. In the meantime Crassus decided to back Catiline, a man who had been disqualified from competing in the consular elections of 65 by an impending trial for extortion in his propraetorian province but was more determined than ever to stand in the elections of 64.

By combining the few extant fragments of Cicero's dramatic outburst before the election with the commentary of Asconius and the first major speech which Cicero made as consul-elect, it becomes clear that Crassus had decided that 63 was to be the year in which he and his friends would take control of the Roman government so effectively and lucratively that they could be as confident against the threat of Sulla's pupil as the Marians had felt against Sulla himself. How much Cicero himself really knew of the full extent of Crassus' machinations in the election of 64 is not clear; but as the Catilinarian bandwagon rolled on with increasing momentum over the passive resistance of the other candidates, he realized that he had nothing to lose by presenting himself as the only really effective opposition to what turned out to be a monopolistic political scheme that went far beyond the control of the consulship. For having just used a tame tribune to veto a senatorial proposal against his electoral bribery, no one knew better than Crassus how rivals in the Senate would count on finding tribunes to do the same to the proposals of his tame consuls in the following year, even if he succeeded in getting both his candidates elected. To be really secure he had to monopolize not only the headship of state but the whole college of tribunes; and the success of his machinations in this direction was revealed when the ten tribunes for 63 took office on 10 December 64 and immediately declared themselves solidly behind a Land Bill to be introduced by one of their number named Rullus which, if passed, would admit Crassus to the same storehouse of power and wealth to which entry had been denied him in 65.

But Crassus was less successful with his consular candidates. Cicero loaded his verbal mortars with every kind of charge from peculation to incest, but with a fine sense of timing he refrained from firing them until a few days before the elections. All were aimed at Catiline and Antonius,

and no sooner had these found their mark than he detonated an
explosion so loud and unexpected that it rocked the whole political scene
and filled the Senate with admiration and fear. This was the accusation
of an abortive conspiracy to assassinate the consuls of 65, and by keeping
it to the very end of the campaign he found to his delight that what
should have had no more effect than a damp squib on the open field
of reason caused utter havoc in the close confinement of the ballot-box.
The result was a resounding victory for the 'new man' at the top of the
poll. He had swung behind him not only the Pompeian interests but a
large part of the conservative senatorial establishment whose complacency
had been shattered by the fear of revolution, and though Antonius still
managed to come a poor second in the poll, the failure of the more
formidable Catiline lost Crassus his chance of monopolizing the consulships. Not that Crassus was disheartened, knowing that he could count
on the almost unprecedented unity of a whole college of tribunes. It was
not until the heads of state took office on 1 January 63 that he appreciated
the strength of the senior consul, who immediately began to wield a
Pompeian axe to dismember a superficially healthy agrarian reform and
reveal the corruption within.

It is difficult to reconstruct the exact provisions of the Bill because we
possess only Cicero's speeches condemning it, but the principles are clear
enough. At first sight it appeared an extremely popular measure, designed
to relieve the problems of poverty and debt by making grants of land to
poor citizens in the best Gracchan tradition. Cicero's criticism was directed
at the machinery by which the allotments were to be made and the methods
of raising the necessary finance, for there was little public land still
available for distribution in Italy and much of what was needed would
have to be purchased from existing proprietors. For this purpose the
tribune Rullus had proposed the establishment of a board of ten, to be
elected by a process which Cicero claimed to be a charter for ballot-
rigging. These decemvirs were to have full powers for five years not only
to decide where to allot land, from whom to buy it and to whom to give
it, but also to raise whatever money they required by selling off certain
public lands in the provinces, levying special taxes on other provincial
lands, confiscating all the outstanding booty of all victorious generals
past, present or future (with the significant exception of Pompey's), and
appropriating income from all new sources of revenue acquired by Rome
in or after 63.

Although Cicero was careful not to mention Crassus by name, he left
no doubt about the identity of the *éminence grise* when he asked 'if
those men who failed to reach Egypt by a straight course really imagine
that they can slip into Alexandria unnoticed under the cover of murky

darkness and fog'. Nor was it only the wealth of Egypt that gleamed in the greedy eyes of the promoters of this Bill. 'Is it not strange,' pursued Cicero, 'that the very men who are seeking this absolute power over foreign nations are those most loud in their complaints that all lands and seas have been put at the disposal of Pompey?' In seeking to control the revenues from all Rome's acquisitions in or after 63 and interfering in many categories of public land abroad they were obviously trying to siphon off the profits of Pompey's conquests and settlements in Asia. And if they exempted Pompey from the provision requiring all generals to disgorge every part of the booty which they did not pay into the public treasury or use on public monuments, it was only because they were wary of provoking him into military action on his return and anxious not to alienate popular support from a Bill which might otherwise appear too obviously designed to strengthen the hands and bank-balances of his enemies.

In one of the most consummate masterpieces of political rhetoric ever delivered Cicero warned the people of Rome that they were being duped by men who sought at one stroke to remove their liberty. By one vote they would be creating ten kings of the Treasury, of the revenues of all provinces, of the entire Republic, of friendly kingdoms and free nations alike. They would be raising ten generals against themselves, against liberty, against Pompey himself, the very man who was the true guardian of that liberty. Were they going to allow Pompey's provinces to be sold while he was still conquering them? Would they countenance an attack on the People's General and his victorious army by ten greedy men armed with only the spear that auctioneers stick in the ground at public sales? And could they ever agree to a Bill containing a provision requiring personal candidature for membership of the board of ten and thereby deliberately excluding the absent Pompey, the one man who would obviously be their first choice in any commission of this importance? No, they would not! And they did not. However attractive it might have appeared to land-hungry and debt-ridden citizens, no Bill could hope to succeed when represented as nothing but a selfish machination of Pompey's enemies by a consul who proclaimed himself to be as devoted to the popular interest as the proconsul himself, whom he had had the honour of commending to them for the Eastern command in 66. And so powerful was the combination of Pompey's prestige and Cicero's oratory that the unity of the tribunes promptly collapsed. After all, to be an unpopular tribune was a paradox, and Cicero had no sooner finished his speech than one of the tribunes swung round like a weathercock as the breath of popular favour changed direction, and threatened to interpose his veto at once if so outrageous a Bill were ever put to the vote.

After the frustration of this scheme, Crassus backed Catiline yet again at the elections of 63, not only as his main hope for 62 but with the idea that as consul-elect in the second half of the current year Catiline might stiffen the resolution of the existing consul Antonius. But when Catiline failed once more and Cicero bought Antonius by offering him his own proconsular province of Macedonia in which to wax fat from extortion in the following year, Crassus had to accept temporary defeat by the People's Consul backed by the authority of the People's General against whom all his schemes for self-aggrandizement had been chiefly designed. Before the year was out he saw Pompey soaring to new heights of popularity when Cicero read out his dispatches announcing the death of Mithridates. He was treated to the sickening spectacle of two of his ten tribunes, so united in their support of his Land Bill at the beginning of the year, now gaily carrying laws to allow Pompey to wear triumphal regalia at various games and ceremonies in Rome itself. He was cheated of any chance of reviving his own legislative schemes in the following year not only by Catiline's failure to make the consulship but by the election to the tribunate of one of Pompey's staunchest supporters, his former legate Metellus Nepos. And as if all that was not bad enough, he saw Cicero making enormous political capital for himself out of the liquidation of the expensive investment which he himself had written off as soon as Catiline had failed again at the elections of 63.

Financially and politically bankrupted by the withdrawal of Crassus' support, the desperate Catiline had turned with a vengeance into the path of violent revolution which Cicero had so effectively, and almost certainly unjustly, accused him of treading just before the elections of 64. Both within and outside the city there was no shortage of combustible material for an able incendiarist. There were men of his own class equally despairing of achieving by constitutional means the power which they regarded as their birthright, and if they could once set some revolutionary movement afoot, there was a reasonable hope for a successful *coup de main*. How successful it could remain against the legions of Pompey was an irrelevant question. Sufficiently desperate men do not cross their bridges until they come to them, and anything could happen to Pompey in the meantime. The important thing was to get into power while he was still at the other end of the world, and when Catiline and his fellow-conspirators began recruiting their forces, they found they could benefit almost equally from the beneficiaries as well as the victims of the Civil War which had made Pompey's fortune. Among the victims of Sulla's persecutions they found ready support from men spanning all classes, from financially and politically disabled young noblemen whose fathers had supported Marius to the desperate inhabitants of Etruria and other parts of Italy who had lost their lands and livelihoods as the price of loyalty to the legitimate government. Among the beneficiaries they could appeal to once prosperous Sullans whose money had gone as easily as it had come, whose little farms had failed to compete with the great estates tilled by slaves, and whose last chance of avoiding bankruptcy had disappeared with the failure of the Rullan Land Bill which could have bought them out. And Catiline himself was a man of rare personal magnetism and popularity among the demagogues of Rome, as the size of Crassus' investment in him so clearly demonstrates. But thanks to the incompetence of the other conspirators and Cicero's own subtle and even provocative handling of the situation, he was no more successful in achieving his ends by force than by legitimate means.

In October 63 Cicero succeeded in persuading the Senate to pass its Ultimate Decree authorizing the consuls 'to see to it that the Republic shall suffer no harm', but while the agents of revolution were raising forces in Italy, Catiline himself remained coolly in Rome to co-ordinate the internal conspiracy, allay suspicion, and try to brand Cicero as an alarmist. As late as 8 November Catiline was still appearing in the Senate and pouring scorn on Cicero as nothing but a naturalized immigrant bringing ridiculous charges against the heir of a family with five hundred years of service to the Republic to prove its *bona fides*. In the meantime he planned the assassination of Cicero, but after the plot had misfired he finally left Rome in order to take personal command of his revolutionary army. By December he had increased to ten thousand the band of ill-equipped desperadoes with which he planned to march on a city thrown into confusion by his accomplices who were to strike from within during the Saturnalian festivities, and if his accomplices had been as able and determined as himself, he might have achieved something. As it was, they so bungled their attempts to persuade the envoys of a disgruntled Gallic tribe to join them that Cicero was able to reveal the whole conspiracy, apprehend the conspirators, and alienate the people from any sympathy with Catiline by raising oratorical spectres of a Gallic horde rejoicing in a burning Rome. He then asked the Senate what to do with the arrested men, for though their guilt was beyond question, his own preference for their immediate execution without trial was of dubious legality even in the state of national emergency signalled by the Senate's Ultimate Decree. But if Caesar was not alone in opposing him, the majority voted for the death penalty, being anxious to dispose of these dangerous men as soon as possible yet secure in the knowledge that it was only the consul who had the *imperium* to put their will into effect. Thus emboldened, Cicero did what they wanted and ended his year as consul on a pinnacle of popularity, supported not only by the approval of the senatorial establishment but by the plaudits of the people, in whose minds he had magnified his admittedly clever handling of a rather pathetic conspiracy into the salvation of Rome from a fate worse than Allia.

The paradoxical significance of the Catiline affair to the story of Pompey is that he had absolutely nothing to do with it. Whereas Pompey's absent influence had always loomed large behind Cicero's previous political triumphs, Cicero's success against Catiline was all his own work, and exactly because it was an achievement that could be made to detract from Pompey's victories it endeared him to Pompey's enemies as much as to those of Crassus. That is not to say that Cicero himself had abandoned Pompey's interest. As his letters show, he was anxious to continue a political alliance with the man he now regarded as the *other* popular hero, but his remarkable success and his acceptance by the senatorial establishment had so far gone to his head that he felt Pompey's friendship was now less a matter of necessity than of choice. This impression was confirmed by the failure of Metellus Nepos' attacks on him. Nepos had secured election to the tribunate on the Pompeian ticket, exactly as Cicero had secured his election to the consulship of the previous year, and because Nepos now saw Cicero as an establishment figure whose much vaunted achievement against the Catilinarians threatened Pompey's prestige, he launched a series of attacks as soon as he took office on 10 December 63.

The first came when Cicero wanted to deliver his public account of his year in office on the last day of his consulship. Nepos immediately interposed his tribunician veto, thus silencing what Dio rightly says would have been a highly self-congratulatory speech, 'for Cicero took the greatest pleasure not only in being praised by others but in extolling himself'. He then proceeded to charge Cicero with the murder of Roman citizens, by whom he meant the conspirators put to death without trial, and he followed that up with a Bill proposing the recall of Pompey to deal with Catiline's army which was still in the field. This last proposal was manifestly absurd, for while it would no doubt have delighted Pompey if he had happened to be entering Italy and fallen in with the Catilinarians as fortuitously as he had run into the remnants of Spartacus' slave-army on his way back from Spain, he would hardly have been pleased if Nepos had succeeded in having him recalled from Pontus for so little cause. All the same it was significant of a strengthening of the senatorial establishment against the Pompeian interest that it used the tribunes Minucius Thermus and Marcus Cato to veto the clerk's reading of this Bill, that Nepos' rented mob of rowdies lost the ensuing battle in the Forum, that the Senate again authorized the consuls 'to see to it that the Republic shall suffer no harm', and that Nepos himself was forced to fly for his life

back to Pompey in the East. It was also significant that one of the two
consuls of 62 was Lucullus' old legate Lucius Murena whom Cicero
had recently defended against a charge of electoral corruption, and that
it was in 63, the year of Cicero's consulship, that Lucullus himself
had at last been able to celebrate his triumph over Mithridates. As for
Catiline, lest anyone should doubt the cynical realism of Dio's definition
of the politician as 'one who forms friendships and enmities according
to the influence of others and his own advantage', it was his old
friend and former running-mate Antonius who commanded the consular army which annihilated a band of men so brave and desperate
that they all fell with wounds in front, and Catiline himself in front of
all.

When news came in 62 that Pompey was on his way home there was
much nervousness and hedging of political bets. We have a letter of about
June 62 to Pompey from Cicero, prudently assuring the returning hero
of his own delight at seeing 'old enemies and new friends cast down
from their hopes by his victorious dispatches' and representing himself
as no fair-weather friend but 'an old adherent whose constant faith in
Pompey's ability to bring a lasting peace had been vindicated in the eyes
of all Rome'. The reference to the disappointment of 'new friends' is a
subtly oblique swipe at the demagogues who had been Crassus' most
ardent suitors until they had turned in fear rather than affection to court
the stronger man: men like the tribunes Ampius and Labienus, supporters
of the Rullan Land Bill at the beginning of 63 but gaily voting unprecedented honours to Pompey the moment Crassus' scheme had
collapsed. They would also include Julius Caesar, who, though a much
more deeply indebted protégé of Crassus, had no sooner entered his
praetorship at the beginning of 62 than he had supported Nepos' Bill to
recall Pompey and proposed one of his own to transfer from Catulus to
Pompey the honour of dedicating the newly rebuilt Temple of Jupiter on
the Capitol. That is not to say that Caesar was then supporting
Pompey for the first time. He had spoken along with Cicero in support
of the Manilian law giving Pompey his Eastern command in 66, but there
is no doubt that Cicero could rightly claim to have been a more consistent
Pompeian in the meantime or that Caesar's most recent Bills had been
proposed, as Dio says, 'not so much for Pompey's sake as Caesar's
own'.

But if Pompey cared little for Caesar, it is clear from the hurt tones of
the rest of Cicero's letter that the conqueror of the East had scarcely
more time for a pompous ex-consul who had already irritated him by a
boastful account of his own achievements against Catiline. And while
we unfortunately lack both that earlier bombastic letter and Pompey's

reply, there is no mistaking the chilling tones of the latter in Cicero's complaint that 'it scarcely showed any indication of your regard for me' and in what follows:

To make it quite clear what I missed in your letter I shall write as frankly as my own nature and our mutual friendship demand. My recent achievements are such that I did expect, both on the score of our intimacy and of their importance to the Republic, some word of congratulation from you in your letter, and I can only suppose that you omitted it for fear of offending anyone's feelings. But I must tell you that what I did for the security of our country has been approved by the considered judgement of the whole world, and that when you return home you will recognize that my achievements were made with so great a degree of wisdom and courage that you, who are so much greater than Africanus, will find no difficulty in allowing me, who am not much inferior to his Laelius, to associate closely with you both in politics and in private life.

Pompey's reply, if indeed he replied at all, is not preserved, but it is not difficult to imagine his reaction to Cicero's insolent proposal to play Laelius to Pompey's Africanus. Pompey was happy enough to be called much greater than the Scipio Africanus Aemilianus who had destroyed Carthage in 146 and Numantia in 133, but he utterly refused to see any more resemblance to Laelius in Cicero than a certain oratorical and cultural similarity. Laelius had been a military man, not only as a legate on Scipio's staff in Africa but a successful general in his own right in Spain. The very last person Pompey would have picked for his most intimate political and private friend was an unmilitary windbag who had done nothing but arrest a few bungling conspirators in Rome while leaving his inept fellow-consul to deal with Catiline's band of ten thousand desperadoes who were doing their best to escape into Gaul just as the remnants of Spartacus' slaves had done. Never, it seemed to Pompey, in the field of political endeavour had so much been made by so many out of so little. Who on earth did Cicero think he was addressing? What were a handful of failed revolutionaries to boast about in comparison with the achievements of 'Gnaeus Pompeius Magnus, *Imperator*, who in thirty years of war had routed, scattered, slain or accepted in surrender 12,183,000 people, sunk or taken 846 ships, received the capitulation of 1,538 towns and castles, and subdued all the lands from the Maeotic to the Red Seas'? If Pompey wanted friends, either political or personal, he would choose his own, and he had complete confidence in his ability to carry all before him at home as successfully as he had done abroad. And at first it appeared that he would. When he wrote to the Senate about the same time as Cicero was writing to him and requested that

the consular elections of 62 should be postponed so that his legate Piso
might reach Rome in time to stand, the Senate at once acquiesced, and
Piso was elected 'unanimously'. But as Dio shrewdly observes, 'Pompey
had recommended Piso not only to his friends but to his enemies, and
all alike stood in fear of him as long as it remained uncertain whether
or not he would give up his legions.'

As we have already seen, Pompey felt sufficiently confident in the power
of his wealth and reputation to ensure that his will was done without
staying aboard his military juggernaut and threatening to crush all
apostates under its wheels. He was aware that he would face opposition
on his return. He knew that his old enemy Crassus would now be as
jealous of his superior fortune as he had always been of his superior
military reputation, for if Pompey's generalship had earned him the
surname 'the Great', it had always before been a consolation to Crassus
that an equal talent in business had justified his inherited surname 'the
Rich'. But now it seemed that *Magnus* had a better claim to the title of
Dives too. Rich as Crassus was – and in 55 Pliny reckons his personal
fortune at the enormous sum of 200 million sesterces in land – Pompey
must now have been even richer, having paid an equivalent sum into the
Roman Treasury, distributed twice as much to his army, and obviously
kept enough for himself not only for his vast public works but to be able
to lend a single creditor like the King of Cappadocia something between
36 and 72 million sesterces. He was not in the least surprised that Crassus
had schemed so hard to get his greedy hands on the wealth of Egypt and
the new provinces while he was away, and he was no doubt delighted to
hear how Crassus was making an even bigger fool of himself by fleeing
Rome with his family and portable property in terror of the man against
whose interests he had worked so hard in vain for the last five years. For
Pompey could not conceive of needing force to help him overwhelm in
person a man who had failed to achieve anything against him while he
was away, and he had similar contempt for his other inveterate enemies
such as Lucullus and Metellus Creticus or that section of the senatorial
establishment whose talents were unequal to their distinguished birth,
and whose natural instincts for self-protection meant automatic opposition to a superior talent advanced by an extremely unconventional career.
Far from fearing these rivals, he looked forward to their discomfiture.
He could outbribe Crassus, overawe Lucullus, oppose Creticus with loyal
members of that divided family, and conciliate the Senate by the prompt
disbanding of his army, an exaggerated show of respect for its prestige,
and a marriage alliance with Marcus Cato, who was rapidly emerging as
the new spokesman of the establishment. And if there was any difficulty,
he could always rely on the devotion of the people in whose name he

had won his victories, whose wisdom he had vindicated, whose bread and circuses he was providing on an unprecedented scale, and whose fears of a blood-bath, usefully exaggerated by the Catilinarian scare, he had dismissed along with his legions. In short, as Plutarch says, 'his greatness and splendour, combined with the warmth of his reception, led him to believe that he could get whatever he wanted from his fellow-citizens'.

There were three things that Pompey wanted when he returned, namely a triumph, a grant of land for his veteran troops, and the ratification of his arrangements in the East. But if the granting of a triumph was a foregone conclusion, Pompey had made all his regulations in the East without bothering to ask the Senate to send him the usual board of ten commissioners to help in the organization of his new provinces, and it was therefore not unreasonable for the Senate to seek to inquire a little more closely into his dispositions instead of ratifying them *en bloc*. Moreover these questions of land and provincial arrangements were of the sort which could be postponed under the pressure of other business once the triumph had been granted, and it must have come as a rude awakening to Pompey to find not only that he was unable any longer to run his own show in his own way but that his show was no longer even the central attraction. And when he now found the Senate totally preoccupied with regulations not for settling the affairs of twelve million people but for the trial of a childish prankster named Clodius who had violated the mysteries of the Bona Dea by dressing in drag and bluffing his way into Caesar's house where the all-female rites were being held, he must have wondered what sort of madhouse he had returned to.

According to a letter written by Cicero to Atticus on 13 February 61, Pompey's first public speech on returning to the city – a speech delivered outside the city-walls while he waited for the formal authorization of his triumph – had been a flop: 'It contained no joy for the poor, no ammunition for the radicals, no gratification for the rich, nothing sufficiently weighty to satisfy the men of good will', the phrase by which he modestly signified himself and those who shared his opinions at the time. But this could well be sour grapes on the part of a Cicero who was still smarting from Pompey's failure to show more appreciation of his achievements in the Catiline affair. For Pompey to have made a highly controversial or partisan speech would have been a curious way to pursue his policy of conciliating all sections of society and burying the reputation of Sulla's pupil which he had already tried to kill by the prompt disbanding of his army. What he probably did was to concentrate on his own achievements in the East, which were a very proper subject for a general awaiting his triumph, and if it was at this assembly that he made his famous claim to have found 'Asia' the remotest of Rome's provinces and left it at the centre of the empire, it must be doubted that the speech fell as flat as Cicero would have liked Atticus to believe.

But Pompey could not keep out of petty politics forever. The affair of Clodius' trial for sacrilege had become a battleground between the demagogues and the senatorial establishment. The majority of the Senate, desiring to secure the conviction of this troublesome rabble-rouser, had framed a proposal to allow the praetor who was to try this case to pick his own jury and use them as a panel of advisers. This, they felt, would be a safeguard against the bribery to which a jury picked in the usual manner by lot would be only too susceptible, and so Clodius' friends found themselves in the unusual role of supporting convention against innovation. Piso, who was a friend of Clodius, was put in a difficult position. As consul he had to present the Senate's proposal to the popular assembly, but because he wanted to see it fail he prevailed upon the tribune Fufius, who was to propose the rival Bill to keep to the usual system, to try to secure Pompey's influence against what had been shown to be the will of the majority of the Senate. He may have thought that Pompey would support him as a personal favour in this as readily as he had supported his candidature for the consulship, and he may even have hoped that Pompey would feel some sense of obligation to Clodius himself, since this was the same P. Clodius Pulcher whose agitation among the mutinous legions of his brother-in-law Lucullus had contributed indirectly to the transfer of the Eastern command in 66. But Pompey was not the man to acknowledge any obligation readily, still less such indirect assistance from an inept commander whom Lucullus had very properly refused to promote; and when the tribune Fufius now 'trotted Pompey out to give another speech in the Circus Flaminius', Pompey wisely confined himself to some suitably vague and general remarks *en grand seigneur* about his respect for the Senate and his complete confidence in its authority. 'And very long-winded he was about it too,' adds Cicero, who should have been the very last man to criticize a speech either for its establishmentarian tone or its length, for there was no Roman alive who so loved the sound of his own voice. Again Cicero's snide remarks disguise what was a safe piece of batsmanship by Pompey against a tricky ball on a sticky wicket, and it was only when he began to play his first match in the Senate that he realized how difficult it was going to be to win a place in the establishment team.

The decree authorizing Pompey's triumph and allowing him to enter the city must have been passed very promptly since Cicero also refers to Pompey's first speech in the Senate in his letter to Atticus of 13 February. This time it was the consul Messalla who asked Pompey's opinion both on the sacrilege itself and on the proposed method of selecting the jury, and once again Pompey tried to present himself as a pillar of the establishment by 'a great eulogy of the Senate's measures in general', not only in this matter apparently but in all that had been done while he had been away, which naturally included the opposition to the Rullan Land Bill, the subsequent outlawing of Catiline, and the execution of the conspirators. At any rate he turned to Cicero when he had sat down and said, ' "I think that covered all those affairs of yours adequately enough, don't you?" ' But Cicero evidently did not think it adequate at all, and his obvious disappointment did not escape the shrewd gaze of Crassus, the very man whose schemes Cicero had done more than anyone to frustrate in Pompey's interest but who now saw his chance to manipulate the hurt vanity of his former antagonist to his own advantage. Crassus was on his feet in a moment and using all his eloquence to drive a wedge between the would-be Laelius and his reluctant Africanus. 'Realizing that Pompey's speech had been well received because he had seemed to be approving my consulship,' wrote Cicero naïvely, 'Crassus got up and spoke of it in the most complimentary terms. He said that he owed his very position as a senator to me, his privileges as a citizen, his freedom, his very life. He never looked at his dear wife, his home, his children without recognizing his debt to me ...' And so it had continued, laid on ever more thickly by the man about whom Cicero had written only three weeks before that 'he was not going to be taken in by this new pretence of friendship that cannot disguise his secret jealousy'. Atticus had himself warned Cicero that Crassus had begun to praise him only when he no longer dared to criticize him, and Cicero had replied that he saw Crassus for what he was, 'a man without grace or straight dealing, wholly unprincipled and totally devoid of honour, courage or generosity'. But now it appeared that Cicero's ability to see through people could be impaired by interposing sufficient layers of flattery, and Atticus must have smiled ruefully at his friend's gullibility when he read his report of Crassus' intervention:

I was sitting next to Pompey and observed that the man was much moved, either at seeing Crassus snapping up the popularity which he had thrown away or because he at last realized the greatness of my achievements when he saw that they were lauded before a delighted Senate by a man who had far less obligation to praise me after having been censured in every one of my speeches to the benefit of Pompey. This day has brought Crassus and me very close together, though I still accepted gratefully whatever tit-bits were offered me by the other either directly or indirectly. As for my own speech, good God! How I showed off before my new listener Pompey! If ever my rounded periods, my smooth transitions, my beautiful antitheses, my constructive arguments stood me in good stead, it was then. Result: Loud Applause! For my whole hypothesis was the importance of the senatorial order, its concord with the knights, the harmony of all Italy, the paralysed remains of the conspiracy, peace and plenty. You know the noise I can make on that subject – in fact, you probably heard it right across the Adriatic!

When or if the questions of grants of land for Pompey's veterans and the ratification of his Eastern settlement were mooted in the earlier part of 61 is not known. Although Pompey had expected opposition from men like Crassus, Lucullus and Metellus Creticus, he had sadly overestimated his ability to conciliate the bulk of the senatorial establishment by fair words. Despite his prompt disbanding of his legions, his eulogies of the Senate's actions and his refusal to support Piso against the Senate's will, his unconventional career and the many unconventional things done in his name during his absence had aroused the protective reflexes of a frightened mediocrity. There were too many senators whose only thought was to oppose what appeared to be the greatest threat at any given time. When it had been Crassus, they had rallied round Cicero and welcomed the supporting influence of the absent Pompey. Now that it was Pompey, they were prepared to rally even behind Crassus as well as such safer defenders as Lucullus, Metellus Creticus and the young Marcus Cato. Cato indeed was too highly principled for his own or his country's good, but while Cicero might criticize a political inflexibility that seemed more appropriate to the Republic of Plato than the Midden of Romulus, it was that very single-mindedness of purpose combined with inde-fatigable vigour which made him such a powerful figure in the Senate when still so low on the ladder of office, for he had held only the quaestorship and tribunate at this time. He was utterly safe, a determined opponent of anything and anyone that appeared to threaten the authority of the Senate, an oligarch so dedicated that he was as incapable of accommodating the aspirations of any other section of society as he was of accepting the most magnificent bribe which Pompey could offer him, namely himself and his elder son as suitors for the hands of Cato's two marriageable nieces. Not surprisingly the nieces themselves were not very pleased at losing the most eligible catches in Rome, and Cato's own wife and ambitious stepsister thought it madness to refuse a marriage-alliance with Pompey the Great, but no amount of feminine nagging or coaxing could move the adamantine Cato to favour what he rightly saw as a means of neutralizing his opposition to Pompey's plans. On the other hand he might have reflected that a marriage-alliance ties both parties, and he could have welcomed the opportunity to shore up the Senate's authority by conciliating a man who by nature and inclination was ill-suited to radical politics, whose eulogies of the Senate had been more than fair words, and from whom there was more to fear by opposition than conciliation. Even Cicero had seen Pompey's natural place as a pillar of the establishment when he had spoken of playing Laelius to his Africanus, and with the benefit of hindsight Plutarch rightly criticizes Cato's folly for spurning an alliance with Pompey and so driving him into Caesar's camp.

Angry at this blow to his pride and the rebuff of all his conciliatory gestures Pompey took to political warfare to secure the victory which diplomacy had failed to win, and it is fascinating to see that his strategy is almost an exact replica of that which Crassus had employed in vain to promote his own interests in Pompey's absence. Pompey now sought to control the consulship by supporting his former legates Lucius Afranius and Metellus Celer (brother of Nepos) in the elections of 61, and the tribunate by backing the candidature of Lucius Flavius, who was working on a Land Bill of his own. And the methods employed were similar. Just as Crassus' bribery of the electorate had reached such proportions that the Senate had begun formulating decrees imposing stiffer sentences for corruption, Pompey was now making even Crassus look miserly by throwing open his gardens to the public and overwhelming all callers with a liberality that contained the promise of more to come when he celebrated his triumph after the elections. 'The means he is using,' wrote Cicero in July, 'are neither authority nor influence but those which Philip said should storm any fort to which an ass laden with money could climb.' Again the Senate reacted with decrees against electoral corruption, two this time and both proposed by Cato. While one legalized the searching of any magistrate's house, the other made it unlawful to harbour bribery-agents at home, but they were not the healthily disinterested reforms that they at first appear.

When Cicero refers to them in this same letter to Atticus of July 61, he is careful to dissociate himself from 'moves which are unpopular because they are thought to be directed against the consul Piso' – a curious remark which reveals three things. The first is the naïvety with which Cicero had assured Atticus five months earlier that Pompey's refusal to support Piso's friend Clodius had created an unbridgeable gulf between the consul and his promoter, for whether Piso's house was really swarming with Pompey's bribery-agents or not, Piso was now clearly prominent in his support of Pompey's protégés for the following year. The second is that Cato's measures were designed not against bribery in general but against this bribery in particular. And the third is that Pompey has now re-enlisted Cicero in his ranks. The sourness of the grapes which had embittered Cicero's earlier letters to Pompey and Atticus on the score of faint praise for his achievements against Catiline had evidently been sweetened by some honeyed words from the Roman Alexander, and if Cicero still makes deprecatory remarks against the scale and openness of Pompey's bribery, he is obviously flattered by a change of attitude on Pompey's part that had the young bloods in the cafés referring to him as 'Gnaeus Cicero'. So great was his vanity that he was quite prepared to believe that 'the political and private intimacy' which he had so desired with Pompey was being firmly established on a rock of mutual respect rather than the shifting sands of mutual interest, and he was mercifully unaware how easily a change in the political climate would wash it away without causing the least concern to Pompey. But for the present Pompey was concerned only to strengthen his own hand. While he may not have regarded Cicero as one of his trump cards like his two consular candidates or his tame tribune, he considered him sufficiently strong to help him win a trick against Crassus and his partners, especially now that Cicero was disenchanted with 'Old Baldy, my former panegyrist', whose bribery of the jury at Clodius' trial had secured the outrageous acquittal of a dangerous and vindictive protégé who would never forgive Cicero for destroying his alibi.

When the election results were announced for the following year, Pompey was confident of achieving his grand slam. Whereas Crassus had succeeded in securing the election of only one (and the weaker) of his consular candidates for 63, both of Pompey's were returned for 60 along with the tribune Flavius, who was admittedly only one of the ten but the strongest card of that suit. While Pompey waited until he could play his hand in the new year, he had the double satisfaction of celebrating the most magnificent triumph ever witnessed in Rome and of watching the gradual disintegration of the enemy partnership as the reasons for Crassus' support of Clodius became clearer and Cato did his intransigent best to alienate the powerful business interests of the equestrian order. In letters written to Atticus in December and January Cicero explains how the publicans had requested the Senate to release them from a contract to farm the taxes of Asia for which they decided they had paid too much to make an adequate profit, and while Cicero thought the whole business 'scandalous and disgraceful', he nevertheless backed them because (as he says) a refusal might have created an open breach between the knights and the Senate and because (as he does not say) they had always backed him. He further reveals how Crassus had also been egging them on, presumably because he had money of his own tied up in the contract but also perhaps as a means of securing their support for his future political schemes, in which it now transpired, to Cicero's horror, that he had earmarked Clodius for the tribunate. It had never occurred to Cicero that this patrician criminal could ever stand for an office for which only plebeians were eligible (for while many of the very noblest families of the Roman aristocracy were of plebeian origin and the old distinction between patrician and plebeian had largely disappeared, one of the few places in which it remained significant was the 'tribunate of the plebeians'). If he had wondered why Crassus had spent so much money to secure the acquittal of a man so utterly damned by his own testimony, he now knew. Already an existing tribune was preparing to make Clodius plebeian by plebiscite, and the more Cicero reflected on the prospect of a vengeful arch-enemy in the tribunate of 59, the closer he edged towards the protective greatness of Pompey, who obviously annoyed him as much as he impressed him by 'wrapping himself round with that precious little painted cloak of his' and maintaining an Olympian calm. For Pompey had no need to fear for 59 when he was confident of holding an unbeatable hand for 60, and it was not until the game had begun that he realized that he had ended up in the wrong suit after all.

The irony is that the political game of 60 turned out to be an almost exact replay of the one Crassus had lost in 63, for Pompey was as disappointed in his consular hopes of Metellus Celer and Afranius as Crassus had been in Catiline and Antonius. If Pompey managed to secure the election of both his consuls where Crassus had succeeded only with Antonius, it did him no more good because he found the abler of his protégés as disloyal as the loyal one was incompetent. The latter was Afranius, formidable at the head of Pompey's legions but such a child in political warfare that he became a favourite butt of Cicero's private jokes, 'a cowardly wretch for a soldier' and so ham-fisted that he gave his great promoter 'one in the eye'. And Metellus Celer waited only until he was safely in office before showing himself a bitter personal enemy of his former chief over a matter of family honour. The previously latent fact was that Celer considered Pompey's divorce of his sister Mucia an ineradicable insult to his family. If this seems an unreasonable attitude in a case where the lady's infidelity was beyond question and the rest of Roman society (including his brother Nepos) could find no fault with Pompey's action, we must remember that Celer's own wife Clodia was the Lesbia of Catullus' love-poetry, and any man who could stand that amount of cuckolding was probably genuine in feeling that nothing which Mucia had done could justify Pompey in putting aside a wife who had borne him three children.

Consequently both the consuls of 60 proved as unwilling or unable to help Pompey as the consuls of 63 had been to assist Crassus, and when Metellus Celer added his consular weight to the united opposition of Cato and Lucullus to prevent voting on the questions of land for

Pompey's veterans or the Eastern settlement, Pompey attempted to turn their flank by means of his tribune Flavius, who brought forward a Land Bill attractively designed to provide land for other citizens as well as Pompey's veterans. But neither Flavius' efforts nor the force of Pompey's still undiminished personal popularity were sufficient to carry it against their opponents' ability to play on the fears of senators who were easily persuaded to see it as a ruse to get for Pompey dangerous new powers of the sort which Rullus' Bill would have secured for Crassus. Celer indeed opposed both the Bill and Pompey so persistently that Flavius had him arrested, and when the imprisoned consul replied by convoking the Senate to a sitting in jail, Flavius promptly set up his tribunician bench in front of the cell-door and prevented anyone from passing. It was obviously a ridiculous situation that could not be allowed to continue, but Celer's pride and his determination to make Pompey climb down made him refuse the offer of other tribunes to set him free. Instead he ordered the wall of his cell opposite the door to be broken down, not so that he could escape – for a tribune was entitled to jail even a consul and to prevent access to him by interposing his own sacrosanct person – but so that the Senate could enter at the back while Flavius was blocking the door, or *vice versa* since Flavius could not be in two places at once. And his persistence paid off. 'When Pompey learnt what was happening', says Dio, 'he felt both ashamed and afraid that the people might take offence, and he therefore ordered Flavius to withdraw.' And though he tried to salvage something from the situation by putting it about that he had called Flavius off at the request of Celer, no one believed him.

This little farce was probably enacted quite early in 60, for on 15 March Cicero was writing of the Flavian Bill as something almost forgotten, an issue which 'had cooled off' in the shadow of a war-scare in Gaul. The belligerent Helvetii had gone on the war-path, conquered Rome's friendly buffer-state of the Aedui, and started to make incursions into the Roman province of Transalpine Gaul. One of the decisions which the Senate took to deal with this emergency was to send ambassadors plenipotentiary to visit the other Gallic nations and dissuade them from joining the Helvetii, and the selection of these ambassadors was left to the luck of a draw from the names of all the ex-consuls. But when an embarrassing mischance brought the names of Cicero and Pompey out first, the whole Senate cried out that they must stay at home. Cicero, needless to say, was only too delighted that he and Pompey were being 'kept as guarantees of the security of the state', but if he was vain enough to believe that he was too precious to be spared, Pompey was under no illusions that he was thought too dangerous to be allowed to go. And

such was Cicero's naïvety that the letter which admits that he joined in
the criticism of Pompey's Land Bill also expresses the belief that Pompey
felt sufficient affection for him to revive his dream of playing Laelius to
Pompey's Africanus as defenders of the establishment. He failed to observe
that Pompey's increasingly flattering expressions of his achievements in
the Catilinarian affair were inspired not by affection or admiration but
by a purely pragmatic desire to neutralize an opponent of his immediate
aims. Although Atticus tried to warn his gullible correspondent against
too great a familiarity with Pompey, Cicero still claimed in June that his
growing friendship with Pompey was making a true patriot of him, and
he asked Atticus what he would say if he could do the same for Caesar,
'who is now sailing so bravely before the wind'. What he did not ask
himself was the direction from which that wind was blowing. Atticus
had asked what had happened to Pompey's Land Bill since the interrup-
tion of the war in Gaul. Cicero replied very casually that there seemed
to be no more interest in it, evidently without pausing to wonder why
Pompey had given up pressing for a measure on which Cicero had said
in March that 'he had set his heart'. If Pompey had given up the Flavian
Bill, it could only have been because he had seen a safer and surer means
to his ends. And if Cicero had been half as astute as he pretended to be,
he would have recognized the flag of convenience under which Caesar's
political ship suddenly left his propraetorian province of Spain without
even waiting for the arrival of his successor, and came racing back to
Rome in time for the consular elections for 59.

12
THE THREE-HEADED MONSTER

To other powers Fate never lent her grudge
To use against the People who held sway
Over each corner of the earth and sea;
O, Rome, you were the cause of your own ills,
The mistress of three masters' common use,
Three men who fatal bargains struck for power
That never yet was shared by such a crowd
Blind by ambition to all mischief done.
Lucan, *Pharsalia*, 1.82–7

After the fiasco of Flavius' imprisonment of Metellus Celer, Dio tells us that Pompey 'abandoned his demands for the passing of the Bill: he now learnt that he had no real power but merely the name and envy resulting from his former authority without receiving any benefit from it, and he regretted having let his legions go so soon and having put himself in the power of his enemies'. But it is hard to believe that Pompey saw what had happened as anything more than a temporary setback, or that he regretted not having kept a military sledge-hammer with which to crack two political nuts which had proved tougher than he had expected. If he had regarded the granting of land to his veterans and the ratification of his Eastern settlement as objects to be secured by a Sullan *coup d'état*, the troops which he had reassembled for his triumph were still available to be reassembled for revolution. But he cherished a longer-term aim – to lay the ghost of Sulla's pupil, to settle down as the acknowledged first citizen and servant of a grateful Republic, and to enjoy the trust and affection of all orders of society as the great Defender of the Constitution. And while he was well aware of the potential effectiveness of loyal soldiers summoned to the Forum as a political rather than strictly military pressure-group, he was unwilling to use compulsion except as a last resort.

If Flavius and the consul Afranius had not proved strong enough to secure Pompey's outstanding requirements against the opposition of Metellus Celer, Lucullus, Cato, Crassus and even the nit-picking naïvety of the orator who wanted to play Laelius to his Africanus, it was simply a matter of finding someone stronger. One obvious possibility was himself. Now that ten years had elapsed since his last consulship Pompey was legally eligible to stand for re-election for 59, and if he put himself forward, he could be almost certain of success. After all, if he had been able to buy his legate Afranius into the consulship, he could surely do the same for himself, supported as he was by an unequalled prestige which he could reinforce with an electoral platform of land for the people (including his veterans) and the tax-farming concessions for which the electorally powerful equestrian business-interests had been lobbying for so long in vain. On the other hand such a move towards personal power had grave disadvantages. In the first place it would provoke the senatorial establishment into opposing him at all costs, and though there was little chance of their preventing his election, his candidature would forfeit all hopes of a reconciliation as surely as his unlikely failure would be the ultimate in humiliation. Then again his election would be only the beginning of more difficulties. His enemies would certainly do their utmost to ensure that he had a strong and implacable fellow-consul, and Pompey knew only too well that he lacked the skill in political warfare that he enjoyed on the battlefield. To be sure of getting his own way he would have to secure not one consulship but two, and the choice of a running-mate was a ticklish business. If he selected a pliant nonentity, he was not only lessening his chances of getting his man elected against a strong opposition but running the risk of finding himself saddled with another Afranius, loyal but ineffectual. If, on the other hand, he chose a strong and politically effective partner, the last thing he wanted was to find himself sharing a tandem with a colleague who might suddenly decide to pedal in the opposite direction as Metellus Celer had done. All the same, the more he thought about it, the more Pompey recognized the need to detach from the opposition the most unscrupulous and the second most influential man in Rome, and if that man was none other than the old rival who had worked so hard against him while he had been away in the East, he was prepared to bury the hatchet in their mutual interest as readily now as ten years ago when they had stood together for the consulships of 70.

Marcus Crassus was as eager to accept a political alliance with Pompey as Pompey was to offer it. Separately they had failed to get their way. Together they were virtually unstoppable, and a hard-headed business-man like Crassus was the last person to let private animosity stand between him and a joint venture of such obvious potential. They both realized that they needed each other as much now as in 71, though this time Pompey had no intention of making their partnership public and official by inviting Crassus to run with him for the consulship. For one thing they would then be stuck with each other in official partnership for a whole year, and there was little chance that their mutual interests could survive their inveterate rivalry for so long in such close proximity. For another there was always the danger, however remote, that Crassus might be elected and Pompey not. But by far the most important consideration in Pompey's mind was that in accepting Crassus as his running-mate for the consulship he might appear to be treating him as an equal rather than an inferior, and he was not prepared to give him that satisfaction. By all means let Crassus join him in a political partnership, but only on the understanding that Crassus was the junior partner and that it would be better still if the partnership could be kept secret by trading under the name and apparently sole management of an able and reliable third party. For Pompey had not forgotten that 'life in the robes of peace has a dangerous tendency to diminish the reputation of those whom war has made great and ill-suited to democratic equality', and there was nothing he relished less than the prospect of seeing his fine triumphal toga besmirched by the mud-slinging that he would have to endure if he became consul in a year that would require a great deal of demagogy to achieve his ends.

Cicero's evidence that Pompey had let the Flavian Bill drop into political oblivion by June without making the slightest effort to rescue it suggests that he had already secured as his political agent for the following year an ambitious consular candidate who was ready to take any amount of political bespattering in return for Pompey's support for his own political and military ambitions. This was Julius Caesar, who had proved himself a formidable politician both as a protégé of Crassus during Pompey's absence and as a supporter of Pompey's tribune Metellus Nepos in 62 in preparation for the return of the conquering hero whose power would eclipse that of his former promoter. Following his praetorship of that year Caesar had been governing Further Spain and stirring up what Dio considered a totally unnecessary war in Lusitania in order to exercise his military talents and earn a triumph. He was a genuine admirer of Pompey's military achievements, and Pompey in turn respected him as an able soldier though of course he never dreamt that Caesar could ever rival his own exploits any more than Afranius or Gabinius or any other of his own legates for whose military abilities he entertained a similarly high regard.

Caesar had announced in December 61 that he intended standing for the consulship of 59, and as the mid-summer elections approached in 60 it seemed to Pompey that this was the very man through whom he might obtain what he wanted. Although it is uncertain whether Pompey had secured Crassus' agreement to his plan before Caesar had returned for the elections, it is highly probable that Caesar raced back to Rome with the assurance not only of Pompey's interest but of Crassus' too. What is certain is that any such arrangements were skilfully disguised, so skilfully indeed that they allowed Caesar's later dominance to convince most of our sources that it was Caesar who made the approach to secure Pompey's support rather than Pompey who initiated the political partnership which was to prove so effective in the following year.

The sequence of events as given by Dio and most of the other sources is that Caesar rushed back to Rome for the consular elections, but because he also wanted a triumph for his victories in Spain he begged the Senate to grant him dispensation from the normal requirement that a candidate must be present in person. Although Plutarch maintains that the Senate as a whole was willing to agree to Caesar's candidature *in absentia*, the request was obviously made at such short notice that Marcus Cato was able to talk it out, not from the pure motives of the disinterested upholder of precedent – the guise in which he usually appears – but because his own son-in-law Bibulus also happened to be standing for the consulship. Caesar was left with an apparently difficult choice between a certain triumph and a possible consulship, but Dio assures us that he did not hesitate for a moment. 'He readily gave up the triumph and entered the city to canvass for office . . . for he hoped that his election to the consulship would enable him to perform many more and greater exploits and celebrate triumphs accordingly.' Then, and only then, did he supposedly 'begin courting Pompey, Crassus and the rest', and he did it

so subtly that although they were at enmity with each other and opposed each other's every wish, he won them over and was elected by them. Nor was he content with this. He actually reconciled the men themselves, not because he desired that they should agree but because he saw that they were the most powerful men, that without the aid of at least one of them he could never come to power, and that if he made a friend of only one rather than both he would meet with more failures than successes. For he knew well enough that all men put more effort into opposing their enemies than into fighting for their friends, not merely on the principle that anger and fear are stronger motives than friendship but also because the degree of pleasure or pain in the success or failure of his efforts is far less for the man who is working on behalf of another than for the man who is working for himself. He also reflected that it was easier to stand in men's way and prevent them from reaching prominence than to lead them willingly into great power, for the simple reason that he who keeps another from becoming great pleases others as well as himself whereas he who exalts another makes him burdensome to both.

And with these cynically realistic observations on the psychology of power-politics Dio concludes that Caesar conciliated both sides, 'with no fear that such inveterate enemies as Pompey and Crassus would ever join forces against him but in perfect confidence that he could first master others through his friendship with them and soon afterwards master them through each other'.

But the evidence, stripped of hindsight, makes this traditional inter-pretation highly improbable. If Caesar gave up the glory of a triumph in order to stand for the consulship as readily as Dio maintains, it can only have been because he was sure of being elected; and if he was sure of being elected, he was already sure of the backing of at least Pompey, and very probably of Crassus too, before he entered the city. That Caesar would have thrown over his triumph in a last-minute gamble to secure the support which Dio himself calls indispensable is as incredible as the implication that Pompey had allowed his Land Bill to lapse into oblivion without having prepared what he considered to be a foolproof scheme for the following year. And for such a scheme to be foolproof required the co-operation of Crassus, which Dio treats as something easily secured once Caesar had pointed out the advantages to them. But two such worldly men as Pompey and Crassus did not need Caesar to tell them that they needed each other. Pompey wanted his Land Bill and the ratifi-cation of his Eastern settlement. Crassus wanted relief for the tax-farmers in whose enterprises he was closely involved, and moreover did not want to be left out of a mutual benefit society which would otherwise channel all the profits of his most promising political investment of recent years into Pompey's coffers. And it is difficult to see Caesar offering his services to the most powerful men in Rome on the eve of an election to which he had committed himself with no more security than the support of Luc-ceius, the rich nonentity of a senator whom he had been courting as his running-mate, much to the amusement of Cicero, since the previous December.

One result of the secret compact between Pompey, Crassus and Caesar was that poor rich Lucceius became the dupe of the year. He had allowed Caesar to convince him that his best chance of success lay in bribing the electorate in their joint names, and while he lavished his money on his running-mate he remained totally ignorant of the extent of Caesar's com-mitment to two more powerful backers, or of theirs to him. Indeed the partnership was kept so close a secret that even Cicero remained unaware of it as late as the following December, and if a political contemporary could so easily be deceived, it is not surprising to find Suetonius, writing his biography of Caesar some 175 years later, remaining either ignorant or unconvinced that his subject had succeeded through the support of anyone but Lucceius. According to Suetonius it was only after the elections that Caesar began courting Pompey 'who was at odds with the Senate because of the delays in confirming his acts after the victory over Mithridates', and then reconciled him with Crassus. Suetonius also says that Bibulus' supporters contributed to an electoral bribery-fund to match the expenditure of Lucceius, and without even mentioning the fact that Bibulus was Cato's son-in-law he adds naïvely that 'even Cato did not deny that bribery under such circumstances was to the public good'. At any rate, Lucceius saw no profit from his largess. The 'stop-Caesar' movement stopped only his running-mate, and when the votes had been counted it was Caesar who emerged at the top of the poll with Bibulus in second place.

For so overwhelming a victory to have been won without the support of Pompey and Crassus is incredible, but if Pompey and Crassus supported Caesar, it is valid to ask how they could have done this so secretly that the partnership remained undiscovered until well into the following year. And this may well have been the consideration which caused a puzzled Suetonius to reject the electoral support of Pompey and Crassus which we find attested by Livy, by the sources followed by Plutarch in his *Lives* of Caesar and Crassus, by Dio (probably following Livy) and by Appian, who makes Pompey take the initiative in promising Caesar his support though he allows Caesar the honour of bringing about the reconciliation with Crassus. But electoral support need not have indicated a political coalition. There can have been no secret that Pompey and Crassus had supported Caesar rather than Bibulus, but there was no reason to assume that they were voting for a political programme already agreed with Caesar rather than simply voting against Bibulus, the candidate of Cato's faction which for different reasons was equally inimical to the interests of both Pompey and Crassus. To Pompey it represented not only the stumbling-block to his two political aims but also the insulting rejection of a marriage-alliance. To Crassus it meant continuing opposition to the demands of the publican lobby, which Cicero tells us he had been 'egging on' to persuade the Senate to cancel the unprofitable contract for farming the taxes of Asia since the previous December. For Pompey and Crassus to use their influence in favour of the strongest rival to Cato's candidate need therefore have revealed nothing of the nature of the secret 'pact' which Dio describes as 'sealed by oaths to manage public affairs among themselves and receive from one another whatever suited them in the circumstances' – especially since they evidently took such care 'to conceal the alliance as long as possible, for they did whatever they decided upon while pretending and suggesting utterly opposite proposals in order that they might remain undiscovered for a long time and complete their preparations'. From Heaven alone they were unable to hide the birth of the 'Three-Headed Monster' which was Varro's name for the coalition that was to dominate Roman politics for longer than even its partners yet realized, but though there was no shortage of portents to mark the occasion, they were as usual recognized only in retrospect by the worldly divines of Rome.

Our lack of any correspondence from Cicero between June, when Caesar was about to return from Spain, and December, just before he entered the consulship, leaves us with no knowledge of Pompey's activities for the second half of 60 until the very end, when Caesar published the Land Bill which he was proposing to introduce as soon as his year of office began. Its purpose, of course, was to satisfy the first outstanding requirement of the new consul's principal backer, and since Pompey was anxious to secure its passage with the Senate's approval, he sought to ensure that Cicero at least would not oppose this new Bill as he had opposed nearly all the provisions of the similar Flavian scheme of the previous spring. But Pompey did not approach Cicero himself. Being reluctant to do anything that might disclose his major shareholding in his political consortium he left it to his managing director to take appropriate action, and Caesar sent his friend Balbus to Cicero with what the latter described as 'firm assurances that he would consult Pompey and me about everything in his consulship, and would try to reconcile Pompey and Crassus'. It is clear from the reference to 'Pompey and me' that Pompey had been flattering Cicero's conceit to make him receptive to Caesar's overtures, and this impression is not contradicted by Cicero's jocular reference to Pompey as 'Iphicrates up to his old tricks again' in connection with a court case in which his influence had acquitted an otherwise unknown friend of Afranius. For Cicero to call Pompey 'Iphicrates' in a confidential letter to an intimate need have been no more unfriendly than a private reference to the Duke of Wellington as 'Old Boots'. Pompey had taken to wearing a special style of boot either for fashionable or medical reasons, and since the Athenian general Iphicrates had invented a new kind of military footwear, it pleased Cicero to air such knowledge in a letter to the arch-philhellene Atticus. What humourless modern commentators have seen as a slap in Pompey's face was nothing more than a friendly dig in the ribs. It is certainly no evidence that Cicero felt anything but friendship to Pompey at this time, and when he considered his response to the publication of Caesar's Land Bill, this friendship weighed heavily with him.

In his letter to Atticus on the subject Cicero frankly observed that there were only three possibilities open to him: to support the Bill, to resist it, or to leave Rome for a spell in the country – an unusually honest admission of his constitutional inability to keep quiet without self-rustication. If he stayed in Rome, he must speak out, and when he considered the pros and cons of the other two possibilities he showed himself well aware that the first had the advantages of 'an intimate connection with Pompey and with Caesar too if I like, a reconciliation with my enemies, peace with the multitude, and a generally easy time in my old age'. In choosing the second he showed himself totally unaware that he was being sounded out as a possible fourth partner in a joint venture that was intended to monopolize Roman politics for at least the next year. Indeed his reference to Caesar's promise 'to try to reconcile Pompey and Crassus' shows how well the secret had been kept, and if Cicero had known that the Land Bill was only the first manifestation of a political programme already agreed between Caesar and his supposedly unreconciled electoral supporters, he would probably not have rejected so easily the request that he should support, or at least not oppose, this piece of legislation. One day he would understand what he had missed and claim credit for refusing to join the Big Three, but at the time he was as blind to the dangers of his own self-confidence as to the turgid mediocrity of the poetry which he wrote in self-congratulation on his consulship and quoted in the letter to Atticus in which he communicated his decision to reject Caesar's overtures in the last month of 60.

Caesar next invited the Senate to discuss a measure which Dio calls unexceptionable to any section of the community either in its aims or proposed method of operation. 'It was in everyone's interest that the city's swollen population, which was responsible for the frequent rioting, should be returned to productive work on the land; that the greater part of Italy, now desolate, should be colonized afresh; and that not only those who had toiled in the campaigns but the rest as well should have the means for an ample livelihood.' And all this, as Dio observes, could be achieved without burdensome expense to the city or loss to the aristocracy. On the contrary, there was a huge surplus of wealth from Pompey's conquests and the new tributes and taxes which they had established, and what could be more just than to spend some of the profits of war on those who had earned them and whose sons would earn more? Moreover the mechanics of the proposed distribution of land appeared as unobjectionable as the principles that lay behind it. The lucrative public land of Campania, which was tilled by tenant-farmers who paid rent to the Roman Treasury, was not to be touched. What was needed would be purchased from owners elsewhere, not under compulsion or at arbitrary prices, but only from willing sellers and for the price at which the property had been assessed in the tax-lists. And the whole operation was to be administered by a board of twenty commissioners, a body large enough to reduce the opportunities for corruption and to provide attractive opportunities for rank and distinction to 'the most suitable men who might share the honour'. This also made it difficult to accuse Caesar of promoting the wealth and power of a small clique as Rullus had so obviously been attempting with his Bill in 63, and the consul of 59 was careful to make it clear from the outset that he exempted himself from consideration when the time came for the composition of the board to be decided. But it was easy for Caesar to claim that 'he was adequately rewarded with the honour of having originated the proposal' when he had been rewarded in advance by his election to the consulship; and since Pompey's ineligibility for the Rullan board had been one of the most powerful weapons with which Cicero had destroyed that earlier scheme, it would now be hard to put any name but his at the head of a list of 'the most suitable men' for Caesar's agrarian board. And that, needless to say, was exactly where Pompey intended his name to be, not only for the dignity of the position but because he wanted to draw his old troops even closer to himself by associating himself as closely as possible with the efficient implementation of the promises he had made them.

But the fact that this Bill was so apparently unexceptionable did not make it acceptable to a Senate which was generally mistrustful of its author. Indeed their very inability to criticize its provisions proved more of an irritant than a salve to many of the senators, and though Caesar coaxed and cajoled and asserted that 'he would not even introduce the Bill to the people unless the Senate was happy with it', Dio tells us that the majority remained non-committal and inactive. For three months they found excuses for delays until neither Caesar's obligation to Pompey nor his own dignity would let him tolerate further procrastination. As long as there had seemed to be a chance of winning the Senate's approval for the Bill, Pompey had been patient in the hope that he would not have to reveal and test his means of beating those with whom he would have preferred to be joined; but when the Bill was finally debated it was the last straw to hear Cato blandly admitting that he had no fault to find with the details of the Bill yet urging its rejection 'on the general principle of leaving well alone'.

The effect of this utterance on Caesar was as stimulating as a red flag flapped in the face of a very angry bull. Reacting exactly as Pompey's tribune Flavius had done when similarly frustrated in the previous year he promptly instructed his lictors to march Cato off to jail, and it was only the spontaneous action of a large number of senators in standing up and threatening to follow him there that prevented a politically unnecessary and counter-productive martyrdom. Instead Caesar contented himself with the pleasure of informing the Senate that it had forfeited its chance to maintain its authority. ' "I made you judges and masters of this law," ' he thundered, ' "so that if any particular did not suit you, it should not be brought before the people. But since you are not willing to pass a preliminary decree, the people shall decide for themselves." ' And after that, says Dio, 'Caesar brought nothing before the Senate but legislated directly through the people.' The gloves were off, the relatively dignified sparring of the Senate House had given way to a free-for-all in the Forum, and it was only a matter of time before Caesar would be revealed as the pugilist of two more formidable and supposedly rival champions, whose appearance at his side in the political prize-ring would deter almost all comers from the surprised and frightened senatorial establishment.

Foreshadowing the combination of powers which would form the basis of the Augustan autocracy Caesar 'turned his consulship into a kind of tribunate', to quote Plutarch's succinct description of what happened. He summoned a popular assembly and promulgated his Bill to a Forum full of the land-hungry or trouble-loving rulers of Rome's empire, amongst whom were several thousands of Pompey's veterans who had spent their gratuities and were more than ready to fight for their promised farms. It was a formidable demonstration of support for the senior consul, and when Caesar had finished expounding the Bill, he gave his senatorial opponents their last chance to relent and indicate their support for a measure which they must now see the hopelessness of opposing. It was also his own last chance to keep his secret partners out of the political debate. He therefore turned to his colleague Bibulus, and asked him to comment on the proposals before the assembled multitude. But Bibulus refused to be intimidated, replying bluntly that he would 'tolerate no innovation of any sort in his year of office'. Caesar begged him to be a little more positive in his attitude and called upon the crowd to join in his entreaties, but Bibulus defied them all by shouting ' "You shall not have the law *this* year even if every man-jack of you wants it!" ' and marched off the platform amid the hoots and cat-calls of the angry mob.

Caesar then brought two other speakers to the rostra. Although it was customary to call for the opinions of magistrates before private citizens, he was not going to waste any more time with possible opponents when he had certain allies of greater authority upon whom to call. And for those who had eyes to see it, the long-secret partnership was now revealed as the supposedly irreconcilable Pompey and Crassus took their places on either side of the consul of their own making. With due propriety Caesar called upon his senior partner first, and Pompey stood up to address an excited and eager audience with what seems to have been a very cleverly designed speech to judge from the opening gambit which Dio preserves:

'It is not I alone, fellow-citizens, who approve this measure but all the rest of the Senate too, since that body voted for land to be granted not only to my own soldiers but to those who also once fought with Metellus Pius [in our Spanish campaign of the seventies]. That this vote was not then put into practice was an unfortunate but unavoidable result of the economic situation at that time, but now that I have made the state extremely rich, it is only right that the promise formerly made to the troops should be honoured, and that the rest should also enjoy the fruits of the common toil.'

In these few words Pompey convicted his senatorial opponents either of inconsistency or downright bad faith. He implied that they had been prepared to promise land only when it was clear that the promise could not be fulfilled, and he presented himself as the champion of the Senate's honour as well as the provider of the means of redeeming its past promises. Then having skilfully disposed of the opposition, he proceeded to go through the details of Caesar's Bill and approve every one, including a final provision requiring every member of the Senate to swear an oath to obey the law and not try to change it at a later date. This was a provision first introduced into agrarian legislation by the Marian tribune Saturninus forty years before, and it had the double advantage of giving the assignees of the land greater security of tenure and presenting the opponents of the Bill with the unenviable choice between eating humble pie and suffering a satisfactorily deflating penalty for refusing to swear. As this was not the sort of provision that was likely to endear the Bill to the Senate it will have been added only at a later stage, certainly after the failure of Caesar's attempt to win a favourable senatorial decree and possibly only at this popular meeting once Bibulus had made it clear that there was nothing to lose. At any event Pompey's wholehearted approval of this and all Caesar's measures was greeted with as much delight as Bibulus' intransigence had given offence, and just as Caesar had entreated the people to join him in persuading Bibulus to change his mind, so now he urged them to beseech Pompey's aid in protecting them and their interests against all who were working to oppose them. They complied with alacrity, and for all that Pompey would have preferred to get his way without becoming personally embroiled in popular politics, he was taking no half-measures now that it had become unavoidable. He delivered another long speech on his services to the state and his tireless dedication to the welfare of the people of Rome, and he concluded with the ominous promise that 'if anyone dared to raise a sword, he could be relied upon to snatch up his shield'.

Plutarch condemns this remark as an 'impulsive outburst, unworthy of Pompey's high esteem', but while he is no doubt right that it 'distressed the nobility' – or at least some of them – as much as it delighted the populace, it hardly qualifies for censure as 'the most arrogant thing he had ever said or done' and 'something for which even his friends apologized on the grounds that the words must have slipped out in the heat of the moment'. Perhaps Plutarch felt that it was raising the ghost of Sulla's pupil, but even if the offending words were 'I shall raise sword as well as shield' as Plutarch maintains, it was scarcely unreasonable to threaten to meet force with force. According to Appian, Bibulus and his faction were already prepared to arm their supporters to thwart the passing of Caesar's Bill, and Dio at least has no fault to find with Pompey's remark. He simply comments that it was immediately echoed by Crassus, and that the approval of 'the two men who were unanimously agreed to be the foremost in the city and the most influential at that time' caused many of the previously reluctant senators to support the Bill, largely through fear of not being on what had suddenly emerged as the stronger side. But Bibulus was not amongst them.

Motivated by personal animosities which were at least as potent as any political principles, Cato's faction displayed that inflexibility of purpose which reacts to increasing isolation by rigidification rather than relaxation. In a desperate attempt to pursue his hopeless opposition Bibulus had procured three tribunes to veto the enactment of the Bill, but the storm of popular displeasure soon broke those flimsy reeds and left him with no resort but to Higher Authority, which he promptly recruited to his cause by observing the heavens for omens. The advantage of this alliance was that it did not require his divine partner to produce any omens at all, favourable or unfavourable. The mere act of watching for them constituted a sacred occasion on which no public business could be transacted, and since there was no time-limit to this pursuit, Bibulus seems to have indicated that he would continue watching the heavens until the end of his consulship if necessary. And that is exactly what he did, after making one last secular attempt to outface Caesar in the Forum when the latter had ignored this ludicrous manipulation of the state religion to party political ends by fixing a day for a plebiscite on his Land Bill.

It seems unlikely that Pompey and Crassus were present on the day of the vote. They had already declared their support for the Bill, and for all Pompey's expressed determination to fight force with force in defence of the people's will he cannot have relished the prospect of being involved in the unseemly fracas which could all too easily break out in a Forum packed with an excited crowd including not only large numbers of his own land-hungry veterans but groups of professional heavies clutching daggers under the folds of their togas. That is not to say that the Three necessarily expected the trouble for which they were prepared. If a reference in the admittedly confused account of Appian is correct and Bibulus had summoned a meeting of the Senate at his house before the date appointed for the plebiscite, he had clearly failed to inspire any general enthusiasm for continued resistance to a Bill to which Pompey and Crassus had won a large number of formerly reluctant but realistic senators. Indeed, Pompey and his partners may well have doubted that Bibulus would turn up on the day, but Caesar had not been speaking for long when he observed the approach of Bibulus, Cato, Lucullus and their party. They were preceded by Bibulus' twelve lictors bearing the bundles of rods and axes that symbolized his consular authority and proved as effective as Moses' staff in turning aside the human waves. But if the people fell back at his approach, it was only partly through respect for the consulship. They hoped to find that he had relented as they watched him mounting the steps of the temple from which Caesar had been speaking, but when he ignored Caesar and began instead a loud tirade against the Land Bill, they first shouted him down and then cheered in delight as someone tipped a bucket of excrement over his head. Now platform-parties at popular assemblies were not usually equipped with buckets of excrement, and it soon became apparent that Caesar's henchmen were highly skilled agents of public vilification. Before Bibulus had time to wipe the filth from his eyes he heard the screams of his lictors being beaten up, and the first thing he saw was the smashing of his consular *fasces* and a terrific fracas in which his friends struggled valiantly to defend themselves against a hail of blows from instruments both blunt and sharp. With as much dignity as he could muster in his beshitten condition he turned to Caesar in a fury, bared his throat, and dared his colleague to cut it. But Caesar simply watched with bland amusement as the would-be martyr was seized from behind, kicked downstairs, and manhandled out of the Forum, which was then sealed off against any further interruptions. Only the indefatigable Cato found a way back through an unguarded back-street, struggled again to the platform and screamed a few more words of defiance, but he soon disappeared over the heads of the crowd like a storm-tossed ship in a howling gale, and there was no more opposition that day. 'And thus,' concludes Dio succinctly, 'the law was passed.'

The significance of this victory went far beyond the immediate legislation over which it had been fought. While Plutarch calls it 'the bait by which the people were caught and tamed so completely that they were ready to support any project commended by Pompey and his partners',

Dio emphasizes the complete collapse of the opposition in the face of
the popular enthusiasm, for when Bibulus convened the Senate on the
following day and tried to persuade them to annul the plebiscite, he found
his words falling on ears conveniently deafened by the noise of the mob.
There remained the necessity to acknowledge compliance with the popular will by swearing to abide by the distributions of land on pain of some
uncertain but evidently serious punishment. According to Appian the
penalty was death, but if it is right to dismiss this as a sensationalizing
exaggeration of such lesser penalties as expulsion from the Senate and
monetary fines which had been prescribed under Saturninus' Land Bill
of 100, there was obviously a sufficient deterrent to cause even Cato and
Metellus Celer to fall into line, despite their repeated declarations of intransigence that continued until the very last day before the penalties were
due to take effect. They then capitulated and took the oath, 'perhaps',
suggests Dio, 'because it is only human nature for men to utter promises
and threats more readily than to carry them out, or else they decided
that they were going to be punished to no purpose, since nothing would
be gained by their obstinacy'. As for Bibulus, he showed his disgruntle-
ment by incarcerating himself in his house for the remainder of his consulship, maintaining his scrutiny of the heavens, and issuing large numbers
of edicts condemning the coalition and all its works. No public meeting
was called without evoking a note from Bibulus declaring it invalid, but
no one took the slightest notice of these fatuous prohibitions, and political life continued with only one active consul, who proved to have an
even stiffer neck than his star-gazing colleague.

As members of the land commission Pompey and Crassus would soon
be leaving Rome, but probably not before they had seen to the safe passing of the two other measures in which they had the chief interest. For
Pompey, of course, the next priority was the long-delayed ratification
of his Eastern settlement, but because he wanted to secure the support
of the knights he probably agreed to allow the tax-farming law to take
precedence, as indicated by Dio. Caesar therefore introduced a Bill freeing
the publicans from one-third of their obligations under their Asian contracts, and just as it had proved useful to pack the Forum with Pompey's
land-hungry veterans for the agrarian law, so now Appian tells us that
interested financiers contributed 'multitudes of trusty servants', who
doubtless included a strong contingent of Crassus' own clients. Caesar
ignored the inevitable note from Bibulus, the assembly met, and the Bill
was passed. Needless to say, the delighted equestrians saw nothing monstrous in the political coalition which could get from the people what
Cato and his faction had blocked for so long in the Senate, and as a *quid
pro quo* for this valuable assistance they supported the Bill confirming

all Pompey's acts. This most probably followed hard on the heels of the tax-farming and agrarian legislation before the farmers of taxes had time to forget their obligations, the prospective farmers of land left Rome, or the fickle farmers of nothing lost their enthusiasm for these heady flights of demagogic democracy. And as Pompey watched the effortless rubber-stamping by plebiscite of something for which he had been struggling to gain acceptance for two and a half years through less skilful agents, he felt he had good reason to congratulate himself on the effectiveness of his new political alliance and particularly his support for Caesar, whom he was daily regarding with increasing favour as his most successful creation.

Although Caesar had not been a cheap investment and must still have been drawing heavily on his political partners to defray the expenses of the popular shows and circuses which Appian insists were far beyond his own means to put on, Pompey would gladly have invested ten times the sum to gain the handsome political dividends which Caesar had yielded, and he had further cause for self-congratulation when it appeared that not all Caesar's dividends were political. Where Crassus had tried in vain to 'sail into Alexandria' under his own flag as censor in 65 and under Rullus' tribunician flag of convenience in 63, Caesar now seems to have used the implicit threat of another plebiscite to persuade a resigned Senate to grant the title of Friend and Ally of the Roman People to King Ptolemy Auletes, who promptly showed his gratitude by a douceur of six thousand talents which Suetonius says 'Caesar extorted from him in his own name and that of Pompey', though almost certainly something will have stuck to Crassus' palm in the course of the transaction. At any rate Pompey was now convinced that he had found in Caesar as promising a protégé as Sulla had found in him, and when Caesar sought a proconsular province that would give him scope to exercise the military talents which he had discovered in Spain, Pompey was only too ready to support him – and for reasons which went beyond what is usually argued to have been a contractual obligation under the terms of the mutual benefit society. After all, Pompey could reasonably have regarded Caesar's assistance in securing his agrarian and Eastern legislation as the discharging of a debt already incurred by his electoral support, and we may be sure that if Pompey now continued to support him as a military as well as a political animal, there was an element of further self-interest in the calculation.

Once Caesar had proved his value as a political investment Pompey began to regard him less in the light of a short-dated stock purchased for fixed returns and more as a long-term investment which would offer security and growth in an uncertain political market. The only difficulty was that Crassus had also ploughed a great deal of capital into Caesar in the past, and while it was true that Pompey and Crassus were temporarily partners in politics, Pompey wanted to be sure of retaining the major interest in this particularly valuable investment which he was now happy to see transferred abroad with the prospect of very rapid expansion. And that is why Caesar was able to acquire a provincial appointment very different from the sinecure of 'Forests and Pasturelands' which a suspicious Senate had designated for the consuls of 59 in a pre-electoral attempt to confine his ambitions in case the wrong man won. By a plebiscite introduced by the tribune Vatinius (who obligingly introduced Bills that were for Caesar's personal advancement) he acquired instead not merely the usual proconsular province for one year but a special five-year commission of the Pompeian type to govern Cisalpine Gaul and Illyricum and to raise a force of three legions to help him do it. And when he decided that this was not enough, the province of Transalpine Gaul and a fourth legion were later added by the Senate itself, whose majority now realized the futility of refusing what would otherwise be granted by the people in a further erosion of its authority. For Caesar to have been able to achieve all this presupposes Pompey's support, and if Pompey supported the granting of so much military power to Caesar when there was not even an existing emergency such as the piracy or the Mithridatic Wars which had justified his own irregular commissions, it was because he felt sure of his man. It is only with hindsight that we see Pompey creating his own destroyer. In 59 he was supremely confident that his own military achievements were as unapproachable as his latent power would be unbeatable in the unlikely event of another civil war, and in blessing Caesar's appointment to Gaul Pompey was no more apprehensive than Sulla had been in sending *him* to Sicily and Africa in 82. On the contrary, he looked upon it as a useful strengthening of his own position at home to have a protégé on active service abroad with a considerable army, and just as Sulla had sought to bind Pompey to himself by bonds stronger than gratitude and mutual interest and respect, Pompey now secured Caesar by proposing to his daughter Julia, whom Caesar was only too delighted to see married to the most powerful influence behind his own advancement.

This marriage was a rather more wholesome affair than Sulla's callous arrangements which had had such distressing results. Julia was already betrothed, it is true, and about to be married to the Servilius Caepio whom Suetonius describes as 'a man who had rendered conspicuous services to Caesar in his electoral contest with Bibulus'; but even the most conspicuous of other men's services were obscured in the perspective of Pompey's support, and Caepio's marriage-plans were doomed the moment that Pompey offered for the hand of his betrothed. As for Julia herself, she received instead a kind and devoted if rather older husband, and in a social milieu where love was a happy accident of arranged marriages she can hardly have been desolated by the last-minute change of spouse. Caepio had cause for annoyance, of course, because it affected the honour of his ancient and influential family, but Pompey promptly pacified him by breaking his own daughter's betrothal to Faustus Sulla and offering her to Caepio instead. And that satisfied everyone except poor Faustus, who had no consolation in seeing Caepio as delighted as Caesar at their marriage-alliances with his father's former pupil (though this turned out to be only a postponement of his own marriage with Pompeia, perhaps because Caepio died young). The Romans were great believers in keeping a successful business in the family, and if necessary a family would be manufactured to accommodate the business, with the curious result in this case that the son-in-law was the senior partner. What Crassus thought of it is not recorded, but he can scarcely have been pleased when Caesar celebrated his new marriage-alliance by changing the order of precedence in which he called upon the senators to speak in the House. According to Suetonius, a consul customarily maintained for the whole year the order which he established on his first day in office, and since Pompey had been keeping a low profile at that time, Crassus had been called before him, presumably in recognition of his censorial dignity. But now Caesar started calling for Pompey's opinion before that of Crassus, and political observers began to see that two of the Monster's three heads were joined like Siamese twins of different sizes, of which the larger had that unmistakable hair-curl of Alexander the Great and the smaller belied its apparent effeminacy by the ferocity of its frown. The third was bald, and if it looked more shrunken and less comfortable than it had done before, its horns still carried their warning twist of hay.

Among the most anxious of these political observers must have been Cicero, whose letters provide our only contemporary literary evidence for the year 59 when they begin in April after a silence of over three months, during which presumably both he and his correspondent Atticus were in Rome. But if we are unfortunate in lacking the continuing correspondence that would have given us a reliable chronology (though not of course an objective commentary) for the events related by later sources for the first part of the year, we can glean from the letters of April and later many useful indications of what happened earlier as well as contemporary information. In April, for example, Cicero wrote bitterly from Antium that 'no one there cares if the land commissioners are alive or dead', gloatingly that his arch-enemy Clodius 'has no place among the twenty', and hopefully that he himself 'may be offered the embassy to

Egypt' – all of which indicates that the agrarian legislation and the lucrative recognition of King Ptolemy had occurred relatively recently. For it is clear that Cicero had only just become aware of the coalition. 'If the power of the Senate was unpopular', he wrote, 'what will it be like now that it has been transferred not to the people but to three irresponsible men?', though by admitting in the same month that he would 'not mind Egypt', 'would consider any offer' and 'might be tempted by a vacancy in the college of augurs' he revealed that it was jealousy rather than moral indignation which prompted his affirmation that 'it would never enter my head to envy Crassus or to repent of not having turned traitor to myself'. There is no doubt that Cicero privately regretted his folly in opposing the Land Bill and therefore Pompey himself. While still unaware of the coalition he had even undertaken the defence of his former consular colleague Antonius, the very man whom Pompey had rightly wanted recalled in disgrace for incompetence and misgovernment in Macedonia two years before, and whom Crassus had never forgiven for failing to support the Rullan Bill and Catiline's electoral campaign in 63. Referring to this case two years later with the belated delicacy of a returned exile Cicero acknowledged that his speech on Antonius' behalf early in 59 had contained 'complaints of certain political abuses', but he maintained that his remarks had been 'misreported by scoundrels to certain worthy men in terms far removed from those I had used'. The reality, according to Dio, had been a vitriolic personal attack on Caesar, and it is not without significance that within three hours of this political solecism the partners had met, decided that Cicero was to be silenced, and unleashed his arch-enemy Clodius by transferring that formidable reprobate to the plebeians by a ceremony in which Pompey himself acted as augur and declared the omens favourable. This meant that Clodius could now stand for the tribunate of 58, and the fear of what that vindictive character might do to him was to hang like the sword of Damocles over Cicero's head and make him cling to Pompey for a protection that was far from certain even if he remained on his best behaviour. But it is thanks to Cicero's indiscretion at Antonius' trial that we have such a valuable and voluble spate of letters from his various country-houses in April and May, for it would be too much of a coincidence if his sudden self-rustication were unconnected with a feeling that discretion was the better part of valour in the face of an offended Three-Headed Monster – and a hope that his absence might make its heart grow fonder.

Cicero's surprised discovery of the political partnership only in April reinforces Plutarch's statement that Bibulus retired from the political stage with eight months of his consulship to run as evidence against the usual view that Caesar's first Land Bill had been passed as early as

January. The appearance of Pompey and Crassus alongside Caesar and their speeches in favour of that Bill must have made their coalition obvious, and if Cicero did not know about the coalition until April, the Bill was not passed until then. Indeed it seems most likely that not only the Land Bill but those concerning Crassus' tax-farming concessions, Pompey's Eastern settlement and Caesar's proconsular command all cascaded into law in a great torrent of democratic legislation over a period of days rather than weeks, with the result that Cicero kept bombarding Atticus with demands for every scrap of news from Rome and wild speculations on the Monster's next moves. The sudden revelation that Pompey and Crassus were not at daggers drawn but hand-in-glove gave rise to a widespread belief that they would be standing together for the consulships of 58, but some shrewder political observer had clearly suggested to Cicero that Servius Sulpicius and Aulus Gabinius were likelier candidates, and one of the orator's numerous letters to Atticus in that eventful April requested his opinion. What Atticus replied we do not know, but it says little for Cicero's political understanding that he should even have considered a joint candidature of Pompey and Crassus as a strong possibility at this time. Pompey had no more intention of seeing Crassus in a position of official equality with him in 58 than in 59, or indeed of undertaking the tiresome burden of the consulship at all. The shrewder observer had been right in believing that Pompey and his partners would secure the election of reliable agents, and he had accurately identified one of them.

Aulus Gabinius was a natural choice as Pompey's man. He had been the tribune of 67 who had proposed the law granting Pompey his commission against the pirates, and he had subsequently proved a loyal and able legate in Pompey's Eastern campaigns. His running-mate, on the other hand, was perhaps a more general compromise candidate of the whole partnership. This was Lucius Calpurnius Piso Caesoninus, a man of impeccable family who was only too happy to secure the consulship by promising to secure his promoters' political interests and by marrying his daughter to one of them. For just as Pompey and Caesar had bound themselves to each other through Julia, so Piso now accepted Caesar's offer for the hand of his daughter Calpurnia, who would not only bind him to Caesar but also, through Julia, to Pompey. With the news of Caesar's betrothal to Calpurnia following hard on the heels of Pompey's to Julia, there was some justice in Marcus Cato's snide comment that the Roman empire was becoming a marriage bureau. But if Cato burned with outrage at 'seeing authority prostituted by marriage alliances and having to watch men helping each other to provinces and armies by means of women' as though this was a new phenomenon in Roman politics, it was Cato upon whom Cicero laid the blame for the 'revolution in the wheel of state' which he so decried: Cato's inflexibility had done more than anything to unite 'those who disregard auspices and laws, hand out kingdoms and tetrarchies like farms, and lavish vast sums of money on one or two people'. Cicero was too self-righteous to acknowledge his own contribution to the situation, and now that he knew that he had missed his opportunity and would receive neither his coveted augurship nor the ambassadorial appointment to Alexandria, he showed his exasperation in an explosion of epistolary spitefulness to the long-suffering Atticus: 'Let them make consuls and tribunes of anyone they like,' he wrote; 'let them cloak filthy old Vatinius' scrofula with the double-dyed purple of an augur's robes, and you will see even Cato lauded to the skies before long!' Pompey, whom he cannot forgive for seeking to control him by fear rather than favour, is now 'the Jerusalemite plebeianizer of Clodius', and in his bitterness at what he sees as 'a poor reward for all those flattering speeches I made on his achievements' Cicero promises 'a most divine recantation'. But it is easy to be brave in a private letter to a trusted friend. Cicero was under no illusions about his need for protection, and he knew that his only hope of finding it was under Pompey's powerful wing.

Grasping now at every shred of evidence for a split in Pompey's partnership or a waning of Pompey's personal popularity that might make 'Africanus' turn again to his 'Laelius' for help and advice, Cicero rejoiced to hear in mid-April that though Clodius was standing for the tribunate for the following year it was not as a protégé of the coalition, for he was said to be threatening to undo all Caesar's legislation. The first word of this extraordinary development had come from Curio, a young aristocrat who had been a supporter of Clodius against Cicero at the trial of 61. He now appears in the guise of an outspoken opponent of the 'proud kings', and assures Cicero that they have the unanimous hatred of the younger generation. Then Cicero is told much more of the same sort by letters from Atticus, who maintains that Pompey and Caesar are so angry with Clodius that they are trying to deny the validity of his adoption by a plebeian family and therefore his eligibility to stand for the tribunate. 'Just let Clodius send me a few witnesses,' replies a cheerful Cicero, 'and I'll swear an affidavit that I heard Gnaeus – Balbus' colleague that is – tell me himself that he had assisted in taking the auspices at the adoption ceremony.' Departing from his usual characterization of Pompey by the name of an oriental magnifico Cicero's sarcasm now delights in depreciating him as someone forgotten except as a colleague of Caesar's henchman, but Cicero was being even more naïvely Micawberish than usual if he really thought that Clodius could oppose the Monster to its face and survive in political life. That there was some foundation for the news beyond dinner-table gossip is not to be doubted, but it is far from certain that the foundation was the rock of truth and not the shifting sands of political strategy. For Clodius to have turned against his sponsors before the elections seems incredible, and if he was openly threatening to reverse Caesar's legislation as Cicero's letters maintain, it can have been no surprise to 'our proud kings', who were no more unsubtle than Clodius was politically suicidal. Indeed their motive for allowing Clodius to make this pretence of opposition is unwittingly revealed by Cicero himself. In a letter of the end of April he expresses his fears 'that the Pasha may run amok when he realizes how people are getting at him and how easily these measures can be upset'. By early May these fears have materialized. 'The Pasha *is* running amok', he writes. 'We may expect anything. He is quite clearly setting up a despotism. What else can be the meaning of this sudden marriage-alliance, the proposals about the Campanian land, this reckless expenditure of money? If that were all it would be bad enough, but he won't stop there. Mark my words, these are just the first steps towards a lot more mischief.' What Cicero failed to realize was that the Pasha *wanted* to 'run amok', needed an excuse, and found it in Clodius' pretended threat to undo the legislation which was providing farms for his veterans and had ratified his Eastern settlement.

Of the three manifestations of 'running amuck' which Cicero diagnoses as symptoms of an approaching despotism the 'marriage-alliance' between Pompey and Caesar is the easiest to recognize. The 'expenditure of money' is ambiguous, but it is unlikely to refer to any purchases of land under the former agrarian law because that piece of legislation had already been superseded by a new one of more sinister significance. More likely it refers to expenditure on the vote-catching shows that Caesar provided 'far beyond his own means', or to the more direct buying of votes for the passing of a new Land Bill and for the electoral campaign of the coalition's consular candidates for the next year. But if both the marriage-alliance and the election of tame consuls could be called 'despotic' in character, it was to secure the passage of the new Land Bill that Pompey wanted the excuse to 'run amok' by using the heavy methods which Plutarch describes as 'filling the city with his soldiers and carrying everything with a high hand'. For this new Bill provided for the distribution of the public land of Campania which had been excluded from the earlier Act, and to understand the 'despotic' character of settling this particular area with Pompey's veterans we need look no further than Cicero's speech against the last politician who attempted to establish a clientele there – the tribune Rullus who in 63 had been used by Crassus to try to establish a power-base in Campania as an insurance against Pompey's return.

Though not as extensive then as its namesake today, ancient Campania was a considerable area of excellent farming land bounded by the Aurunci mountains in the north-west, the Apennines of Samnium in the interior, and the spur of Sorrento to the south-east. Its centre was Capua, a town some 120 miles south-east of Rome on the Appian Way and once a proud and powerful ally of the Republic until it defected to Hannibal in 216 and gave Rome the excuse to destroy it in revenge five years later. Since then its former territories had been designated Roman public land and let out to tenant farmers whose rents provided a useful source of revenue to the Roman Treasury. But it was not so much the loss of revenue against which Cicero had inveighed in 63 when Rullus had proposed distributing the territory in freehold lots to the Roman proletariat and elevating Capua from a provincial market-town to the status of a Roman colony by the infusion of five thousand citizens. His main point had been the danger of establishing 'the trusty friends' of Rullus' party in Capua, 'a city so well able to organize and make war'. Raising the old spectre of the Hannibalic Wars he had gone on to picture Capua once more as a rival to Rome, a citadel of Rullus' henchmen 'always disposed to violence and ready for revolution whenever their benefactors gave the word'. He had also condemned the hypocrisy of a measure supposedly designed to provide for the landless poor of Rome by dispossessing the existing tenants, 'men of the most honest, reliable and unassuming type, excellent both as farmers and soldiers'. And it is in that last remark that we find the answer to the much-discussed question of what happened to the tenant-farmers who were now dispossessed when Caesar's second Land Bill was successfully passed. While Pompey had wanted a nearby settlement for a devoted veteran army, Caesar had wanted a new army to take to Gaul with him in the following year, and he knew of no better potential recruits than the tenant-farmers of Campania, 'excellent both as farmers *and soldiers*'.

Cicero at last began to realize how cleverly Pompey had been directing the political drama from behind the scenes, and complained bitterly to Atticus:

Asked if he [Pompey] agreed with Caesar's laws he replied that he could not answer for Caesar's methods. The agrarian law? Yes, that seemed sound, but whether it could be vetoed by a tribune or not was no concern of his. The Alexandrian question? Yes, it was high time that a settlement was made with King Ptolemy, but really it was no business of his whether Bibulus was watching the heavens at the time or not. The tax-gatherers and the reduction of the amounts they had contracted for? Yes, they were a class that he wished to oblige. When asked what would happen if Bibulus were to come into the Forum on that occasion, he simply replied that he was no prophet. And now what has the Pasha to say for himself? That he imposed a tax on Antilibanus in distant Syria that will make up for the lost revenues from land on our doorstep! I can't see how he will get away with that one. 'Oh, I'll keep you lot quiet with Caesar's army,' says he.

And in that final remark true words were written in jest. For Pompey had not only arranged to settle such large numbers of his own army-veterans on rich farms in Campania that he would one day be able to make his famous boast that he had only to stamp his foot and armies would spring up from the soil of Italy to serve him. He had also arranged that Caesar would have a new army on active service as an extra safe-guard to the interests of his patron just as Pompey himself had secured the position of Sulla, and in the meantime Caesar's potential army would serve a useful political role in Rome. After all, however much the dispos-sessed tenants of Campania might resent their treatment, they could not afford to oppose the wishes of the one man who could offer them a lucrative military replacement for the agricultural livelihood which he had removed.

Not surprisingly the Campanian Land Bill and the way it was carried into law by the formidable presence of Pompey's veterans did nothing to enhance Pompey's popularity among sections of society other than the beneficiaries and his own personal adherents. In June Cicero was back in Rome, and in a letter to Atticus who was going abroad on business he complained of the general sense of helplessness against the will of the Monster. His mention of a greater freedom of speech is an indication of the threat of violence by which the opposition had been cowed while the Campanian Law was passed in the previous month, and a later allusion to a conspiracy to assassinate Pompey in mid-May suggests that the opposition had been more than vocal. 'But if disgust is getting the better of fear,' he continues, 'it does not alleviate the universal despair.' He tells how the Campanian Law required all candidates for office to take an oath never to suggest any scheme to remove the tenure of the land assigned under its provisions, and how only one, Marcus Laterensis, chose to withdraw from the elections rather than swear. He also praises Curio as the only senator bold enough to speak openly against the Monster, before whose formidable appearance even Cato seems to have kept a discreet silence, as indeed did Cicero himself when not confiding to his friend.

Cicero was becoming increasingly afraid of what Clodius would do to him unless he accepted one of the two positions of security which Caesar had offered him for the year of Clodius' tribunate. One was a post on Caesar's own general staff for the following year, the other an opportunity to go abroad on an ambassadorial sinecure, and Cicero was under no illusions that they had been offered for altruistic reasons. The former would be safer and meant that he need not leave Rome, but it would compromise his political independence. The latter would be less compromising but as effectively silencing and also less secure, since he would not enjoy the immunity conferred by the military appointment. But if Cicero proceeds to scorn both these offers in his letter to Atticus and declares his intention to stay and defy Clodius to do his worst, he also asks Atticus not to mention this to anyone else, doubtless because he wishes to keep his options open as long as possible.

By July Pompey was away at Capua, where he and his fellow land commissioners were busily establishing his veterans in a Roman colony and apportioning the Campanian farmland. And as Pompey's old soldiers were replaced in the capital by an influx of dispossessed tenant-farmers, it is not surprising that his popularity reached a low ebb among the changing populace. According to Cicero 'even Bibulus is now exalted to the skies', and if the noticeable lack of enthusiasm in imparting this information is typical of a man 'who found it hard to bear the praise of any man but himself', there was at least the satisfaction of reporting that Pompey's stock had never been lower. 'To my great sorrow,' he wrote with gloating sarcasm, 'my darling Pompey has shattered his own reputation, and I am very much afraid that our rulers may find it necessary to try the effect of fear.' And he proceeded to make a virtue out of what was a necessity in the face of his preoccupying fear of Clodius: 'I myself do not quarrel with them on account of my friendship with Pompey, though I refrain from strong expressions of approval in order not to compromise my previous actions.'

But there were no such restraints on the dispossessed mobs who packed the circuses and theatres, and Cicero could report some general hissing at a gladiatorial show given by Gabinius and one particularly pointed attack on Pompey delivered by an actor reciting some verses from a play 'that might have been specially written for Pompey'. With a keen satirical sense the actor had emphasized such lines as 'By our misfortunes art thou great', and 'Thy boldness still in time to come/Wilt thou lament', and 'If neither law nor custom can restrain'. They were received with terrific applause and encored several times until the fun suddenly stopped at Caesar's entrance, for no one dared make fun of Pompey in Caesar's presence any more than they would have done if Pompey had been there in person. But if Caesar was annoyed when his entrance was greeted with a 'frozen silence' that was itself an insult of sorts to the demagogue who was used to applause, he was furious when Curio entered soon after him 'to the kind of ovation which Pompey himself used to receive when the Republic was still sound'. Within hours a letter was being expressed down the Appian Way to Capua. Caesar was reporting this outrage to Pompey and suggesting, so Cicero believed, a series of punitive measures which revealed that his attitude was that of the emperor Caligula: 'Let them hate provided they fear.' And since the Roman knights had so far forgotten their gratitude for the tax-farming concessions that they had joined in the standing ovation for Curio, there was a rumour of a proposal to rescind the laws which gave them seats of honour at theatrical performances and guaranteed the sale of corn at fixed prices. But Pompey was not as untroubled by unpopularity as Caesar, whose famous retort to criticism was that 'it is only to be expected of inferiors that they will cast mud at their betters in order that they may appear to be their equals'. Pompey did not enjoy mud-fights at all, and when he heard about the incidents at the games and the theatre and the insulting edicts which Bibulus kept posting up about him outside his house, he steeled himself to return to Rome and address the popular assembly in person in an attempt to recover his old prestige.

According to Cicero the result was disastrous:

Our friend, having always been carried along on a wave of admiration and glory and being totally unaccustomed to disrespect, is a broken man, disfigured in body, crushed in spirit, and not knowing where to turn. He sees that to advance brings him nearer to the cliff-edge, yet to retreat is a confession of weakness. The men of quality are his enemies. The riff-raff are no longer his friends. You see how soft-hearted I am. I could not keep back my tears when I saw him delivering a speech on Bibulus' edicts on 25 July. He used to carry himself so proudly in that place where he once enjoyed such boundless popularity and universal respect. But now how abject he was! What a sorry figure he cut – in his own eyes too, quite apart from what his audience thought. What a sight it was – pleasing to Crassus alone but not to others. He was a fallen star, a man who had slipped more by accident than design into his coalition with Caesar. I felt as I imagine the painter Apelles might have felt if he had seen his Venus daubed with mud, for I could not endure without deep distress the disfigurement of a man on whose adornment and embellishment I had lavished all the colours of my oratorical art. And while I realize that no one looks upon it as my duty to remain friends with Pompey after the Clodius business, my affection for the man is still such that no injury could extinguish it. All the same, the fact remains that Bibulus' scathing edicts about him are now so popular that you simply cannot get past the place where they are posted up for the crowds of people reading them. Pompey himself finds them so distressing that he is wasting away with grief, and I must say I too am far from pleased – and not only because they cause so much pain to a man I always loved. Pompey is an impulsive man who is as unaccustomed to abuse as he is terrifying once he gets a sword in his hand, and I very much fear that he may give free rein to his present mortification and anger.

Now Cicero was no literary Apelles, who was famed for his use of
a secret varnish which gave a beautifully soft tone to his works of art.
In correspondence as in the courtroom Cicero painted everything in the
most vivid splashes of hyperbole, and Pompey's address may not have
been quite as disastrous as he represented it. On the other hand, the composition contains enough realistic features to suggest that the central
figure was not wildly overdrawn. Crassus' enjoyment of a dismal performance by Pompey is certainly credible, not because the coalition was
breaking up but because Crassus always gloated over the misfortunes
of others, even his friends; and since he was a man 'who thought he might
surpass all other men by his combination of family and wealth', he must
have resented not being the senior partner in the coalition. Moreover it
is clear that Pompey failed in his attempt to win popular support against
Bibulus' defamatory edicts, despite the fact that Bibulus had ordered a
postponement of the elections until 18 October, which Cicero tells us
would normally have been a very unpopular measure. Pompey's more
dignified appeal was as ineffective as Caesar's inflammatory proposal that
the mob should go and set fire to Bibulus' house – a suggestion that would
have met with an enthusiastic response only a few weeks earlier but now
raised scarcely a murmur of support. It seems then that there is something
more substantial than wishful thinking in Cicero's assertion that 'those
men who are all-powerful have become all-hated yet without giving any
hope of a change'; and if so, it is also possible that he was right in pictur-
ing Pompey as 'thoroughly disgusted and sick to death of it all'.

In August Cicero elaborated on this theme to Atticus, and his letter
indicates a growing intimacy between an unhappy Pompey and himself:

> The first thing to tell you is that our friend the Pasha is heartily sick of his
> position and longs to be restored to the pedestal from which he fell. He confides
> his distress to me and at times openly asks me for a remedy, but I do not think
> there is one. Next you must know that the whole of their party, both the prin-
> cipals and their followers, are outstaying their welcome, and though no one
> actually opposes them, there never was a greater unanimity of feeling or popu-
> lar expression of it than there is now.

There is no reason to doubt either that Pompey was genuinely uncomfortable about his political reputation or that he confided in Cicero. After
all, it seems unlikely that he had abandoned his long-term objective of
achieving establishmentarian respectability, and he saw Cicero as a useful
agent who might do much to reassure the Senate that his recent demonstration of power had been purely defensive, a means of attaining honourable ends against unreasonable opposition. But what Cicero failed to realize was that Pompey was not going to defend him against Clodius without

some more positive recompense than the political silence which Cicero was now observing. In confiding his distress Pompey was seeking public support and he presented Cicero with an opportunity to show it by inviting him to replace a deceased colleague on the land commission. But Cicero refused the position as bravely or as blindly as he had refused Caesar's offer of a post on his proconsular staff. No offence may have been meant, but offence was certainly taken, particularly as mere commiseration was entirely inadequate in the face of a second alleged conspiracy against Pompey's life within three months.

Inevitably the fullest account of this curious affair, in which large numbers of prominent nobles were accused by a certain Vettius of plotting to put Pompey permanently out of his misery, is in one of Cicero's letters, and because there is so much disagreement about the true nature of the allegations, it is worth quoting in full the relevant part, written to Atticus in August or September 59:

That fellow Vettius, our famous informer, evidently promised Caesar that he would frame the young Curio. He therefore wormed his way into the young man's friendship, and saw a good deal of him, as the facts prove. Then after a while he reached the point of declaring his determination to set upon Pompey with the help of his slaves and kill him. Curio told his father about it, and his father told Pompey. The matter was then reported to the Senate. When Vettius was hauled up, he at first kept denying that he had ever passed the time of day with Curio, but not for long. He soon asked permission to turn state's evidence. There was a howl of objections, but nevertheless he proceeded to testify that a band of young men had been formed under Curio's leadership. Among the first members were Paullus, Quintus Caepio (Brutus, I mean) and Lentulus, the son of the *flamen* (with his father's knowledge). Then he said that Septimius, Bibulus' secretary, had brought him a dagger from the consul's own hand. That of course was farcical – just as if Vettius would have been short of a dagger if the consul had not sent him one! Besides, it was considered incredible that Bibulus would have been involved since it was he who had warned Pompey to be on his guard against plots on 13 May, and Pompey had thanked him. At any rate young Curio flatly denied Vettius' accusation, and the flaw in Vettius' story which was particularly seized upon was his allegation that the young men's plan had been to attack Pompey in the Forum during Gabinius' gladiatorial show, and that Paullus was the ringleader. But everyone knew that Paullus was in Macedonia at that time. The Senate then decreed that Vettius should be committed on his own admission of having been in possession of an offensive weapon, and that if anyone released him, it should be considered an offence against the state. The general view is that the original plan was for Vettius to have been arrested in the Forum with the dagger and his slaves and then to have asked to turn state's evidence, and it would have worked if only the Curios had not reported the affair to Pompey before the event.

So far, so good: the Senate's decree was read out to the assembly. But the next day Caesar brought Vettius to the rostra and set him on that public platform to which a mere fellow-consul like Bibulus cannot aspire! Here Vettius said all he wanted about the affair in a way that made it obvious that he had been carefully primed and schooled. To start with he left out Caepio, whose name he had been most emphatic about in the Senate, so that it became clear that a busy night with much nocturnal coaching had intervened. Next he named names on which he had not breathed the faintest breath of suspicion in the Senate – Lucius Lucullus (who, he alleged, used to communicate with him through Fannius, the assistant prosecutor in Clodius' trial) and Lucius Domitius, whose house was supposed to have been the base of operations. As for me, he did not actually accuse me by name but said that a certain voluble ex-consul who happened to live near the present consul had told him that what was needed was a Servilius Ahala or a Brutus. Then right at the end, when he had been called back by Vatinius after the assembly had been dismissed, he added that he had heard Curio say that Piso, my son-in-law, and Marcus Laterensis were also involved. The upshot of it all is that Vettius is now up before the praetor on a charge of violence, and after his conviction he will doubtless ask leave to turn state's evidence. And if that is granted, there are likely to be some prosecutions. But though I am not the man to underestimate likely dangers, I can't say that this is something that greatly worries me.

Unfortunately Cicero does not tell us how the affair ended, and the sole point of unanimity among our other vague and discordant sources is that Vettius died mysteriously in prison before he could stand trial. Beyond that there is disagreement not only about the agency responsible for the informer's untimely demise – Suetonius suggests Caesar, while Appian and Dio suspect some of the accused – but on the more fundamental question whether there was a genuine conspiracy at all or it was all a fabrication either of Vettius' own making or at the behest of others. Dio alone suggests that the conspiracy was genuine, and though the complacency of Cicero's letter to Atticus invalidates Dio's claim that Cicero and Lucullus were behind it, it is not inconceivable that Curio junior and a group of young hot-heads really did conspire to assassinate Pompey and Caesar (for it would have been suicidal to eliminate the one without the other).

The arguments which Cicero uses to exonerate the suspects are far from conclusive. The fact that it was Curio's father who had first alerted Pompey against Vettius is no proof that what he told Pompey was the whole truth. If the father had discovered that his son was implicated in a genuine plot, there would be no better way to protect him from the results of his folly than to do exactly what he did, warn Pompey of his danger, and put the whole blame on Vettius. Moreover it was not long since Cicero had told Atticus how Curio had come to assure him of 'the younger generation's hatred for the proud kings', and Curio had done nothing to disguise his opposition. As for Paullus, Lentulus and Caepio Brutus, the absence of the first in Macedonia at the time of Vettius' arrest does not preclude an organizational role, the second had little cause to love the man whose protégé Gabinius was his father's rival in the consular elections for 58, and the third had both a strong personal motive and a retrospective capacity for assassination: he was the son of the Brutus whom Pompey had executed after receiving his surrender in the war against Lepidus in 77, and he would one day assassinate Caesar. And even Bibulus is not above suspicion. He more than anyone had cause to hate the men who had turned the year which should have been the crowning glory of his career into one that was parodied as the consulship of 'Julius and Caesar', and when Cicero ridicules the accusation that the self-martyred consul had sent Vettius the intended murder-weapon by special messenger, he had evidently forgotten his own oratorical image of the admittedly metaphorical dagger which Catiline 'had dedicated with Heaven only knows what secret rites in preparation for plunging it into the body of a consul', namely himself, in 63.

But this is not to say that there really was a conspiracy against Pompey's life, only that Cicero's arguments against it are not ones which he could have found any difficulty in questioning if they had been presented by a rival in a court of law. It may well be that Vettius' story was, as Cicero suggests, a complete fabrication, but if so it is impossible to follow Cicero in accusing Caesar of instigating it as a means of framing Curio. On the principle of *cui bono?* it might appear credible that Caesar and Pompey sought to revive popular support and silence their political enemies by the scheme, but if they had really been behind Vettius from the outset, he would certainly have been properly primed and would not have needed to change his evidence overnight after his appearance before the Senate. It seems more likely that Vettius had been operating on his own initiative until his arrest. His whole career had been that of an unscrupulous political opportunist who would sell anything or anyone for sufficient pieces of silver. Sulla's proscriptions had provided him with a golden opportunity for self-enrichment, and when he had run through one ill-gotten fortune, he joined Catiline's revolutionaries in the hope of making another – and did not hesitate to denounce his leader as soon as he found that he had backed the wrong horse. And now it was probably as another way of restoring his failing fortunes that he conceived the idea of exploiting the political situation of 59 by cultivating the young Curio and other opponents of the coalition: he would either egg them on into a real conspiracy which he could then reveal, or at least incriminate sufficient of them by his contact so that he could pretend to be their agent and turn state's evidence for an appropriate consideration from interested parties. Unfortunately for him Curio senior heard of the real or pretended conspiracy and attempted to save his son from either just or unjust suspicion by reporting the matter to Pompey, who in turn informed the Senate which proceeded to arrest and examine Vettius. And this is the stage at which Caesar is most likely to have stepped in to try to make political capital out of this sudden windfall.

There is no reason to doubt Cicero's careful note of the omissions and additions in the list of the accused which Vettius had evidently revised by the time Caesar brought him out to give testimony before the people on the following day. It was ironic in the perspective of history that Caesar should have insisted on the removal of the name of his future assassin, but the reason was very probably to avoid embarrassment to the branch of the Caepiones into whose house Pompey had betrothed his daughter, for Brutus had become a Caepio by adoption. As for the many additions it is not hard to find the motive for the inclusion of Lucullus, Cicero, Piso Frugi (who was Cicero's son-in-law) and Marcus Laterensis (the one candidate for office who had withdrawn from the elections rather than take the oath to abide by Caesar's second Land Act). It was an excellent opportunity to frighten these actual or potential opponents into silence. These men cannot have been seriously suspected by Pompey and Caesar, for Caesar would then have taken good care to keep his informer alive. As it was, Vettius met a convenient end after furnishing a useful example of what could be done more effectively if the opposition did not fall into line.

The timing of this warning was just right for the elections, at which Pompey, Caesar and Crassus successfully mobilized their human and financial resources to secure the consulships of 58 for Gabinius and Piso Caesoninus and to restore their waning popularity to its former brilliance. While Pompey's veterans were no doubt summoned to Rome for the occasion, Caesar's new army was already there and needed little extra inducement to follow the wishes of its general. Cicero might have been telling Atticus in October that 'nothing could be more desperate than the plight of the Republic and nothing could exceed the hatred felt for those responsible', but after the elections the incident which he related to Quintus to show how 'utterly the Republic is lost' also reveals that Pompey's popularity was restored. It concerned a certain Gaius Cato, 'a man of no judgement yet a Roman and a Cato', who wanted to prosecute Gabinius for electoral bribery. He was so angry about being denied access to the magistrates from whom he needed to ask permission for the prosecution that he denounced Pompey publicly as a 'dictator', and he only just escaped being lynched.

As this eventful year drew to its close Pompey could feel satisfied with the past and confident of the future. Although the year had not been without difficulties, he had secured all his main objectives. His great Eastern settlement had been ratified. His veterans had been provided with their promised farms, and they in turn were providing him with a formidable political clientèle within easy calling distance of the capital. As for the future, two loyal and able consuls had been elected for the following year along with a fiery tribune who could be unleashed on potential opponents as necessary. It was altogether highly satisfactory, and Pompey was particularly pleased with himself for having found such an effective protégé as Caesar, through whom all these political successes had been won. That he was nurturing a deadly rival is recognizable only in the perspective of history. At the time, Pompey looked upon Caesar as Sulla had looked upon him, as a safe investment which was paying handsome dividends; and handsomest of all in Pompey's tender eye was his new wife, with whom he had fallen passionately in love. With his political struggles seemingly over, his popularity restored, and a delightful companion for his leisure, the same man who had so recently mocked Lucullus for retiring into a life of luxurious ease was himself now only too happy to desert the political scene for the peace of his villas and gardens – at least until he awoke with a start to the unpleasant realization that mice will take advantage of even the most monstrous cat if it disappears leaving only a toothless grin of contentment to remind them of its existence.

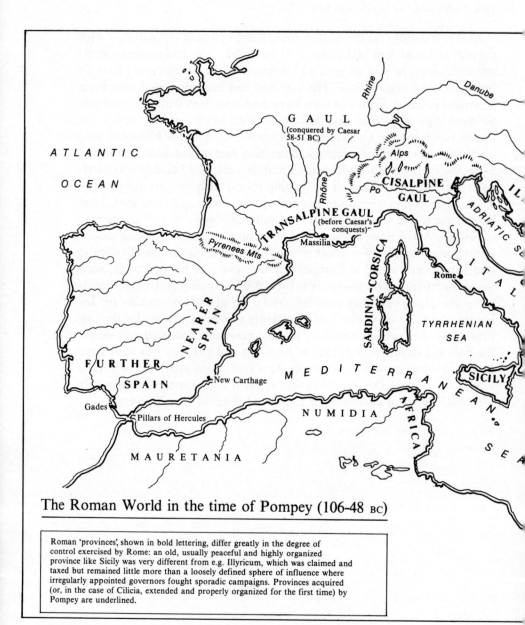

The Roman World in the time of Pompey (106-48 BC)

Roman 'provinces', shown in bold lettering, differ greatly in the degree of
control exercised by Rome: an old, usually peaceful and highly organized
province like Sicily was very different from e.g. Illyricum, which was claimed and
taxed but remained little more than a loosely defined sphere of influence where
irregularly appointed governors fought sporadic campaigns. Provinces acquired
(or, in the case of Cilicia, extended and properly organized for the first time) by
Pompey are underlined.

Italy

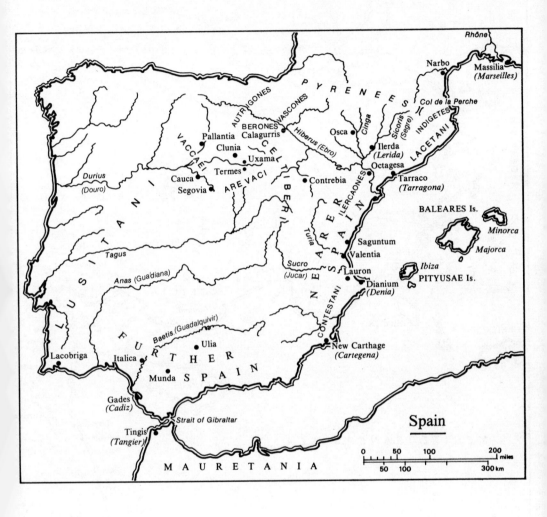

Spain

The East

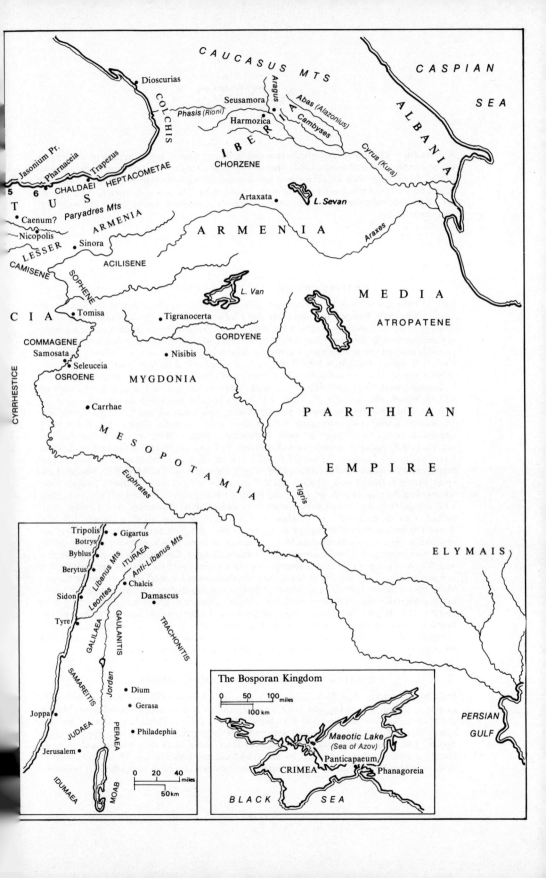

CAUCASUS MTS

CASPIAN

SEA

Dioscurias

COLCHIS

Phasis (Rioni)

Seusamora

Aragus

Abas (Alazonius)

IBERIA

Cambyses

Harmozica

ALBANIA

CHORZENE

Cyrus (Kura)

Jasonium Pr.

Pharnaccia

Trapezus

HEPTACOMETAE

CHALDAEI

5 6

T U S

Caenum?   Paryadres Mts

Nicopolis

LESSER   ARMENIA

Sinora

CAMISENE

SOPHENE

ACILISENE

Artaxata

L. Sevan

ARMENIA

Araxes

MEDIA

ATROPATENE

CIA

Tomisa

L. Van

COMMAGENE

Samosata

Seleuceia

Tigranocerta

GORDYENE

OSROENE

MYGDONIA

Nisibis

Carrhae

PARTHIAN

CYRRHESTICE

MESOPOTAMIA

EMPIRE

Euphrates

Tigris

ELYMAIS

Tripolis   Gigartus

Botrys

Byblus

ITURAEA

Anti-Libanus Mts

Berytus

Libanus Mts

Chalcis

Sidon

Leontes

Damascus

Tyre

GALILAEA

GAULANITIS

TRACHONITIS

SAMAREITIS

Jordan

PERAEA

Dium

Gerasa

Joppa

JUDAEA

Philadephia

Jerusalem

IDUMAEA

MOAB

0   20   40 miles

50km

The Bosporan Kingdom

0   50   100 miles

100 km

Maeotic Lake
(Sea of Azov)

Panticapaeum

CRIMEA

Phanagoreia

PERSIAN

GULF

BLACK   SEA

NOTES

Abbreviations: The abbreviated references to ancient literary sources and collections of inscriptions will be comprehensible to the specialists who will use them. Modern works are cited by the authors' names, occasionally with an abbreviated title but usually with the date of publication of their works, full details of which will be found in the Bibliography. The only idiosyncratic abbreviations are TP and SB, referring to the collections of Cicero's correspondence by Tyrell & Purser and Shackleton Bailey.

CHAPTER ONE (pp. 1–11): A SCHOOLING IN WAR

Date of birth (29 Sep 106 by unreformed calendar): Vell 2.53; Pliny *NH* 37.13. **Family**: on relationships of the Pompeii and possibility that P's father and Q. Pompeius Rufus (cos 88 with Sulla) were second cousins once removed or third cousins (hardly relevant politically) see summary of recent research in Ward 1977, 123 n 84. P's own family was not of the old nobility. Grandfather probably reached praetorship and governed Macedonia *pro praetore* in 117 (*SIG* 1².318; Groebe 1909; Gelzer 1941; Broughton *MRR* Supp (1960) 48). Father had become praetor by 92 at latest (*MRR* 2.19 n 3). Mother was Lucilia, of senatorial family (Vell 2.29), probably niece of the satirist C. Lucilius: see further Gelzer 1941. P was apparently an only son. He had a sister who married a C. Memmius, who served as P's legate in 82–1 in Sicily and was killed serving as his quaestor in Spain (Plut *P* 11; *Sert* 21; Orosius 5.23.12). **Marius and Sulla**: see esp. Plutarch's *Lives*; also for Marius: Carney 1962, Ooteghem 1964, Kildahl 1968; for Sulla: Oman 1903, Baker 1927, Carcopino 1931, Lanzani 1936; for both: Gabba 1972. **African War**: see also Sallust *Jug* esp. 102–13; Livy *Ep* 62, 64–7; Appian *Numidica* (frags); Vell 2.11–12; Dio fr 89; Florus 1.36; Orosius 5.15.1–19, 321–5; Diodorus 35.39; Gsell, vol 7; on significance of Marius' army reforms and development of professional armies see Gabba 1973, Harmand 1967. **Cimbric War**: see also Livy *Ep* 63, 65, 67–8; Dio frs 90–2; Florus 1.38; Vell 2.12; Orosius 5.16, 327–31. **Italian (Social) War**: see also App *BC* 1.34–54 (esp. 40, 47, 50 and 52 for P's father's role); Florus 2.6; Diod 37.2; Oros 5.18, 335–40; Livy *Ep* 71–6; Cicero *Phil* 12.27 (anecdote about P's father); Vell 2.13–17, 29 (P trained in war by his father; cf. Cic *Man* 28); *CIL* 1²., 560ff (inscribed sling-bullets); *ILS* 8888 (P in his father's *consilium* at siege of Asculum; see further Criniti 1970); on origins of war see also Gabba 1973, 70–130. **Mithridatic War**: for background and Sulla's efforts see esp. App *Mithr* 1–63 (and Greenidge & Clay for sources year by year); also ch 6. **Civil War**: for first stage see also App *BC* 1.55–75 (esp. 63 for Sulla's attempt to replace Strabo; 66–8 for Strabo's defence of Rome and death); Livy *Ep* 77–80; Val Max 9.7, ext 2 (Strabo blamed for death of Q. Pompeius Rufus); Vell 2.17–23; Sallust *Hist* (M) 2.21 (recall of Strabo: see also Badian 1955 for attribution to P's father in 88 rather than to P's own recall from Africa); Florus 2.9; Dio fr 102; Oros 5.19, 341–5; Plut *P* 3 (saves father's life), 2 and 4 (trial and marriage; for distinguished advocates see also Cic *Brutus* 308); for summary of research into background to the Civil Wars see Badian 1962, reprinted in Seager 1969, 3–51; see Katz 1976 for recent study of the internal politics of 88–7; Bauman 1973 on exact nature of 'hostis' declarations; also Gelzer 1941 for P and his father.

CHAPTER TWO (pp. 12–29): BEARDLESS *IMPERATOR*

Main literary sources: App *BC* 1.71–96; Vell 2.22–9; Livy *Ep* 80–9; Plut *Marius* 43–6; *Sulla* 22.1, 24.4–25.1, 27–33; *Comp Lys and Sulla* 3.3 (auctions); Cic *Brut* 308 (tranquillity of Marian *triennium*); Plut *Crassus* 4–6; *Sert* 6.1; Oros 5.19–22, 345–54; Florus 2.9; Dio frs 106–10. Specifically on P: Plut *P* 2 (courtesan) 5–14 (n.b. 7.3 corrected by *Sulla* 28.1–3; App *BC* 1.85); App *BC* 1.80 (P joins Sulla with one legion, later three: more likely than starting with three as Plut *P* 6.4; operations against Carbo, in Africa, and triumph under age), 87 (P not mentioned at Aesis, only Metellus; cf. Plut *P* 7.3), 88 (defeats Marcius at Sena Gallica), 90 (Spoletium; ambushes

Carbo's relief-force), 92 (Clusium), 95–6 (Sicily and Africa); Vell 2.24 (raises army; P's character);
Livy *Ep* 85 (joins Sulla with 3 volunteer legions), 89 (captures Carbo; defeats Domitius; awarded
triumph); Plut *Sulla* 29.2 (P and Sulla, marching to converge on Samnite army at the pass, decide
Telesinus to march on Rome), 33.3 (P ordered to divorce Antistia and marry Aemilia: contrast
Caes 1); *Comp Lys and Sulla* 2.4 (Sulla's jealousy of P); *Cras* 6.3–4 (Crassus' jealousy of P); Dio
fr 107 (raises army in Picenum, joins Sulla, becomes 'the Great'); Cicero *Man* 28 and 61 (résumé
of achievements); Eutropius 5.8 (executes Carbo and recovers Sicily: '*secundus a Sulla*'); Val Max
9.13.2 (executes Carbo); 6.2.8 (once called '*adulescentulus carnifex*' by enemy in court-case); Oros
5.20.4–7, 348 (Antistius executed in Rome; P defeats Carbo's cavalry, probably at Aesis before
joining Sulla or possibly in a later campaign with Metellus; pursues Carbo's retreating forces after
news of Sacriportus had relieved Metellus); 5.21.11–14, 351 (Sicily and Africa; role of Bogud;
surrender of Bulla Regia: n.b. Hiertas = (H)iarbas of other sources). **Size of Marian forces**: Sulla
(*Memoirs*, quoted by Plut *Sulla* 27.3) and Florus (2.9.21) are incredible. App *BC* 1.82 ('250 cohorts
of 500 men' ready for Sulla's return; 'considerably augmented later') bears comparison with forces
raised in the Caesarian and Octavian Civil Wars; cf. Appian's figures for the full mobilization
authorized by the Senate against Caesar in Jan 49 (*BC* 2.24: 130,000 Italian soldiers), and in 85–4,
unlike 49, there was time to raise them. **Date of P's triumph**: sources differ between 81 (Livy
Ep 89), 80 (Licinianus p. 31, Flemisch) and 79 (*de Viris Illustribus* 77.2). Badian (1955, 1961)
favours 81. I agree that Sallust *Hist* (M) 2.21, sometimes adduced to support 80, more likely refers
to attempted recall of P's father in 88; but Frontinus *Strat* 4.5.1 may refer to consuls of 79
(emendation '*Servilio et Claudio*' more likely than Badian's, and copyist's transposition of last two
letters of P's age is as likely in Livy as in *de Vir Illustr*. Surely P could not have been back in Rome
and ready to triumph by 12 March 81. Plut's '40 days' (*P* 12.5) could be 'graphic' (cf. 26.4; and
unreliability of other apparent exactitudes, e.g. assignment of Scipio's surrender to P at 7.3); but
delay until spring 79 is too long. I suggest that P returned late in 81 (probably before Mauretanian
debacle, since he was not sent to assist the Sullan general against Sertorius), disbanded army
(no source says he put military pressure on Sulla, *pace* Smith 1960), and recalled it to triumph on
12 March either 80 or 79 (time-lag also allowing change of troops' attitude from universal loyalty
to threatened disruption of procession: Plut *P* 13–14): 79 more likely because of Frontinus' possible
mention of consuls, and P's popularity with electorate at consular elections later that year. For
other discussions of P's triumph and Sulla's attitude see Twyman 1972, Smith 1960 (unconvincing
attempt to use equestrian triumph as dating criterion); for coins (issued most probably in 71: see
Crawford *RRC* 82) commemorating P's African victory (politically less highly charged by then
than the recent victory over Sertorius) see *RRC* no 402; Castritius 1971: the rider on the reverse
probably signifies P's elder son; *lituus* and jug may signify P's augurate; on nature and origins of
Roman triumphs see Warren 1970. **Marriage with Mucia**: I agree with Carcopino (1931) 186–95
that evidence of age given by Pompeia's betrothal to Caepio in 59 (when she was already
betrothed to Faustus Sulla: Plut *P* 47.4) and by Appian's statement (if correct) of Sextus's age
when put to death late in 35 (*BC* 5.144) gives *terminus ante quem* for conception of all three
children sometime in 77, before P left to fight Sertorius (though not necessarily before he set out
against Lepidus, for Mucia could have visited him in camp in Italy). I also agree that P more likely
married Mucia after returning from Africa than straight after Aemilia's death in 82, but for
different reasons. Arguments from silence are dangerous (and Plut does not mention Mucia in the
P until chs 42–43, discussing divorce in 62), but it remains hard to believe that an immediate
remarriage would not have been mentioned in *P* 9, which deals with Antistia's divorce and Aemilia's
marriage and death. Instead Plut indicates that P was sent immediately to Sicily. P had surely had
enough of marriage for a while and was glad to get away without saddling himself with a third
wife whom he would immediately have to leave. Carcopino argues that P's marriage with Mucia
changed Sulla's mind about allowing P a triumph because it represented the formation of a
united front against him by P and the Metelli and various other *nobiles* – a development which he
sees reflected in Cic's *pro Roscio* (on which see also Ward 1970A and 1977, 66–7). But this theory
contradicts Plut (*P* 14), who indicates that P talked Sulla into allowing the triumph immediately
on his return; and there is no reason to suppose that Cic was being hypocritical as well as careful
in suggesting that Sulla did not know the details of what Chrysogonus was doing or that, when he
did find out, he cared any more about the fate of this former favourite than about the more
deserving Q. Lucretius Ofella (App *BC* 1.101). If Sulla made an exception to his laws in P's case,
it can only have been while he still considered P a stabilizing element and was trying to compensate
for P's legal disqualification for high office by allowing him a splendid surname and the honour of

a triumph. It cannot have been after P had blotted his copybook so seriously by supporting Lepidus in the 79 elections that Sulla had struck his name out of his will: it is inconceivable that while Sulla remained alive the Metelli or any other pressure-group among the aristocracy could have forced him to concede an exemption from his laws. Lepidus was allowed to become consul because he had done nothing illegal, not because Sulla had lost the ability to intervene violently. Nor does Scaevola's closeness to Cinna mean that P was joining an anti-Sullan coalition by marrying his daughter: Scaevola had been killed by the Marian Brutus, presumably to stop him joining Sulla along with the Metellus (Pius) to whose clan she was also related. Sulla no doubt approved P's marriage-alliance with the Metelli and therefore with himself: it was what he and his wife Metella had been trying to achieve by forcing him to marry Aemilia. I suggest P married Mucia in 80, soon after his victorious return and the granting of his triumph by a delighted Sulla anxious to win him to acquiescence in his constitutional reforms. On the Caecilii Metelli see Ooteghem 1967.

CHAPTER THREE (pp. 30–39): THE LEPIDUS AFFAIR

Main literary sources: Plut *Sulla* 33–8; *P* 15–17; Livy *Ep* 89–91; App *BC* 1.97–101 (Sulla's administration), 103–6 (retirement, death and funeral), 107 (Lepidus); Pliny *NH* 26.138 (Sulla's phthiriasis); Val Max 9.3.8 (Sulla's death), 8.15.8 (P's appointment to Spain); Florus 2.11 (Lepidus); Licinianus pp. 32 (Sulla's cremation, explained: cf. Cic *Legg* 2.56–7), 33–4 (Lepidus); Sallust, *Speech of Lepidus* (*Hist* (M) 1.55); *Speech of Philippus* (ib 1.77); also *Hist* (M) 1.65–7, 69; Exsuperantius p. 3.22 (Lepidus); Oros 5.22.1, 352 (retirement of Sulla); 5.22.16–18, 354 (Lepidus); Suet *Jul* 3 (Caesar returns to Rome but refuses to join Lepidus). Cic *Man* 62 and *Phil* 11.18 (P's appointment to Spain *'pro consulibus'*: cf. Plut *P* 17.4). **Sulla's constitutional legislation**: for sources see Broughton *MRR* 2.74.5; Greenidge & Clay 211–22; on disputed extent of tribunate's emasculation see Gruen 1974, 23–9 (résumé with bibliography), though importance attached to it by Sulla was surely greater than Gruen allows; see also McDermott 1977. **P's extraordinary commands**: Boak 1919 remains convincing that command against Lepidus was *imperium pro praetore* on precedent of African campaign (though Plut *P* 16 is inconclusive); see Twyman 1972 against Smith 1960, who tried to make P a legate of Catulus (on basis of SCU's failure to specify P, despite its specifying no one at all except the present head of state and the immediately preceding consul) with extravagant conclusions that P 'was guilty of mutinous behaviour and treason' in his subsequent refusal to disband when Catulus told him to (Plut *P* 17.3, itself not evidence that P was legate of Catulus). On P's Spanish command Twyman 1972 rightly argues against Badian 1958, 277, and Sumner 1964 who saw it as political attack on Metellus Pius, but his prosopographical enthusiasm goes too far in using connections between Philippus and P and Appius Claudius to interpret the granting of 'chief authority' under the SCU (Sall *Hist* (M) 1.77.22) to the *interrex* Appius Claudius as a means of securing P's command against Lepidus: n.b. while Philippus doubtless favoured P's appointment, no source gives him a special role in proposing it as they do for the subsequent command against Sertorius; Philippus' role in moving the SCU (and later in speaking for P's appointment in Spain) was probably his right as senior ex-consul (he had been consul in 91); the *interrex* was naturally given 'chief authority' in the decree because he was the head of state (and the fact that he was head of state for only five days is irrelevant in an official motion). On Lepidus and his movement see also Criniti 1969. For reaction against prosopographical mania initiated by Münzer 1920 see Meier 1966; also Broughton 1972 for useful introduction to the method and its limitations.

CHAPTER FOUR (pp. 40–57): WAR WITH SERTORIUS

Main literary sources: Plut *Sertorius*; *P* 17–21; App *BC* 1.108–15; Livy *Ep* 91–4, 96; also fr 18 (Teubner/Loeb); Florus 2.10; Sallust *Letter of P* (*Hist* (M) 2.98); *Speech of Cotta* (ib 2.47), 6–7 (financial difficulties at home: see also 2.45); Oros 5.23.1–15, 355–7; 6.2.12, 373 (treaty between Sert and Mithr); Frontinus *Strat* 2.1.2 and 2.3.5 (Metellus' defeat of Hirtuleius in 76), 2.3.10 (general Sertorian tactics against P), 2.5.31 (S's stratagem against P's foraging parties at Lauron), 2.11.2 (P's stratagem at Cauca), 2.5.32 (final battle with Perperna); Cic *Balb* 5 (Memmius in Spain); *Verr* 5.153 (P's friendly reception of deserters from Perperna's army after S's death). **Gallic War**: see esp. App 1.109; Sall *Letter of P* 4; Lucan 8.808; Cic *Man* 28, 30; Pliny *NH* 3.18 (trophy on Col de la Perche); Caesar *BC* 1.35 (Massilia claimed to have received territory from P at this time); Dio 36.28.1 ('increased your possessions'). Identification of P's new route across the Alps is impossible: Appian's vague statement 'between the sources of the Rhône and the Po' could refer to any of the rival candidates, Little St Bernard, Mt Cenis or Mt Genèvre. Elbel 1975 suggests that P not only enlarged Transalpine Gaul but gave it a separate provincial organization for the first time, that the 876 cities indicate a detailed inventory of captured territory, and that trouble in Gaul in the 60s, e.g. with Allobroges, may indicate that those parts of Gaul were feeling weight of Roman government for the first time; see also vol II ch 6. **Chronological problems** of P's campaigns in Spain: with only epitomes of Livy 91–7 extant we lack the detailed account indicated by fr 18 (other sources being concerned only with major encounters). 76: Disposition of forces at 'beginning of spring' (middle of Livy fr 18) must refer to 76 and not 75. Frag begins with Sert taking Contrebia, which was part of campaign in Nearer Spain in 77 to subdue recalcitrant cities, strengthen his allies and re-equip his men in preparation for the arrival of P, then marching slowly through Gaul and campaigning on the way. Appeals to P by Berones and others were thus in winter 77/6, before P had entered Spain and while he was presumably in winter-quarters on other side of Pyrenees. Confirmation that Livy's reference here to Perp's being sent to join Herennius in defending Ilercaones was in spring 76 and not 75 (where it is usually placed on assumption that Perp gave way before P until compelled to stand and defend Valencia) is found in reference to P's ability to be supplied with provisions by sea while Sertorius' commissariat was in difficulties. In 75 Plut (P 19.6; Sert 21.5) says situations reversed by Sert's pirate-allies, who closed all ports to Roman supply-ships and gave Sert the chance to operate well supplied in the devastated coastal plain; and this is reflected in P's letter to Senate written at end of 75 (see below). 75: Sources confused. Plut Sert 19 gives battles of Sucro and Turia as examples of Sert repairing defeats, former against P, latter against P and Metellus. He then describes Sucro, and in 21 describes a battle in plains of Saguntum. Despite Saguntum's distance from R. Turia I identify this battle with the Turia referred to in 19 and mentioned in Sall Letter of P (Hist (M), 2.98) 6 and Cic Balb 5. In both, Sucro and Turia are given as the two great battles of the year: a 'Saguntum' is not otherwise mentioned except by Appian (1.110), where he describes Turia but the text gives a 'near Seguntia', an obvious mistake (see below). Plut (P 18) indicates that battle of Valentia took place near beginning of campaigning season of 75, since P rushed to attack Sert at Sucro 'elated by this success'. Sallust places it third in the list of Sucro, Turia and Valentia in Letter of P 6, but this need not mean that there was a second battle of Valentia after Turia: Valentia might have been listed last because against Herennius and thus less important than Sucro and Turia against Sert himself. It is Sallust (ib) who says that Valentia was destroyed. Livy's epitomator (92) mentions what are clearly the battles of Sucro and Turia without naming them (though it is he who gives Clunia as the name of the 'strong city in the mountains' in which P and Metellus besieged Sert some time after Turia: Plut Sert 21.3–4). That leaves only Appian 1.110 irreconcilable: he has P and Metellus fighting together at Sucro rather than P alone (as in all other accounts), and P wounded in thigh rather than hand. It seems more likely that he is confused than that there was a second battle fought at the Sucro after Metellus had joined P. Plut (despite loose expression 'after the battle' in P 19.5) says distinctly that P and Sert drew up their forces but Sert retired on approach of Metellus (Sert 19.6). Appian also says that Metellus plundered Perperna's camp after Sucro, but no other source supports this: probably a confusion with Afranius' plundering of Sert's camp (Plut Sert 19.5). Appian seems to be confusing several elements of Sucro and Turia, which he relates as 'near Seguntia [sic]'. **Reaction of Senate to P's letter**: Plut (P 20) attributes favourable reaction to consul Lucullus' angling for Mithridatic command. Sallust (Hist (M) 2.98) agrees that Lucullus was not anxious to have P back but does not mention a particular claim for the Mithridatic command, surely rightly since Octavius was still alive when P's letter was read out in Senate at beginning of 74. Plut's chronology is clearly inexact as he goes on immediately to events of 72 without indicating any lapse of time. **Date of Mithridates' alliance with Sert**: for sources see Greenidge & Clay 248–9; Gelzer 1932 (on 'cession' of 'Asia'); Broughton MRR 2.99 (Sertorius); Magie RRAM 1.322–3; 2.1203 n 1; Scardigli 1971; Gabba 1973, 245 n 316. My own view is that Mithridates' approach to Sert did not come until after death of Nicomedes (possibly very late in 75 but more probably early in 74: see Magie 2.1200 n 49) and after P's letter to Senate written in winter 75/4. While I accept that Rome was worried about Mithridates' growing power in 75 (Sall Speech of Cotta, Hist (M) 2.47.7), I do not believe that he approached Sert for alliance before Rome's annexation of Bithynia in 74 caused declaration of war. To have done so would have been a casus belli in itself, and an unnecessary one. Moreover, though arguments from silence are dangerous, surely if negotiations between Mithr and Sert had taken place in 75 (as e.g. Greenidge & Clay, Broughton, Schulten) Sallust (who clearly knew about them: Hist 2.71 and 78 with M's commentary) would have made much of them in the *Letter of P* and its reception by the Senate (ib 2.98). I put the treaty between Mithr and Sert in 74. On chronology see further Bienkowski 1891; Holmes 1.369–84; Scardigli 1971; on whole war see Stahl 1907; for biography of Sert see Schulten 1926; for assessments (as diverse as the Appian and Livy traditions) see Berve 1929; Treves 1932; Schur 1942, 222–56; Ehrenberg 1935, 177–201; Gabba 1973, 103–22; Gillis 1969; for Sertorian coinage, reflecting the necessary compromising of ideology of a Roman civil war by strong Iberian appeal, see Gaggero 1976; for Mauretania, Ascalis etc. see Gsell 7.270–3.

CHAPTER FIVE (pp. 58–71): SPARTACUS AND CRASSUS

Crassus' early career: see biographies by Plut (1–7), Adcock 1966; B. A. Marshall 1976; Ward 1977 (well documented); also Rubinsohn 1970 (suggests '*propraetor pro consule*'). **Servile War**: see esp. Livy *Ep* 95–7; App *BC* 1.104 (Sullan veterans settled in Italy: ready source of Crassus' new legions), 116–20; Florus 2.8; Frontinus *Strat* 1.5.20–2; 1.7.6; 2.5.34; Sall *Hist* (M) 3.90–106; 4.20, 21 (age of Crassus' veterans?), 22, 30–41; Plut *Crass* 8–11; *P* 21.1.–3; Oros 5.24, 359–61; Vell 5.30.6; Eutrop 6.7; Cic *Parad Stoic* 45 (cf. App *BC* 1.118); n.b. rebels called 'Germans' and 'Gauls' in Plut and Oros, i.e. enslaved Teutones and Cimbri; see further Bonghi 1881, Mischulin 1952, Brisson 1959 for monographs on Spartacus; also Holmes 1.386–90 (analysis of evidence for campaigns); Staerman 1969 (doctrinaire marxist interpretation); Rubinsohn 1971 (Italian nationalism theory: equally unconvincing). **P's return, triumph, electoral promises and consulship**: see Plut *P* 21–3; *Crass* 11–12; App *BC* 1.119–21; Cic *Verrines* (first given on 5 Aug, *terminus post quem* for recomposition of courts) 1.31 (P's votive games), 38–44 (senatorial mismanagement of courts since Sulla), 45 (P's electoral promises); 2.5.153 (clemency to defeated Sertorians in Spain); *pro lege Man* 62 (triumph; cf. Pliny *NH* 7.96); Vell 2.30.1 (triumph 29 Dec); 2.30.4 (restoration of tribunes' powers; see also McDermott 1977); Dio fr 36.25.3 (triumph); Val Max 8.15.8 (triumph); Sall *Hist* (M) 3.48 (*Speech of Macer*: see also Rossi 1965); frs 4.42 (cf. Plut *P* 21), 43 (tribune Palicanus probably summoned the assembly outside the city for P), 44 (presumably P's speech), 45 (spirit of reconciliation?), 46 (corruption of senatorial courts?), 47 (seeking popularity), 48 (cf. Plut *Crass* 12.1), 51 (deteriorating relations between P and Crassus); Ps-Asconius (Stangl) 189 (history of tribunician agitation); Livy *Ep* 97 (Senate waives legal objections to P's candidature); Gellius 14.7.1 (Varro's commentary; on him see Astbury 1967; Boissier 1861); *Schol Gronov* (Stangl) 328 (cf. Suet *Jul* 41.2 where Caesar's exclusion of *tribuni aerarii* from courts in 46 supports this reference against most other sources, which state that the *lex Aurelia*, which P 'let pass', restored courts entirely to knights; for other sources see Greenidge & Clay 272–3, plus Dio 43.25.1; on history of extortion courts and role of equites see also Balsdon 1938, Brunt 1965A and Broughton on Brunt, all in Seager 1969; also Laffi 1967, who goes too far in denying conflict of class-interests); Suet *J* 5 (Caesar's agitation for tribunician legislation and support for *lex Plautia* restoring Lepidan exiles; see further Broughton *MRR* 2.128 (Plautius) plus Sall. *Hist* (M) 3.47 and Cic *Verr* 2.5.151–2; also Taylor 1941 on this and Caesar's early career in general); see also Vollenweider 1969 for intaglio representing P's appearance as knight before the censors. **P's recall from Spain**: Plut (*Crass* 11.2) says that before the gladiators escaped from his siege-lines 'Crassus had written to the Senate that they should summon Lucullus from Thrace and P from Spain, but was now sorry he had done so'. But at *P* 21.1 Plut says nothing about P's being recalled, only that 'he led his army back to Italy, where *as luck would have it* he found the servile war at its height'. App (1.119–20) supports formal vote to bring P into the war (though his vague expressions are not proof of plebiscite as distinct from senatorial resolution, let alone for plebiscite against Senate's will as e.g. Ward 1977, 91); also '*on account of this vote* Crassus tried in every way to come to an engagement with Spartacus so that P should not reap the glory of the war'. On timing of Senate's resolution Cic (*pro lege Man* 30) supports my belief that P was formally recalled from Spain, not just ordered to help when he happened to arrive back of his own accord: 'Italy ... when in the throes of the shameful and perilous slave-war *sought aid from P though far away*, and saw that war reduced and brought low by the expectation of his coming, dead and buried on his arrival.' I suggest that Senate voted recall of P and M. Lucullus as soon as it heard that Crassus had failed to bring Spartacus to battle and was digging in for a long siege, with the further danger that Spartacus might escape to Sicily and revive the wars of 135–2 (Diodorus 34–5). App (1.121) says that Crassus' campaign lasted 6 months, and since pursuit of Spartacus down into Bruttium cannot have taken long, there would have been ample time for P to bring his army back from Spain and catch fugitives from the final battle if he had been recalled as soon as the siege began. If Crassus wrote suggesting the recall of P and Lucullus, he probably knew or guessed that it would happen anyway. **Election to consulship**: see Sherwin-White 1956, 5–8, against the anachronistic but usual view that P and Crassus demanded their consulships under threat of force (e.g. Syme 1939, 29; Last *CAH* 9.332–4); App (1.121) has clearly telescoped the consuls' deteriorating relationship in office and the reconciliation-scene at the end of 70 (when their armies had long since been disbanded) with their appearance at Rome at the end of 71 and their demands for deserved honours; see also Rossi 1965. But n.b. the ability to threaten force may not only enhance the prestige of a man who genuinely renounces it but discourage the unconvinced from running the risk of putting him in a position to change his mind; large numbers of troops were also large numbers of organized voters; an absence of military threats and the recognition by P and Crassus of a common interest in standing together for the consulship at the end of 71 need not mean (as e.g. Adcock 1966, 28, 31) that there was no hatchet to bury between them: the tradition of their natural rivalry (cf. *Iliad* 6.208–11) dating from the Sullan Civil War is too strong to be dismissed (e.g. Plut *Crass* 6.4, 7.1; *P* 21.2, where P's pompous letter to the Senate was hardly the gesture of an old friend; App 1.120–1). As soon as they had achieved their desired honours, their relations relapsed into the old rivalry as they sought in their different ways the status of *princeps* (cf. Vell 2.30.6; Plut *P* 22.1, 23.2–4; *Crass* 12.4) until they were again reconciled at the end of 70, this time by the agency of a third party rather than by their own joint recognition of an immediate community of interest.

CHAPTER SIX (pp. 72–90): PIRATES AND POTENTATES

Mithridatic War and Lucullus: see App *Mithr* 64–90; Plut *Lucullus* 5–35; Livy *Ep* 93–5, 97–8; Dio 36.1–17; Florus 1.40 (esp. 14–21); Oros 6.2–3, 373–7; Memnon (Jacoby) 434F27–31, 37–8; Sall *Hist* (M) 3.17–42, 3.52–60, 4.4–16, 4.56–80, 5.1–16; Eutrop 6.6–12; Cic *pro lege Man* 26 (L ordered to disband Valerian legions; cf. Sall *Hist* (M) 5.13, also mentioning transfer of Bithynia and Pontus to Glabrio; also Cic *Sest* 93 for example of Gabinius' methods of moving assembly against L); Magie *RRAM* esp. 321–55 (campaigns), 250–3 (administration in Asia and its political repercussions); Broughton *MRR* 2.106–8 (notes on dating); Eckhardt 1909–10 (L's Armenian campaigns); Ooteghem 1959 (biography of L); Hayne 1974A (on Glabrio's politics); Boak 1919 (appointments of L and Cotta in 74); Reinach 1890 and Castagna 1938 (monographs on Mithridates); Olshausen 1972 (mainly bibliographical); Gruen 1974, 131 (incredibly presenting Glabrio as willing accomplice in a 'holding operation' by Gabinius to keep L's command for P: Gruen cites Glabrio's marriage connection with P, as if P's having married his pregnant wife who promptly miscarried and died would endear him to the role of political stooge! If Gabinius really did propose Glabrio's command, it was a necessary sweetener to avoid the opposition of both consuls instead of just one). **Piracy**: see Strabo 14.5, esp. 668–71; 14.3, 664–5; 12.6, 568–9; Dio, 36.20–3; App *Mithr* 63, 70 (cf. Plut *Sert* 7 and 21.5; *P* 19.6; Memnon fr 43; and for negotiations with Spartacus see Plut *Crass* 10), 78, 92–3; *Sicula* 6 (Crete); Plut *P* 24–5; Diodorus 36.3, 40.1; Livy *Ep* 68 (appointment of elder Antonius in 102; see also Cic *de Orat* 1.82; Obsequens 44; see also inscriptions relating to piracy-laws of 101–100: Hassall *et al* 1974; Sherwin-White 1976), 90, 93, 97 (appointment and failure of younger Antonius in 74; see also *IG*².4.1.66; *SEG* 11.397; *SIG*³.748; Plut *Ant* 1); Florus 1.41 (growth of piracy in 'Golden Sea'; descriptions of ornate pirate-ships), 42; Vell 2.31 (n.b. identical nature of Antonius' command in 74 and P's in 67, presumably therefore proconsular); Eutrop 6.3 (Servilius); Sall *Hist* (M), 1.127–32; 2.81, 87 (Servilius); 2.47 (Cotta's speech: situation in 75); 3.1–16 (Antonius in 74; n.b. 5–6 for attempts to aid P and Metellus in Ligurian Gulf and Spain); Cic *Verr* 2.1.89 (Murena); 2.1.56–7, 2.4.21, 2.5.66, 2.5.79 (Servilius); 2.5.91, 97–8, 100 (piracy in Sicilian waters), 2.2.8 ('*imperium infinitum*' of Antonius in 74, also depredations in Sicily; cf. App *Sic* 6), 2.3.213–15 (Antonius did more harm than good); *pro lege Man* 32–3, 53, 55; Ps-Asconius (Stangl) 259 (Antonius' '*curatio infinita totius orae maritimae*'; cf. 202); also Magie *RRAM* 239–40, 281ff, 341; monographs on piracy by Ormerod 1924, Ziebarth 1929 and Maroti 1972; also Maroti 1968 (piracy oracle), 1969 (Delos), 1970 (role of piracy in Mithridatic War), 1971 (on Antonius' *imperium*; see also Boak 1919, Jameson 1970A, Ehrenberg 1953). **Metellus and Create in 69**: Plut *P* 29.1–2; Dio 36.1a, 36.17a; Livy *Ep* 98–100; App *Sic* 6.2; Vell 2.34.1; Cic *pro Flacco* 6, 30, 63; *pro lege Man* 46; Diodorus 40.1; Florus 1.42.4–6; Eutrop 6.11.1; Oros 6.4.2, 378. **P's appointment** (*lex Gabinia*): see Dio 36.23–37; Plut *P* 25.1–26.2; Cic *pro lege Man* 52 (Hortensius' opposition), 44 (popular demand for P; immediate drop in corn-price cf. Plut *P* 26.2, 27.2; also Sall *Hist* 5.25); *post Red in Sen* 11 (suggestion of financial advantage to

Gabinius); App *Mithr* 94; Vell 2.31–2 (cf. Val Max 8.15.9; Plut and Dio cited above); Sall *Hist* (M) 5.17–26 (but n.b. fr 19 could refer either to *populus* or P or Gabinius; fr 20 is surely from speech of Gabinius, not of P; fr 27 is further example of Piso's antagonizing the people until they attacked him); Asconius (Clark) 64 (Trebellius' rash promise). On the nature of P's command Vell (2.31) is specific: '*imperium aequum in omnibus provinciis cum proconsulibus usque ad quinquagesimum miliarium a mari*': that it was not *maius imperium* (as e.g. Loader 1940, Jameson 1970A) is clear from refusals of Metellus and Piso to co-operate (as Boak 1919). The only legal difference between the positions of Antonius in 74 and P in 67 was not in the geographical scope of the command or its proconsular rank but in the status of the recipient. Antonius, as praetor enjoying *imperium* by popular election, had been the correct hierarchical choice to take a commission to act on behalf of the absent consuls (and his *imperium* was surely *pro consule* from the outset in order to be effective *vis-à-vis* proconsular, not merely propraetorian, governors); P was given a (literally) extraordinary *imperium* by plebiscite, which ignored all the existing magistrates in 67. On legislative process at Rome see e.g. Botsford 1909, esp. 139–50 (procedure at *contiones*), 465–8 (simple procedure for turning a *contio* into a voting assembly), 432 (P's appointment). **Piso:** see further Gruen 1968 for references. **Gabinius:** see Badian 1959 (early career), Williams 1973 (a political biography). **P's forces:** Plut *P* 25.3; Dio 36.37; App *Mithr* 94.

CHAPTER SEVEN (pp. 91–100): VICTORY AT SEA

Main literary sources: App *Mithr* 94–6; Plut *P* 26.3–29.6; Florus 1.41; Vell 2.32.4–6; Dio 36.37; Cic *pro lege Man* (esp. 34–5 on length of war); Lucan 2.576–9; Livy *Ep* 99; Oros 6.4.1, 377; see also Magie *RRAM* 298–301; Ormerod 1924, 235–47; Maroti 1972; Groebe 1910; Ziebarth 1929, with collected inscriptions; also on Roman sea-power generally in this period see Thiel 1946. **P's naval dispositions:** App lists 13 legates (*Mithr* 95), corresponding to Plut's 13 operational areas (*P* 26.3). Of the 13 legates named by Florus (1.41) 9 are common to App's more reliable list: the other four are P's two sons (too young at this time), Caepio (probably confused with the Servilius who was P's naval commander in the Euxine in 65: Plut *P* 34.5) and Marcus Cato (now a military tribune in Macedonia: Broughton MRR 2.149). The remaining 11 or 12 legates out of the 24 (Plut) or 25 (App) probably remained on the proconsul's general staff and were assigned to special military or organizational duties as needed (as L. Octavius, sent to Crete). See further Ormerod 1923 and 1924; Broughton *MRR* 2.148–51; Breglia 1970/71; Reynolds 1962 (for Marcellinus and Cyrenaica). **P's resettlement of pirates:** see App *Mithr* 96 (Soli; also Mallus and Epiphaneia near east coast of Level Cilicia, Adana further inland up the Sarus valley, and Dyme in Achaea); Strabo 8.7.5, 387–8 (Dyme and Soli); 14.5.8, 671 (Soli: careful selection of new settlers; renaming; famous citizens); Vell 2.32.4 (vindicates P against carping critics, whom Cicero belatedly joined in hypocritical contrast to eulogies in *pro lege Man*; see *de Officiis* 3.49: '*nos, qui piratas immunes, socios vectigales habemus*'); see further ch 10. **Quarrel with Metellus over Crete:** Plut (*P* 29) blames P for small-mindedness in trying to rob a deserving general of his just rewards; Dio (36.17a–19) accuses Metellus of unscrupulous greed for power and gives detailed account of Octavius' actions; see also Dio 36.45 for P's supposed intention to sail against Metellus. Livy *Ep* 99 says the lost book contained the exchange of letters between the proconsuls and 'P's statement justifying his action' in sending Octavius to receive surrender of the Cretan cities; on precise nature of P's *imperium* see ch 6; on Metellus Creticus and the Metelli in general see e.g. Meier 1966, Ooteghem 1967, Gruen 1969, Twyman 1972: n.b. P's feud with Creticus did not stop Celer and Nepos from serving as P's legates in the East (see Broughton on legates for 67–63); also ch 10 on Nepos' tribunate in 62). **Official claims** of ships captured or destroyed: Pliny *NH* 7.93 (846 ships 'taken from the pirates': rounded to 800 by Plut *P* 45.2; exaggerated to 1,300 'destroyed by fire' by Strabo 14.3.3, 665. App (*Mithr* 117) describes inscriptions carried in P's triumph as recording the capture of '800 ships *with bronze beaks*': if valid, this must refer to whole period of P's wars from 67 to 63). For Sextus' future glorification of his father's naval victories see e.g. Dio 48.19.2 (calls himself 'son of Neptune since his father had once ruled the whole sea': cf. 31.5; 48.5); App *BC* 5.100; Pliny *NH* 9.55; Crawford *RRC* no. 483 (coin of 44–3 depicting P's head with a trident and the legend 'Neptuni' on obverse, naval battle on reverse).

CHAPTER EIGHT (pp. 101–121): GENERALISSIMO IN THE EAST

Main sources: Cic *pro lege Manilia* (*de imp. Cn. Pompeii*; see also Jonkers 1959 for social and economic commentary); *Fam* 1.9.11 (claiming to have supported P with an eye to his own advancement); *pro Sestio* 58–9 (P's settlement with Tigranes); Dio 36.45–54 (best account of the campaigns in Pontus and Armenia and the most reliable chronology); Plut *P* 30–4 (n.b. confused chronology with Albanian campaign in 34); Luc 35.7–36.7; *Comp Luc and Cimon* 3–4; *Caes* 11.5–6 (cf. Dio 37.52.2 and Suet *J* 7.1); App *Mithr* 97–101, 104–5 (founding of Nicopolis and Armenian campaign wrongly put after expeditions of 65 against Albanians, Iberians and to Colchis); Vell 2.33 (includes charge that Luc prolonged war for personal gain: cf. Plut *Luc* 35.4, where Valerians supposedly told him 'to fight the enemy by himself, since he alone knew how to get rich from them'), 37, 40; Florus 1.40 (esp. 21–7); Livy *Ep* 100–1; Strabo 12.5.2, 567 (Danala: site of conference between P and Lucullus); 12.3.28, 555 (Lesser Armenia; M's treasuries there, esp. 'Sinoria'; Dasteira in Acilisene, position held before final battle; P's foundation of Nico-polis); 11.14.10, 530 (Armenia's wealth: Tigranes' indemnity of 6,000 talents and bounty to P's troops); Frontinus *Strat* 2.5.33 (P's cavalry battle against M), 1.1.7 (M's escape from P's blockade at site identified by Strabo as Dasteira), 2.1.12 (P's chase, ambush and night-battle), 2.2.2 (advantage to P's troops of a downhill charge in the final battle: loose expression 'in Cappadocia' refers to the later Roman province, which was more extensive than the kingdom); Eutrop 6.13; Oros 6.4, 378; Waddington et al 1².20 (M's coins show he had recovered his kingdom and was again minting in Pontic year 231, which began in Oct 67: none recorded for previous two years). **Cicero's early career:** see biographies by e.g. Smith 1966, Gelzer 1969A, Shackleton Bailey 1971, Stockton 1971, Lacey 1978, also Ward's articles on Cic's earlier relations with P (1968–70). **Caesar's early career:** see e.g. (for inflated views of his importance) Taylor 1941 and 1957, Sumner 1966; see also Gelzer's biography (1968), with Syme's review of original German edition (1944); Ward 1977, esp. 120–5. **Comparative military strengths of P and M:** M's forces were inferior overall from the outset (Dio 36.47) though superior in cavalry. Front (*Strat* 2.5.33) and App (*Mithr* 97) give M 30,000 infantry and 3,000 cavalry; Plut (*P* 32.1) gives same infantry but 2,000 cavalry; Vell (2.37) simply speaks of the king's '*new* army of great strength' (cf. Plut *P* 31.6). For résumé of modern calculations of P's force from the 16,000 talents distributed to his troops on leaving Asia Minor (App *Mithr* 116) see Magie *RRAM* 2.1220, n 5; but 50,000 could well be too high for beginning of campaign, when (I believe) the legions from Cilicia had not yet joined P. (On meaning of 'Cilicia' before P's formal annexation of Cilicia proper see Magie *RRAM* 1.285ff, 375–6; Sherwin-White 1976, 10–11; also ch 10); for P's re-enlistment of Valerian legions see Dio 36.46.1; for different interpretations of evidence for P's great battle see Magie *RRAM* 2.1221–4, nn 7, 8 (with bibliography); for monographs on M see Reinach 1890; Zancan 1933–4; Castagna 1938; for Pontic history see also Meyer 1879; Anderson et al 1903–10; on P's campaigns see also Anderson 1922; Holmes 1923, 1.201–8, 426–33; for history of Armenia's political relations with Rome see Asdourian 1911.

CHAPTER NINE (pp. 122–146): THE NEW ALEXANDER

Transcaucasian campaigns of 65: see Dio 37.1–5; Plut *P* 34.1–36.1; Strabo 11.3, 499–501 (Iberia); 11.4, 501–4 (Albania; esp. 11.4.5 for military strength and P's great battle; for heavy cavalry see also 11.14.9, 530; cf. Plut *Crass* 35.6–8 for similar Parthian cavalry, also Tarn 1930, 73–6); Front *Strat* 2.3.14 (against Albanians; cf. Dio 37.4; Strabo 11.4.5, 502); Plut *Crass* 23.6 (similar conceal-ment of main army by Parthians); App *Mithr* 103 (campaign misplaced in 66 before P's advance against Tigranes), 116–17 (statistics from P's triumph); Diodorus 40.4 (fuller details of an official inscription); Livy *Ep* 101; Florus 1.40.28; Oros 6.4.8, 379–80; Eutrop 6.14.1. **Return to Lesser Armenia and Pontus for winter** 65–4: see Plut *P* 36 (Stratonice's surrender of fortress identifiable with 'Sinora' of 32.8, the 'Symphorion' of Dio 37.7.5 and the 'Sinoria' of Strabo 12.3.28, 555, which also describes Lesser Armenia), 37–8 (Caenum and Amisus; see also Strabo 12.3, 541ff generally for description of Pontus and esp. Eupatoria-Magnopolis, Cabeira-Diospolis, Kainon Chorion (Caenum): 12.3.30, 556ff); Pliny *NH* 25.5–7, 23.149 (M's scientific research). **Burial of Triarius' troops:** see Plut *P* 39.1–2 (for their defeat see Luc 35.1; App *Mithr* 89; Dio 36.12–13: 'near Gaziura'). **'Conquest' of the Medes and Commagene:** Vell 2.40.1 ('invasion of Media'); App *Mithr* 106 ('fought against' both Antiochus and Darius), 114 ('fought battles against ... Medes'), 117 (Antiochus and Darius in official list of 'kings conquered'; contrast absence of Seleucid

Antiochus or Elymaeans); Dio 37.52 (Gabinius' expedition to Tigris, which I associate with conquest of Media); 36.2.5 (Commagene's earlier submission to Luc: n.b. Pliny's account (NH 2.235) of L's siege of Samosata seems to be a confusion with Tigranocerta, for which see Dio 36.1b); Diodorus 40.4; on Commagene see also ch 10. **Relations with Parthia**: Dio 37.5–7 (n.b. P's wintering at 'Aspis' at end of 64 is a misplaced reference to his wintering at Amisus in the previous year – clearly shown by association with Stratonice's surrender of 'Symphorion'); Plut P 36.2, 33.6; also Dobias 1931, Ziegler 1964. **Levantine campaigns**: Plut P 38.2–41.5; App Syr esp. 49–50, 52–70 (brief history of Seleucid dynasty ending with P's annexation of new province); Diodorus 40, frs 1a-b (struggles between Antiochus XIII and Philip II, with rival Arab supporters, esp. Sampsiceramus: for Cic's snide references to P as 'our Sampsiceramus' see Att 2.14, 16, 17, 23), 2 (Aristobulus and Hyrcanus approach P at Damascus; see Josephus JA 14.34 for A's gift); Jos JA 13.320–14.28 (Jewish affairs from accession of Alexander Jannaeus to rivalry of Hyrcanus and Aristobulus; Nabataean intervention in support of H; cf. JW 1.85–127); 14.29–79 (Roman intervention from Scaurus to P's capture of Jerusalem; cf. JW 1.127–58); Strabo 16.2.18, 755 (suppression of Libanus Arabs; description of Massy as plain); Dio 37.7a (epitome following disintegration of narrative: lost chapters concerned annexation of Pontus to Bithynia and subjection of Syria and Phoenicia); 15–17 (Arab and Jewish campaigns: very little on former, which is chronologically misplaced); Eutrop 6.14.2 (n.b. P's delight in Daphne, suburb of Antioch); Pliny NH 33.136 (n.b. text says only that Ptolemy maintained 8,000 cavalry at his own expense at time of P's campaigns about Judaea, not that he sent them to P; see App Mithr 114 for Ptolemy's gifts of 'money for P and clothing for his army', also explanation why P did not intervene in Egypt); Justinus 40.2 (P's scathing dismissal of Seleucid Antiochus XIII); Florus 1.40.29–31; Livy Ep 102; Oros 6.4.8, 380. See further Liebmann-Frankfort 1968A (Roman empire's eastern boundaries from 188 to end of P's conquests); Stark 1968 (Euphrates frontier); Bouché-Leclercq 1913 (Seleucid history); Downey 1951, 1963 (history of Antioch); Will 1972 (Rome and Seleucids, also (briefly) Kucharczak 1976; Bellinger 1949 (end of Seleucids); Rizzo 1963 (sources of history of P's conquest); Gutschmid 1887 (Osroene); Frankfort 1963 (Sophene); Bachmann 1973 (Commagene). For Nabataeans see ch 10. For Jews see esp. Abel 1947 (P's siege of Jerusalem), plus Magie RRAM 1228 n 23 and Drew 1951 on date of Temple's capture; Medico 1964 (study of sources); Smallwood 1976 (history of Jews under Roman rule); also Ginsburg 1928; Burr 1972; Abel 1952. For the Alexander parallel see also D. Michel 1967; Cunningham 1971; Weippert 1972; Dreizehnter 1975.

CHAPTER TEN (pp. 147–167): THE GREAT SETTLEMENT

Mithridates and the Crimea: App Mithr 102, 107ff; Dio 36.50.2; 37–11–14; Livy Ep 102; Reinach 1890, 397, 402ff; Magie RRAM 1229 n 25; Havas 1968 (arguing that M's plan to attack Italy was not without logic); for reaction to news of M's death see (for P's and his army's) Plut P 42.3–43.3; App Mithr 113; (for Rome's) also Cic de prov cons 27 (ten-day thanksgiving); pro Murena 34 (general feeling about M); Fam 5.7.1 (Cic's congratulatory letter to P); App Mithr 113 (Pharnaces recognized, but freedom for Phanagoreia); Suidas s.v. 'Kastor Rhodios' (commander of Phanagoreia designated Friend of the Roman People). **Colchis**: App Mithr 114; Eutrop 6.14.1; for Aristarchus' coins see Head HN 496; Golenko 1974. **Pontus-Bithynia**: Strabo, 12.3.1, 541 (Pontus divided into 11 city-states); for previous centralized government and problems of creating a governmental substructure suitable to Roman provincial administration see Magie RRAM 179ff, 369ff; Jones CERP 157ff; also (with caution) Fletcher 1939; for coastal region towards Colchis see Strabo 12.3.1, 541; 12.3.13, 547 (Pharnacia and Trapezusia to Deiotarus, also part of Gazelonitis); 12.3.18, 549 (nature of tribes); for the 11 city-states the most likely candidates are: Nicopolis (Strabo 12.3.28, 555; App Mithr 105, 115; Dio 36.50.3; also ch 8; n.b. also that placing of Nicopolis 'in Lesser Armenia' by Strabo and Appian, and 'in Cappadocia' (i.e. the Cappadocian province of his own day) by Dio, need not exclude it from P's Pontic province: it was in what had been Lesser Armenia under M, but P was not bound to M's arrangements; see further Magie RRAM 1233 n 35 against Jones CERP 422 n 20); Cabeira-Diospolis and Eupatoria-Magnopolis (see ch 9); Amisus (Strabo 12.3.13–14, 547; also Head HN 497 for 'Roma' coins minted under proconsuls of 61–59 and 56); Amaseia (Strabo 12.3.39, 561); Zela (11.8.4, 512; 12.3.37, 559–60); Megalopolis (ib: incorporates Colopene and Camisene); Amastris and Sinope (12.3.10–11, 544–6); Arrian Periplus 22 (evidence that Sinope's territory extended to the Halys in the 2nd century AD); App Mithr 92–3; Memnon, Jacoby 434F37: n.b. there is little to prove that Amastris and Sinope were members of the eleven but their earlier and later importance makes it likely); Neapolis

(Strabo 12.3.38, 560); Pompeiopolis (12.3.40, 562). If Strabo had said 12 instead of 11 cities I should have included Heracleia, said by him to have 'marked the western edge of M's kingdom and to have been incorporated in the Pontic province by P' (12.3.2, 541), but it seems an improbable replacement for any of my eleven, least of all Nicopolis. (For doubts on accuracy of Strabo's statement about Heracleia as formerly Mithridatic see Jones *CERP* 152–3; for divergent views on composition of the eleven see Magie *RRAM* 1232–3 n 35); for Comana see Strabo 12.3.32, 34, 36, 557–9; for trade-routes running east–west from Armenia to Bithynia and north–south from the Pontic ports to Upper Mesopotamia (i.e. routes on which the 11 cities were sited) see Magie *RRAM* 1083 (n 33), 1078 (n 25); for uniform Pompeian constitutions in combined Bithynia-Pontus see Dio 37.20.2 (confirming continuation until at least the early 3rd century AD); Pliny *Letters* 79–80, 112, 114–15 (early 2nd century AD); Jones *CERP* 159ff; Magie *RRAM* 1231 n 34; Vitucci 1957, 442–4; A.J. Marshall 1968; for original bequest of Bithynian kingdom by Nicomedes see App *Mithr* 7; Livy *Ep* 93; Eutrop 6.6.1; Cic *contra Rullum* (*de leg agr*) 2.50 (delivered early in 63: evidence that *publicani* were already enjoying revenues from royal domains of Bithynia; see also Jones *CERP* 156 for suggestion that companies' vested interests may have influenced P's organization); Vitucci 1953 (history of Bithynian kingdom); for subsequent interference with P's network of city-republics in Pontus by Caesar and Antony see Jones *CERP* 166ff, 426–7. **Paphlagonia**: see App *Mithr* 114 (Attalus made ruler: Magie *RRAM* 1234 n 37 argues for division between two princes, but Jones *CERP* 424 n 29 rightly contradicts him from Strabo 12.31, 541 and Eutropius 6.14.1, clearly a conflation of two accounts). **Galatia and Deiotarus**: Strabo 12.3.1, 541 (Galatians given to hereditary tetrarchs); 12.3.13, 547 (part of Gazelonitis to Deiotarus, also Pharnacia and Trapezusia, when he already held his ancestral Galatian tetrarchy of the Tolistobogii); 12.5.1–2, 566–7 (description of tetrarchies: P gave Mithridatium to 'Brogodiatarus', tetrarch of the Trocmi); App *Mithr* 46 (M's massacre of Galatian nobles and tetrarchs in 86; cf. Plut *Mul Virt* 23), 114 ('P made D and others tetrarchs of the Gallograecians'); Eutrop 6.14.1 (P made D 'king of Lesser Armenia'; cf. Cic *Phil* 2.94; *de Div* 2.79; [Caesar]· *Bell Alex* 67.1, all referring to Lesser Armenia as D's kingdom): Magie (*RRAM* 1237–8 n 41) rightly discounts quibbles of Adcock 1937, Jones (*CERP* 422 n 20) and others who doubted that P assigned this to D because Cic says that the Senate awarded it to him (*l.c.*) and the title of king (*Att* 5.17.3; *de har resp* 29; *pro rege Deiotaro* 10): all P's *acta* in the East technically required validation by Senate); see further Magie (*l.c.*) on inscriptional evidence. **Cappadocia**: for curious circumstances of Ariobarzanes' accession see Justinus 38.2; Strabo 12.2.11, 540; Head *HN* 751 (coin giving title 'Philoromaios' and regnal years); for vicissitudes of his reign and constant loyalty to Rome see Magie *RRAM* 206, 321, 335, 349, 374–5; for Lucullus' gift of Tomisa to Ariobarzanes see Strabo 12.2.1, 535; on P's grants to him see for Sophene App *Mithr* 105 (though n.b. not Gordyene too; see Reinach 1890, 393 n 1); for area of Lycaonia round Cybistra see Cic *Fam* 15.2.2; *Att* 5.18.1; 5.20.2 (all referring to Cybistra 'in Cappadocia'); for importance of trade-route passing through Cilician and Syrian Gates see Magie *RRAM* 276–7, 1152 (n 36); see further Liebmann-Frankfort 1968 and 1975. **Antipater**: for P's grant of wilder territory including Derbe and Laranda between Isauria and Cybistra to this chieftain see Cic *Fam* 13.73.2; Strabo 12.1.4, 535 ('Antipater the pirate'); 12.6.3, 569; 14.5.24, 679; *IGR* 4.1694. *Cilicia*: see ch 7 for P's resettlement of pirates; for eras of Zephyrium, Mopsuhestia and Alexandria see Head *HN* 734, 724, 716 (all 67); for Pompeiopolis 729 (era 65; n.b. coins with P's portrait), also *IGR* 3.869 (its freedom), and Langlois 1853; for Tarsus as capital see Cic *Att* 5.16; for extent of so-called province of 'Cilicia' before P's annexations see Cic *Verr* 2.95 (Verres as proquaestor in 'Cilicia' in 80–79 harried 'the Milyad, Lycia, Pamphylia, Pisidia and Phrygia'); see also Liebmann-Frankfort 1968B. **Tarcondimotus**: see Cic *Fam* 15.1; *IGR* 3.901 (inscription of Hieropolis); Dio 54.9.2 (Augustus in 20 restores 'to the son of Tarcondimotus all the Cilician kingdom which his father had held except certain coastal districts, which he gave to Archelaus' of Cappadocia: since Archelaus ruled a piece of Rugged Cilicia between Seleuceia and Soli, Jones (*CERP* 202–3) argues that this was formerly a possession of T); 41.63.1 (T, 'a ruler of part of Cilicia', provides great help with ships for P in the Civil War: he must therefore have had coastal possessions); Head *HN* 716 (Caesarean era of Aegae beginning 47 may suggest subjection to T before then). **Commagene**: see ch 9; also (for Antiochus' acquisition of Seleuceia) Strabo 16.2.3, 749; App *Mithr* 114 (n.b. the addition 'and the parts of Mesopotamia he had conquered' is invalidated by other sources); see also Bachmann 1973 (outline of the region); Toros 1976 (Antiochus' coins and the Armenian resemblance). **Osroene**: see Dio 40.30.1 ('Abgarus had pledged himself to peace with the Romans in the time of P'); also Gutschmid 1887; Liebmann-Frankfort 1968A. **Northern Syria**: for freedom of Seleuceia-in-Pieria see Strabo 16.2.8, 751; for Cyrrhestice see Cic *Att* 5.18 (called 'the nearest part of Syria' to Cilicia); for rule of Sampsiceramus at Emesa and Arethusa see Strabo 16.2.10, 753 (connected with P's settlement by Cic's frequent references to P as 'our Sampsiceramus', i.e. the Pasha: e.g. *Att* 2.14, 16, 17, 23); see also Seyrig 1959; for Lysias and fate of Silas see Jos *JA* 14.40; for destruction of citadel of Apamea, ib 14.38; for origin and coinage of Tetrapolis of Seleuceia-in-Pieria, Antioch, Apamea and Laodicea see Head *HN* 778. **Ituraeans**: see Jos *JA* 14.39 (jaundiced allusion to Ptolemy's payment of 1,000 talents; also P's execution of tyrant of Tripolis); Strabo 16.2.10, 753 ('Heliopolis and Chalcis, belonging to Ptolemy who possessed Massyas and the mountainous territory of the Ituraeans'); 16.2.18, 755 (P's destruction of Botrys, Gigartus etc.); Head *HN* 783 (coin of Ptolemy, 'Tetrarch and High Priest'); Jones *CERP* 254, 258, 456 n 44 (restoration of Ituraea); for liberation of Canatha see Head *HN* 786 (Pompeian era and epithet 'Gabinia'). **Jews**: see ch 9; also Jones *CERP* 257–8, 455–6 (n 42), who adds to Josephus' incomplete list of cities freed by P (*JA* 14.75–6; *JW* 1.155–6) the cities rebuilt by Gabinius (*JA* 14.88; *JW* 1.166) and Abila, which used the Pompeian era (see Head *HN* 786); for imposition of tribute on Jerusalem see Jos *JA* 14.74, also summarizing P's reorganization of Jewish state; for the Decapolis in the 70s AD see Pliny *NH* 5.74 (admittedly variable, but then said to comprise Damascus, Philadelphia, Raphana, Scythopolis, Gadara, Hippos, Dium, Pella, Galasa (Gerasa) and Canatha); on foundation-members and development of Decapolis see Jones *CERP* 259, 456–7 (n 45); Bietenhard 1963. **Naba-taeans**: see for conclusion of campaign Jos *JA* 14.80–1; *JW* 1.159; for Nabataean history and civil-ization see Starcky 1955 and 1971; for coins minted by P's legate Scaurus in 58 depicting Aretas kneeling in submission see Crawford *RRC* no 422. **Tyre and Sidon**: Jos *JA* 14.95; *JW* 1.361 (freedom respected by Antony when he awarded rest of coast to Cleopatra); Dio 54.7 (removed by Augustus). **Ascalon**: Pliny *NH* 5.68 (still free in 1st century AD and maintaining original era of freedom, 104: Head *HN* 804). **Gadara**: Jos *JA* 14.75; *JW* 1.155; Head *HN* 787 (adopted 'Pompeian' epithet as well as era); for influence of Demetrius in general see Plut *P* 40 (cf. *Cato Minor* 13: re Cato's visit to Antioch, for date of which see Broughton *MRR* 2.165 n 5). **Distribution of cash**: see App *Mithr* 116 ('at the end of winter he distributed rewards to the army: 1500 Attic drachmas to each soldier and in proportion to the officers, the whole coming to 16,000 talents'); Pliny *NH* 37.16 (200m HS given to the state, 100m HS to the commanders and quaestors, and 6,000 HS (= 1,500 drachmas) to each soldier); Plut *P* 45.3 (Rome's existing revenues from taxes of 50m drachmas (200m HS) were increased by 85m dr (340 HS) by P's acquisitions, i.e. from *c*. 8,333 to 22,500 talents); P also gave to the Treasury 20,000 talents in coined money and vessels of gold and silver (i.e. 480m HS) in addition to his payments to the troops, which Appian put at 16,000 talents. The difference between Pliny's 200m HS put in the Treasury and Plut's 480m could have been a further sum handed over at the time of the triumph (possibly in the form of the gold and silver vessels rather than the coin, although the greater part of this sum could be accounted for by the 75,100,000 drachmas of silver coin which Appian says were carried in P's triumphal procession at the end of Sep 61: *Mithr* 116). If so, the state will have received 480m HS, the army 384m HS, and P will not have left himself short: for P's enormous personal wealth (reflected in the loans which he made, e.g. to Ariobarzanes III of Cappadocia) see further Badian 1968, 82ff; for unconvincing reductions of Pliny's figures both for cash and people see Dreizehnter 1975. **Return to Rome**: see Plut *P* 42.4–43.7; *JHS* 27 (1907), 67, no 7 (inscription from Miletoupolis; *ILS* 9459); *CIG* 3608 = *IGR* 4.198 (inscription from Ilium); *ILS* 8776 = *IGR* 4.54 (honoured at Mytilene as Saviour and Founder after defeating the world's enemies by land and sea); App *Mithr* 116 (embarked at Ephesus); Cic *Att* 1.12 (dated 1 Jan 61: reveals P's return in Dec 62 and general approval of his divorcing Mucia: cf. Plut *P* 42.7); Dio 37.20.

CHAPTER ELEVEN (pp. 168–196): TRIUMPH AND ANTICLIMAX

Triumph: Plut *P* 45.1–46.1; App *M* 115–17; Dio 37.21; Vell 2.40.3–4; Pliny *NH* 7.97 (inscription), 98 (date), 99 (speech; cf. Cic *Att* 1.14); 12.20 (ebony), 111 (balsam); 33.12 (slave holds Tuscan crown of gold over *triumphator*s head), 151 (silver statues of Mithr and Pharnaces I, chariots of silver and gold); 36.41 (the 14 statues in P's theatre); 37.11ff (gems, pearls, murrhine ware etc. exhibited on 29 Sep, P's birthday); Diodorus 40.4 (inscription; cf. Pliny *NH* 7.95); *Act Tr* (Degrassi) 84f, 566; Livy *Ep* 103; Cic *Balb* 9; *Sest* 129; see also Deutsch 1924, Warren 1970 (on origins and symbolism of Roman triumphs), Dreizehnter 1975; for financial proceeds and distribu-tions see ch 10; for Panares and Lasthenes see Florus 1.42 (capture by Metellus); Dio 36.19.3 (P's use of a tribune to reserve them for his own triumph); for P's public works: vol II ch 3. **Events**

at Rome during P's absence: see Dio 36.42–4; 37.8–10, 21–45 for the best ancient narrative. **Year 65**: for Crassus and Transpadanes see esp. Dio 37.9.3 (cf. Cic *Balb* 50); re Egypt see Cic *contra Rullum* (*de lege agraria*) 1.1 and 2.44; *de rege Alex* (frags; see esp. *Schol Bob* 91–3 Stangl); Suet *J* 11; Plut *Crass* 13.1 (n.b. Adcock 1966, 33–6, rightly distinguishes enfranchisement question, which was a censorship matter, from Egyptian question, which was not; Plut's 'annexation' may exaggerate a proposed 'regularization' of relations with the existing king); for Cic starting canvass for 64 elections see *Att* 1.1; for short-lived intention of running with Catiline, 1.2; for so-called First Catilinarian Conspiracy see Asc (Clark) 83 (Crass improbably suggested as its 'author'), 92; Dio 36.44.3–5; Sall *Cat* 18–19; Suet *J* 9; Cic *Sull* 11, 81; *Mur* 81; on improbabilities see e.g. Stockton 1971, 74–6, 78); for Caesar's aedileship and games see Suet *J* 9–11 (also restores Marian trophies; cf. Vell 2.43.4); Dio 37.8; Plut *Caes* 6.1–3; Sall *Cat* 49.3; Pliny *NH* 33.53. **Year 64**: on Cic's electioneering see Q. Cicero *Com Pet* (on which see Henderson 1950, Balsdon 1963, Richardson 1971) esp. 5, 14, 15 (importance of demonstrating P's interest; cf. Cic *Att* 1.1; *pro lege Man*; Asc *in Corn* 57ff Clark); also Cic *in toga cand* (attacking Cat and Ant) 82–94 (esp. 83; Crass and Caes support Cat and Ant against Cic; tribune used to block anti-bribery legislation: cf. 85–6, 88); Plut *Cic* 10–11; for Cat's supposed conspiracies see Sall *Cat* 17 (Crassus implicated), 26.1; Cic *Cat* 1.11 (supposed plot against Cic as consul-elect, though see *Mur* 52 for virtual admission that breastplate was more to impress electorate than because he was really afraid); n.b. also that Caesar, president of *quaestio de sicariis*, stopped prosecutions of Sullan agents on appearance of Crassus' main protégé: see Suet *J* 11; Dio 37.10.2; Asc 90–1C. **Year 63**: Cic *contra Rullum* (esp. 1.6, 13; 2.17, 23–5, 46, 49, 52–3, 59–62; 3.16; for Pompeian interest); Plut *Cic* 12.4 (Cic buys Ant with province; but n.b. probably several months later than indicated here); Cic *pro Murena* (n.b. 37 and 69 on contribution of Luc's triumphing troops to Murena's electoral success); Plut *Luc* 37 (L's triumph after long opposition); Cic *Luc* 3 (claimed major role in unblocking L's triumph; anti-Catiline rather than anti-P move?); for Catiline see esp. Sall *Cat*; Cic *Cat*; also e.g. Stockton 1971, 99–142; for Caesar see on pontifical election Dio 37.37.1–2; Plut *Caes* 7.1–3; Suet *J* 13, 46; Vell 2.43.3–4; re Cat see Cic *Att* 12.21; *Cat* 4.7–10; Sall *Cat* 49–51; Suet *J* 14, 17; Plut *Caes* 7–8; *Cato Min* 22–4; *Crass* 13.2–3; Cic 20–1; App *BC* 2.6; Dio 37.36; on Caesar's attack on emergency powers of S.C.U. through trial of Rabirius for murder of tribune Saturninus in 100 see Dio 37.27; Cic *pro Rab perd*; for Bill of Ampius and Labienus (P's regalia) see Vell 2.40.4; Dio 37.21–34. **Year 62**: for end of Cat see esp. Dio 37.39–42 (n.b. on Cic's inflation of Cat's importance); Sall *Cat* 57–61 (battle with Ant); for Cic's letter to P see *Fam* 5.7; for Clodius and Bona Dea scandal see Cic *Att* 1.13; Plut *Caes* 10 (resulting divorce); also Cic *Att* 1.14, 16, 18 (Clodius' trial in 61; Crassus bribes jury); for Caesar's pro-P measures as praetor see esp. Suet *J* 15–16; Dio 37.44; Plut *Cat Min* 27–8; for Metellus Nepos' tribunate see Cic *Fam* 1.2; Dio 37.38.2; 37.42–4; Plut *Cat Min* 26–9; *Cic* 23; Suet *J* 16; Asc 6C; on Piso's consular candidature and P's request for postponement of elections see Dio 37.44.3 (request granted; cf. Plut *P* 44.1 and *Cat Min* 30.1–2, though surely mistaken to suppose that P made request so that he could be there to support Piso in person); n.b. also Creticus' long-delayed triumph: Cic *Pis* 58; *Act Tr* (Degrassi) 84f, 566; Vell 2.34.2; 2.40.5; Dio 36.17a; Sall *Cat* 30.3–4 (Creticus evidently still waiting when deployed against Cat in 63). On identification of 'your friend' in Cic *Att* 1.13.4: n.b. that though Cic asked Att to be responsible for 'the followers of our friend P' in *Att* 1.1 of 65, and speaks of P in similarly disparaging terms in mid-May 60 (*Att* 1.20), 'your friend' here could be sarcastic and/or business reference to Crassus, and the 'lavish praise and secret jealousy' are surely more appropriate to Crassus in a letter dated 25.1.61 since P is still cool towards Cic's achievements at this stage whereas Crassus goes out of his way to eulogize them (see *Att* 1.4 of 13.2.61). **P's plans and policies on return**: see esp. Cic *Att* 1.14 (first public speeches; but cf. Pliny *NH* 7.99 for possible quotation); Plut *P* 44 (cf. *Cat Min* 30; perhaps Cato's 'sister' was stepsister Servilia: see Asc 19C; Münzer 1920, 336ff; Syme 1939, 26–7, though I doubt Syme's vendetta); on opposition to P see esp. Sall *Cat* 17.7; 19.1 (Crass a 'deadly enemy'); Plut *Cat Min* 29.3–31.1 (Luc and Cato); *P* 43.1 (Crass), 46.3 (Luc and Cato); *Luc* 37–8, 42.4–6 (Crass and Cato lead opposition when Luc proves sluggish); Dio 37.49–50 (P's aims; opposed by Luc, Celer and Cato; Flavius' failure); Vell 2.40.5 (L and Creticus); Cic *Fam* 5.7 (letter to P; on 'old enemies and recent friends' see also Gruen 1970, Parrish 1973, Mitchell 1975, Ward 1977 (199ff) for different interpretations); on P's attempt to secure aims through consuls and tribunician legislation in 60 see Cic *Att* 1.13, 14, 18, 19, 20; 2.1; Dio *l.c.* **Further modern scholarship**: on Transpadane and Egyptian questions see Hardy 1916; Ward 1977, 122–3, 128–37; also vol II, chs 2 and 4; on Catiline see Hardy 1917; Pareti 1934; Salmon 1935; Allen 1938; Frisch 1948; Meier 1962; Yavetz 1963;

Seager 1964, 1973; Havas 1967; Hutchinson 1967; Waters 1970; B. A. Marshall 1974; Ward 1977, 135–52, 171–92; on Rullan proposal see also Hardy 1912–13; Sage 1921; Afzelius 1940; Gabba 1966; Sumner 1966; Luzzatto 1966; Ward 1977, 152–62; on search for P's absent influence on criminal prosecutions see Gruen 1974, 261ff, also (on the trial of Archias supposedly politicized as attack by the Pompeian interest on the Lucullan circle) see J.H. Taylor 1952, Dorey 1955; on Cato see also Afzelius 1941; on Cic's 'Laelius-Africanus' delusion see also Ward 1968; for Clodius see further ch 12 and vol II, ch 1.

CHAPTER TWELVE (pp. 197–227): THE THREE-HEADED MONSTER

Origin of coalition (so-called 'first triumvirate') and Caesar's election: see esp. Dio 37.54–8 (cf. Cic *Att* 2.1 of June 60, also 2.3 of Dec 60, for secrecy of reconciliation between P and Crassus); Plut *P* 46–7; *Luc* 42.6; *Caes* 13–14; *Cat Min* 31; *Crass* 14; Livy *Ep* 103; App *BC* 2.9 (Varro's *Tricaranus*; see also Astbury 1967); Vell 2.44; Suet *J* 19; Cic *Att* 1.17 (on Lucceius see also McDermott 1969; Piauko 1969); 2.9 (Apr 59; cf. *de prov cons* 41); *pro Flacco* 32 (from which Brunt 1965B, 17, and Adcock 1966, 41–2, make unwarranted assumption that Crassus went to arrange political deal with P before P's return: contradicted by Plut *P* 43.1 (cf. *Luc* 42.4–6; App *BC* 2.9 etc.); also improbable that P would listen to overtures from an old rival who had tried *and failed* to work against him *in his absence*); for modern controversies see also Stanton & Marshall 1975 with bibliography, to which add Bersanetti 1924; Sanders 1932; Hanslik 1955; Mitchell 1973; Gruen 1974, 88ff; Zecchini 1975; Ward 1977, 193–226. **Agrarian legislation**: Dio 38.1–7; Suet *J* 20; App *BC* 2.10–12 (n.b. voting and coercive power of P's troops); cf. 1.29 (Saturninus' Bill); Plut *P* 48 (P's soldiers); *Caes* 14; *Cat Min* 31–3; *Cic* 26.4; Livy *Ep* 103 (n.b. more than one law; cf. Plut *Cat Min* 33.1; *Caes* 14); Cic *Att* 2.3, 13, 16, 18, 19 (P at Capua, presumably on land-commission); *Sest* 61; *de prov cons* (commission of 5: executive of Dio's 20 esp. for Campanian land; or separate board?; Gellius 4.10.8 (Cato's opposition: cf. Suet *J* 20; Plut *Cat Min* 33; also Afzelius 1941); for Bibulus' *spectio* see Dio 38.6.1; Cic *Att* 2.16 (1.5.59; cf. *de har resp* 48; *de domo sua* 39–40; also Greenidge 1901, 172–4)); P's unpopularity among mob June–Sep (Cic *Att* 2.18–23) attributable to veterans' departure to Campania and influx of dis-possessed tenants; restored popularity in autumn (n.b. Cic *QF* 1.2, and success of P's candidate) may reflect recall of veterans for elections (as e.g. in 56 against Clodius' gangs: *QF* 2.3; cf. Caes *BC* 1.14 for P's veterans at Capua in 49) and recruitment of dispossessed into protégé's army with pay and plunder prospects. **Tax-farming legislation**: see esp. Dio 38.7; Suet *J* 20; App *BC* 2.13; n.b. Crassus not specified as direct beneficiary, but financial involvement indicated by his zeal: Cic *Att* 2.1, 16 ('egging on the knights'). **Eastern settlement ratified**: Dio 38.7 (no opposition); App *BC* 2.13; Plut *P* 48. **Ptolemy of Egypt recognized**: Cic *Att* 2.5, 16; Suet *J* 54 (n.b. dating uncertain); Dio 39.12.1 ('certain Romans'). **Lex Vatinia**: Dio 38.8 (full details); Suet *J* 22; App *BC* 2.13 (pre-ceded by shows 'far beyond Caesar's own means'); Plut *Cato Min* 32 (Cato's public warning: 'tyrant in the citadel'); *P* 48 (indicated as part of a whole legislative programme carried with help of P's troops); Cic *Att* 2.18 (gives June as *terminus ante quem*: Cic already offered staff-appoint-ment); on chronology of legislation and elections in 59 see also Marsh 1927; L.R. Taylor 1951, 1968; Meier 1961. **Marriage-alliances**: see esp. Dio 38.9; Suet *J* 21–2; App *BC* 2.14; Plut *P* 47 ('to everyone's surprise'); *Cato Min* 31; *Caes* 14 (Cato's protest: cf. App *l.c.*); Cic *Att* 2.17 (early May: 'sudden' marriage-contract); n.b. Servilius Caepio not Brutus (as Münzer 1920/63, 338–9, followed by Syme 1939, 58): the adopted Brutus was only 'Caepio', not 'Servilius Caepio'; surely ancient sources (esp. Plut, Brutus' biographer) would have identified the tyrannicide; and Brutus hated P so much for having killed his father in the Lepidan War that he would not even speak to him until after outbreak of Civil War (Plut *Brut* 4; *P* 16, 64); this Caepio's fate unknown: we know Faustus Sulla eventually married Pompeia, but not how soon after this or whether she married Caepio first: perhaps Caepio died before wedding-day or P simply changed his mind. **Vettius**: see Cic *Att* 2.24; Dio 38.9–10; Suet *J* 20; App *BC* 2.12; Cic *Vat* 24–6; Plut *Luc* 42.7–8; for conflicting modern interpretations see e.g. Allen 1950; Rossi 1951; Brunt 1953; McDermott 1949, 1972; L.R. Taylor 1950, 1954, 1968; Meier 1961; Seager 1965; Rowland 1966; Ward 1977, 236–42. **Clodius**: see also on P's role at adoption, Dio 38.12; Cic *Att* 2.9, 12; 8.3 (cf. 2.5); on timing after Cic's gaffe see *de domo sua* 41; Suet *J* 20; for Cic's obsession with Clodius throughout the year see esp. *Att* 2.5, 7, 9, 12, 14–15, 18–25; *QF* 1.2; for view that Clodius' supposed opposition was genuine (as Cic believed: *Att* 2.12) see e.g. Lintott 1968, 198ff; Stockton 1971, 179; Ward 1977, 231ff.

BIBLIOGRAPHY

NB Journal abbreviations follow the generally accepted conventions of *L'Année Philologique*

ABEL, F.-M., 'Le siège de Jérusalem par Pompée', *RBi*, 54 (1947), 243–55.

ABEL, F.-M., *Histoire de la Palestine, depuis la conquête d'Alexandre jusqu'à l'invasion arabe*, vol. 1 (Paris, 1952).

ADCOCK, F.E., 'Lesser Armenia and Galatia after Pompey's settlement of the East', *JRS*, 27 (1937), 12–17.

ADCOCK, F.E., *The Roman Art of War under the Republic* (Cambridge, Mass., 1940).

ADCOCK, F.E., *Roman Political Ideas and Practice* (Ann Arbor, Michigan, 1964).

ADCOCK, F.E., *Marcus Crassus, Millionaire* (Cambridge, 1966).

AFZELIUS, A., 'Das Ackerverteilungsgesetz des P. Servilius Rullus', *C&M*, 3 (1940), 214–35.

AFZELIUS, A., 'Die politische Bedeutung des jüngeren Cato', *C&M*, 4 (1941), 100–203.

ALLEN, W., 'In defense of Catiline', *CJ*, 34 (1938), 70–85.

ALLEN, W., 'The Vettius affair once more', *TAPhA*, 81 (1950), 153–63.

ANDERSON, J.G.C., CUMONT and GRÉGOIRE, *Studia Pontica* (Brussels, 1903–10).

ANDERSON, J.G.C., 'Pompey's campaign against Mithridates', *JRS*, 12 (1922), 99–105.

ASDOURIAN, P.P., *Die politischen Beziehungen zwischen Armenien und Rom von 190 v. Chr. bis 428 n. Chr.* (Venice, 1911).

ASTBURY, R., 'Varro and Pompey', *CQ*, 17 (1967), 403–7.

BACHMANN, H.G., 'Kommagene. Porträt einer antiken Landschaft', *AW*, 4 (1973), 11–20.

BADIAN, E., 'The Date of Pompey's first triumph', *Hermes*, 83 (1955), 107–18.

BADIAN, E., 'The early career of A. Gabinius (cos. 58 B.C.)', *Philologus*, 103 (1959), 87–99.

BADIAN, E., 'Servilius and Pompey's first triumph', *Hermes*, 89 (1961), 254–6.

BADIAN, E., 'From the Gracchi to Sulla (1940–59)', *Historia*, 11 (1962), 197–245. Reprinted in Seager (1969), 3–51.

BADIAN, E., *Roman Imperialism in the late Republic* (Ithaca, N.Y., and Oxford, 1968).

BAKER, G.P., *Sulla the Fortunate* (London, 1927).

BALSDON, J.P.V.D., 'The History of the Extortion Court at Rome, 123–70 BC', *PBSR*, 14 (1938), 98–114, reprinted in Seager (1969), 132–48.

BALSDON, J.P.V.D., 'Roman history 65–50 B.C.: five problems', *JRS*, 52 (1962), 134–41.

BALSDON, J.P.V.D., 'The Commentariolum Petitionis', *CQ*, 13 (1963), 242–50.

BALSDON, J.P.V.D., *Julius Caesar. A political biography* (New York, 1967).

BAMMEL, E., 'Die Neuordnung des Pompeius und das römisch-jüdische Bündnis', *ZPalV*, 75 (1959), 76–82.

BAUMAN, R., 'The *hostis* declarations of 88 and 87 B.C.', *Athenaeum*, 51 (1973), 270–93.

BELLINGER, A.R., 'The end of the Seleucids', *Transactions of the Connecticut Acad. of Arts and Sciences*, 38 (1949), 51–102.

BENNETT, H., *Cinna and his Times* (Diss. Chicago, 1923).

BERSANETTI, G.M., *Quando fu conclusa l'alleanza fra Cesare, Pompeo e Crasso?* (Palermo, 1924).

BERSANETTI, G.M., 'La tradizione antica e l'opinione degli storici moderni sul "Primo Triumvirato"', *Rivista Indo-Greco-Italica di filologia* (1927), III–IV, 1–20; (1928), I–II, 21–42.

BERVE, H., 'Sertorius', *Hermes*, 64 (1929), 199–227.

BEVAN, E.R., *The House of Seleucus* (London, 1902).

BEVAN, E.R., *A History of Egypt under the Ptolemaic Dynasty* (London, 1927).

BIENKOWSKI, P.R. von, 'Kritische Studien über Chronologie und Geschichte des Sertorianischen Krieges', *WS*, 13 (1891), 129–58, 210–30.

BIETENHARD, H., 'Die Dekapolis von Pompeius bis Trajan. Ein Kapitel aus der neutestamentlichen Zeitgeschichte', *ZPalV*, 79 (1963), 24–58.

BOAK, A.E.R., 'The extraordinary commands from 80 to 48 B.C.', *AHR*, 24 (1918–19), 1–25.

BOISSIER, G., *Étude sur la vie et les ouvrages de M.T. Varro* (Paris, 1861).

BONGHI, R., *Spartaco* (Atti Della Reale Accademia di Science Morali e Politiche di Napoli, 16, Naples, 1881).

BOTSFORD, G.W., *The Roman Assemblies* (New York, 1909).

BOUCHÉ-LECLERCQ, A., *Histoire des Séleucides, 323–64 av. J.C.* (Paris, 1913).

BOUCHENAKI, M., 'Relations entre le royaume de Numidie et la république romaine au Ier s. av. J.C.', *RHCM*, 7 (1969), 7–9.

BREGLIA, L. PULCI DORIA, 'I Legati di Pompeo durante la guerra piratica', *AFLN*, 13 (1970–71), 47–66.

BRISSON, J.–P., *Spartacus* (Paris, 1959).

BROUGHTON, T.R.S., 'Senate and Senators of the Roman Republic: the prosopographical approach', *Aufstieg und Niedergang der römischen Welt* (ed. H. Temporini, Berlin and New York, 1972), 1.1.250–65.

BROUGHTON, T.R.S., *The Magistrates of the Roman Republic* (New York, 1951–2) and *Supplement* (New York, 1960): *MRR*.

BRUNT, P.A., 'Cicero: *ad Atticum*, 2.24', *CQ*, 3 (1953), 62–4.

BRUNT, P.A., 'The equites in the late Republic', *Second International Conference of Economic History, Aix-en-Provence, 1962* (Paris, 1965A), vol. I, 117–49; reprinted in Seager (1969), 83–115, with comment by T.R.S. Broughton, 118–30.

BRUNT, P.A., '*Amicitia* in the late Roman republic', *PCPhS*, N.S. 11 (1965B), 1–20. Reprinted in Seager (1969), 199–218.

BRUNT, P.A., *Social Conflicts in the Roman Republic* (London, 1971).

BURR, V., 'Rom und Judäa im 1. Jahrhundert v. Chr. (Pompeius und die Juden)', *Aufstieg und Niedergang der Römischen Welt* (Berlin and New York, 1972), 1.1.875–86.

CARCOPINO, J., *Sylla ou la monarchie manquée* (Paris, 1931).

CARCOPINO, J., *Histoire Romaine*, vol. 2 (Paris, 1935).

CARCOPINO, J., *Jules César* (Paris, 1968).

CARNEY, T. F., *A Biography of C. Marius* (PACA, Supp. I, 1962).

CARY, M., 'The land legislation of Julius Caesar's first consulship', *Journal of Philology*, 35 (1920), 174–90.

CASTAGNA, M., *Mitridate VI Eupatore, re del Ponto* (Portici, 1938).

CASTRITIUS, H., 'Zum Aureus mit dem Triumph des Pompeius', *JNG*, 21 (1971), 25–35.

CHAPOT, V., *La frontière de l'Euphrate, de Pompée à la conquête arabe* (Bibl. des Ecol. franç. d'Athènes et de Rome, fasc. 99, Paris 1907).

CRAWFORD, M.H., *Roman Republican Coinage* (Cambridge, 1974): *RRC*.

CRINITI, N., 'M. Aimilius Q.F.M.N. Lepidus "ut ignis in stipula"', *MemIstLomb*, 30 (1969), 319–460.

CRINITI, N., *L'Epigrafe di Asculum di Gn. Pompeo Strabone* (Milan, 1970).

CUNNINGHAM, D.R., *The Influence of the Alexander Legend on some Roman Political Figures* (Diss. Seattle, 1971).

CUQ, E., 'La loi Gabinia contre la piraterie de l'an 67 avant J.-C., d'après une inscription de Delphes', *CRAI* (1923), 129–50.

DAGUT, M.B., 'The Habbakuk scroll and Pompey's capture of Jerusalem', *Biblica*, 32 (1951), 542–8.

DAVISON, J.A., 'Cicero and the *lex Gabinia*', *CR*, 44 (1930), 224–5.

DEGRASSI, A., 'Fasti Consulares et Triumphales', *Inscriptiones Italiae*, 13.1 (Rome, 1947).

DEUTSCH, M.E., 'The death of Lepidus, leader of the revolution of 78 B.C.', *Univ. of California Publ. in class. phil.*, 5.3 (1918), 59–68.

DEUTSCH, M.E., 'Pompey's three triumphs', *CPh*, 19 (1924), 227–9.

DOBIAS, J., *Dejiny Rimské Provincie Syrské* (History of the Roman Province of Syria), vol. 1 (Prague, 1924).

DOBIAS, J., 'Les premiers rapports des Romains avec les Parthes et l'occupation de la Syrie', *ArchOrient*, 3 (1931), 215–56.

DOREY, T.A., 'Cicero, Pompey and the *Pro Archia*', *Orpheus*, 2 (1955), 32–5.

DOWNEY, G., 'The occupation of Syria by the Romans', *TAPhA*, 82 (1951), 149–63.

DOWNEY, G., *Ancient Antioch* (Princeton, 1963).

DREIZEHNTER, A., 'Pompeius als Städtegründer', *Chiron*, 5 (1975), 213–45.

DREW, D.L., 'Pompey's capture of Jerusalem on tenth Tishri?', *BFAC*, 13 (1951) 1, 83–8.

EBEL, C., 'Pompey's organization of Transalpina', *Phoenix*, 29 (1975), 358–73.

ECKHARDT, K., 'Die armenischen Feldzüge des Lukullus', *Klio*, 9 (1909), 400–12; 10 (1910), 73–115, 192–231.

EHRENBERG, V., *Ost und West. Studien zur geschichtlichen Problematik der Antike* (Brünn, 1935).

EHRENBERG, V., '*Imperium maius* in the Roman Republic', *AJPh*, 74 (1953), 113–36.

FLETCHER, W.G., 'The Pontic cities of Pompey the Great', *TAPhA*, 70 (1939), 17–29.

FRANK, T., *Economic Survey of the Roman Empire* (Baltimore, 1933–40).

FRANKFORT, T., 'La Sophène et Rome', *Latomus*, 22 (1963), 181–90.

FRISCH, H., 'The first Catilinarian conspiracy: a study in historical conjecture', *C&M*, 9 (1948), 10–36.

GABBA, E., 'Nota sulla rogatio agraria di P. Servilio Rullo', *Mélanges d'archéologie et d'histoire offerts à A. Piganiol* (1966), vol. 2, 769–75.

GABBA, E., 'Mario e Silla', *Aufstieg und Niedergang der Römischen Welt* (ed. H. Temporini, Berlin and New York, 1972), 1.1.764–805.

GABBA, E., *Republican Rome, the Army and the Allies* (translated by P.J. Cuff, Oxford, 1973).

GAGÉ, J., 'Sylla, Pompée et la théologie de la victoire', *RH*, 177 (1936), 279–342.

GAGGERO, G., 'Aspetti monetari della rivolta sertoriana in Spagna', *RIN*, 78 (1976), 55–75.

GELZER, M., 'Die *lex Vatinia de imperio Caesaris*', *Hermes*, 63 (1928), 113–37.

GELZER, M., 'Hat Sertorius in seinem Vertrag mit Mithridates die Provinz Asia abgetreten?', *PhilWoch*, 52 (1932), 1129–36.

GELZER, M., 'Cn. Pompeius Strabo und der Aufstieg seines Sohnes Magnus', *APAW* (1941), no. 6.

GELZER, M., 'Das erste Konsulat des Pompeius und die Uebertragung der grossen Imperien', *APAW* (1943), no. 1.

GELZER, M., *Pompeius* (Munich, 1959; first published 1949).

GELZER, M., *Caesar: Politician and Statesman* (trans. P. Needham, Cambridge, Mass., 1968).

GELZER, M., *Cicero: Ein biographischer Versuch* (Wiesbaden, 1969A).

GELZER, M., *The Roman Nobility* (trans. R. Seager, Oxford, 1969B).

GILLIS, D., 'Quintus Sertorius', *RIL*, 103 (1969), 711–27.

GINSBURG, M.S., *Rome et la Judée* (Paris, 1928).

GOLENKO, K.V., 'Aristarchus of Colchis and his coins', *VDI*, 130 (1974), 95–110.

GREENIDGE, A.H.J., *Roman Public Life* (London, 1901).

GREENIDGE, A.H.J. and CLAY, A.M., *Sourses for Roman History 133–70 B.C.* (revised by E.W. Gray, Oxford, 1960).

GROEBE, P., 'Eine Athenische Ehreninschrift des Sex. Pompeius, des Grossvaters des Triumvirs', *AM*, 34 (1909), 403–6.

GROEBE, P., 'Zum Seeräuberkriege des Pompeius Magnus', *Klio*, 10 (1910), 374–87.

GRUEN, E.S., 'Pompey and the Pisones', *California Studies in Classical Antiquity*, 1 (1968), 155–70.

GRUEN, E.S., 'Veteres Hostes, Novi Amici', *Phoenix*, 24 (1970), 237–43.

GRUEN, E.S., 'Pompey, Metellus Pius and the trials of 70–69 B.C.: the perils of schematism', *AJPh*, 92 (1971), 1–16.

GRUEN, E.S., *The Last Generation of the Roman Republic* (Berkeley and Los Angeles, 1974).

GSELL, S., *Histoire ancienne de l'Afrique du Nord* (Paris, 1928, reprinted Osnabrück, 1972).

GUTSCHMID, A. von, 'Untersuchungen über die Geschichte des Königreichs Osroëne', *Mém. de l'Acad. Imp. des Sciences de St.-Pétersbourg*, 35 (1887).

HANSLIK, R., 'Cicero und das erste Triumvirat', *RhM*, 98 (1955), 224–34.

HARDY, E.G., 'The policy of the Rullan proposal in 63 B.C.', *Journal of Philology*, 32 (1912–13), 228–60.

HARDY, E.G., 'The Transpadane Question and the Alien Act of 65 or 64 B.C.', *JRS*, 6 (1916), 63–82.

HARDY, E.G., 'The Catilinarian conspiracy in its context: A restudy of the evidence', *JRS*, 7 (1917), 153–228.

HARMAND, J., *L'armée et le soldat à Rome de 107 à 50 avant notre ère* (Paris, 1967).

HASSALL, M., CRAWFORD, M. and REYNOLDS, J., 'Rome and the eastern provinces at the end of the second century BC', *JRS*, 64 (1974), 195–220.

HAVAS, L., 'Pompée et la première conjuration de Catilina', *ACD*, 3 (1967), 43–53.

HAVAS, L., 'Mithridate et son plan d'attaque contre l'Italie', *ACD*, 4 (1968), 13–25.

HAYNE, L., 'The politics of M'Glabrio, Cos. 67', *CP*, 69 (1974A), 280–82.

HEAD, B.V., *Historia Numorum* (London, 1963): *HN*.

HENDERSON, M.I., 'De Commentariolo Petitionis', *JRS*, 40 (1950), 8–21.

HOLMES, T. RICE, *The Roman Republic* (Oxford, 1923).

HUTCHINSON, L., *The Conspiracy of Catiline* (New York, 1967).

JAMESON, S., 'Pompey's *imperium* in 67 : some constitutional fictions', *Historia*, 19 (1970A), 539–60.

JONES, A.H.M., *The Cities of the Eastern Roman Provinces* (revised, Oxford, 1971): *CERP*.

JONES, A.H.M., *The Roman Economy* (Oxford, 1974).

JONKERS, E.J., *Social and Economic Commentary on Cicero's 'de imperio Cn. Pompei'* (Leiden, 1959).

JONKERS, E.J., *Social and Economic Commentary on Cicero's 'De Lege Agraria Orationes Tres'* (Leiden, 1963).

KATZ, B.R., 'Studies on the period of Cinna and Sulla', *AC*, 45 (1976), 497–549.

KILDAHL, P., *Caius Marius* (New York, 1968).

KNIGHT, D.W., 'Pompey's concern for pre-eminence after 60 B.C.', *Latomus*, 27 (1968), 878–83.

KRAFT, K., 'Taten des Pompeius auf den Münzen', *JNG*, 18 (1968), 7–24.

KROMAYER, 'Die Entwicklung der römischen Flotte vom Seeräuberkriege des Pompeius bis zur Schlacht von Actium', *Philologus*, 56 (1897), 426–91.

KUCHARCZAK, T., 'Starożynta Syria wobec ekspansji Rzyml', *Meander*, 31 (1976), 41–55 (with Latin summary).

LACEY, W.K., *Cicero and the End of the Roman Republic* (London, 1978).

LAFFI, U., 'Il Mito di Silla', *Athenaeum*, 55 (1967), 177–213.

LANGLOIS, V., 'Soli et Pompéiopolis', *RA* (1853), 358–63.

LANZANI, C., *Lucio Cornelio Silla dittatore* (Milan, 1936).

LEACH, J., *Pompey the Great* (London, 1978).

LIEBMANN-FRANKFORT, T., *La frontière orientale dans la politique extérieure de la République romaine, depuis la traité d'Apamée jusqu'à la fin des conquêtes asiatiques de Pompée* (Mém. de l'Acad. Roy. de Belgique, Cl. de lettres, Série 2.59, Brussels, 1968A).

LIEBMANN-FRANKFORT, T., 'La Provincia Cilicia et son intégration dans l'empire romain', *Hommages à M. Renard* (Brussels, 1968B), 447–57.

LIEBMANN-FRANKFORT, T., 'Les étapes de l'intégration de la Cappadoce dans l'empire romain', *Hommages à C. Préaux* (1975), 416–25.

LINDERSKI, J., 'Constitutional aspects of the consular elections in 59 B.C.', *Historia*, 14 (1965), 423–33.

LINDERSKI, J., 'Were Pompey and Crassus elected in their absence to their first consulship?', *Mélanges offerts à K. Michalowski* (Warsaw, 1966), 523–6.

LINTOTT, A.W., *Violence in Republican Rome* (Oxford, 1968).

LOADER, W.R., 'Pompey's command under the *lex Gabinia*', *CR* (1940), 134–6.

LUZZATTO, G.I., 'Ancora sulla proposita di legge agraria di P. Servilio Rullo', *BIDR*, 69 (1966), 85–108.

MAGIE, D., 'The final defeat of Mithridates by Pompey', *CW*, 37 (1943–4), 237–8.

MAGIE, D., *Roman Rule in Asia Minor* (Princeton, 1950; reprinted New York, 1975): *RRAM*.

MANSUELLI, G.A., *La politica di Cneo Pompeo Magno* (ed. E. Pettorelli, Bologna, 1959).

MARÓTI, E., 'A recently found versified oracle against the pirates', *AAntHung*, 16 (1968), 233–8.

MARÓTI, E., 'Der Sklavenmarkt auf Delos und die Piraterie', *Helikon*, 9–10 (1969–70), 24–42.

MARÓTI, E., 'Die Rolle der Seeräuber in der Zeit der Mithradatischen Kriege', *Ric. stor. ed econ. C. Barbagallo* (Naples, 1970), 481–93.

MARÓTI, E., 'On the problem of M. Antonius Creticus' *imperium infinitum*', *AAntHung*, 19 (1971), 252–72.

MARÓTI, E., *La piraterie avant la guerre civile* (in Hungarian) (Budapest, 1972).

MARSH, F.B., 'The Chronology of Caesar's Consulship', *CJ*, 22 (1927), 504–24.

MARSHALL, A.J., 'Pompey's organisation of Bithynia-Pontus. Two neglected texts', *JRS*, 58 (1968), 103–7.

MARSHALL, B.A., 'Crassus and the command against Spartacus', *Athenaeum*, 51 (1973), 109–21.

MARSHALL, B.A., 'Cicero and Sallust on Crassus and Catiline', *Latomus*, 33 (1974), 804–13.

MARSHALL, B.A., *Crassus: a political biography* (Amsterdam, 1976).

McDERMOTT, W.C., Vettius ille, ille noster index', *TAPhA*, 80 (1949), 351–67.

McDERMOTT, W.C., 'De Lucceiis', *Hermes*, 97 (1969), 233–46.

McDERMOTT, W.C., 'Curio *pater* and Cicero', *AJPh*, 93 (1972), 381–411.

McDERMOTT, W.C., 'Lex Pompeia de tribunicia potestate (70 B.C.)', *CP*, 72 (1977), 49–51.

MEDICO, H.E. del, 'La prise de Jérusalem par Pompée d'après la légende juive de la ville inconquise', *BJ*, 164 (1964), 53–87.

MEIER, C., 'Zur Chronologie und Politik in Caesars ersten Konsulat', *Historia*, 10 (1961), 68–98.

MEIER, C., 'Pompeius Rückkehr aus dem Mithridatischen Kriege und die Catilinarische Verschwörung', *Athenaeum*, 40 (1962), 103–25.

MEIER, C., *Res Publica Amissa* (Wiesbaden, 1966).

MEYER, E., *Geschichte des Königreichs Pontos* (Leipzig, 1879).

MICHEL, D., *Alexander als Vorbild für Pompeius, Caesar und Marcus Antonius. Archäologische Untersuchungen* (coll. Latomus 94, Bruxelles, 1967).

MILTNER, F., 'Cn. Pompeius Magnus', *RE*, Erste Reihe, 21.2 (1952), 2062–2211 and 2549–52; sons (2211–13; 2213–50); father (2254–62).

MISCHULIN, A.W., *Spartacus. Abriss der Geschichte des grossen Sklavenaufstandes* (Berlin, 1952).

MITCHELL, T.N., 'Cicero, Pompey and the rise of the First Triumvirate', *Traditio*, 29 (1973), 1–26.

MITCHELL, T.N., 'Veteres Hostes, Novi Amici (Cic. Fam, V.7, 1)', *Historia*, 24 (1975), 618–22.

MOMIGLIANO, A., 'Ricerche sull'organizzazione della Guidea sotto il Dominio romano (63 a.C.–70 d.C.)', *ASNP*, 3 (1934), 183–221.

MÜNZER, F., *Römische Adelsparteien und Adelsfamilien* (Stuttgart, 1920; reprinted 1963).

NEVEROV, O.I., 'On the iconography of Mithridates VI', *TE*, 13 (1972), 110–18.

OLSHAUSEN, E., 'Mithridates VI und Rom', *Aufstieg und Niedergang der römischen Welt* (ed. H. Temporini, Berlin and New York, 1972), 1.1.806–15.

OMAN, C.W.C., *Seven Roman Statesmen of the Later Republic* (London, 1903).

OOTEGHEM, J. van, *Pompée le Grand, bâtisseur d'empire* (Brussels, 1954).

OOTEGHEM, J. van, *L. Licinius Lucullus* (Brussels, 1959).

OOTEGHEM, J. van, *Caius Marius* (Brussels, 1964).

OOTEGHEM, J. van, *Les Caecilii Metelli de la République* (Brussels, 1967).

ORMEROD, H.A., 'The distribution of Pompeius' forces in the campaign of 67 B.C.', *Liverpool Ann. of Arch. and Anth.*, 10 (1923), 46–51.

ORMEROD, H.A., *Piracy in the Ancient World* (Liverpool, 1924).

PARETI, L., *La Congiura di Catilina* (Catania, 1934).

PARRISH, E.J., 'Crassus' new friends and Pompey's return', *Phoenix*, 27 (1973), 357–80.

PASSERINI, A., 'Caio Mario come uomo politico', *Athenaeum*, 12 (1934), 10–44, 109–43, 257–97, 348–80.

PIAUKO, G., 'Lucius Lucceius', *Meander*, 24 (1969), 326–34.

POULSEN, F., 'Les portraits de Pompeius Magnus', *RA* (1936), 1.16–52.

POZZI, E., 'Studi sulla guerra civile Sillana', *AAT*, 49 (1913–14), 183–221.

REINACH, T., *Trois Royaumes de l'Asie Mineure: Cappadoce, Bithynie, Pont* (Paris, 1889).

REINACH, T., *Mithridate Eupator, roi de Pont* (Paris, 1890).

REYNOLDS, J., 'Cyrenaica, Pompey, and Cn. Cornelius Lentulus Marcellinus', *JRS*, 52 (1962), 97–103.

RICHARDSON, J.S., 'The *Commentariolum Petitionis*', *Historia*, 20 (1971), 436–42.

RIZZO, F.P., *Le fonti per la storia della conquista pompeiana della Siria* (*Kokalos*, Supp. 2, Palermo, 1963).

ROSSI, R.F., 'La congiura di Vettio', *AFLT*, 21 (1951), 247–60.

ROWLAND, R.J., 'Crassus, Clodius and Curio in the year 59 B.C.', *Historia*, 15 (1966), 217–23.

RUBINSOHN, Z., 'A note on Plutarch, *Crassus*, X.1', *Historia*, 19 (1970), 624–7.

RUBINSOHN, Z., 'Was the *Bellum Spartacium* a servile insurrection?', *RFIC*, 99 (1971), 290–99.

SAGE, E.T., 'Cicero and the agrarian proposals of 63 B.C.', *CJ*, 16 (1921), 230–36.

SALMON, E.T., 'Catiline, Crassus and Caesar', *AJPh*, 56 (1935), 302–16.

SANDERS, H.A., 'The so-called First Triumvirate', *MAAR*, 10 (1932), 55–68.

SANFORD, E.M., 'The career of Aulus Gabinius', *TAPhA*, 70 (1939), 64–92.

SCARDIGLI, B., 'Sertorio, Problemi cronologici', *Athenaeum*, 49 (1971), 229–70.

SCHULTEN, A., *Sertorius* (Leipzig, 1926).

SCHUR, W., 'Das Zeitalter des Marius und Sulla' (*Klio*, Beiheft 46, Leipzig, 1942).

SEAGER, R., 'The First Catilinarian Conspiracy', *Historia*, 13 (1964), 338–47.

SEAGER, R. (ed.), *The Crisis of the Roman Republic* (Cambridge, 1969).

SEAGER, R., '*Iusta Catilinae*', *Historia*, 22 (1973), 240–8.

SEAGER, R., *Pompey: A Political Biography* (forthcoming, Oxford, 1979).

SEYRIG, H., 'Caractères de l'histoire d'Emèse', *Syria*, 36 (1959), 184–92.

SHACKLETON BAILEY, D.R., *Cicero's Letters to Atticus* (Cambridge, 1965–8): SB, *Att.*

SHACKLETON BAILEY, D.R., *Cicero* (London, 1971).

SHACKLETON BAILEY, D.R., *Cicero: Epistulae ad Familiares* (vol. 1, Cambridge, 1977): SB, *Fam.*

SHERWIN-WHITE, A.N., 'Violence in Roman Politics', *JRS*, 46 (1956), 1–9. Reprinted in Seager (1969), 151–9.

SHERWIN-WHITE, A.N., 'Rome, Pamphylia and Cilicia', *JRS*, 66 (1976), 1–14.

SMALLWOOD, E.M., *The Jews under Roman Rule* (Leiden, 1976).

SMITH, R.E., 'The *lex Plotia agraria* and Pompey's Spanish veterans', *CQ*, 7 (1957), 82–5.

SMITH, R.E., *Service in the Post-Marian Roman Army* (Manchester, 1958).

SMITH, R.E., 'Pompey's conduct in 80 and 77 B.C.', *Phoenix*, 14 (1960), 1–13.

SMITH, R.E., *Cicero the Statesman* (Cambridge, 1966).

STAERMAN, E.M., *Die Blütezeit der Sklavenwirtschaft der römischen Republik* (Wiesbaden, 1969).

STAHL, G., *De bello Sertoriano* (Diss. Erlangen, 1907).

STANTON, G.R. and MARSHALL, BA., 'The coalition between Pompeius and Crassus, 60–59 B.C.', *Historia*, 24 (1975), 205–19.

STARCKY, J., 'The Nabataeans: a historical sketch', *The Biblical Archaeologist*, 18 (1955), 84–106.

STARCKY, J., 'La civilisation nabatéenne. État des questions', *AArchSyr*, 21 (1971), 79–86.

STARK, F., *Rome on the Euphrates* (New York, 1968).

STOCKTON, D., *Cicero, A Political Biography* (London, 1971).

STOCKTON, D., 'The first consulship of Pompey', *Historia*, 22 (1973), 205–18.

SUMNER, G.V., 'Cicero, Pompeius and Rullus', *TAPhA*, 97 (1966), 569–82.

SYME, R., *The Roman Revolution* (Oxford, 1939).

TAYLOR, J.H., 'Political motives in Cicero's defense of Archias', *AJPh*, 73 (1952), 62–70.

TAYLOR, L.R., 'Caesar's early career', *CP*, 36 (1941), 113–32.

TAYLOR, L.R., 'The date and meaning of the Vettius affair', *Historia*, 1 (1950), 45–51.

TAYLOR, L.R., 'On the Chronology of Caesar's first consulship', *AJPh*, 72 (1951), 254–68.

TAYLOR, L.R., 'On the date of *ad Atticum*, 2.24', *CQ*, 4 (1954), 187–8.

TAYLOR, L.R., 'The rise of Julius Caesar', *G&R*, 4 (1957), 10–18.

TAYLOR, L.R., 'The dating of major legislation and elections in Caesar's first consulship', *Historia*, 17 (1968), 173–93.

THIEL, J.H., *Studies on the History of Roman Sea-power in Republican Times* (Amsterdam, 1946).

TOROS, H., 'Tigran's crown in Commagene', *SAN*, 7 (1976), 65–6.

TOYNBEE, J.M.C., *Roman Historical Portraits* (London, 1978).

TREVES, P., 'Sertorio', *Athenaeum*, 10 (1932), 127–47.

TWYMAN, B.L., 'The Metelli, Pompeius and Prosopography', *Aufstieg und Niedergang der römischen Welt* (ed. H. Temporini, Berlin and New York, 1972), 1.1.816–74.

TYRRELL, R.Y. and PURSER, L.C., *The Correspondence of M. Tullius Cicero* (Dublin and London, 1904–33).

VITUCCI, G., 'Gli ordinamenti constitutivi di Pompeo in terra d'Asia', *RAL*, 344 (1947), 428–47.

VOLLENWEIDER, M.L., 'Un épisode de la vie du général Pompée le Grand', *Hommages à Marcel Renard*, Coll. Latomus 51, 52 & 53 (Bruxelles, 1969), III, 655–61.

WADDINGTON, W.H., BABELON, E. and REINACH, T. *Recueil général des monnaies grèques d'Asie Mineure* (Paris, 1904).

WARD, A.M., *Ad Familiares* 5, 7. *Cicero, Pompey, Posidonius and the Scipio–Laelius myth* (Diss. Princeton, 1968).

WARD, A.M., 'Cicero's support of the *lex Gabinia*', *CW*, 63 (1969), 8–10.

WARD, A.M., 'The early relationships between Cicero and Pompey until 80 B.C.', *Phoenix*, 24 (1970A), 119–29.

WARD, A.M., 'Cicero and Pompey in 75 and 70 B.C.', *Latomus*, 29 (1970B), 58–71.

WARD, A.M., *Marcus Crassus and the Late Roman Republic* (Columbia and London, 1977).

WARREN, L.B., 'Roman Triumphs and Etruscan Kings: the changing face of the Roman triumph', *JRS*, 60 (1970), 49–66.

WATERS, K.H., 'Cicero, Sallust and Catiline', *Historia*, 19 (1970), 195–215.

WEIPPERT, O., *Alexander-imitatio u. röm. Politik in republikan. Zeit* (Diss. Würzburg, 1972).

WELLESLEY, K., 'The extent of the territory added to Bithynia by Pompey', *RhM*, 96 (1953), 293–318.

WILL, E., 'Rome et les Séleucides', *Aufstieg und Niedergang der römischen Welt* (Berlin and New York, 1972), I.1.590–632.

WILLIAMS, R.S., *Aulus Gabinius: A Political Biography* (Diss. Michigan State University, East Lansing, 1973).

YAVETZ, Z., 'The failure of Catiline's conspiracy', *Historia*, 12 (1963), 485–99.

ZANCAN, P., 'Mitridate Eupatore', *AIV*, 93 (1933–4), 1217–32.

ZECCHINI, G., 'La data del cosidetto primo triumvirato', *RIL*, 109 (1975), 399–410.

ZIEBARTH, E., *Beiträge zur Geschichte des Seeraubs und Seehandels im alten Griechenland* (Hamburg, 1929).

ZIEGLER, K.H., *Die Beziehungen zwischen Rom und dem Partherreich* (Wiesbaden, 1964).

LIST OF QUOTATIONS

The following list gives the sources page by page of all direct quotations (whether the author's name is specified or not) and all citations of authors by name in the text.

104 Dio 36.45.1–2
    Plut *P* 32.1
106 *ib.* 31.1
    Dio 36.45.2
107 Plut *P* 31.4
    id. Luc 35.7
    Dio 36.46.2
    Plut *P* 31.6–7
    Vell 2.33.1–4
    Plut *Luc* 36.5
108 *ib.* 33.2
    (*cf.* Dio 36.16)
    Plut *P* 31.5
    (*cf. Luc* 36.4)
109 Dio 36.47.2
110 Front *Strat* 2.5.3
111 App *Mithr* 99
    Front *Strat* 1.1.7
112 Dio 36.48–9
    Plut *P* 32.3–7
    App *Mithr* 99–100
    Front *Strat* 2.1.12
    Dio 36.49
113 *ib.*
    Plut *P* 32.7
    App *Mithr* 100–1
114 Florus 1.40.24
    Plut *P* 32.8
    Dio 36.50.1
    Florus 1.40.20
115 Strabo 12.3.28, 555
    Dio 36.51.1
116 *ib.*
    Florus 1.40.21
    Plut *P* 33.2
117 Dio 36.52.2
118 *ib.* 36.52.4
    Vell 2.37.4
    Plut *P* 33.4
    id. Comp Luc & Cimon
    3.4
    Strabo 11.14.10, 530
    Vell 2.37.5
120 Dio 36.54.1
122 Plut *P* 34.4
    App *Mithr* 101
    Dio 37.1.2
    Plut *P* 34.5
123 Strabo 11.3.5, 500–1
    Dio 37.1.3
    ib. 37.2.2
124 *ib.* 37.2.5
125 Strabo 11.3.4, 500
    App *Mithr* 103
126 Dio 37.3.2–3
    Plut *P* 35.1
    Strabo 11.3.5, 500
    ib. 11.4.5, 502

127 Plut *P* 35.1
    Dio 37.3.5
128 Strabo 11.4.5, 502
    ib. 11.14.9, 530
    Dio 37.4
    Front *Strat* 2.3.14
129 Dio 37.4.1
    Front *Strat* 2.3.14
    Strabo 11.4.5, 502
    Plut *P* 35.2
    Dio 37.5.1
    Plut *P* 36.1
    Strabo 11.4.6, 503
130 *ib.* 12.3.28, 555
    Vell 2.40.1
    App *Mithr* 106, 114, 117
    Dio 37.5.2
131 Plut *P* 33.6
    Dio 37.6.1
132 Plut *P* 36.6
    App *Mithr* 115
    Plut *P* 36.7
    Strabo 12.3.31, 556
    Plut *P* 37
    Pliny *NH* 25.5–7
    (*cf.* 23.149)
    Strabo 12.3.30, 556
133 Plut *P* 38
134 App *Syr* 49
135 Diod 40.1b
    Jos *JA* 14.29
    id. JW 1.127
    id. JA 14.37
    Plut *P* 39.2
136 *ib.* 38.3–39.1
137 App *Mithr* 106
138 Jos *JW* 1.127
139 Dio 37.7.2
140 Strabo 16.2.18, 755
    Jos *JA* 14.38–40, 48ff
141 Cic *Att* 2.14, 16, 17, 23
    Jos *JA* 14.34
    Plut *P* 39.3
142 Jos *JA* 14.46
    id. JW 1.136
    id. JA 14.51
143 *Psalms of Solomon*
    2.1–2
144 Tac *Hist* 5.9
145 Jos *JA* 14.78
    Plut *P* 41.1
147 *ib.* 42.1
    Cic *de prov cons* 11.27
148 Dio 37.11.2
    App *Mithr* 109
149 *ib.* 112–13
    Plut *P* 42.3
150 App *Mithr* 113

151 Strabo 12.3.1, 541,
    ib. 12.3.18, 549
152 *ib.* 12.3.1, 541
153 *ib.* 11.8.4, 512
154 *ib.* 12.3.36, 559
    ib. 12.3.32, 557
    ib. 12.3.34, 558
155 *ib.* 12.3.13–15, 546–7
159 App *Mithr* 96
160 Cic *Fam* 15.1.2
164 Plut *P* 40.4–5
165 *ib.* 42.3
    JHS 27 (1907), 64, no 7
    CIG 3608 (*IGR* 4.198)
    Plut *P* 42.4
166 App *Mithr* 116
    Plut *P* 42.6–7
    Cic *Att* 1.12.3
167 Plut *P* 43.1
    Dio 37.20.3–6
    Plut *P* 43.3
168 Vell 2.53.3
    Plut *P* 45.1, 5
    Vell 2.40.4
169 Plut *P* 45.2–3
170 Pliny *NH* 7.98
    App *Mithr* 117
171 *ib.*
172 Pliny *NH* 7.98
    ib. 37.13
173 Cic *pro lege Man* 28ff,
    61–3
    Plut *P* 46.1
    ib. 45.4
    Dio 37.21.2
174 App *Mithr* 117, 115
    Pliny *NH* 12.20–1, 111
    ib. 37.11
175 *ib.* 37.12–16
176 Diod 40.4
177 Q. Cic *Com Pet* 13–14,
    51
178 *ib.* 51
    Cit *Att* 1.1
179 *id. in toga cand*
    Asconius 82ff (C)
    Cic *contra Rullum*
180 *ib.* 2.3
181 *ib.* 2.44, 46, 25, 15; 3.16;
    2.25, 62; 1.6; 2.24
184 Dio 37.38.2
185 *ib.* 37.39.3
    Cic *Fam* 5.7
    Dio 37.44.2
186 Cic *Fam* 5.7
    Pliny *NH* 7.97
187 Dio 37.44.3
    Pliny *NH* 33.134

188 Plut *Cato Min* 30.1
   Cic *Att* 1.14
189 Pliny *NH* 7.99
   Cic *Att* 1.14
190 *ib.* 1.13; 1.14
191 *ib.* 2.1
192 Plut *Cato Min* 30.6
   Cic *Att* 1.16
   ib. 1.14
193 *ib.* 1.16
   ib. 1.17, 18
194 *ib.* 1.18; 1.20
195 Dio 37.50.3
   Cic *Att* 1.19
196 *ib.* 2.1
   ib. 1.19
197 Dio 37.50.5–6
199 Plut *P* 23.4
   Dio 37.52.3
200 *ib.* 37.54.1–55.3
   Plut *Cato Min* 31.3
201 Dio 37.56.1–2
   Cic *Att* 1.17
202 Suet *J* 19.1–2
   Livy *Ep* 103
   App *BC* 2.9
   Cic *Att* 2.1
   Dio 37.57.1
   ib. 37.58.1
203 App *BC* 2.9
   Cic *Att* 2.3
204 *ib.*
   Dio 38.1.3–5
205 *ib.* 38.1.6, 7
   ib. 38.1.2 (*cf.* 2.1)
   ib. 38.2.3–3.1

206 *ib.* 38.3.3, 4.1
   Plut *P* 47.3
   Dio 38.4.3
207 *ib.* 38.5.1–2
   ib. 38.5.4
208 Plut *Caes* 14.6
   id. P 47.5
   App *BC* 2.10–11
   Dio 38.5.5, 4.5
209 App *BC* 2.11
   Dio 38.6.4
   Plut *P* 48.2
210 Dio 38.6.4
   App *BC* 2.12
   Dio 38.7.2
   ib. 38.7.4–5
   App *BC* 2.13
211 *ib.*
   Suet *J* 54.3
212 *ib.* 21
213 *ib.*
   Cic *Att* 2.6
   ib. 2.7
   ib. 2.5
214 *ib.* 2.9
   ib. 2.5
   ib. 2.4
   id. de domo sua
   41
   Dio 38.10.4
   Plut *P* 48.4
215 Cic *Att* 2.5
   Plut *Caes* 14.8
   (*cf.* App *BC* 2.14)
216 Cic *Att* 2.9
   ib. 2.12

217 *ib.* 2.14
   ib. 2.17
   App *BC* 2.13
   Plut *P* 48.1
   Cic *contra*
   Rullum
218 *ib.* 2.77, 82, 84
   id. Att 2.16
219 Plut *P* 57.5
   Cic *Att* 2.18
   ib. 2.24
   ib. 2.18
220 *ib.*
   ib. 2.20
   Dio 38.12.7
   Cic *Att* 2.19
221 Suet *Gaius* 30.1
   (from Accius *Atreus*,
   ap. Cic *Phil* 1.34)
   Dio 38.11.1
   Cic *Att* 2.21
222 Dio 37.56.4
   Cic *Att* 2.22
   ib. 2.23
223 *ib* 2.24
224 *ib.*
   Suet *J* 20.5
   App *BC* 2.12
   Dio 38.9
   Cic *Att* 2.24
225 *ib.* 2.8
   Suet *J* 20.2
   (*cf.* Dio 38.8.2)
   Cic *Cat* 1.16
226 *id. QF* 1.2
227 Plut *P* 48.4–5

INDEX

Note: After locating a reference in the text through this index the reader should also check the detailed notes to the appropriate chapter.